and watch for game   that

PAUL BROWN HAS NEVER SHIED
AWAY FROM CONFLICT—ON THE
FIELD OR OFF.

HE DOESN'T DO IT NOW.

This book is Paul Brown speaking, telling what he knows
and all he knows about the years of football glory already
glowing with the golden aura of legend.

He pulls no punches in revealing the struggles he's had
with owners—and with certain players.

He holds back no secrets in spelling out his formula for
success.

He will leave you with no defenses against realizing how
grueling the game of football can be—and how great.

Once again Paul Brown has done what he does best. He
has produced an all-time winner.

PB: THE PAUL BROWN STORY

Other Sports Books from SIGNET

☐ **INSTANT REPLAY: The Green Bay Diary of Jerry Kramer edited by Dick Schaap.** From the locker room to the goal line, from the training field to the Super Bowl, this is the inside story of a great pro-football team . . . "The best behind the scenes glimpse of pro football ever produced."—*The New York Times* (#E9657—$2.50)

☐ **PAPER LION by George Plimpton.** When a first-string writer suits-up to take his lumps as a last-string quarterback for the Detroit Lions, the result is "the best book ever about pro football!"—*Red Smith*. "A great book that makes football absolutely fascinating to fan and non-fan alike . . . a tale to gladden the envious heart of every weekend athlete."—*The New York Times* (#J7668—$1.95)

☐ **PLAYING PRO FOOTBALL TO WIN by John Unitas, with Harold Rosenthal.** A bruising inside look at the pro game by the greatest quarterback of them all. Revised and updated. (#W7209—$1.50)

☐ **SCREWBALL by Tug McGraw and Joseph Durso.** "You gotta believe!" when baseball's star reliever and super flake rips the cover off the game he plays and life he's led . . . "It's the best!"—Roger Kahn, author of *The Boys of Summer* in *The New York Times* Includes an action-packed photo insert. (#Y6421—$1.25)

☐ **THE PERFECT JUMP by Dick Schaap.** What happens to a world-record-breaking athlete when he's reached that once-in-a-lifetime perfection he can never achieve again? The glory and heartbreak of an athlete who reached the top and had nowhere left to go. With an exciting sports photo insert! (#E7248—$1.75)

Buy them at your local bookstore or use this convenient coupon for ordering.

THE NEW AMERICAN LIBRARY, INC.
P.O. Box 999, Bergenfield, New Jersey 07621

Please send me the SIGNET BOOKS I have checked above. I am enclosing $_____ (please add 50¢ to this order to cover postage and handling). Send check or money order—no cash or C.O.D.'s. Prices and numbers are subject to change without notice.

Name _____

Address _____

City _____ State _____ Zip Code _____

Allow 4-6 weeks for delivery.
This offer is subject to withdrawal without notice.

PB: THE PAUL BROWN STORY

PAUL BROWN
with Jack Clary

A SIGNET BOOK

NEW AMERICAN LIBRARY

TIMES MIRROR

NAL BOOKS ARE AVAILABLE AT QUANTITY DISCOUNTS
WHEN USED TO PROMOTE PRODUCTS OR SERVICES. FOR
INFORMATION PLEASE WRITE TO PREMIUM MARKETING DIVISION,
THE NEW AMERICAN LIBRARY, INC., 1633 BROADWAY,
NEW YORK, NEW YORK 10019.

Copyright © 1979 by Paul Brown and Jack Clary

All rights reserved. For information address
Atheneum Publishers, Inc., 597 Fifth Avenue,
New York, New York 10017.

This is an authorized reprint of a hardcover edition published by
Atheneum Publishers, Inc. A hardcover edition was published
simultaneously in Canada by McClelland & Stewart Ltd.

SIGNET TRADEMARK REG. U.S. PAT. OFF. AND FOREIGN COUNTRIES
REGISTERED TRADEMARK—MARCA REGISTRADA
HECHO EN CHICAGO, U.S.A.

SIGNET, SIGNET CLASSICS, MENTOR, PLUME, MERIDIAN AND NAL
BOOKS are published by The New American Library, Inc.,
1633 Broadway, New York, New York 10019

First Signet Printing, August, 1981

1 2 3 4 5 6 7 8 9

PRINTED IN THE UNITED STATES OF AMERICA

*To my family who has endured the ups and downs
of this wonderful experience . . .
and to my coaching colleagues and the players
who have made it all possible*

Contents

PB: THE PAUL BROWN STORY

PROLOGUE

A Coach's Credo

I KNOW MANY PEOPLE WERE surprised when I retired from coaching after the 1975 season. The Cincinnati Bengals had won eleven of their fourteen games and made the play-offs that year, and the team's best days seemed to lie ahead. We had worked for eight years to turn the club into a real contender, and I'm sure there were many, including some of my dearest friends, who thought I would stay with it at least until we had gotten into the Super Bowl and prove to those who had said otherwise nearly thirteen years before that the game had not passed me by.

Such thoughts never entered my mind, however. I simply felt that it was the proper time to step down, and even then I made the decision only after the season had ended. It was an easy decision because I made it myself. I had nothing more to prove, and I wanted to go out on a successful note. I was the only person who had ever had the privilege of starting two franchises from scratch in professional football and of seeing the one become a great champion and the other arrive at the brink of becoming a champion. The cataclysmic events in Cleveland in 1962 had long since passed, and what we had accomplished in only a few years in Cincinnati had pretty well satisfied my friends and me about the soundness of the principles and methods of our football. I stepped away quietly, and I know that startled many. Maybe I was overly sensitive, but I couldn't face the idea of a major media event and all that went with it. I elected to slide out sideways with as little fanfare as possible, as is my nature.

There were other factors involved in my decision, too. I had not lost my zest for coaching or the challenge that came from each game, but I had seen the sport change drastically since I had returned to football in 1968, and not much of the change was for the good. Society had become different, and with it, some of the fun that I had always found in my profession had begun to wane. We were getting a different type of player from the colleges, and a certain percentage of them were not what I considered college material. They had been exposed to education, but not actually educated. One player of mine, for example, said, after he retired, that he wanted to return to his university to get his degree—but that it would take him three to three and a half years to get it! That man had already completed four years of college when he had been drafted, and I can't imagine what he had been doing during that time. His type of athlete was becoming increasingly common.

In addition, the players were now represented by a union, even though they were in fact independent contractors. A few years ago the players held a strike, and even today some of our wives won't speak to the other wives because of it. A large majority of the players had also acquired agents, and a few of them were more loyal to those agents or their union than to their team, the people who paid them, or the communities they represented. They frowned on many of the proud principles I used to enforce on the Cleveland Browns and in the early years of the Bengals. With the areas of player control beginning to diminish, I couldn't picture myself adhering to a system which I didn't believe benefited everyone, and I knew better than to agonize over it. I had returned to football not to become miserable, but to pursue my lifelong profession and the work I loved so much.

Added to all this was the fact that I was getting older, and a certain segment of society seems automatically to dislike you as you progress in age. Sometimes it seemed that if we won, they said it was in spite of my age, and if we lost, it was because of it. *I* didn't feel any different at sixty-five from the way I had at forty-five, but society certainly did. The final straw was that at times I wondered if I might not be an albatross around the neck of my team; often our opponents used me to get their own teams psyched to play us: one last shot at the old man, you might say. So, I made the decision to step down and to try to make a contribution from another direction. The success of the franchise and the overall success of professional football became my paramount interest.

In my role as Bengals' general manager and part owner with voting trust control, I have stayed on top of all our corporate decisions regarding football matters and have devoted my time to protecting and building the franchise. I operate as most general managers do, and I have made a special point of giving our coach the right to command and operate his football team. I felt from the beginning that the coach should have the same freedom for his coaching work that I had always wanted for myself.

I am helped in my work by my second son, Mike, our club legal counsel and assistant general manager, and by my youngest son, Pete, who is the director of player personnel and in charge of our draft. Both areas are critical for a team's success, and by spending more time on them, I can help us surmount the growing problems which have radically changed our game. The end result of everything I do is to help us become the best team in professional football. Until his unexpected death in 1978, I was also assisted by my oldest son, Robin, who acted as a scout. He died at the relatively young age of forty-six, and burying him was the toughest thing I have ever done.

My basic philosophy, the one I have stressed with every team I have ever coached, is simple: everything we do must be in terms of our team and of doing our best. Obviously, the teams were convinced of its appropriateness because our record speaks for itself. Personally, that philosophy has helped me achieve success at every level, and after more than twenty-five years as a head coach and owner in professional football, I am independent and able to enjoy my life as I wish. Wealth and the material benefits which have accrued to me from football have never been paramount in my life, however. Though the niceties of life have helped my family—my only other consuming interest outside of football—nothing has ever meant as much to me as what I accomplished during my years at Massillon High School and Ohio State University, where I had the only two coaching jobs I ever really wanted. And though my success has brought me a measure of recognition, which is nice, it certainly isn't necessary in order for me to be satisfied with my life.

Why were we so successful over so many years in a profession not really given to individual success?

Many of the things I'm going to say here are going to come up later in the book as well, in their appropriate contexts, but I think it's important to lay them all out now at the beginning, so you'll know who I am. The one key reason for our success was this: I always believed that football was just as much a "people business" as an exact science of plays and formations. Contrary to some misguided public perceptions of me as the taskmaster who treated players like automatons, I worked harder at every phase of the "people business" than at anything else, from the first time I ever looked at a player in junior high school until the final day I coached the Cincinnati Bengals.

Other reasons were important, too, such as my attitudes about coaching and the way I approached my job. I was strong-willed and single-minded and possessed a fierce sense of independence. I believed strongly in the things that were necessary for us to win, and I refused to tolerate any exceptions to those beliefs.

In a pure football sense, that meant I always called the offensive plays, although our quarterbacks had the flexibility of changing the play at the line of scrimmage depending on the given situation. In this is the true artistry of my profession: the ability to do the right thing at the right time at the right place for the greatest possible number of times under the stress of a game. That applies to the defense, too, and I was a party to everything we did there in every game, although an assistant relayed the signals.

Before we could ever succeed on the playing field, however, we had to have the right caliber of people for our squad. Early on, I received two fine pieces of advice about dealing with young people. The first came from Dean Elizabeth Hamilton, speaking at a Miami University chapel program when I was a student. She said: "The eternal verities will always prevail. Such things as truth, honesty and good character will never change no matter how people and times change."

The second came from my high school coach, Dave Stewart, who taught me in his own inimitable way that football was a game and should be fun and that this could be done only by surrounding yourself with good people. My old flanker, Dub Jones, used to say, "When the bad people outnumber the good people, you have got a real problem."

I never flinched in my belief in these basic premises. The hard proof of their efficacy is that we were more successful over a longer period of time than anyone who had ever coached high school and professional football. Our Massillon teams won eighty games in nine years; the Browns went to the world championship game—today called the Super Bowl—eleven times in twelve years and were league champions seven times; the Bengals rose from an expansion team to a division champion in just three seasons and twice more reached the play-offs; and Ohio State won its first national championship in only the second of my three years coaching the Buckeyes.

I cite the records only because what my coaches and I accomplished during those years came from the way we handled our players. To know and appreciate all that went into our football—in high school, college and the pros—and why we were successful, it is necessary to understand the principles that guided our teams. Everything had to do with people—from properly assessing a man's character, intelligence and talent to getting him to perform to the best of his ability and in a way that benefited our team. "The team" was everything.

I know that over the years much of our success was due to the individual excellence and leadership of such players as Otto Graham, Dub Jones, Marion Motley, Bill Willis, Lou Groza, Dante Lavelli, Kenny Anderson and our other great stars, but equally important, all of them were fine people as well. We wanted every one of our players to be both, a good player and a good person, whether he was all-pro or the last guy on the team, because I discovered early in my coaching career just how delicate the mechanism of a football team was and how much effort had to go into maintaining a correct balance between so many different personalities. The only way to do that job was to pick the right kind of people. My beliefs about that have never changed, regardless of how our society has changed.

In professional football, we tried to put our beliefs into action during the annual college draft. I considered the draft of college players the life's blood of our game and the only way to build a firm foundation of talent. When we first joined the National Football League in 1950 and drafted players to-

gether in a Philadelphia hotel ballroom, some teams made
their selections from a copy of a football magazine. We
startled everyone when we walked in carrying our notebooks
listing each player by position and in order of preference.
The next year there were quite a few notebooks at other
tables.

We wanted our players to be intelligent, fast, coachable, to
have good size and a good character—in other words, to be
solid citizens and solid football players. We always looked
into a potential player's character before we drafted him, particularly in the early rounds. Most players don't change too
much once they enter professional football, and those who
are problems in college nearly always will be problems in the
pros. Fortunately we had very few of that type because I
know many college coaches, and in later years many of my
former players became coaches. If I wanted to find out about
someone, I'd simply call one of my friends, and all he would
have to say was, "He's not your kind of guy," and we'd steer
clear. The danger came when coaches felt they owed something to their players and so recommended them wrongly as
high draft picks or when the coach himself wanted to look
good by having someone from his team drafted high by the
NFL. Having my friends and former players available for advice paid off and saved us many headaches, particularly during the seventies, when we began getting players who didn't
want to be timed in the 40-yard dash, or to take an IQ test,
or who had possible drug or alcohol problems.

We always preferred "raising our own"—drafting players
we were reasonably sure of and who believed in our system.
There is no foolproof way of knowing what is in a player's
heart, but we always had a pretty good idea because of the
reliability of our overall testing program. Even before they
were drafted, we gave all our players intelligence tests so that
we could determine their capacity to learn. Poise under stress
is the key to maintaining a consistent and winning level of
play, and that in turn is linked to the capacity to learn; those
who don't have it are invariably the first to make the big mistakes in a close game because they can't handle the pressure.

At Massillon I had a psychologist make up some tests and
then combined the results with a boy's grade record. Together, they gave us an idea of the kind of boy we were
coaching. I followed the same rule when recruiting a player
for Ohio State: First I looked closely at his high school

records; then I added our own testing program. In those days the student-athlete was the rule, and we went after the best in both categories.

Everywhere we did our testing we found that players with low intelligence progressed only so far in our football, then quickly leveled off. Knowing a man's capacity to learn before we drafted him helped us calculate his potential.

I never believed that certain positions were only for the lower IQ players, and others for the higher. I felt we were better off with reasonable intelligence throughout our team, though I tried to make certain that the core of our team was in the upper percentiles. Only in absolutely necessary cases, when the player had particular athletic skills that could get him through rough situations, did we keep those with low IQs. Some of the most intelligent people ever to play for us were defensive linemen like Bill Willis, Bob Gain and Paul Wiggin, and then, of course, our great quarterbacks, Otto Graham and Ken Anderson; Ken, in fact, nearly knocked us over when his variance test results ranked in the upper one-tenth of the top 1 percent. Offensive linemen, too, particularly the center, had to be intelligent because of split-second blocking changes before the ball is snapped. Linebacker is the most complex defensive position because it requires smarts, poise and reaction under pressure.

In judging physical talent, I placed great emphasis on my belief that players at all positions should be fast and quick. This is called team speed, and I guess I am somewhat of a "speed freak." We looked for foot speed, above all, because it is the key to success in professional football. In Cleveland, guards like Lindell Houston, Weldon Humble, Abe Gibron, Bob Gaudio and Jim Ray Smith were timed in 4.7 and 4.8 seconds for the 40-yard dash. Our tackles, Lou Groza and Mike McCormack, were both 4.8 for the 40 and played at 255 pounds. Tight end Dante Lavelli ran the 40 in 4.6, and Ray Renfro, who succeeded Dub Jones as flanker, ran a 4.5-second 40, as did Isaac Curtis. Jones himself ran 4.6, and the list could go on: Marion Motley, Jim Brown, Bobby Mitchell, Bob Cowan, Essex Johnson—all were sprinters.

We had the same kind of speed on defense: Bill Willis, a world-class sprinter at Ohio State; Len Ford, who had been an offensive end at Michigan and with the Los Angeles Dons before playing defensive end for us; Tony Adamle and Walt Michaels, both fullbacks in college before becoming linebackers; and two of our defensive backs, Tommy James and Warren Lahr, both of whom ran the 40 in 4.6 seconds, or less. When we put all that together on defense, we never had to worry about someone's breaking a big play against us, and on offense, we knew we could make that big play with just one shot. I've always believed that overall team speed, together with size and weight, is the difference between great teams and ordinary teams.

If a player had speed and quickness, but wasn't football smart, however, or vice versa, I instructed our scouts not to recommend him. I also told our scouts, when possible, to make sure they saw the player stripped, so they could check his muscle and bone structure. If a college lineman didn't have a heavy bone structure, for instance, they knew right away he didn't belong in professional football. A player in uniform or street clothes can hide both his deficiencies and his strengths. The best example was Warren Lahr, a defensive back with the Browns. He didn't look like much in street clothes, but his tremendous body just rippled. Marion Motley took one look at him naked and, laughing, said, "I don't fight no man until I see him stripped."

The only exception to all these rules was someone we called a "player." That was a man whose times in the 40-yard dash might not have been impressive, nor his quickness something special, but who had great instincts. Some of these "players," such as Bob Gain and Alex Agase of the Browns, consistently seemed to be in the right place at the right time. These players stood out whenever they were on the field.

Even when drafting a "player," however, we were always careful not to upgrade anyone's ranking just to fill a specific need. If we rated a particular center as a third- or fourth-round choice, we made sure we didn't pick him in the first or second round, even though we might have needed a center. We tried to select the best player available and hoped it would be one who would strengthen us at a particular position. The exception was quarterback. If there was an outstanding candidate on the board when it came our time to select, I thought long and hard about choosing him, even if we already had a great one on our team. A quarterback is a unique property in professional football.

When drafting, I never had any prejudices about a player's college background, though we did scale down our evaluations of a player from a small college—we had no idea what would happen when he stepped into games in front of huge crowds or played against players better schooled and used to more pressure. There were too many good players from small schools to ignore their potential. Ken Anderson, the Bengals' quarterback, is a notable example. Because he played at a high school which could support only a six-man football team, he was overlooked by every major college and wound up at Augustana College, a tiny Illinois school. Ken actually went to Augustana on a basketball scholarship, but because he was a great natural athlete with a tremendous mental capacity, he easily fitted his school's need for a quarterback. We just did beat the Atlanta Falcons in drafting him—and he has easily fitted our needs as well. Other fine players from small schools have included Warren Lahr from Western Reserve and Frank Gatski and Eddie Ulinski from Marshall College.

For all our success with these players, however, I always felt our best chance came with players who were used to the big-time atmosphere, particularly those from the Big Ten, Big Eight, and Southwest conferences and from the major independent schools. I liked these schools partly because I wanted players familiar with the cold weather and rough field conditions we encountered late each year in Cleveland and Cincinnati; partly because I was partial to kids from a mid-American background, I knew what we would be getting in terms of life-style and general philosophy. The schools in those areas attracted the best football players, and the best coaches as well, many of whom I knew and could rely on for correct evaluations.

By contrast, and with reasonable exceptions, such as Isaac Curtis of the Bengals and Paul Wiggin of the Browns, I was reluctant to dabble with players from the West Coast. Invariably they played for a year or two, got a taste of some cold weather or missed the life-style of California and began demanding to be traded to teams on the West Coast. Such behavior is disruptive to a team, especially if the player is an integral part of a particular unit; you can't ship every player to California just because he misses the sun and the surf.

The "me first" mentality is endemic to the philosophy of higher education today, and it has not only affected our game over the last decade but made our drafting procedures much harder. In my judgment, we are not getting the same quality of person that we once had in professional football, although in the last few years the situation has eased somewhat. With larger squads and a greater number of teams, we have ended up with more fringe players, many of whom are looking only for what they can get—the lawsuit types—not for what they can give to their team. In many ways, this mentality reflects what they are being taught by their educators; part of the problem, too, is that schools are enrolling people who don't qualify for college. They are being taught things beyond their depth, and as a result, they can only become problem people. The Browns and the Bengals probably had fewer difficulties than most teams, but only because we worked so hard at the "people" job and stood fast behind our principles.

I should point out one thing, however: I've never been afraid to take on somebody with a questionable reputation as long as I knew he had the potential to be a fine player and that he was not really a disruptive person. I have always believed that young men want to work in an atmosphere of reasoned discipline and order and respond better under those conditions.

Two good examples are Don Paul, one of the best defensive backs ever to play for the Browns, and Len Ford, a tremendous defensive end who is now in the Hall of Fame. Paul came to us from the Chicago Cardinals with a reputation as a problem maker, but we discovered the root of his problem: He simply did not like his losing team or its future. With the Browns, he became a driving force in both our daily practices and our games and turned into a team leader. Ford also had an attitude problem when he played with the Los Angeles Dons of the All-America Conference. Len was a tremendous offensive end, but his team got beaten so badly so often that he'd get down on himself and everyone else. I sympathized with his discouragement, and I kept thinking, "Maybe if he were with a better team, like the Browns, he'd play well." As it turned out, we were able to select him in the allocation draft of players from the defunct AAC when we joined the NFL. My judgment about him was correct because when we switched him to defensive end, he responded by becoming one of the greatest ever to play in the NFL.

There were some, however, who came to us and played well for a year or two because we were contenders, then reverted to their old form, and we moved them on. They just did not understand what we expected of them as players or even as ordinary citizens. What we expected, and stressed at all times, was the team concept; it took an intelligent person to understand why it was necessary to sublimate himself for the overall good of the team. The only people who couldn't play for us were the selfish or the disloyal or those who could not adjust their individual skills to our team concepts. Many fine players in professional football started with the Browns or the Bengals but were moved on for one or more of those reasons. We simply replaced them, sometimes with better players, sometimes not, but always secure in the knowledge that we had our kind of person.

The selfish player is the worst, like a cancer; a few of them can quickly devastate a football team. All they think about is how many times they ran outside or inside, how many times the ball was thrown to them or how many times they were allowed to block for a decisive play. I wanted players who blocked for other runners and didn't worry how many times they carried the ball. Marion Motley was that kind of player. He never cared whether he gained 100 yards or 20; all that counted was: Did we win?

I didn't even like our coaches to make an issue of statistical milestones. I was criticized one day for taking Bobby Mitchell out of a game against the Washington Redskins when he was only a few yards shy of establishing a new rushing record. I didn't know anything about the record at the time, but even if I had, I wouldn't have risked the possibility of his being injured simply to break a record in a game that had already been won.

To foster the team concept further, I tried to discourage cliques among our players. In training camp, we used to ask the players to eat at different tables with different people every day. I wanted them to have a feeling for one another because in order to survive in football, players have to be able to depend on one another.

With so many different personalities on a team, however, it was only natural that we'd have one or two who couldn't get along with anyone not of the same emotional or philosophical stripe. I tried to slow these people down at training camp by telling them in my opening talk that we sold tickets to Republicans and Democrats, communists and capitalists alike, and that there was room for everyone to exist. Some people you never could help, though.

I was sensitive to everything that went on in our locker room, and anytime I felt there might be some sort of confrontation brewing, I'd step in and try to make a joke about

it. We always seemed to have problems when a heavyweight
fight was coming up, for instance; everyone seemed to have
strong views on a favorite fighter and why he should win.
Some people on a team take these things a little too personally, and all you need is one man's feelings hurt for any
length of time to have a problem. I've seen players become
estranged over matters just as trivial as that, and that is
anathema for a team that must work so closely together.

I tried to be loyal to our players, and I expected, and in
nearly every instance received, the same loyalty in return. I
wanted nothing to do with anyone who wasn't true to his
team; we simply cut him off by moving him to another team
or releasing him outright. It happened on only a few occasions, though usually when a young player got carried away
by someone offering him more money to play in Canada. In
one case, however, a former player was paid to spy on our
practices prior to the 1957 championship game against Detroit. When we found out about it, the player said it was because he desperately needed the money for his family and he
was deeply embarrassed about it. I felt sorry for him, and
we've since made our peace—but as a result, our opponents
knew every short-yardage play we would use and in what order. I'm not sure Jim Brown would forgive him, even now.

I made it a point never to lie to or mislead our players,
and any coach who does will lose them the moment they find
out. The players must believe in the coach if he is to lead
them, and he must convince them that everything they are
doing for him is totally correct. Every day before practice,
from training camp to the last day of the season, from my
first teams in Massillon through my final season in Cincinnati, I talked to our players: sometimes about football; often
about matters which touched on their lives as a whole. I
didn't moralize with them; I was simply interested in getting
their best efforts and in giving us the best possible chance to
win. Most of all, I wanted them to know that everything on
this team would be honest and aboveboard and that I expected their total cooperation. As long as I was allowed to run
the team without interference, which was the case except in
our final season in Cleveland, the feeling of mutual respect
and responsibility that resulted was a key reason for the
success which stretched over so many years.

For all that, however, I've been criticized for not hobnob-
bing with our football players, accused of being cold and

aloof because I didn't pal around with them or slap them on the back every time they did something well. When Jim Brown was playing, he once told people, "Why, I've never even been invited to his home." Neither was any of our other players, however. I've often had my former players as guests in my home after their careers ended. Many of them are my dearest friends now, but our relationship is different and allows for such niceties.

I'm sure Jim understands now that this is the way it had to be: the player doing his best to win, the coach running the show. There is a time and a place for everything, and I couldn't hobnob with just one player and not with all of them. I certainly never meant to act aloof to any player. It was strictly my nature. My first wife, Katy, and my present wife, Mary, knew all our players and got along with them very well, but only in terms of meeting them as they came from the dressing room or talking with their families. At Cleveland we'd have a big family picnic at training camp every year for our players and staff, and I'd get to know their wives and children then. When it was over, we went back to business. I felt that was the proper way to handle those relationships.

It was different with our coaching staff. They were my closest friends, as well as my associates, and they were welcome as guests in our home, and my wife and I were welcome in their homes. When I coached in Massillon and at Ohio State, we got together socially at least once a month, and in Cleveland I always held a Christmas party for our coaches and their families. Their children still talk about those parties.

Another principle I always followed, from the day my first team gathered at Bowling Green College in 1946 until my final training camp at Wilmington College with the Bengals in 1975, was incorporated in my opening lecture to the players. I never left anything to their imagination; I laid out exactly what I expected from them, how I expected them to act on and off the field and what we expected to accomplish each day of the season. I always told them "why" we asked them to do something. I consider this one of the most important principles of coaching. That word appeared more than any other in our playbook, and we used it in everything: "Why we work at running," "Why we do our routine warm-up daily," "Why we take calisthenics," "Why we practice our daily drills." In our early years in Cleveland, the players wrote the answers to those questions in their playbooks, and even today most can repeat a question and answer it verbatim as it was dictated three decades ago. When we told our players "why," they were more willing to accept everything we asked them to do and to get into the spirit of the game. Good football requires that acquiescence.

During a normal coaching day I spent a lot of time with the players. I made it a point to look into the training room and see how our injured guys were coming along. It also served to keep any potential malingerers at bay. I spent time with them in the locker room, and we'd talk about football situations or about their families because I was interested in them and I wanted them to know it.

If I saw a player not doing his job or if I didn't like the way he looked when he came to practice, I'd call him into my office, and we'd reach an understanding about how things should be. The same was true if a player didn't think he was getting a square deal; I'd talk to him, and we'd try to resolve the problem. I demanded the same respect, obedience and team attitude from every man and expected full compliance with those demands. Over the years enough players have come back home and said thank you, so that I feel I've done some good in the world, more than just being paid for a job.

Some of these players have told me there was a quality to playing for the Browns and the Bengals that actually transcended football and became a part of their life-styles. I always stressed to our players, for instance, that they should be good examples for the kids who saw them away from the football field. That's why I had rules against smoking in public, swearing or bad language and required coats and ties on the road. I wanted our players to show class. College players had a good reputation, but the public perception of the professional football player back then was of a big, dumb guy with a potbelly and a cheap cigar. That kind of person disgusted me, and I never wanted anyone associating our players with that image, so I always tried to make our pro teams collegelike.

Our teams had training rules, too, and we enforced them even though they were grown men; they knew it was important for them to take care of themselves. Some players painted me as a harsh disciplinarian, but that wasn't true because I never asked anything of them that I wasn't willing to do myself. We probably had fewer fines for breaking rules in Cleveland and Cincinnati than any teams in the league, but when it happened, the fine was never rescinded or put into a kitty so everyone could have a party when the season ended. I made sure the player knew that he had made a mistake; I also made sure he knew I wasn't mad at him, and then we went on as if it hadn't happened.

Les Horvath once missed a flight to the West Coast when he was playing for the Browns, and not only had to pay his own way but had to pay a $100 fine for not traveling with the team. Our guys couldn't wait for him to arrive because they wanted to see his reaction to having to pour out nearly $200, which was a lot of money back in 1949, just for sleeping late. Les wasn't going to give them any satisfaction, though. "You know, that airline was so happy to have a former Heisman Trophy winner on one of its flights that I rode for free," he told the players, and the meeting broke up in laughter. Les paid his fine without bitterness, and his attitude was typical of our players who made a mistake.

The biggest fines I ever imposed were $500 penalties for lost playbooks. Once one of our more serious rookies unaccountably allowed his book to lie around, and some of the players took it without telling him. That caused a stir because the poor guy came to me, really upset that he had lost his playbook and that it was going to cost him $500. Just as I was ready to levy the fine, however, the veterans returned his book, but the player had learned his lesson.

One of the rules which many outside people took too seriously was really more of a joke. That was our so-called Wednesday rule—connubial abstinence. It came about because of Weeb Ewbank's camaraderie with some of our big linemen when he was tackle coach. Because I told the players so often that the coaches wouldn't ask anything of them they wouldn't do themselves, the linemen ribbed Weeb and said they'd abstain if he would, but that he wasn't about to do. No one could have enforced a rule like that, but some people actually believed it. Maybe that's how I got to be known as "cold and brutal"!

The players knew—because I told them—that their futures depended on how well they took care of themselves and adhered to our principles. That was easier to enforce many years ago, when, with only ten or twelve teams and smaller rosters, there were plenty of hungry players vying for just a few jobs. No one wanted to take the chance of being fired.

Our rules were enforced without regard for a player's status or reputation; I knew that if the players knew the rules were for everyone and applied without discrimination, they would respond. Everyone's time was equal, and if Jim Brown came late to a meeting, as he did only a few times, he got fined $50, the same as the last man on the roster.

I dismissed players, too, for breaking training rules. At Ohio State, one of my former Massillon players, a fine end named Charley Anderson, sneaked out the night before a game and did some celebrating at a night club in Columbus. When I found out about it the day after the game, I waited until our team was assembled for its next meeting and then said to him, "Charley, you violated our training rules. Have you anything to say?"

"No," he replied.

"Then for the benefit of this squad and the future of our football, you are dismissed," I told him. "Get out!"

He walked out of the room, and that was it.

Another time, before our first AAC championship game, Jim Daniell, our team captain, who had also played on my first Ohio State team, was arrested for getting into an altercation with the police after he had been drinking. Two other players, Lou Rymkus and Mac Speedie, were with him, but according to the police report, they had tried to act as peacemakers and were not involved in the fracas.

It became page one news in the next morning's papers, so when I had the team assembled that morning, I said to Jim, "You violated our training rules, and you are the team captain. We can't have that. For the welfare of this team and the future of our football, you are dismissed."

He walked out of our locker room. He did receive a full winner's share after we beat the AAC New York Yankees for the title, but I just could not reconcile the leader of our team with such behavior because a captain has a special obligation to be exemplary in his behavior. Years later I received a nice letter from Jim saying that he was involved with youth work and had been successful in his career. I wrote back and said I held no hard feelings about that incident, and I was happy that he didn't either. Subsequently, for reasons I still can't fathom, he turned around and blasted me for making him live with something he said had been a blight on his life. I don't know what he expected me to do. I suppose his resentment and bitterness stemmed from my not dismissing the other two players, but there was no reason to. It's too bad that something like this should cause a man to be so bitter for so many years. After all, the coach didn't break the rules.

My principles never wavered in this respect. I was not as rigid on matters such as dress codes or hair styles during my final seasons as head coach of the Bengals, but I made every effort to weed out problem players before a season began. If the player became difficult during the season, I talked with him and tried to get him squared away. If that didn't work and it was near the end of the season, we played out the schedule and then moved him. If it was early and his actions became flagrantly disobedient, it was not hard to bid him good-bye. Fortunately we had very few of that kind.

Indeed, our approach to the game was so ingrained in our players that we never had to resort to what is an overused term—motivation—or the use of phony slogans or pep talks. You can't prepare a player that way. The only way to do it is to be so thorough in your work beforehand as to make him totally confident of himself and those around him. Our great players got ready from within themselves. I know that today's players would roll off their chairs laughing if a coach got up and began making some of those old-fashioned pep talks. Players sense when they're not doing the job, and often all I had to do was look at a player for him to get the message. Sometimes he read more into the look than I intended, but that served a purpose, too.

I always told our players that the first day back to practice after a game was the day to begin preparing themselves mentally and physically for the next game. The real pros do this, and they don't need to have someone wind them up. A class person understands what it takes to win. Not every player on a team will be a self-winder, but a team had better have more than its share, as we did, if it wants to be successful.

I had my own ways of keeping players keyed up if they needed it, but I was direct and to the point, with no gimmicks or shouting or profanity, because that never was my style. If I saw a player beginning to slip, I sometimes told him straight out, in front of the team, that he had better improve or we'd find someone else to take his place. Some of my former players have told me that this snapped them back into the groove. I've also been characterized as a needler, but

I always felt a few gentle barbs were enough for the class players, and if it took much more than that to get a guy moving, then we didn't want him on our team.

Mike McCormack, the finest offensive tackle I've ever seen in football and our team captain at Cleveland, never has forgotten a film session we held following a game against the Baltimore Colts. In it, I critiqued his play against Gino Marchetti, Baltimore's great defensive end. Gino had had a pretty good day—and a rare good one against McCormack—and as the film unwound, Mike remembers my saying, "Michael, you are our team captain, and we expect more from you than you showed on Sunday. We always felt confident, if the opposition had a tough man and he was opposite you, that you were going to do your job, that you could handle him. We relied on you, but you let us down; you hurt the team. . . ."

"I kept wishing you'd gotten up there and just screamed at me," Mike told me later. "But you didn't. You didn't even raise your voice, and nothing you said was vicious. But every little barb dug deeper and deeper until I wanted to go out of that room right then, find Marchetti and take him apart."

At the same time I was never reluctant to give a player a lift with a compliment because I appreciated what my players did for our team. Sometimes it was just "thank you" to a man who had played exceptionally well or some words of praise to a boy's parents or to the man's wife when I saw her next. I'm sure there were times when our players wondered if their old coach really knew how hard they tried or if he appreciated all their efforts. I did, and I want them to know that if I was too harsh on them at times, it was only my own strong-willed determination for all of us to succeed that moved me to it. It was my nature. I didn't mean anything personal by it, and if I thoughtlessly offended anyone, I hope he'll realize it was only the spirit of the moment and nothing more. In fact, I always told our players that any harsh words spoken during the heat of a game should be forgotten once the game ended because they usually rose more out of emotion than reason.

One of the reasons I was so successful in dealing with our players was that I had complete authority. Except at the end in Cleveland, when nonfootball people kept interfering with our football operation, it was understood, from my superiors in high school and college to the ownership of the Browns, that everything pertaining to football would be under my control. That way the players always understood exactly where the authority was vested. There can be only one place for a player to go for an answer, and that has to be the coach. I doubt whether any coach can succeed unless he has control of the player-coach relationship. In Cincinnati our coaches have always taken part in our drafts and are consulted on all trades, and once the personnel are selected and finalized, they are on their own to operate.

Success also breeds success. Some call it the winning habit, and we always had it. It came from confidence and the state of mind among our players that said we would win and by whatever means necessary. When Otto Graham was the Browns' quarterback, every player trusted implicitly that he would find a way to win, and he usually did. This confidence was so strong that once, in an AAC game, when we trailed the San Francisco 49ers 31-0 early in the second half and I was fuming, Edgar Jones said to me, "Aw, don't worry, coach, Otto will pull it out." We were down by thirty-one points, but the players still had that kind of trust in the man and in themselves—because they knew what it took to produce a victory. As it happened, we didn't win that day, but there were other times, such as in the 1950 championship game against the Rams when Otto drove our offense nearly the length of the field in the final seconds so that Lou Groza could kick the game-winning field goal. A team must have that confidence in itself if it wants to be consistently successful over a long period of time.

I enjoyed winning—and very much disliked losing—but I did not allow either of them to obsess me. I was a silent loser, believing that if you won, you said little, and if you lost, you said even less. Once I reviewed the movies, I cut off that game—win or lose—and went on to the next one. A victory at any price had no value for me, nor did I put down our team if it played well, yet lost. If the latter happened, I told our players to hold their heads high and walk out of the stadium proud that we had done our best; there was nothing to be ashamed of and no apologies to make. If we played sloppily, however, and were just fortunate enough to win, I told our players as soon as the locker room door closed, "We had a bad day. I'm not proud of how you looked doing it, so let's not get carried away with the fact that we lucked out. Let's get ourselves back down to the ground and go to work again."

Some people just never understood this philosophy and chose instead to criticize everything—from our winning too much, to my calling the plays from the sidelines, to the way I looked. Years from now this group will probably still be trying to poke holes in our system. I will always be proud, however, of all that our system of football accomplished, not only because we won and left a lasting imprint on the game but because of its effect on the lives of the men who played for us at each level of competition. They are the proofs that our methods and beliefs were correct. Many of them became my closest friends; some were or are successful coaches; others achieved great success in other careers. What matters most to me is that they still call me, and they still remember many of the good moments and the lessons which transcended blocking and tackling.

ONE

The Early Years

THE PRINCIPLES I APPLIED TO coaching were the same ones I had been reared with. They reflected my early years growing up in two small mid-American Ohio towns: Norwalk, midway between Cleveland and Toledo, where I spent my first nine years, and Massillon, a much larger town by comparison, where my athletic instincts and interest in football were honed by Dave Stewart. Norwalk was a sleepy little town of only a few thousand persons, a place of Saturday-night band concerts in the park, elm-lined streets, squeaky-clean doorstoops, large homes and a main thoroughfare of well-ordered shops and small businesses. It was little more than a stop along the Wheeling and Lake Erie Railroad, for which my father, Lester, was a dispatcher.

When my father was transferred to Massillon, about sixty-five miles southeast of Norwalk, however, I found a totally different existence. Massillon was a wealthy, thriving steel town with a healthy blue-collar work ethic and, to my pleasure, some fine sports teams, including the Massillon Tigers, one of professional football's first franchises; a healthy semipro baseball team called the Agathons, which attracted many major-league players on their way up or down; and an assortment of good high school teams, particularly a football team that had for years turned out tough, hardnosed players who later went on to colleges in Ohio, Indiana and western Pennsylvania.

I was enthralled with life in both places. I spent summers on my grandfather's farm when I lived in Norwalk and got to explore some of the mysteries of bluegill fishing along the Vermilion River, as well as frog catching and hiking through

21

the woods on the edge of town. I grew up to appreciate the healthy and wholesome life-style of a small community, where a Saturday night on the town meant the band concert, browsing in the local department store, an ice cream soda and listening to my parents and their friends exchange the latest gossip or discuss the day's issues.

At the same time I have never lost my love for the city of Massillon, and while I have enjoyed and always been a part of every community in which I have coached, that city is my real home, and someday I will be buried there, next to my first wife, Katy. I return at least once a year to tend her grave and to visit old friends, and though the city has undergone vast changes in style and appearance, my memories are pleasant because some of my finest and happiest moments were spent there, both as a young boy and as a football coach. I have been an honored citizen for many years, but the city has produced famous people, too, including Tommy Henrich, the great New York Yankees' outfielder, actress Lillian Gish and Ben Fairless, the late president of the United States Steel Corporation.

I knew both Henrich and Fairless very well. Ben Fairless lived around the corner from us, but his name was Ben Williams at the time. When his mother became ill, he was sent to live with some relatives near Massillon whose name was Fairless, adopted their name and in time became president of Central Steel Corporation, the mainstay of Massillon's economy. When that company merged with U.S. Steel, Ben soon became president, but he often returned to the city and the school, several times even sitting on our bench during Massillon's big games against Canton-McKinley.

Tommy Henrich has been a lifelong friend, and one of my memories of him was when he afforded me the rare opportunity of sitting in the Yankee dugout during a game in 1940. Katy and I were in New York for the World's Fair and decided to go to Yankee Stadium early one afternoon to watch the Cleveland Indians; when we got there, we found Henrich engaged in a pepper game near the stands behind home plate. I walked down to the front row, cupped my hands and said, "Yes, he's a great fielder."

Tommy stopped, turned around and, without looking, shouted, "Where are you?"

He brought me down into the dugout, we talked and then the great Yankee manager Joe McCarthy invited me to stay and watch the game from there. In the late innings of that game, one of the Indians hit a high fly ball to right center field, where Tommy and Joe DiMaggio were standing and just watching the ball, and it looked as if neither of them would catch it until DiMaggio finally stuck out his glove and pulled it in. The Yankees won the game, 2-1, and afterward I said, "Mr. McCarthy never said a word when you guys gave that fly ball the Alphonse and Gaston routine and almost lost it."

"Oh," he replied, "it would have been a physical error if Joe had missed the catch. It would have been a mental error had neither of us reached out for the ball, and then you would have heard some words when we got back to the dugout."

That was the first time I became conscious of how a coach should react under such circumstances. In football, particularly, physical errors are in the nature of the game, and though you try to avoid them, a coach cannot always fault a player who is trying to make the play. The only physical error I never could tolerate was fumbling because it often meant the runner was carrying the ball carelessly, or he hadn't built up his arm strength to a point where the ball couldn't be jerked loose. We never made any allowances for mental errors.

Henrich and Fairless were just a couple of Massillon's best-known citizens. Harry Stuhldreher, the quarterback of Notre Dame's Four Horsemen, was another. Maybe I still am a small-town guy at heart, but from knowing these men and others who were just plain, ordinary citizens, I've always been convinced that growing up in a small-town environment is a fine life for a young boy. Certainly for this young boy, totally intrigued by anything that could be moved, caught, jumped over or learned, it was heaven.

My mother, Ida, was a pleasant, happy woman who enjoyed having friends and relatives visit and loved games and competition. Whenever we had company, the card table came out of the closet, and soon a game of euchre, pinochle, gin or 500 rummy would be in progress. She was the competitor in my background and taught me to love any game that was fun. When I came home from college, I always found the card table set up and waiting.

"Paulie boy," she'd say, "how about a little game before you go out?"

And we'd play.

My father was a very meticulous person, as any railroad dispatcher, responsible for split-second timing and switching trains from one track to another without mishap, must be. He was always serious-minded, very disciplined and ordered, and later it was not hard to see those traits in my own coaching. If a lineman was told to split six inches from the player next to him, it had to be six inches, not a quarter of an inch more or less. If an end had to run 11 yards downfield, then cut 6 yards to the sideline, everything was measured, timed and worked out to that precise distance. Our great passing offenses were built on this precision, but its principles had their roots in my father's side of the family.

Lester Brown—his last name originally had an *e* at the end of it, but it got dropped somehow along the way—was first-generation English, the same heritage as my mother, whose family name was Sherwood. All the Sherwoods were very easygoing. She was born in Milan, Ohio, a neat, picturesque mid-American town just a few miles east of Norwalk and the birthplace of inventor Thomas Edison. She did not know him well but, as a young girl, had met him at one of the lectures he gave during his periodic returns home. Her family home still stands outside that little town, and in fact, so does the house at 7 Elm Street where we lived in Norwalk.

Though my parents had different personalities, ours was a typical English household; my father was the unquestioned head, but my mother had a full say in our upbringing. My sister, Marian, and I were always close to them, and they gave us their total and unabashed love, understanding and guidance throughout our lives. We led a very ordered existence, and both parents were even-handed and fair in their discipline, convincing me that everyone's life needs the same.

Some of my happiest times in Massillon, even after I was grown, were spent at Sunday dinner with my parents. The family tradition continued after Katy and I were married, and later we brought our own family to my parents' home in Massillon. My sister and her husband, Sherlock Holmes Evans, a lawyer and graduate of the New York School for the Dramatic Arts, would also be there, as would his parents, who owned a small circus and from whom Sherlock had inherited his love of and interest in all things theatrical. Sometimes dinner would move, and we'd all gather at our home, or at my sister's, or at Sherlock's parents—that always intrigued me because the Evanses kept a variety of small trained animals there, dwelling in perfect harmony with their human masters. Regardless of where we were, dinner never ended until my father pushed back his chair.

Since both my mother's and my father's families were in the Norwalk area, I also had great times with my aunts and uncles and, of course, my grandparents. Some of those relatives were unique and interesting people in their own ways. My uncle Melvin, for example, was a stonemason and seemed to impress everyone in the family because he worked on his own. I always thought he carried the stone-cutting and -laying business a bit too far because he seemed to get carried away every time he saw a piece of stone or something that looked as if it needed stonework. He probably would have been a tremendous worker, though, during the Renaissance, when the great cathedrals of Europe were being built; everything he did was elaborate. Uncle Melvin also belonged to the volunteer fire department and seemed to live for the moment the bell rang and he had to fight a fire. One day it rang, and he got on the fire wagon only to have it bring him right back to his own home. We never let him forget that.

My favorite relative was my aunt Helen, my father's sister, who always took great care of me. Her husband, Clarence, was a milkman, and I sometimes rode with him early in the morning when he made his rounds by horse and wagon. Usually it was dark, and I'd be scared to death in some yards when a dog would suddenly start barking.

My aunt Helen and her sister Myrtle developed one of those unfathomable family feuds and stopped speaking to each other for years. Once, when I was head coach at Ohio State, I came back to Norwalk to speak, and Helen, so thrilled that her darling little nephew Paul was the center of attention, went all around making a big fuss about it. I was speaking from the stage of the local high school when I looked down at the front row, and there on one side of the hall sat Helen, beaming from ear to ear, and there on the other side sat Myrtle, looking up at me as if to say, "This I gotta hear!" Don't think that wasn't a bit unnerving!

Both my parents were very conscious of the need for a sound education. My father was an avid reader with an unquenchable desire to broaden the base of his knowledge. He also loved to attend public lectures and supported the lyceum programs in Norwalk, the backbone of the community culture in those years. He helped create an atmosphere in our home which indoctrinated me on the need for a college education, so there was never any doubt, from my earliest years, that I would go on to get my degree when I finished high school. Every day, before going to work, he wrote an assignment for me on a slate that hung in our kitchen. These projects included such things as sprouting the potatoes, which in the wintertime was a spooky job because they were stored in our dark, dank cellar, where even the smallest spiders played havoc with a small boy's imagination. When he came home, he checked to see whether the jobs were satisfactorily completed. Then he'd give me a few pennies or a nickel, and we'd go through a little ritual.

"What are you going to do with the money?" he'd ask, extending a small lion-shaped bank toward me.

"I'm putting it in my bank so I can have enough saved to go to college," I'd reply as I dropped the coins into the bank.

My father had hoped I would become a lawyer and was a bit disappointed when I accepted a teaching and coaching position at Severn Prep after graduation from Miami University. I was married then, however, and had been bitten by the coaching bug. I'm sure he thought I would get over it after a few years, and in fact, when I became coach at Massillon, I did begin law studies at night. I had to abandon them the following year, however, because the school appointed me basketball coach and my nights were occupied from then on. I never resumed them again, though I later received a master's degree in secondary education and administration from Ohio State.

Once he saw that it was to be my way of life, however, my father, in his introspective way, became enthusiastic about my coaching career and never tried to dissuade me from it. Both my parents attended our games at Massillon, my dad sitting quietly, but proudly, in the background, and my mother, more exuberant and emotional, letting her feelings show. My father died shortly after my appointment as head coach at Ohio State. Katy and I had called him to tell him about the birth of our youngest son, Pete, and after congratulating us, he said that he wasn't feeling good and was going into the hospital for a checkup. Later that same night we got a call saying that an embolism from phlebitis in his leg had broken loose, hit his heart and killed him. My mother, before she passed away in 1964, did live to see our great days in Cleveland, where she joined Katy and our family for one game each season. She listened to the rest of them on the radio and, to work off her nervous energy, busied herself with household projects. It became a family joke. With her irrepressible fervor, all of us were certain that a few plates got cracked during crucial moments of a game. She lived and died with us.

My parents harbored some hopes early in my life that I might become a musician. At least I was given weekly piano lessons, and my teacher, Mrs. Oberlin, probably spent her time hoping that I wouldn't show up. I can still play a little bit today, but then I discovered athletics and found the fun of competing to be better than the daily practices required to master the piano. My father made me a set of high jump standards when I was about eight years old, and I practiced high jumping by the hour. I thought I was doing pretty well until Glen Amsden, the boy next door, who was on the high school team, put the rod at my top height and easily jumped over it. I was a wee, skinny kid and just astounded at such a jump.

One day the town held a track meet for its children, and I entered, along with my best friend, Fletcher Bowers. Fletcher never seemed too interested in sports, and I didn't think he'd offer much competition, but when we both ran in the 50-yard dash, he zoomed out in front of everyone and easily won the event. What a jolt that was! It never deterred me, however, from almost living in the schoolyard and playing every kind of sport there, and if the snow covered the ground, I took up bobsledding or ice skating or whatever else was available.

I was just about six years old when my father bought me my first football, and I used it until the bladder wore out, then stuffed it with rags and leaves and went on playing as if nothing had happened. Five of us from the same neighborhood in Massillon—Harry Stroble, Delmar Halpin, Warren Ott, Jim Hollinger and I—often played together, and oddly enough, each of us later became a football coach. By the standards back then, we might have been considered a wild group. One of the boys nearly killed himself using an umbrella for a parachute and leaping from a second-floor fire escape, another fractured his skull when demonstrating how to guide his sled between two trees while he was blindfolded and another was knocked out when he fell head first into a storm sewer while hanging by his toes from the grating and trying to rescue our well-used football.

When we didn't have a football, we stuffed a stocking cap with leaves, and it served the same purpose. We played everywhere we were welcome and stayed until the welcome expired. There were no quarters or halftimes, and the game ended only when the one who owned the ball or stocking cap had to go home. We used trees for sideline markers, and more than once a play came to an abrupt halt because someone was looking the wrong way and slammed into one of the trees. I used to haunt the home of one family in particular whose son owned nearly every available piece of sports equipment; sometimes I'd show up at seven o'clock in the morning, ready to play.

Though my parents accepted my intensity about competitive sports, they never allowed it to override my schoolwork. Their influence at home was directly responsible for my feeling that teachers were special people. Everyone then held teachers, principals and all school personnel in the highest esteem. They were considered leaders in the community and highly respected.

Several years ago I returned to Norwalk to receive a Distinguished Citizens Award and mentioned the name of my first-grade teacher, Miss Butler, who back in 1914 was just a slender dark-haired young girl of twenty or twenty-one. After I had finished speaking, several people came up to me and said that they, too, remembered Miss Butler and the effect she had had on their attitudes toward school. Teachers like Miss Butler molded young people; her influence was one of the reasons I became a coach and teacher. When I began at Massillon, coaching was a privileged profession and rendered a service to young men. I have said many times that the best job I ever had was coaching at Massillon High School because it was the job in which I was able to do the most good in the world. I never cared about my financial rewards because the job just consumed me.

The main impetus for my development outside my home came from Dave Stewart, who coached all sports at Massillon when I was a student. Dave was a tall, lanky, rawboned man who wasn't too much older than his players back then, but he had the knack of getting them interested in something and then becoming a part of their fun. He was always direct in his teaching and in his critiques and, away from his players, fearless when trying anything that interested him. He never allowed protocol or reputation to color his friendships. and for years his first words to me always seemed to be: "Well, Brown, what have you done this time?"

Dave had been a center for Grove City College in Pennsylvania back in the days when all it took was a quick name change for a player to move from school to school or to play a college game on Saturday and a professional game on Sunday. In fact, Dave used to laugh about the time he went to Bethany College in West Virginia to play guard for a couple of games because the team was short-handed and then arrived back at Grove City just in time for two days of practice before the season opened. The first game, of course, was against Bethany. Dave said the Bethany players spent most of the game trying to figure out if he was the same person who had played for them the previous week and, if so, what had happened to him, and how had he gotten to Grove City so quickly?

Dave thought nothing of it, however, and it was this undaunted spirit and the fun he brought to his work that so impressed me. He was a teaching coach and a stickler for fundamentals. He always told us why he asked us to do certain things, and as you've already seen, it's a key principle in my own coaching I don't think he ever knew that he had such a rapt and willing pupil when I played for him, but I absorbed every word and every action that took place in practice. When I was in college, and Dave had left Massillon to become head coach at Sharon High School in western Pennsylvania, he enlisted me to help with his early fall coaching. I gave back to his players every single thing that he had ever taught me and poured into it all the fun and enjoyment he had imparted to me as a player. It was then that he sensed my intensity and total absorption with football coaching and was moved to recommend me for my first job at Severn Prep, in Annapolis, and later, for the head coaching job at Massillon.

To get back to when I first met Dave, though, my first football exposure came as a sophomore when I went out for the team. Football, of course, was the big sport at Massillon, and every kid dreamed of playing for the Tigers. I weighed about 120 pounds, but my intense interest in the sport and the fact that my friends were also trying out for the team were enough for me. Dave made arrangements for us to use a Boy Scout camp at Turkeyfoot Lake for two weeks during training camp, and each boy was charged $5 a week for food.

My parents were genuinely concerned about my lack of size and at first refused to allow me to attend the camp. This was a mortal blow to my spirit, and I couldn't sleep or eat for two or three days running, until my mother became so concerned she finally convinced my father that it was the only way I could survive. We drove up to the camp in my father's old Model T Ford and paid Dave $10. I'm told that my dad gave him a big wink behind my back because Dave took one look at this skinny little kid and said, "Well, Mr. Brown, I certainly hope he doesn't get hurt. We've got some big boys here, and they don't discriminate on who they hit or how hard they do it."

That didn't throw any chill into me, though, and my father knew by that time that I was determined to see this adventure to its conclusion. Dave put me on the fifth, and last, team as a quarterback, but I was so happy to be playing football and so enthralled with my new coach and his life that numbers meant nothing. Dave really did my father a favor by taking me because he never actually thought I had a chance to make the team then, if at all. I certainly wasn't ready for varsity competition. It wasn't too long, however, before he sensed my obsession with football and became intrigued.

In the season's sixth game, against Wellston, Massillon had a comfortable lead, so he decided to send me into the game to throw a pass. What could he lose? As it turned out, nothing; the pass went for a touchdown. I'm sure I was quite a sight, trotting off the field looking as if I had done this all my life. I didn't consider it anything special, though. I thought this was the way it was supposed to happen, though I know my parents almost fell out of their seats at Agathon Field, first out of surprise at seeing me get into the game and then at watching me throw that touchdown pass on my first play.

I got my first varsity *M*, the most coveted possession of my young life, as a freshman pole vaulter on the track team. When I first began vaulting, I reached 10 feet, and Dave told me that if I reached 11 feet, he would take me to a restaurant for supper. In no time at all, I made the mark, and the biggest night of my life took place when I left my house all dressed up to go out with Coach Stewart to Bender's, Massillon's favorite eatery at the time.

Coach Stewart made me pay a price for my letter, however. The letter-award ceremony was held in the school audi-
torium in front of all the students, and I desperately wanted
my first pair of long pants for this event. My parents declined, however, and I had to show up in a pair of freshly
washed knickers. Dave said a few words about each winner
before handing him the varsity *M*, and when it was my turn,
he did the same, then held out the letter to me. As I reached
for it, he drew it back and walked away. I was taken aback,
and the kids in the audience roared with laughter at this
skinny little guy looking up rather hopefully at his coach.
Dave walked back, said a few more nice words and once
more held out the letter. When I reached for it a second time,
he again drew it back and walked away, and the kids laughed
even harder. Dave did it a couple more times before finally
handing me the letter, but to tell the truth, I was so excited
getting that monogram that I hardly minded his little joke.
My mother sewed the letter on a white sweater that afternoon, and I wore it everywhere. I even wore it when I went
to Norwalk to visit our families in the summer, on the hottest
days. Of course, it was all a young kid's pride, but it was
very important to me.

If one of my biggest thrills came in track, one of my biggest disappointments did, too. In my senior year we went to
Columbus for the state championships. I had added the broad
jump to my pole vault and was jumping a bit over 20 feet
and vaulting about 11½ feet. I felt pretty good about my
chances because no one in our area of the state had matched
my best distances that season. The day was very windy, and
in the broad jump the wind blew in my face as I sped down
the runway and took off—strong enough to hold me almost
still—and I hardly reached the sawdust. I lost the event to a
winning jump of just over 18 feet, well within my range.
Then, using a bamboo pole with a plug in the end and feeling
I could make up for that disappointment in the pole vault, I
left the ground to soar over the bar, was all but batted back-
ward by the wind and lost that event, too.

I also played basketball and baseball at Massillon. I had
developed into a good foul shooter because of the hours of
practice I had spent at the hoop my father had installed on
the shed in our backyard. I practiced shooting until the bladder of the basketball wore out, then resorted again to the
leaves-and-rags solution and kept right on shooting. The rules

in those days allowed a designated foul shooter, and I got the job, as well as the captaincy in my junior year. My most memorable game was against Akron West, in which I not only guarded their star player, Howard Harpster, who later became an All-American football player at Carnegie Tech, and held him in check, but scored most of our points in a 22-21 upset.

In fact, I was probably better at basketball than at football, but my first love was football. In my junior year I became the starting quarterback, and by then I had everything in order, or at least I thought I did. In one game I actually sent a guard off the field with orders for Dave to send in a substitute because he appeared groggy and I didn't think the boy could keep up with us.

"You know, Brown," Dave reminded me many times over the years, "I saw that player trotting off the field, then you coming over and telling me you wanted a substitute and I said to myself, 'What in hell is going on? He's taken over the world. He had to stop the game and make a substitution, and then we could go on and play.' But I sent in the new player just to see what you were thinking, and you were correct."

That was a special occasion, but I had established such a rapport with my coach by that time that I really think he trusted my judgments. Dave held to the popular philosophy, advanced most prominently by Knute Rockne in his relationship with Harry Stuhldreher at Notre Dame, that the coach and his quarterback should spend as much time with each other as possible, so the player might become his coach's alter ego on the playing field. That idea wasn't bad, particularly if the player had the leadership qualities to help the coach establish his program with the other players. As it was, Dave, who had a car and took three or four players with him to college games on many occasions, often took me to his home in western Pennsylvania, so that he saw plenty of his quarterback.

Each time I got a closer look at this man's way of life, and I was amazed more than ever that someone could actually be involved with football all his life and make a living at it. The more I saw of this, the more determined I became that it would also be my way of life, and so the harder I worked and the closer attention I paid to all that Dave taught me. He trusted me so much that one summer he went to Europe on vacation and gave me his job as treasurer of the Agathons' baseball team. That was quite an honor for a sixteen-year-old boy who was just a senior in high school, but the team made money, and I did a meticulous job.

We had our fun moments, too. When I worked with his Sharon High School teams, the two of us often got into a kicking contest after practice. Dave, with his long legs, was a tremendous punter, and he had taught me the techniques when I had done the punting at Massillon. Ostensibly, we were just taking turns kicking, but I know that neither of us ever intended to let up on the other. In those years he still could outkick me, but I gave him a battle, and we used to laugh about it when we finished. Dave never lost his interest or forgot the basic techniques of punting, and the last time I ever saw him alive he began advocating to me the teaching of better techniques in college football because he felt the punters in professional football had become so mediocre. I really couldn't argue with him.

Dave Stewart was not the only important person in my life at Massillon High School. During one of the school's periodic fire drills during my junior year I wound up standing next to a petite, pretty sophomore with light brown hair and blue eyes and a sparkle and a joy to her that really appealed to me. Her name was Kathryn Kester, and we chatted while waiting to file back into our classrooms. We were quite taken with each other that day, and she went home and told her parents, who operated a greenhouse and family orchard on the east side of the city, that she had met a boy named Paul Brown and that she was going to marry him. Her folks laughed at this impulse, though they should have known better: Her own mother had gone to a baseball game and had seen her father catching for one of the teams, then marched home and told her family that she had seen this wonderful boy named Pete Kester and that she was going to marry him.

We started dating soon after our first meeting; in those days that meant going to a movie or ice skating or to a Sunday night social in the Episcopal Church, getting a sandwich and a milk shake and being home by ten-thirty. Katy, who loved the outdoors, was an excellent athlete and a particularly good skater and swimmer, and we never had to look for something to do.

She was my girl during my last two years of high school, and in the summers I visited her folks' summer cottage at Turkeyfoot Lake, and the two of us swam and boated by the

hour. Katy was a senior in high school when I left to attend
Ohio State in 1926, just a few days away from my seventeenth birthday—but we knew then it was going to be far
from the last time we saw each other.

I was directed to Ohio State by my father, who thought it
offered the best education, though, personally, I was just as
interested in the athletic programs there. It was an exciting
day when I boarded the train in Massillon for the four-hour
ride to Columbus, but it also happened to be the first time I'd
ever been away from home for any extended period of time.
It didn't take long for me to become terribly homesick, even
though I was rushed by several of the fraternities and seemed
on the way to settling into college life. I used to write to my
dad and tell him how disappointed I was in college and that I
was ready to come home, but he dismissed my pleadings.

"When the bed gets too hard for you to sleep and the food
so bad that you can't eat, then I'll know you're homesick," he
wrote back, and at one point, things almost seemed that bad.
With Rollie Brown, a friend from Massillon who came to
Ohio State with me, I used to walk nearly four miles each
Sunday from the campus to the Pennsylvania Railroad station
just to watch the trains come in from Massillon in hope that
it would cure our homesickness.

Being homesick wasn't as bad as not being allowed to try
out for Ohio State's freshman football team, though. I was
too small for that caliber of football, they told me, and it was
a mortal blow to my pride. I probably felt it more because I
roomed with Bill Edwards, a great football player, who also
had played at Massillon. Bill was several years older than I
was and not too interested in the school's scholastic requirements at that time. He lived only to play football and later
transferred to Wittenberg. He went on to become a distinguished college and professional coach—including a stretch
on my staff at Cleveland.

I wanted to leave Ohio State, too, but for different reasons.
It was just too big for me, and I wanted to go where I could
feel a part of the school's life. I had visited Miami University
in Oxford, Ohio, during my freshman year and there had
seen Ray Cronin, who had been a star football player in Norwalk. He convinced me that I could be happy at Miami, and
the clinching fact was that the school itself looked just the
way I had always pictured a college. Since Miami was part of
the state's school system, my credits were transferable from

Ohio State. The hardest job was convincing my father, who didn't like the idea at first but relented after he was satisfied that my first year's work would not be lost.

My first day at Miami started a love affair with my alma mater that is as strong today as it was during my three years as a student. To get there on my first day, I had taken the train from Massillon to Hamilton, outside Cincinnati, then boarded a bus for the ride to Oxford. The bus was filled with Miami students, and when the campus buildings came into sight, one of the students, who was a cheerleader, shouted, "Crimson Towers, everybody up!" and the students stood up and began singing the school's song. I didn't know the words, of course, but the fact that those students had such reverence and loyalty for their school that they were moved to sing the moment they saw it left its mark. Cynics see incidents like this only as Broadway or Hollywood musical-comedy material, but that really was the feeling students had for their schools back then, particularly for one as picturesque and as pleasant as Miami.

The school was everything I had ever imagined college would be, and later, when I was coaching the Bengals, I was proud to serve a nine-year term as a member of the board of trustees and to be honored with an honorary doctorate degree. I have always felt that I owed Miami something, and I've never refused any request from its administration.

Though I was not eligible for varsity competition my first year, I worked with the freshman football team. I also learned a great lesson the first day of practice when Merlin Dittmer, the coach, issued me a jersey, though he had to search to find one small enough to fit me because I weighed just 145 pounds. He could easily have turned me away, as Ohio State had done, but he refused to allow a person's size to prejudice him. When I became a high school coach, I never turned away a boy because he seemed to lack the size. I guess I always knew there might be another like myself, whose heart and intensity for the game were larger than anything that showed on the outside.

In my first varsity season our coach, Chester Pittser, who had lost his first two quarterbacks, Eddie Wohlwonder and Weeb Ewbank, by graduation, had planned for me to play behind Oscar Glick, who was a senior. Before the season's first game, however, another player lost a cleat from his shoe, the post struck Oscar in the back of the leg and Oscar had his Achilles' tendon severed. He was finished for the season, and I became a starter. Oscar today is an executive with Procter & Gamble in Cincinnati.

Mr. Pittser, who was an outstanding person, modeled his football from his experiences at Illinois with Bob Zuppke, so that as the quarterback I lined up behind the center, then shifted to a blocking back or tailback, depending on the play. I was listed in the program as 150 pounds by now and could take the contact without being seriously injured. I served not only as a combination running back and blocking back but as the passer, signal caller, punter and punt return man—and I held for place kicks. By this time I had developed a pretty good broken-field running style, which helped with the punt returns, and I also had begun to develop my own single-mindedness about what I thought our team should do during a game.

Several times these ideas clashed with Mr. Pittser's, such as in a game against Denison when, in the face of a strong wind, I called for a quick kick, and it backfired, setting up Denison for a touchdown. The next time I had the ball, I tried to pass against the wind—though our game plan was distinctly laid out to play cautiously until we had the wind at our backs—but my arm was hit, and the ball was batted up in the air, intercepted a split second later and returned for a touchdown. We fell behind, 14-0, in the space of five minutes and lost the game, 14-7.

That didn't deter me, though. There were times when I'd see something in our opponent's defense that gave me the impulse to try something outside of Mr. Pittser's game plan, and even though more of them worked than didn't, it only made him madder than ever. I was living by Dave Stewart's principles, though, that football was supposed to be fun and you shouldn't be afraid to try different things. I often ran from punt formation instead of kicking and threw long passes on first down. I was never afraid to throw the football because I was confident the pass would be completed—even when it wasn't. I carried the same philosophy into professional football. Mr. Pittser was a dear friend of mine for the rest of his life, and we always agreed that we had basic philosophical differences about the way football should be played; he was conservative, and I was not.

A good example of our differences came in a game against Wittenberg in 1928. The plan was to attack their defense cautiously and try not to make any mistakes that would give them cheap touchdowns. Wittenberg was a big game for me because my friend Bill Edwards and half a dozen other Massillon players were on the team, including Jim Price, the team's quarterback and punter. One of our receivers was Jim Gordon, who would later be a 400-meter runner for the 1932 American Olympic team. I figured no one on either team could touch him for pure speed, so the first two times we had the ball, I sent him straight down the sideline and threw the ball as hard as I could so he could run under it, make the catch and go for touchdowns. We won the game, 18-0, and I had the satisfaction of outpunting Jim Price as well. I never felt I went against Coach Pittser's orders because I wasn't taking any chances—I simply knew the defensive back on that side could not run with Gordon.

We finished that season with six victories in eight games, and the Associated Press put me on its second team for Ohio small colleges. In my senior year we won seven of nine games, and six of those were shutouts. Again, the key game was against Wittenberg. We had heard their players were going to "get Brown" this time, though I never believed my friends from Massillon would inflict any deliberate physical harm. The first couple of times I handled the ball, though, there was some wild piling on and flailing of arms and elbows before the officials cooled things off with 15-yard penalties. Neither team could do much until midway through the third quarter, but then Wittenberg punted, and I caught the ball on the run, gave a couple of their players a quick hip fake and took off down the sidelines to put us in good field position for a field goal by Bob Corry. As it turned out, those were the only points in the game. A couple of weeks later on Thanksgiving Day, I finished my collegiate football career with a 14-6 upset over the University of Cincinnati, despite having to play on a sprained ankle.

Ironically, both Chester Pittser and Dave Stewart passed away within a few months of each other in 1978. I count myself fortunate to have had them as dear friends for so long, and I know they took great satisfaction in seeing one of their pupils do so much with the lessons they had imparted.

The rest of my college life was a happy, fulfilling experience. I played center field on Miami's baseball team as a junior but stayed off the team as a senior so that I could concentrate on my schoolwork. During my junior and senior

years I was manager of the Delta Kappa Epsilon house; that
took care of my room and board. My accounts were audited
periodically, and we accumulated enough of a surplus in our
senior year to build a solarium on the house as our memento.
The house has since been torn down. I spent one summer
working for a contractor who built sidewalks, another as a
grounds keeper on a golf course, and spent a couple of summers on the Great Lakes ore boat *William F. Stifel*, which
carried coal to Duluth, Superior and Port Arthur and brought
back wheat and iron ore to the Lake Erie ports. I was an ordinary seaman and spent most of my time swabbing decks
and chipping and painting the hull. That was one of the most
pleasant periods of my life, and I often slept out on the deck
so as not to miss the ghostly beauty of the nights on the
lakes. The food was excellent, and the lakes were so pure
then that we could drop a bucket and bring up our own
drinking water. I'll never forget what it was like steaming
into Duluth at four-thirty on a clear morning, with the lights
of the city marching up the hills from the waterfront. Years
later, when we came to Buffalo for an All-America Conference game, I saw that old ship docked at one of the piers.

During those summers Katy came up to see me whenever
the boat docked in Sandusky, Huron or Cleveland. Katy had
started at Western Reserve Nursing School in Cleveland at
the same time I had transferred to Miami University, and
though we had been about as geographically separated from
each other as it was possible to be within the state of Ohio,
she had always come to Oxford for the major social events,
and when football season was over, I had gone home to Massillon as often as I could to see her.

There was no doubt by that time that we wanted to get
married, but the rules of both our schools in those days forbade it until graduation. The nursing school was very strict on
that subject, and at Miami, though several fellows got married before graduation, they had to keep it hushed up until
they had their degrees in hand. Weeb Ewbank, who was
ahead of me at Miami, was married for two or three years
before graduation, and no one ever found out until afterward. Katy and I decided we would take our chances, though
each of us had a year left to go, and with our parents' cooperation we were married quietly on June 10, 1929, in St.
Matthew's Episcopal Church in Wheeling, West Virginia.

It was a wonderful union that lasted for nearly forty years.

Despite a brittle diabetic condition for the last twenty-nine years of her life, Katy was always a kind, gentle person, quick to laugh and to enjoy life, and never had an unkind word for anyone. The word *serene* best describes her. She was the perfect wife for someone as intensely devoted to his work as I was, who at times probably brought too much of that intensity into my home. She never allowed it to bother her, regardless of the circumstances, and she was totally loyal to me and devoted to our family's every need. On many a Friday night, when Massillon had a game, she simply cleared the supper dishes into the sink so she would not miss a second of anything that happened at the stadium. "The dishes will be there when I return, and I'll do them at that time," she'd say, shooing her family out the door in front of her. "This is more important."

Until diabetes took her eyesight, about the time we came to Cincinnati, she attended every home game our teams ever played. Sometimes she brought some knitting and quietly worked on it during the game, always attentive to what went on, but never displaying the emotions which churned inside her. She knew that if things were not going well, everyone would look at the coach's wife to see what she was thinking, and she never wanted to let on one way or the other. Of course, when we were scoring touchdowns and making big plays, her face lit up, and everyone knew exactly what she was thinking.

Katy was a wonderful partner in helping rear our family. She always managed to maintain the delicate balance that is so often elusive in families whose father is constantly in the public eye. I never placed any importance on my prominence, but children can be affected in different ways. Katy and I were determined that our three boys lead normal lives. Sometimes it was difficult, especially when they were playing sports, because they couldn't help being linked with me, but at home no one got a swelled head or ever took advantage of our good fortune. Katy watched over our three boys like a mother hen; one time when our middle son, Mike, was injured during a football game, she even marched right into the locker room after the game to make sure he was all right and was being properly cared for.

Most of that was still in the future, however. Toward the end of our first year of marriage, and the end of my senior year in 1930, my grades were high enough for me to qualify for a Rhodes scholarship, and I considered applying. By now the Great Depression had gripped the nation, however, and survival had become the only rule, so when, a short time later, I was recommended for a post as teacher and coach at Severn Prep in Maryland, I took it. Katy had received her RN nursing degree from Western Reserve, and the two of us were ready to test our strengths against the world. Perhaps it wasn't the ideal time for a young couple to start their life together, but we considered ourselves fortunate because a lot of college graduates were simply joining the millions of the nation's unemployed. I had put aside my father's wishes for a law career because I was determined that I had to try football as a way of life. It turned out to be the best decision I ever made.

TWO

Massillon:
The Beginning

THE FIRST STROKE OF GOOD fortune in my career came when
I landed the teaching and coaching job at Severn Prep. It was
a rudimentary beginning, but it helped me get the valuable
experience that two years later led to my being hired in my
hometown, Massillon. I hadn't taken the education courses at
Miami, so couldn't teach in the state of Ohio, but outside the
state was no problem, and the two years of teaching at
Severn gave me time to become accredited. After Dave Stewart had written a glowing recommendation to Roland Teal,
Severn's headmaster—and the school had found that Katy
was a registered nurse, who could run the infirmary during
school hours—we were most welcome. We were provided
with a small apartment, and we ate our meals with the
students. Our other compensation, $1,200 for the school year,
was very small, but for a young couple starting out in those
times, we had everything we needed.

Severn was primarily a prep school for the Naval
Academy, with a middle-school program added on for the
children of naval officers on sea duty. I taught history, English grammar and English literature and assisted Bill Hoover
with the athletic program. When Bill slowly began to show
the effects of cancer, from which he died a short time later,
my role in the football program increased. I was assigned, as
well, to coach the offense in lacrosse, a totally new experience
which I found most enjoyable, and late in the school year I
convinced Mr. Teal to start a track and field program and
ran that, too.

41

Though our football was good for our level of competition, it bothered me that no one seemed to be as engrossed in the program as I was or made a big fuss if we won or lost. There was the usual boyish enthusiasm from the students, but the administration and the community lacked the total commitment I felt was necessary to have a topflight program. Of course, they pointed out to me that most of the students at Severn were there to be prepared academically to pass the Naval Academy entrance exams and that sports were just a part of that overall picture. I accepted that, grudgingly perhaps, because my students were serious about their classwork, and I was serious when I taught them—in fact, I had to hustle to keep up with most of them, and overall, I really liked the atmosphere that grew out of this academic intensity. I just felt—and proved later—that the same intensity could be applied to football and athletics in general and still provide the same rich rewards for the students.

Out of the eighteen games we played at Severn during my two years, we won sixteen and tied one, and some of the players later went on to become stars at Navy. One was Dick Pratt, one of my favorite young men, a quarterback who later became an admiral. Another was Slade Cutter, whom I still see for an occasional round of golf, a bubbling, exuberant young man who not only became a great end and kicked for the midshipmen but during World War II was one of our most decorated submarine commanders. In Navy football history, he is probably best remembered for his field goal that beat Army, 3-0, in 1934. When Slade came to us from Elmhurst College in Illinois, he was supposed to have preferred playing the flute to playing football, but we made him a tackle and, on some goal line plays, even our fullback because he was so strong.

I also came away from Severn with my first successful football system. I had watched Jimmy deHart's Duke team mesmerize Navy with a version of the close double wingback formation, which used deceptive ball handling and quick movement of the backs to hide the ball from the defense. I found a coaching clinic where it was being taught, learned it and became so convinced of its merits that I sold the concept to Dave Stewart as well; the first year he installed it, his Sharon team went unbeaten. I also found—and convinced Dave—that lacrosse was the best possible competition for football players who had had no spring practice. People in

Maryland looked on lacrosse as a sport that was peculiarly their own, but we had consistently winning teams with many players who had never even played lacrosse until they came to Severn Prep.

My second year there had almost ended when I was told that Massillon was seeking a new head football coach. I didn't waste a moment arranging to be interviewed for the job because I wanted to work where football was the focal point of the entire community.

Washington High School in Massillon had won only one game in 1931, its squad was run-down and dispirited, its 3,000-seat stadium was never filled and its athletic budget was $37,000 in debt from an investment in a lighting system. Dave Stewart wrote another stirring letter of recommendation for me, this time to Dr. H. W. Bell, president of the school board. I've kept that letter, not because of what is said about me, but for what it said about the characteristics of being a good coach. It is better than anything I have ever heard at any clinic or read in any book. Part of it bears repeating because I always found it useful in my own coaching life.

Dave wrote:

> A coach must play the role of many characters and be able to adapt himself; through him, the boys obtain the moods and inspirations that are so necessary. For example, off the field I am moderately friendly with the boys, enough for them to know that I am human and sympathetic. On the field, I do not know them as personalities. I'm a different kind of person. There are no favorites. It is all work with a goal in view. A team is keyed up only as the coach is keyed up. . . . You must so control them that when you walk into a sober dressing room, a smile on your face will start them all chirping and smiling; and a somber appearance in a gay dressing room will bring silence. That is a pretty good sign of control. In my opinion, Brown will command to that extent. . . .

There were other candidates, too, and various factions sought to push their own favorites. When it came time for a selection, Dr. Bell called Dave and read him the list of candidates.

"Which of those would you pick?" he asked him.

"I'd take Brown," Dave replied.

And that was it. Even though Dave Stewart had left Massillon almost seven years before, Dr. Bell thought enough of his opinion to select me. That was typical of Dr. Bell, who had a tremendous influence on my life.

As president of the school board Dr. Bell influenced the entire educational system in Massillon, including physical education. He even bought his own tickets to the games, and he always showed up at a local drugstore where an informal "quarterback club" met on the mornings following a game to discuss what had happened. He wanted to know what the people were thinking, and he was never swayed by petty politics or cronyism, as he amply demonstrated by naming me as head coach against the pressures of many within the town. I'm sure there was resentment that during the Depression a young man of twenty-two, with just two years of prep school coaching experience, had taken the job that older and more experienced men had sought.

On a personal level, Dr. Bell also became our family's physician and thus very close to all of us. He delivered two of our sons, Robin and Mike, and cared for us all when we were sick. His insights were wonderful and always seemed to teach a lesson. One day Mike, who was just four, thought he was Superman, tied a sheet around his neck for a cape, then tried to fly off a neighbor's garage roof. He crashed to the ground and broke a leg. Katy summoned me from the football practice field, where one of the players I had been coaching was a great punter and end named Horace Gillom, then called Dr. Bell.

I sped to the hospital just in time to see him putting a cast on Mike' broken leg. When I came into the room, Mike looked up at me and said, "Gee, Daddy, I'll bet you're glad it wasn't Horace."

Dr. Bell, amused, looked at me and said, "PB, I'll bet that's true."

Dr. Bell gave me another lesson when I had to miss my only game in nine years at Massillon because of a severe case of the flu. I had a temperature of 100 plus, but I was set on going to that game, sick or not, before Dr. Bell forbade it.

"Everybody is useful, PB," he told me, "but no one is necessary."

"But, doc," I pleaded, "I have to be with my team. I can't afford to have anything happen at this stage of our season."

"I don't care," he replied. "As your doctor I'm telling you that you can't get out of bed."

"Well," I persisted, "I have to know how things are going

if I do stay here. Can you arrange for a telephone hookup so I can talk to everyone at the half and help them that way?"

That was arranged, and when I got on the phone at the half, the first thing I asked was, "What's the score?"

"We're ahead, forty-seven to nothing," one of my assistants, Hugh McGranahan, told me.

That really gave me a perspective on how important I was as compared to how important I thought I was. Katy got a big laugh out of it, and she always liked to tell Dr. Bell how crestfallen I became when I heard that score. I really hadn't been, but it was a very good lesson in life from a very learned man.

Scores of 47-0 were still in the future, though, when Dr. Bell hired me in 1932. My salary was supposed to be $2,150 for the year, but because the school year had been shortened to eight months to save money, it actually came out closer to $1,600. I felt so fortunate to have a job in those Depression years, though, that I never even gave the money a second thought.

Going home was a happy experience for a young man who loved his school as much as I did—and still do. I coached the same way in Massillon as I would later in college and professional football, and I'm every bit as proud and happy about what we accomplished during my nine years as head coach at Washington High School as anything I ever achieved at Ohio State, Cleveland or Cincinnati.

When I started, I was so wound up in my new job that my enthusiasm and intensity camouflaged my inexperience. Besides coaching, I taught history and English for the first few years, and since many of my former teachers were still on the faculty, my professional relationships were very good, as was my relationship with the school board and, of course, with Dr. Bell.

That first season looked as if it might be pretty rocky at first, however. Our uniforms were deplorable because there was insufficient money to purchase new equipment. Before our first practice we put everything in piles, and our better players had the first selection. In our next-to-last game of that season one of the players came to me and said, "Coach, can I have some of those boards for my pants?" The boy had played almost the entire season without any of the old thigh guards, and he had never known the difference until he saw one of his teammates inserting them into his pants before a game.

Before the first game that year—a 20-7 victory over Wooster, a team that competed below our class a couple of years later—we even had to wet down the field to keep the dust from sweeping over the spectators. The stands were dilapidated, and the playing field was just dirt and rocks with bare markings. With all this, however, we won our first five games and tied one mainly on enthusiasm and better organization. It certainly wasn't on our size—we averaged less than 150 pounds per man. The problem was so serious when we played Alliance High School, which had a 190-pound running back named Larry Russell, that it resulted in many of our players getting injured. After those first six games we lost all the rest, yet we had sparked enough enthusiasm in Massillon to be able to charge $1 for our big game against Canton-McKinley High School. That was a lot of money for a high school game in the Depression years, but we filled our stadium, and since each team always kept its own gate receipts, that meant we had $3,000 available to begin outfitting our players with new equipment for the following year.

It was at that time that another figure entered my life: L. J. Smith, the new superintendent of schools, with whom I would develop an especially warm relationship for the remaining eight of my nine years at Massillon. LJ came to Massillon just before the start of my second season. We had worked so hard in 1932 to obliterate the spirit of defeatism that had gripped the athletic program that I was worried what direction a new boss would take with our football program. I was so intent on having it run the way I wanted that I didn't waste a moment finding out his intentions.

"LJ, I want to get to know you and find out whether we can get along in a comfortable and harmonious manner," I said to him as soon as he picked up the telephone.

"All right, Paul," he replied, wondering, I'm sure, just who I was and what this was all about. "What do you want?"

"Well, I want to come over and talk to you about the problems that might arise in the future," I told him. "I want to do my part, and I wonder what I can do to get you thinking as I do."

"Well, that's not difficult, Paul," he said. "I'm interested in the promotion of football just as much as you are. And I'm sure you're interested in the school system just as much as you're interested in football. There is no reason why the relations between the superintendent of schools and the football coach in Massillon cannot be totally harmonious. I have great respect for you, and even before I came, I knew of your work since becoming head coach."

That set the tone for the next eight years, and knowing that the lines of communication were always open between the two of us certainly made my job easier. We decided at the start that if there were ever areas of disagreement, we would settle them between us and not make a public fight of them in the newspaper or at open meetings. We didn't always agree on every program, but we always settled our differences on what was best for Massillon. Those differences never were serious, and even the most mundane requests, if they had merit, were accepted.

A good example of his cooperation occurred when we were attending a game at Pitt. I saw one of their students dressed in a panther costume, but it wasn't very convincing. Our mascot was the tiger, and looking at that bedraggled panther gave me an idea.

"I wonder, LJ, if we couldn't have a real tiger skin for some of our kids to wear," I said.

"I think we should," he replied, "and I know a taxidermist in Denver who will get us one."

That was it. Mr. Smith wrote to the man, described what we wanted, and we had our tiger skin. It cost us $500, but there was never a question about the expense, and that ferocious-looking tiger skin roamed the sidelines at Massillon until it was replaced, just a few years ago. Being able to get even the little things done with cooperation like that was one of the key reasons I was so successful during my nine years at Massillon. To this day one of my proudest continuing friendships is with L. J. Smith.

With LJ's help, and the $3,000 we had collected the year before, the program turned upward, and as we became more successful and generated more revenue, everything got better. We purchased new equipment each year, and eventually we had the most meticulously dressed football team in the state of Ohio, and as I found out when I became head coach there, that included Ohio State. Not only were our pads, shoes, jerseys and pants the best made, but our equipment included such things as reversible coats for cold or rainy weather and warm-up jerseys with each player's last name sewn on the back.

At the end of each season we passed the previous year's equipment on to one of the three junior high school teams in our system, so that every third year each team got nearly new equipment. That sparked wonderful enthusiasm in those youngsters. Some of the equipment didn't always fit those little guys snugly, but they knew they were getting the best, and that was just as important in their development.

I was able to do this because within a few years all athletics in Massillon were in my domain. I had seen, while a student, how a coach in one sport could work against a coach in another sport to get the best athletes, and I had determined that would never happen to me. My control was built gradually, beginning in the middle of my second year, when the basketball coach was fired and the school board asked me to take over immediately. That ended my night school law studies.

Then, in 1934, came the job as director of athletics at Washington High School. Being in charge of every major sport didn't mean I did all the actual coaching; what it did mean was that I had the overall responsibility for each team. The players knew it; that meant they could not, as before, be disrespectful to one coach and then play for another coach in another sport. Nor could any coach do any politicking to induce the best players to play for his team. Everything was put on a fair and equal basis, and our overall athletic program benefited from this centralized control.

Our basketball team, with Carroll Widdoes, and later Bill Rohr, doing a lot of the technical work, went to the state tournament at Columbus my last five years at Massillon, gained the semi-finals three times and made it to the finals once under this system. Hugh McGranahan, my line coach in football, oversaw much of the track and field team, and we all helped run the baseball program. In every case, however, I had to know and approve of everything my assistants did, and the players knew they had to answer to me.

The final appointment was as director of recreation for the entire city. I held all these jobs simultaneously and never once felt overburdened or overworked. My responsibility was the physical education program for every school in Massillon, and I visited each one of them on a regular basis. I knew who the good athletes were from the time they were little boys. Over the years our program consistently proved that it produced better-conditioned and better-coordinated students than schools that did not place as much emphasis on physical education. Even more, it also cut down the mischief kids got into away from school and brought out the natural leaders who responded to the various competitive situations these programs encouraged. Those young people had great pride in their accomplishments because it helped them to do things they never thought were possible.

A good example of this was Horace Gillom as a little boy. He proudly showed me at recess one day how he could punt a football. No one had ever taught him any of the fundamentals, but he was pretty good, so I took him aside and demonstrated the proper method. "Hold the ball in your fingertips, and don't allow it to rest against the palm of your hand," I told him. "Turn the laces a bit to the right, and hold it with the point slightly upward, so that when the ball drops, your foot will hit it perfectly." When he started doing it the correct way, he became a great punter. I've always felt that even as a high school player he was as good as he was at Ohio State and with the Cleveland Browns, and in my mind there never has been a better punter than Horace.

Some people have said that no one could control an athletic program today in the same total way I did then, and I don't know if that is true or not. I do know this: It would certainly be more difficult than it was then, but if I were starting all over again, I'd still try to run everything. It was the only way. It wasn't even easy back in the 1930s, though, because some of the older people on the board of education tended to get a bit touchy when I'd come in with a new idea. Having men like Dr. Bell and L. J. Smith helped smooth the ruffled feathers, however, and the fact that we were able to produce a winning and revenue-producing program that totally captivated the community also undercut the opposition. After being downtrodden for so long, everyone wanted success, and we provided it.

The benefits of our success came back many times over to the community and the school system. Massillon became so wrapped up in our football you might say it became its prime industry. There was no such thing as juvenile delinquency because the athletes were the leaders and they were very disciplined. On the day of a game the main streets were awash with orange and black flags; each merchant displayed one outside his place of business. A huge black sign in the town square announced that this was the home of the Massillon Tigers and prominently displayed our schedule. The tiger motif and the orange and black colors were everywhere, and don't think it didn't have an effect on our opponents when they came to town! The city still displays this spirit and interest, and it is hard to ride through Massillon without knowing that you are in Tiger country.

Massillon was probably the only community in the country, or so it was thought at the time, that had the ingredients to develop such a phenomenon. It had always had a great football tradition that reached back to the earliest days of professional football and the spirited rivalry between the Massillon Tigers and the Canton Bulldogs, and that tradition had persisted in the high schools in both communities.

When Dave Stewart left Massillon to become the coach at Sharon, Pennsylvania, the bottom dropped from the high school program, and no one seemed to care. When we began our string of successes, however, the pride revived, and the spirit of the old Massillon Tigers suddenly took on new meaning. People in the community came forward, willing to support us with their interest and their money; students expressed willingness to accept the teaching and leadership necessary to propagate this excellence. It wasn't too long before this new spirit became a reality not just for ten weeks, but for all year long. It permanently touched every part of the town's soul.

To capitalize on this feeling, Carl Young of the school board, two or three other friends and I formed a Booster Club. Within a couple of years its membership had grown to more than 1,000 people. We had only one objective: to boost, not only the football team but every activity at Washington High School. Each person paid dues according to what he could afford; the average was about fifty cents per person. Football was the catalyst. Every Monday night I showed movies of our previous game and talked about our upcoming opponent, always in glowing terms because I didn't want any complacency from either our team or our fans. We had anywhere from 500 to 1,000 persons at these film sessions; once, at an outdoor meeting, we even had 2,500. On one occasion we had an out-of-town game, and the club actually chartered a train to attend the game. Our postseason dinner in 1939 was so large it had to be held in three locations simultaneously, and the guest speaker was Ohio's governor, John Bricker. Whenever a school tax levy came up for a vote, the Booster Club got behind it and helped push it through, and even today Massillon has a very active Booster Club.

Such support helped pave the way for building a new stadium and recreation complex when our old field became too small. Within two years we had begun jamming crowds of more than 7,000 people into that dusty old park, which had barely held 3,000 when I became head coach. Dr. Bell was the prime mover in getting the city to purchase the land and then in finding available Works Project Administration funds to help finance it. Our new 21,000-seat home was completed in 1937, and just a few years ago it was renamed Paul Brown Tiger Stadium. I'm proud, but I always felt it would have been more appropriate to have it named after Dr. Bell.

I had total input into everything about that stadium, and I made sure it was more up to date even than stadiums at our largest universities. We had a spacious locker room, training room and classroom for our players, as well as comfortable dressing facilities for the visiting team. Our band also had a dressing room and its own practice field adjacent to the football practice field because we always felt that we had not only the best football team but also the best marching band, and we wanted the musicians to feel they were just as much a part of our success as our players. Under George Bird, the Tiger Swing Band became one of the most impressive musical organizations in the country and introduced a fast, high-stepping tempo to its marching that literally wowed crowds wherever it played. Our playing field was in better condition than the one at Ohio State because our grounds keeper, George Rohr, whose son Bill was one of our coaches and later director of athletics at Ohio University, kept our grass in perfect condition in order to make it a fast track and take advantage of our great team speed.

Everything that went into this complex reflected our desire to be the best. The land around it is still used for recreational purposes; there are picnic tables and benches for use at any time, as well as vast parking areas suitable for pregame tailgate parties. We wanted anyone coming there at any time to enjoy himself.

In 1940, my final year as head coach, we totaled more than 182,000 people at our games in that stadium, an average of 18,200 from a town of 26,000. In the state, only Ohio

State attracted more people to football games than we did. With tickets priced at $5 for an adult season ticket, $1.25 for a student's season ticket and $1 for a single admission, we generated more than $100,000 in revenue.

With that money, we were able to support nearly two dozen extracurricular activities, from the school newspaper to the camera club to the model airplane club. We built an observatory, added a speech and debating program that produced a national championship debating team and financed an a cappella choir that became renowned throughout the state. We even sent it on a concert tour to Hawaii. We brought in famous speakers, poets and other notables for our chapel programs and paid them from these funds. Harry James and his orchestra played at one of our year-end football proms. By law, those activities could not be supported by tax money, but the revenue generated by our football program made them all possible.

Dr. Bell often noted that many of our football players went on to college, while 75 percent of the other graduates did not. He felt it necessary to provide something for that majority over and above the required classroom routine.

"Our extracurricular activities are the ice cream and cake on top of a good meal," he always said.

We did all this for one reason: We wanted to have the best because we wanted our students to see nothing but the best and be content with nothing less than the best—whether in football or any other area.

There is a lesson here, and it is directed at the apologists who demean a winning football program, even at the high school level, as being beneath the aims of a good education. Football, like every activity within a school, has it place, and if properly directed and administered, it can return benefits to its students and its community that last forever.

The quality of the education, of course, also helped me as a football coach. Even with all my emphasis on physical education in our school system, I never placed any less emphasis on the classroom side of a student's life. I wanted all students to have the best kind of education because it gave our program the kind of players we wanted—intelligent boys who reacted and understood quickly all that was taught. As I mentioned at the beginning of this book, that's the kind of player I sought throughout my coaching career. We carried the idea of a complete education to every level of our school system, and while it may not always have been the difference between winning and losing, it played a significant role in a player's development.

Another key element in our continuing success—in fact, perhaps *the* key element—was our junior high school football program. This program existed when I came to Massillon to coach, but it was loosly structured. The junior highs were vital as a feeder system for our varsity, so to become competitive, I started by personally selecting the junior high coaches. Everyone was to teach the same techniques and use the same system that we employed on the high school level. The quality of these men became a key to the program's success, and each of them went on to become a successful head coach later in his career.

The junior high school program was open to everyone from the sixth through the ninth grades, and no one was ever cut. I've heard it said that I drove those kids, but that's ridiculous. I never even saw the teams until the end of the year, when they played each other. I made sure the teams were for *fun*, and that they entertained and engaged as many youngsters as wanted to participate. We taught them rudimentary lessons about physical coordination before we ever advanced any football techniques, and it made no difference if they were good players or not. We wanted as many kids as possible to enter the program and to enjoy it. The important thing was to give them an opportunity to occupy themselves and to improve in a sport they might want to play.

We always knew who the best players were by the time they reached the ninth-grade level, and at that point we began grooming some of them to meet our needs when they came to the varsity the next year. Tom James was one such player. We started working him as a tailback when he was in the ninth grade; because of his tremendous speed and great running ability, he became a starting wingback as a junior, the starting tailback as a senior—and then went on, of course, to become a great running back for us at Ohio State and a superb defensive back at Cleveland.

One player who did not come from our junior high school program, however, was Lindell Houston, the fastest offensive guard ever to play for me. He moved to the Massillon area in January 1937 from Wolf Lake, Illinois, and his family lived on a farm. Lindell was reluctant to enter high school, but it was the only way he could play his favorite sport, basketball.

John Tannehill, one of our assistant basketball coaches, looked at this strapping young sophomore and asked, "How much do you weigh?"

"About one-seventy-five," Lindell replied.

"You mean one-fifty-five?" John said.

"No, one-seventy-five the last time I stepped on a scale," the boy repeated.

John still couldn't believe it, so he took Lindell to Carroll Widdoes, who was in the middle of conducting a physical education class.

"Hey, Wid," he said, "look at this guy. He says he weighs a hundred seventy-five pounds."

Widdoes couldn't believe it either, and he brought me out of a history class to settle the matter. I had Lindell remove his trousers, and when he stepped on the scale, it registered 176 pounds. Much of his weight and muscle density was in his legs. I asked him if he had ever played football. He said no, but he wouldn't mind giving it a try if he could play basketball for the remainder of that winter.

We had two weeks of indoor football drills that spring, and one day I put Lindell in a wrestling match against a senior end. Coming off the farm, where he lifted bales of hay nearly every day, Lindell was exceptionally strong and pinned the older, bigger boy in nineteen seconds. I could hardly believe it, and I had them wrestle again. This time it took him twenty seconds to end the match. That was enough for me, and though he didn't know anything about football, we started to train him to be a guard. He worked with some seniors throughout the summer and became our starting left guard in the fall, playing in the first football game that he had ever seen.

He did very well. In the second game, against Alliance, our right guard broke his leg, so I said to Lindell, "You know the plays to the right, so just switch your assignment, and I'll put a tackle in the stationary guard's position." It was that easy with this great young player, and he played both left and right guard for the rest of the season. The next year we wanted to utilize his great speed, so we played him at offensive guard and defensive end. I guess his biggest moment came against Canton, when he tackled Marion Motley and knocked him out of the game. It was the only time in Motley's football career that had ever happened—or would happen again—and Marion never found out who had sent him from the field until the two of them became teammates on the Browns.

Lindell played on our national champion Ohio State team in 1942, from which he was selected as an All-American guard, and later made all-pro in both the All-America Conference and the National Football League.

Many of our best players, such as Lindell Houston, lived on farms on the city's outskirts, but most were born and reared in Massillon. We sometimes were accused of bringing in players whose eligibility had expired in another section of the country or of having the steel mills transfer to Massillon men whose sons were great football players. Those accusations were simply false—everyone who played for us at Massillon did it legitimately. Believe me, if we had done it any other way, you can be sure someone would have found out because you don't win as often as we did without having people snooping about to see if they can turn up something wrong.

With an occasional exception, such as Lin Houston, everyone went through our junior high school program, and players were invited to our varsity team solely on the basis of what they had done during those four years. Outsiders had a difficult time making our team because they had not been exposed to the meticulous training our boys got in that program. During our unbeaten years in the late thirties, nearly every member of our squad either started in our school system or entered before his junior year. I should also point out that like all Ohio school teams, we filed reports on the ages of all our players with the state scholastic athletic association, and our team members' ages never averaged any more than our opponents'.

Another basis for the success of our program was law and order, and because I had the parents' backing from the start, that meant in the boy's home as well. Before each season we had a dinner to which each player brought his parents or guardian. There I laid down our training rules for the season, as well as the rules for studying, conduct, even for what time the players had to be home at night. I told the parents what was necessary for being a starting player and a substitute, and because they considered it a privilege for their sons to be on our football team, we won their complete cooperation.

Our training rules were comparatively simple by standards back then. There was no smoking or drinking at any time, in or out of season, and anyone who violated those rules was automatically dismissed from the team. During football season we allowed no riding in automobiles, going to dances or dating. Every player had to be home by nine-thirty and in bed by ten o'clock each night. We prescribed a study program from seven-thirty to nine each evening and insisted that the parents oversee it. I'm sure those rules will raise some eyebrows in today's society.

We had a sign in our locker room: "You represent the best football town in the United States. Never disappoint your people by the way you represent it." That feeling was shared by the townspeople, and I knew immediately if our players went astray because every waitress in town knew them, and they were not shy about naming anyone who did not observe the spirit of our rules. Our players took all this very seriously, and we rarely had a problem. If we did, the boy responsible quietly disappeared from the team.

In the off-season we conducted a sports program for all the football players not competing in basketball to encourage their conditioning and promote some healthy competition. I opened the gymnasium three nights a week, and from seven-thirty until nine o'clock we had wrestling and boxing tournaments, volleyball, gymnastics, running and basketball. It was a healthy and a wholesome atmosphere for these young men, and I liked it so much I competed right along with them.

Before the start of each season I took the seniors to my father's fishing cottage near Norwalk, on the Huron River. We didn't play or practice football, just fished or played softball. It was a relaxing way for everyone to tune up for the season, and those seniors knew it was something special. When our fall practice began, they showed the way to the other players.

Each fall nearly sixty players turned out for practice, and we had to pare our squad to about forty. Even when a boy made the varsity as a sophomore, he usually had to work and wait for a chance to be a starter. Those who were starters as seniors or juniors never let down because they knew there were other good players itching to replace them. It was a very competitive situation.

My assistants were an integral part of our team, and much of the program's success was due to them. They each had specific assignments for the day's session, and we didn't finish practice until the assignments were thoroughly covered, although out practices never exceeded ninety minutes. On Sunday nights the coaches came to my home, and we reviewed the scouting report on our upcoming opponent. Those were our only evening meetings because the men also carried full teaching schedules at the high school and had to care for their families.

Our staff was young, yet very close, and we had an informal rule: Once a month one of us would have to propose a social activity that involved everyone, something different. Once it was bobsledding, another time roller skating, and one of the coaches even took us to a professional wrestling match in Akron. I had never been to one before, and neither had our wives. One of the matches on the card involved two woman wrestlers. One didn't show up, so the promoter put a man into the ring against the woman. We were sitting in the front row, sort of bug-eyed at all this because every time the man would try to put a hold on the woman wrestler, the crowd would yell a horrified "Oh-oh-oh-oh," and the poor guy would let go. In the meantime, she was tossing him all over the ring.

I got a big kick out of it, and though a couple of the wives in our group were a bit shocked, things like this gave us a warm feeling for one another, something I tried to promote wherever I coached. I was successful at it, too, until the final year with the Browns, when some divisiveness was fostered on our staff. At Massillon, however, our coaches were loyal, hard-working young men whose preparation and commitment were complete in every respect. A school doesn't win eighty games in just nine years, including the final thirty-three in a row, unless everyone puts forth a total effort for every game.

The night before a game I always took our signal caller on the field and stood at various spots, gave him downs and distance for a first down, then asked what play he would call from that spot. We walked up and down the field for two hours playing that imaginary game so he would get a mental picture of what it might be like the next day. I learned that technique from Mr. Pittser at Miami, who used to do the same thing with me before every game.

Later I called the plays myself by developing a wigwag set of hand signals from the sidelines. This was the forerunner of our messenger guard system of shuttling plays into a game. I developed the system in high school because it was tough enough being a coach without being at the mercy of a young boy who just picked plays out of a hat with no real idea of what he was trying to do. I knew from having called the signals in high school and college just how much a quarterback did not see on every play, while coaches, sitting in a spotting booth atop a stadium or watching the point of attack at the line of scrimmage from the sidelines, had a total view of what was happening.

We also started the idea of playbooks in Massillon. They were small ring notebooks similar to the kind every student uses in school. I always believed that the football practice field was just an extension of the classroom and that the laws of learning were applicable. Once the player copied down the play, it was his responsibility to learn it. I wanted the player to see the play, hear it, diagram it on paper, learn it physically and then do it until it became rote. In the years to come, we had playbooks at Ohio State and Great Lakes and were the first to introduce them into professional football. When we first entered pro football, our opponents carried comic books onto trains and planes or played cards, while we carried our playbooks and took examinations about our game plan. Our guys took a lot of ribbing about that until we started winning so often, and then we saw fewer comic books and more playbooks.

Our system of plays and play-calling intrigued everyone as soon as Massillon moved to the forefront. I once invited one of my junior high school coaches, Jimmy Hollinger, into our locker room before a game because he had scouted our opponent and he was curious to see how we had set up our first few plays. My method was always to detail the first three plays carefully, making sure to tell the team exactly what I expected of each one.

"I'm going to turn my back and not look because I want to hear it," I told my players, meaning that I wanted them to explode off the ball and into our opponent with such force that it could be heard on each play. That day the first play gained about 40 yards, the next picked up about 20 and we scored on the third.

A few years later Jimmy became the head coach at the Medina, Ohio, high school, and took with him all the principles he had learned in Massillon, including the pregame talk. At the first opportunity he lined up the same three offensive plays I had used and told his players that he, too, was turning his back so he could hear them piling into their opponents.

"When I turned around, it was fourth down and twenty,"

he told me years later, laughing until the tears rolled down his cheeks. "I couldn't believe it. It wasn't supposed to work out that way. On top of that, we lost the game, and I stayed out on the field alone until the stadium lights were turned off. When I went into the locker room, the players were having a party, eating ice cream and cookies, and feeling they had played a good game while I never felt worse in my life.

"I raised the devil with them and got called on the carpet for doing it by the school's principal. 'Mr. Hollinger,' he said, 'this isn't Massillon, and these people don't understand what you're talking about. They thought it was a good game, and the boys played hard. The local dairy always brings ice cream to them, win or lose.' But before I left Medina, that entire town began to feel somewhat the way about its school and community as Massillon had felt about the Tigers."

Our football style at Massillon, as with all the other teams I ever coached, was built on fundamentals. We used to hear about a so-called Massillon system, but there was no such thing. We taught the same football system as any other high school, with a few variations, but we were simply more meticulous in our teaching procedures. Lin Houston was a perfect example of someone who mastered them. I've said he was fast, but he was also one of the finest guards technically I've ever seen in my life. He developed a little scrape on his cheekbones from constantly brushing the defensive man's pants at exactly the right place in his charge. This charge involved a little dip at the last moment, and the scrape meant our blocker had executed our technique exactly as we had taught it. Great emphasis was placed on the offensive and defensive line charge. We worked at it much as you groove a golf swing.

In the off-season we put blocking sleds around in strategic places and instructed the players to work out three times a week, with fifty blocking charges each time. I even put a sled in an open field across the street from Katy's parents' greenhouse—the kids never knew when I might be there, watching them, so, believe me, that sled was well used.

Our offense was based on speed and power, but there, too, mainly on execution. I took the double wing concepts I had brought from Severn and added to them some of Nobel Kizer's ideas for getting back to the weak side of an unbalanced formation, which he had used successfully as head coach at Purdue. Although I also incorporated some of Jock

Sutherland's line blocking theories, I never liked the long, slow way it took his reverses to reach the point of attack, so I found a quicker way to get there by using Kizer's methods. Our offense really consisted of what I judged to be the best parts of several systems.

We had exceptional high school fullbacks to carry out that offense. Bob Glass, who later played at Tulane, Rocky Snyder, who played at Purdue, and Pokey Blunt just riddled teams that tried to overshift on us. We later added a wrinkle before the ball was snapped in which the quarterback stood behind the center in a T formation with the two tackles behind him. When the quarterback shifted to the blocking back's position, the tackles took their place on either side of the center, using a five-count rhythmic pattern, three counts to get aligned and the last two to wind up and take off. The defense had no way of knowing until the last possible moment how we would be aligned.

Our teams were totally dedicated to the game. We didn't even own a water bucket, and our players never knelt or lay down on the playing field unless they were injured. This became a psychological factor, not only for our boys but for our opponents because they knew we worked at being physically tougher, better conditioned, faster and more meticulously trained. We played a lot of teams that were beaten in their own minds even before the kickoff.

As we became more successful, we sought out teams that had gone unbeaten for a couple of years and put them on our schedule. Size of school never meant anything to us because many of the teams on our schedule, such as Canton-McKinley, Mansfield, Warren and Steubenville, had larger enrollments than Massillon's 800 students. Canton had nearly 3,000, and many of those other schools had two or three times as many as we did. We were often outweighed dramatically, but that meant nothing because of our speed and dedication to fundamentals.

With our big stadium, we could make attractive financial offers to these worthy opponents and attract topflight competition. We offered them a flat guarantee of up to $3,000 against 40 percent of the gate, which, in those years, was a lot of money for any high school to take away from one game. Many of the schools we contacted couldn't believe the money offer, and I recall the superintendent of schools of one new rival expressing total disbelief.

"Oh, no, you don't," he told me. "Don't give me any of that percentage talk. I'll take my three-thousand-dollar guarantee, and that's it."

I knew that he really didn't understand what we were offering, so I told him, "If the percentage is greater than the guarantee, I'll give you the option of taking the larger amount."

"No, sirree, none of those tricks with me," he said most emphatically. "It's going to be the guarantee, or we won't play."

Of course, we paid the guarantee, but the man missed taking home almost twice as much money, and he told me afterward that he just couldn't believe any high school game could generate such revenues. Before I left Massillon, I scheduled games against Marblehead, Massachusetts, and Cedar Rapids, Iowa, both of which had tremendous winning streaks. I was gone when those games were played, but Massillon, unbeaten the year after I left for Ohio State, won both.

Another game of importance for me, for different reasons, was against Dave Stewart's team in Sharon, Pennsylvania. We were ahead 28-27 at halftime, and as we walked off the field, Dave, who was still my idol, called over, "Who's the scorekeeper, Brown? He's the most important guy in the ball park."

We won the game and won again when he brought his team to Massillon. These were the only two times I ever coached against him, and I know the satisfaction that comes from the pupil's beating the master. I went through it countless times later, in professional football, when former players and coaches of mine tried to beat our teams. During the game everything must be all business; past relationships mean nothing because you are trying to win. When the game is over, there is time for warmth and friendship, and that is only proper.

For all our victories, however, success was never automatic. I remember Alliance leading at the half of our 1939 game, for instance, because we had gotten into a predictable pattern with our play-calling and our offense had become ineffective. I heard later that people in the stands were sure I was in the locker room at halftime giving our kids a tongue-lashing, but that never was my way of operating.

"This isn't your fault; it's mine because of our play-calling," I told the kids. "We'll change our style."

In the second half we doubled the score. Instead of run-

ning on first and second down, as we had been doing, we
passed on the first two downs and ran on third down. In high
school, particularly, teams cannot adjust readily to changes
like these. No coach, however, can ever do radical surgery on
his game plan during a short halftime break; if he tries, he is
only asking for chaos and disaster. On every level, it comes
down to doing the right thing at the right time at the right
place, for the greatest possible number of times. As I've said,
this is the true artistry of coaching. In this game we even put
a player deliberately offside on a punt so we could run a
special play. Instead of kicking the second time, Gillom faked
the punt, and while his leg was still in the air, he handed the
ball behind his back to James, who made a huge gain on a
reverse. I had seen Buck Shaw's Santa Clara team do that to
LSU in the Sugar Bowl, although I never had been sure
Buck's team had done it on purpose. We did.

We always tried to have something ready in case we were
in trouble and needed a quick touchdown. We had what has
become a well-known flea-flicker play, which was born in a
victory over Canton. In its original form, our tailback took
the direct snap from center and began running a sweep to the
right, then handed the ball to the wingback on a reverse. The
wingback lateraled the ball to the left end as he was coming
around on a reverse, and the left end then stopped and threw
the ball to the right end. At Cleveland we modified the play
so that Otto Graham made the initial hand off and was the
one who got the ball back after the double reverse, so he
could throw the pass. During the Cincinnati Bengals' first
eight seasons we used that play at least a dozen times, and it
rarely failed. It is now part of many NFL offenses, in various
forms, and it is still as exciting and surprising to watch as it
was when we first tried it against Canton.

Massillon's success naturally attracted college football re-
cruiters from nearly every part of the nation. At one time
more than fifty of our players in one season were playing college football. Those boys weren't just good football players,
though; they were also good students. Don Snavely, one of
two brothers who played for Lou Little at Columbia, and
Augie Morningstar, who played at Purdue, were ranked first
in their class scholastically, Several of our players went to
Columbia, strict entrance requirements and all, and played
for Little, one of college football's greatest technicians. Bob
Glass went to Tulane, and George Slusser went to Dartmouth

for a year before joining our program at Ohio State. Both were killed during World War II, but George was one of the finest high school passers I ever saw.

I knew my players well, and I judged which colleges I felt each boy had a chance to succeed in. I had catechized those young men about going to college, just as my father had catechized me. In the off-season I'd pile three or four into my car every weekend, and we'd visit schools in Ohio and western Pennsylvania. I took Howard Brinker and Fritz Heisler, both of whom later coached with me in professional football, to Miami University, where they became fine players. I even helped get jobs for the students who needed them to get through college. It was my final stroke to help those boys succeed.

The best high school team I ever saw was our 1940 team, the last team I coached in Massillon. For the first half of the season our starting eleven didn't even have to play after the first two quarters of the game, and I seriously doubted whether my first team at Ohio State the following year could have beaten that team because it was so meticulously coached in our system and had far greater speed. And that Buckeye team lost only one game against major college competition.

Such thoughts were not idle daydreaming because in those days it was not uncommon for a good high school team to scrimmage a small college team. In the spring of 1940 we quietly arranged a scrimmage against Kent State and scored more than fifty points, before their people stopped the game with some of the fourth quarter still to be played. Kent State won eight of its nine games that season and was champion of the Ohio Conference. We also scrimmaged Wooster and Mount Union colleges, and Akron University actually called off a scrimmage when it found out what had happened to Kent State. There was nothing to gain by beating us, the players said, and too much at stake if they lost.

Jim Schlemmer, sports editor of the *Akron Beacon-Journal*, who had arranged that abortive Akron scrimmage, did arrange for us to play Alliance High School in Akron's Rubber Bowl. Alliance had a great team, and its star was a boy named Willis Hume, who later played at the Naval Academy. Our defense stopped Hume with hardly a yard, and a sellout crowd of 28,000 watched Tommy James score twenty-seven points in the fourth quarter in our 47-0 victory. The most memorable part of the game was Horace Gillom's punting.

He sent his kicks above the light towers, and I'll never forget the expression on the face of Alliance's safetyman as he watched that ball disappear and then reappear out of the lights. The huge crowd was awestruck at his performance.

Perhaps our two most important games that season were against our principal rival, Canton-McKinley, and Toledo's Waite High School. The previous year we had been invited to participate in the Buckeye Bowl at Ohio Stadium to decide the state champion, but since we were not allowed to play postseason games, Waite High School defeated Portsmouth High School and declared itself the best team in the state.

There was some feeling in Massillon about that, particularly when Grant Walls, a member of Toledo's board of education, began writing letters to the *Cleveland Plain Dealer* proclaiming Waite's dominance. Grant, who later backed the efforts of the Ohio Coaches Association to make me head coach at Ohio State, got bags of mail from the people in Massillon disputing his claim.

We knew that the best way to answer him was for the two teams to play, but our schedules appeared to be incompatible in 1940. Waite had only one open date late in the season, but it was a day we were scheduled to play Canton-Lehman High School. The temptation was too much. We paid Lehman their guarantee, took them off from the schedule and arranged a game with Waite at Tiger Stadium.

It poured the day of the game, but 5,000 people stood in line from early afternoon until the ticket windows opened to buy the remaining 2,500 seats. We won, 26-0, with a tremendous performance from Ray Getz, and if it hadn't been for the rain, we probably could have scored well over fifty points. Even with the downpour, we ran up 340 yards rushing and stopped Waite's running game from getting even one first down.

By the time we got up to our final game against Canton-McKinley, we were not only unbeaten that season but unscored upon. Canton's big star was Athy Garrison, who was the state's leading scorer that year, and we had worked all week in practice to stop him. Early in the game he ran a sweep, found himself hemmed in, cut back against our over-aggressive pursuit—and ran for a touchdown. I knew immediately this meant we were too high, and it was a grim moment on our bench; not only had we been scored on, but now we were behind. As the players gathered around me, I said, "That was just something that happened. We won't bat an eye. Just keep after them relentlessly."

They really did, and we won the game, 34-6. It was our thirty-third straight victory, and only an outbreak of the flu in 1937 had kept that streak from reaching sixty. At that time we had won twenty-six consecutive games coming up to a game against the New Castle, Pennsylvania, high school. As was the custom, we had taken the team to an afternoon movie before the Friday-night game, but before the picture was even half over, we had had to send many of them home because they were so sick.

When we played that evening, some of our best players were home in bed, but even then we lost the game only because one of our substitutes failed to react to a reverse pass play we had signaled him New Castle was going to run. We knew that when New Castle's Lindy Laurel went to wingback, that was the play that was coming. I signaled to our player, and he waved back indicating that he understood, but when the play came, he just froze, while one of New Castle's ends caught the touchdown pass. Early in the first quarter we had had another chance to win erased when a drive to the one-yard line had been killed by a penalty. I often felt that the penalty was called because the official, feeling the game was going to be a runaway, like so many in those years, had decided to step in early and take control. Whatever the reason for our falling short, the record still says we lost, but I've always regretted there wasn't some way to note the circumstances. That game taught me one real lesson: The public is interested in only one thing—whether you win or lose.

THREE

Ohio State: The Only Job I Ever Wanted

MY FIRST TWO YEARS AS head coach at Ohio State were the happiest, most exciting and rewarding period of my life, better in some respects than the great years in Cleveland because coaching the Buckeyes had been my ultimate dream. Until the war changed the program in 1943, Ohio State was all that I had ever imagined, and the sweet taste of those first two years still lingers whenever I get together with my players from the 1942 national championship team at our periodic reunions at the university.

College life then was far different from today. College football was king, and university students really loved their school and their team. The nation had just emerged from the Depression, and those kids knew about misery and privation. Going to college became something special to them; they seemed to feel it was a privilege, and their love was reflected in their spirit: Those were the days of the great pep rallies and huge bonfires, when students weren't afraid to stand up and show their affection for school and team.

Ohio State has always been special in this respect, and back in 1941 and 1942 everyone was caught up in the spirit of the Buckeyes. When our team won, it was front-page news in both Sunday papers, picture spreads and banner-headlined stories crowding out the news of Europe and Asia at war. In those days the media considered the team their team and looked at the game just as the campus and the community did.

Ohio Stadium held 72,000 people at that time, and we

filled it every week. I was so wound up I rarely paid any attention to the crowd because as far as I was concerned, those people were just supposed to be there to help us. I'll never forget our student body chanting, "Our man is Paul Brown, our man is Paul Brown," thundering down from the student section of that magnificent arena. It would stir me so much I was ready to get right into the game with our kids. As a matter of fact, when our team ran onto the field for my first game in 1941, I was so carried away that I ran out to the middle of the field with the players. I didn't realize what I had done for a moment, and I suddenly thought, "What am I doing out here?" and edged back to the sidelines.

The magic of Ohio Stadium, the special intensity emanating from that huge bowl filled with all those people, had been a part of me ever since the one freshman year I had spent at Ohio State, a seventeen-year-old kid trying desperately to get onto the freshman team. Even though I had considered their refusal to give me a uniform the cruelest injustice, my love for the place had never diminished.

Then, when I was coaching at Massillon, I went to summer school at the university, and in the evenings I'd often go to the stadium, walk around the playing surface and then sit on the Ohio State bench. I'd close my eyes and imagine myself coaching the Buckeyes and visualize what it might be like with the stadium jammed and the game unfolding before me.

And now I had my chance to find out.

I was projected into the Ohio State coaching picture as much at the insistence of the Ohio Football Coaches Association, the 500 members of which included every high school coach in the state, as from my own record at Massillon. The association considered it a duty to provide Ohio State with the best players and expected, in turn, the football team's record to reflect that effort. There had been growing dissatisfaction with Francis Schmidt's coaching ever since Ohio State's last-minute loss to Notre Dame in 1935, and it all culminated with Michigan's 40-0 beating in the final game of 1940. I was at that game, incidentally, and watched Tom Harmon give the greatest one-man performance I have ever seen in a college game.

Ohio State had fine football players, but that embarrassment proved too much, and Schmidt was fired. Shortly afterward Jimmy Robinson, the coach at Canton-Lehman High School and the association's president, presented my name to

Lynn W. St. John, the university's athletic director, and proceeded to round up support from all over the state. It wasn't exactly an ultimatum, but the association made it pretty clear that if Mr. St. John wanted its continued support, he'd better give my nomination strong consideration.

We had just finished another perfect season at Massillon and some have suggested, perhaps tongue in cheek, that what my fellow coaches were really doing was trying to get rid of me. Actually, of course, the reason they went to bat for me was that they felt a high school coach from their own state should be given an opportunity to turn things around.

Naturally our local paper, the *Massillon Independent*, made it a major issue. I also received a tremendous amount of support from Jack Mollenkopf, then coach at Toledo-Waite High School and a lifelong friend, who later was a successful coach at Purdue. Jack wielded some muscle because his school was not only one of the state's best but close to our archrival Michigan as well, and he therefore could direct players to either school if he wished.

Ohio State had not been the first college to offer me a coaching job. A couple of years earlier Muskingum College, a small, pleasant school in the southeastern part of the state, had called and asked me to come for an interview. Katy and I had driven there and found a picturesque little college town in a rural setting. However, I'd heard about the community's restrictions on smoking and drinking. I'd even been told that sometimes people visiting homes there had had to go down to the basement to have a cigarette, so they could blow the smoke into the furnace. I didn't smoke, but this policy sounded pretty narrow and puritanical—and then I thought about Dave Stewart, my old high school coach, who did plenty of both! He'd never come to visit us under those conditions. The clincher came when the president told me my salary would be only half of what I was making at Massillon, and I declined.

However, when Mr. St. John finally came to my home in Massillon for our first interview, he could have had my services for nothing, simply for the opportunity of coaching the Buckeyes. I always felt he came only to let people know that I had been considered for the job, but I think that attitude changed after his visit to our home because he often told friends later that he had been struck by the tremendous warmth and feeling generated by my wife. He became very fond of Katy; she was very much a homebody, and he, being from the old school, found this appealing. Katy was always a tremendous asset to me.

The only thing that Saint never forgot about that day was Katy fixing his favorite dish for lunch, or at least he said that she had. "I want you to know," he later told my friend Luther Emery, then the *Independent*'s sports editor, "that Mrs. Brown had as much to do with Paul getting the job as those unbeaten seasons."

I firmly believe that was true.

After our first meeting we arranged periodic get-togethers in Wooster, about twenty-five miles west of Massillon, at the home of a Wooster College professor who was a very good friend of Mr. St. John's. We had privacy and got to know each other's feelings about what went with coaching at Ohio State. I knew that I was the prime candidate, though Mr. St. John reportedly considered others. Don Faurot, the head coach and athletic director at Missouri, was the favorite among these, and ironically, our first game in 1941 was against his team. Others mentioned were Alan Holman, coach at Franklin & Marshall; George Hauser, Bernie Bierman's line coach at the University of Minnesota; and Wes Fesler, who had been an assistant at Harvard but had just taken a job at Wesleyan.

In the minds of some, naturally, there was the question of whether a high school coach could assume a job of such magnitude. I had no misgivings about making the leap from high school because I had such total confidence in myself and in my football beliefs, but this conviction wasn't shared by everyone. Dr. H. W. Bell came to me and said, "PB, I am concerned about your getting this job because you are wound too tightly. I don't know whether you can stand this, physically."

"Well, doc," I replied, "if I've got to go, that's one of the better ways I can think of."

I have often thought that perhaps Dr. Bell was trying to make things easier for me in case I didn't get the job. I never once doubted that I would be hired, and I'm certain this confidence reflected itself in all my discussions with Mr. St. John. Our talks never touched on technical football matters, nor did we look at a single film of Massillon's games. Instead, he spent the time judging me strictly on my record, my character, my family and what the community thought of us.

He wanted to know the kind of person he would have to

live with on a day-to-day basis at the university, and more than anything, he was probably intent on being certain I understood the limitations which the Big Ten placed on such matters as recruiting football players. He didn't realize then that, from previous relationships with coaches such as Fritz Crisler at Michigan, Bo McMillan at Indiana and Mal Elward at Purdue, all of whom had actively recruited my Massillon players, I knew exactly how Big Ten coaches operated. They got no innocent babe in the woods when I became one of their number.

Saint also sought my theories on how I'd handle losing, how I motivated players and how I would deal with college students after so many years of working with high school kids. Again, none of this had ever struck me as a problem because I was certain that once I got to Ohio State, we would win and therefore would attract the best players.

Throughout our sessions he never once let on that he knew the man he was interviewing was really a very intense, one-dimensional person who had succeeded over so many years because he believed nothing was as important as his football program. Through many of my early years as a coach I had no other interests. I went fishing, but I could hardly wait to get back to work. I played golf, but I was probably as intense and obnoxious in a golf or bridge game as I was coaching football. If I had hired me at that time, I'd have done it and then gotten far away.

In fact, after I had been at Ohio State for about a year, Saint made the observation—which was totally correct—that our winning had less to do with my actual performance as a coach than with my determination and belief in what I was doing. This competitive, compulsive attitude permeated all the players and coaches on our team.

Throughout all our meetings and considerations, Mr. St. John continued to be pushed by the Ohio Coaches Association, and to this day I don't know whether he really did want me originally. I've always felt that once he made up his mind that he would live with me as a person, he took the tack that if I succeeded, everyone would be happy, and if I failed, then he was blameless because he had given the association the man it had wanted, and the responsibility would have to be shared.

By the time the NCAA convention in late December came around, Saint had just about made up his mind, but to get more of an idea of what kind of people Katy and I were away from Massillon and how compatible we'd be with other university officials, he invited us to be his guests for the meetings in New York City. It had become very apparent that I was going to get the job, and I was interviewed by several newspapers. I think Saint also wanted me to get a feel of how to conduct myself with the big-city media and wanted to observe for himself how I would react to such notoriety. I'll never forget Katy and me standing out in Times Square on New Year's Eve with thousands of other people welcoming in the new year, both of us as excited as we'd ever been in our lives.

Once Saint actually recommended me, the final step was convincing the university's athletic board, but since I had known two or three of its members from graduate school, that was a very pleasant experience. Some other top professors in the graduate school, with whom I had been friendly at that time, also offered unsolicited recommendations, and the board was convinced I was worthy of the job.

My appointment was announced on January 14, 1941, and at age thirty-three I became the youngest head coach in the history of the Big Ten. My salary was $6,500, only about $1,500 more than I had been making at Massillon, but that wasn't important. I don't believe I ever discussed salary with Mr. St. John, but I did request and receive a full professorship. All my life, money had been a secondary thing; I needed it to provide the necessities for my family, but what counted was football. It was such an obsession with me that it never seemed like work.

I was in Columbus when the announcement was made, but I couldn't get home to my family because of icy roads, and Katy had to hear about it that afternoon from Luther Emery at the *Independent* just as she was leaving for the beauty parlor. Even such momentous news didn't keep her from being on time to have her hair done, however. When I arrived home the next day, I was worn out from the events of that past month and came down with the flu. That kept me in bed for several days—a brief respite before we embarked on a busy schedule of public appearances. The first time Katy and I went up to the university, for instance, it was to a "Meet Paul Brown" rally broadcast by radio to a national audience. Perhaps the most memorable event was a luncheon held by the Agonis Club in Columbus at which I was a surprise guest of honor. To carry off the surprise, I was seated anonymously in the middle of a huge throng, and next to me happened to be Johnny Jones, a man-about-town gossip columnist for the *Columbus Dispatch*. He was a tremendously loyal Ohio State fan and prided himself on knowing everything about the school's athletic teams.

Johnny was soon trying to impress everyone at the table with all sorts of "inside information," before a couple of people mischievously asked if he knew Paul Brown.

"Know him well, we're great friends," he boasted.

Of course, I had never met him before, and he obviously didn't recognize me, despite the scores of photos that his own newspaper had been running for over a month. The other men goaded him on with some leading questions about what Paul Brown would do with his new football team.

"Don't worry about anything," Jones said. "I've been close to him for years, and he told me that he was going to do this, and do that . . ." and he kept on and on. Soon everyone in the place knew that Johnny was being suckered. When I was called to the dais to speak and rose from his own table, it brought down the house. For the rest of Johnny's life no one ever let him forget that day, and he was always introduced as "Paul Brown's friend."

From that point on, I was totally consumed by the job, and looking back, I'm sure I was a real demanding nobody who made life miserable for anyone who dared cross my path with something I didn't believe in. However, I hadn't lost a game in almost four years at Massillon, and anyone who goes through something like that begins to feel pretty sure of himself. If I believed in something, I did it. The answers came out quickly and clearly then because I had thought about everything I wanted to accomplish and how to get it done, with regard not only to how to win a football game but to how my football team would operate.

The latter was my chief concern for the first few months as head coach, and it became the foundation for success at Ohio State and everywhere that I coached. Everyone—players, students and alumni—had to absorb my beliefs, and I was so determined that again, I'm sure I was very obnoxious.

From the start I set out to convert everyone to my ways. The first time I addressed the Cleveland chapter of the Ohio State alumni association, I said that being the finest football coach meant more to me than being president of the United

States and that if I weren't coaching at Ohio State, I would be coaching someplace else.

When I talked to the students, I urged them not to be afraid to yell for their team or to worry about being sophisticated or to think that cheering was high schoolish. I also told them, "Don't be afraid to remind any players who are out of line or not in the spirit of our training rules that they owe it to the school to straighten themselves out."

In my first talk to the players I insisted that football was not solely a game of plays, but a game of technique, perfect timing and good blocking that would move against any defense. My rules at Ohio State were the same as they had been at Massillon: The best eleven men, regardless of race, creed or affiliation, would be in the starting lineup—and that starting lineup would be trained to play for sixty minutes, no matter how hot, cold or wet the day was. Substitutions would be made only when the need arose, not to give anyone a rest. I stressed that everything each of them did had to be directed toward the good of the team. I have always made it a point in selecting my players to find those who were not only what I call contact men—physical players—but who were also good people and unselfish in their efforts. There is nothing incompatible in being a good person and being a hard-nosed football player. The more of those any team has, the more successful it will be.

In those years, playing college football for a university like Ohio State was a happy, wholesome experience for the boys. The commercialism we have today did not exist. Players were not given full scholarships, room and board and spending money; instead, they worked for everything they received, unless their parents could afford to pay their expenses. We supplemented whatever money they had with a jobs program, and that was the only aid available. Ernie Godfrey, one of my assistant coaches and a dear friend, who spent his life working for Ohio State, was in charge of the jobs program because of his great rapport with the business community in Columbus. The jobs paid $50 to $75 a month—a boy could survive on that much money back then—and we checked to make sure the players fulfilled their obligations to them. If anyone didn't, he had to have a pretty good reason. When our players reported for football in September, most had worked in summer jobs we'd helped them get. Lin Houston, Don McCafferty, Charley Csuri and Dick Eisner worked on

Ohio highway repair gangs one summer. Others, like George Lynn, my 1942 captain, came from Niles, Ohio, and knew about life in front of a blast furnace. Paul Sarringhaus spent a summer working in a paper mill. By the time they came to school in the fall they were rock hard and really appreciated playing football.

There were no special privileges for any of my players at Ohio State. I made a point of letting my former Massillon players know they would receive no special treatment; they were at the university because we thought they had the opportunity both to get an education and to contribute to our football program. Each understood fully that he would become a starter only if he were the best man at the position. That had been the law of the range back in Massillon. Nobody could take exception to that, and at Ohio State even the players who didn't know me realized it would be a square deal.

We stressed that point whenever we recruited a boy for our team and made certain that he and his parents understood it. Recruiting was an enjoyable experience during my years at Ohio State. The pressure, the under-the-table payments, the soul-selling—these didn't exist as they do today. I had been at the other end of the line, where coaches came to me, and I knew who got the deals, who made them and what they were, but we had a set of rules at Ohio State, and we lived by them.

One of my first public commitments on recruitment was to announce that I considered the entire state of Ohio to be the boundaries of the Ohio State campus. There was no reason why all the good football players with good grades had to go to eastern schools. I knew every topflight player in the state, and I went after them. We divided the state among our coaches and made them responsible for seeing that no football player in their area who could help our program went any place other than Ohio State. I worked where I could do the most good. If we really wanted someone like Lou Groza, I went to Ernie Godfrey and said, "Ernie, get him." We didn't really care how, but Ernie was tenacious, and he did it legitimately. He would buzz around a guy's family so much the boy would be sent to Ohio State just to get rid of Ernie.

The Ohio Coaches Association, having pushed for my appointment, had committed itself to helping, and we got the players we wanted. Another big asset was the reputation our football program at Massillon had formed in everyone's mind. Dante Lavelli, for example, had scholarship offers to Notre Dame, Williams and Dartmouth, but he began to change his mind after Mike Palermo, a basketball official in Cleveland who had seen him perform magnificently in a tournament, told him he should attend his own state school. And when we sent someone down to his home in Hudson, Ohio, he said it was my coming to Ohio State that had finally tipped the scales in our favor, and he joined our program.

We had the same good fortune with Bill Willis. Bill had agreed to attend the University of Illinois on a scholarship that had been arranged in part by his coach, Ralph Webster, himself an alumnus of that university. When my appointment to Ohio State was announced, however, Webster steered him to us. Ralph was very impressed with the manner in which we treated our black players at Massillon and with our policy of judging them only by their football talent. It had really never occurred to me, however, to judge a player in any other manner.

This was not always the case back then. I recall one time in particular when Bill, a dash man for Ohio State's track team and one of the fastest men in the world, was in Philadelphia for the Penn Relays. He and Ralph Tyler, the only black members of the team, were forced to accept separate accommodations, and no one looked after them. As a result, they got separated from their teammates after the meet and suddenly found themselves alone and virtually without any money in a strange city, 600 miles from home. Bill called me, and I wired money so they could pay for their room and get home. You can be sure I let Ohio State's track coach know I didn't appreciate *any* of our football players being abandoned like that. Bill today is a member of both the college and professional football Halls of Fame, a former All-American and the director of the Ohio Youth Commission. He is also one of my dearest friends. I tried to persuade him to join our first coaching staff in Cincinnati, but he was devoted to his work in Columbus and declined.

Bill was just one of several great young players we recruited that year, and many of them later formed the nucleus of our first team in Cleveland. In 1941 six of my Massillon players from the 1940 team came to Ohio State; they included Tom James and Horace Gillom, both of whom became great players at Cleveland. We also recruited or developed other future Browns such as Gene Fekete, Tony Adamle, Lindell Houston, George Cheroke, Ollie Cline, Bob Gaudio and Les Horvath. Adamle, who is a very fine physician today, came from Collingswood High School in what was then the toughest part of Cleveland. He was a tough, hard-nosed player in college, just as he would be in professional football, but always directed himself primarily toward his medical career. Fekete was one of Ohio's most sought-after players in 1941, and I really worked to get him to Ohio State. I made several visits to his home and got to know his parents very well. He's now a high school principal in Columbus. Gaudio, another special player, became a splendid offensive guard for the Browns and was a mervelous technician in that highly skilled position. There were times at Cleveland when we had what amounted to an all-Ohio State offensive line, with Willis and Groza at offensive tackle, Houston and Gaudio the guards and Lavelli the tight end.

From the very beginning we set out to build our Ohio State team as we had built our teams at Massillon, with speed at every position. I had heard Jesse Owens explain his theories about how to increase a man's speed, and I always believed a player could improve himself in that department. A 250-pound tackle couldn't run with a 175-pound halfback, but each man could learn to lessen the distances between himself and the fastest men in his weight class if he followed the fundamentals of running. It wasn't a quality we had inherited from Francis Schmidt, however. He hadn't been the speed freak that I was.

I certainly don't want to disparage any of the players who joined us from the Schmidt era—all of them responded to our program—but for the first time I found that inheriting another man's talent often meant undoing the habits that had been formed over several years. It meant a total relearning process under some very intense conditions. Francis Schmidt certainly hadn't been as detail-conscious as I was, or as demanding, nor had he put the same emphasis on teaching or execution. In our system everything had to be done a certain way. We stressed classroom work and study away from the field and emphasized working with small units. Schmidt, however, worked on the team theory and used to hold up big six-foot cards behind his team in practice so each player could see his assignment. He had about 350 plays, and his practices often ran two and a half hours, with little emphasis on individual technique. Sometimes his players had to improvise simply because they couldn't understand what they were supposed to do. One of his players once made a mistake on a play in practice, and Schmidt jumped all over him.

"But, coach," the player said, "it's on the card that way."

Francis turned and looked at the card and said, "Well, the card's wrong."

I was familiar with Schmidt's football—I had discussed it with him, watched films and been a guest lecturer at several of his football clinics—but I never grasped it, really. Built on a complex system of ball handling and laterals, it was intriguing and fun to watch, but also very error-prone; that, of course, was anathema to me.

Our personal styles were very different, too. One of my former Massillon players, Wendell Lohr, who was an end on one of Schmidt's teams, told me about one of his Ohio State teammates who always made it a point to sit beside Francis and talk to him about what was happening.

"Gosh, coach, they just got around Lohr again," he'd say, or, "They got inside Lohr this time, coach. Did you see that?"

In one particular game, this went on until Schmidt could stand no more. "Son, I can't stand you," he told the player, and moved to the other end of the bench. He stayed there for a few minutes, thought about it and then walked back to where the player sat.

"Kid," he said, "I'm the coach. *You* move to the other end."

Francis was also a very earthy man, prone to the kind of muleskinner language that I never tolerated, in neither our practices nor our games. Because he never demanded the same discipline I did, and class and lab schedules were never planned, his players often missed two or three days of practice each week. I endured this situation during our first spring practice but thereafter saw to it that every player finished his classes by three o'clock each afternoon and came ready for football practice. We never interfered with the players' curricula. In fact, we required them to attend every class, every day, and we checked with their professors to make sure they did, both in and out of football season. I always felt that players who lay around a fraternity house or a dorm and skipped classes were the kind who would begin to erode a football team. A boy's dedication to studies should be no less than his dedication to football. He not only makes himself a better person, but makes the team better.

Schmidt sent me a telegram of congratulations when I got the appointment as head coach, but I never saw him afterward. He moved to the Far West, coached for a time at the University of Idaho and died a few years later.

His ways were firmly entrenched when I took over, and one of the first things I sought to change was his approach to conditioning. For years Ohio State players had been beefy because that was how Francis liked them. Not me. I met Jack Stephenson, our captain-elect, on the first day I had the job.

"What's your weight, Jack?" I asked, eyeing him from top to bottom.

"About two hundred thirty-six pounds," he replied.

"Well, you'll have a lot more lateral movement when you get down to about two-sixteen," I told him. "When that Michigan game comes around next November, you'll be the leanest, hungriest boy we know."

Soon everyone was losing weight. I kept stressing the words *lean and hungry,* and finally, one of the squad, rather bemused, asked why I was so insistent on the point.

"I'll tell you why, and this may jump you ahead in life a little bit," I told them. "The she-wolf fights best on an empty belly."

They all laughed, but they got the message. We had a small litany of homemade sayings on the subject that they got to know by heart: "When you're lean and hungry, you fight the good fight," and "When you're fat, you think fat, and when you think fat, you get gotten." When I meet those players today, they still remember and roll them right out. We can laugh and kid about all this now, but it was deadly serious back then.

That "lean and hungry" philosophy touched every area of practice. As at Massillon, there were no breaks, no water buckets even for games on the hot late-summer afternoons in September, and our players could not sit or kneel during time-outs unless they were injured. If a player was hurt, then he lay down and we took care of him. Everything was built on a spartan, tough, fight-your-way-to-the-death basis, and as the attitude seeped into the players, they began to realize they didn't need any comforts on the field. When they saw other teams hit the water bucket, they said, "We'll take care of them."

That same philosophy would later apply to the Browns as well. I remember once arriving at the stadium at the same time as the Baltimore Colts and watching several Baltimore players get off their bus smoking cigars. Our guys had their playbooks in their hands, and that was about all. I said to them, "We can lick any team that gets off a bus smoking cigars." And we did.

One of my real concerns during those first few months at Ohio State was whether our returning players had suffered any long-lasting effects from that brutal defeat by Michigan the season before. Consequently, everything we did for a while was directed at sweeping out defeatism and the stigma of the previous season. It even affected how we purchased equipment and selected hold-over coaches.

I was surprised to discover that Ohio State's equipment was not as good as Massillon's, but the reason became evident: In a big institution the coach often doesn't pay enough attention to this phase of the program, so the people who do the selling find they can set up deals with people on the inside. Schmidt had obviously never involved himself with the equipment, so some sweetheart deals had developed over the years. I put an end to them and persistently demanded thereafter that only the best and most expensive equipment be purchased—and I was the judge of what constituted "the best." Coming from the football coach, this caused quite a stir.

I supervised the fitting of every player, the overriding principle being that our players should feel as comfortable as I would want to be if I were playing. Our shoes and pads were the lightest to give our players speed, comfort and safety. We had satin pants with two-way stretch in the back, which were a bit ahead of the times, and I even designed our jersey numbers to resemble those we had had at Massillon.

We always wanted out players to think they were something special, to be so proud that they knew everything had to be the best, from the equipment they wore to the way they took calisthenics to the way they conducted themselves off the field to the dedication they gave to their team. It was my way of letting those Ohio State boys know the old ways were gone.

Our assistant coaches became just as involved as I did. I brought Hugh McGranahan, Carroll Widdoes and Fritz Heisler from Massillon but still faced the nagging question of which of Schmidt's staff to keep. I felt it important to have at least one holdover, so that there would be a source of information about the past, but I hesitated at first to make any commitments. That stirred up some people because at the same time I was adding new coaches to the staff, including Paul Bixler, who had been an assistant to Jimmy Aiken at Canton-McKinley High School, and Trevor Rees, a former Ohio State star, who had been coach at Shaw High School in Cleveland. I knew these men and believed in them.

One of the holdovers I wasn't sure about at first was Ernie Godfrey. It wasn't because I didn't like him. Ernie was a sweet, wonderful man, whom I had known for years and who was totally dedicated to the university's football program. The problem was that a number of players used to make fun of his speech. Ernie was the master of the malaprop. "Scatter out in bunches," he'd tell the players. "Indiana runs two-thirds of its plays on the ground and three-fifths of them in the air," he'd counsel them. "Run around the field ten times if you have to walk twelve of them," he'd order.

Once Ernie was gazing around the stands at an Ohio State-Notre Dame game in Columbus. The freshman team at Ohio State got complimentary tickets behind the Buckeyes' bench, but like many college kids who needed money, they sold them to scalpers, and checking their section, Ernie found not a single young face in sight. He turned to Schmidt with a worried, absolutely serious expression on his face and said, "That is the oldest freshman team I ever saw. We did a very poor job!"

I was worried that the players might not take him seriously enough, but I soon learned that although they mimicked him, they also loved him, and he became an outstanding coach for us. Lou Groza credits him with much of his success as a place-kicker.

I also kept Fritz Mackey and Eddie Blickle from Schmidt's staff. Blickle unfortunately died in an automobile crash shortly after joining us, but Mackey, who had been Schmidt's line coach, proved very valuable. He knew the players I had inherited, and his sound judgments on each man's capabilities were totally accurate. I had known him, as a matter of fact, since my freshman year at Ohio State, when I had been pledging his fraternity, Phi Delta Theta. He slept in the bunk below me in a dormitory room and talked in his sleep, and since I was just a kid, I was all ears.

He'd say, "So-and-so, I never told you I loved you. Yes, I

loved you, but I never told you that. Now you're going to have to understand this." I think I lived his love life that year, and believe me, I was all ears because I was just a kid. We still joke about that whenever we see each other, and his wife, Elaine, who says she's heard the same things I did, over and over, says he still talks in his sleep.

As was the case in Massillon and later in Cleveland, my best and closest friends were my coaches, and once a month each of us took a turn hosting a dinner party. Of course, the personalities were all very different, but the chemistry of the group was right. McGranahan was a rough-and-tumble Irishman, and he contrasted vividly with Widdoes, who was very straitlaced, proper and superethical I always figured that if I cut a corner too close, Wid would let me know, and that was very good for me in my new job.

During much of that first winter in Columbus, before my family and our belongings came from Massillon, Wid bunked with me in our new home. He was a very sensitive man, and even though his coaching future looked great at Ohio State following his 1944 unbeaten season, he left major college coaching because he preferred to work on the small-college level.

McGranahan was just the opposite. He'd do anything, but he did it in good humor. Any player with a problem gravitated to him, and he steered them toward our thinking. His humor was earthy, and I'll never forget a traditional tea party for our team held at the home of President Bevis. Mrs. Bevis had plates of little finger sandwiches, cookies and petits fours out, and of course, our guys went over that spread like a horde of locusts. Within a matter of minutes just one cookie remained.

"Would you look here?" Mrs. Bevis said so sweetly. "With all those big strong boys here, there's still one cookie left. What shall I do with it?"

McGranahan, who knew the players hadn't really wanted to go to that party, put his hand to his mouth and said to those standing behind him, "The first guy who says what I think you're going to say is out of line."

From the start my relations with both President Bevis and Mr. St. John were excellent. I was coach only a few weeks when Saint and I went to a Big Ten meeting in Mankato, Minnesota. He was a voracious cigar smoker—a box a day, I once heard—and we had to share the same cabin. The air be-

came a little thick in there at times, but since this was the
first time the two of us had ever been on the road together, I
was determined that I would get along with him.

The first night we were asleep in our cabin when I awoke
to hear gurgling noises from his side of the room. To me they
sounded like a death rattle. Saint was getting along in years,
and I figured an elderly man could very well be on his way
out, so I lay quietly until I heard him begin to breathe normally. I finally fell asleep only to be reawakened by the same
noises. Again I waited until his breathing was normal before
resuming my sleep.

This went on all night, and I slept little, but when I finally
awoke in the morning, he was on the porch of our cabin,
pounding his hands against his chest, breathing in that wonderful Minnesota air and saying what a tremendous day it
was going to be. Nothing was wrong with him, nor had there
been the entire night. I was exhausted, and he was in terrific
shape. As I continued to travel with him, I got used to his pe-
culiarities, though there were still times when I'd awaken in
the middle of the night. Sometimes he'd just be lying there
smoking a cigar. Maybe those box-a-day stories weren't all
that far-fetched.

This outing with Saint was also my first social contact with
Fritz Crisler of Michigan, a great coach, and I found him to
be quite a prankster despite his austere professional look on
the football field and the intense rivalry between our two
schools. At the Big Ten meeting Crisler arranged the living
accommodations, and most of the time he put the coach and
athletic director of a delegation together in a cabin. Two of
the athletic directors, however, Nelson Metcalfe from the
University of Chicago and Weenie Wilson of Illinois, it was
said, hadn't spoken to each other in years and certainly were
not friends. Fritz put them in the same cabin. We never did
find out what happened when the door closed each night because they never said a word. When the meeting was being
set up, Crisler had also had us contribute $10 apiece for the
person who caught the biggest fish—only we never saw a
penny of it because Crisler and his buddies used it all up par-
tying en route to the conference.

I also got my first glimpse at that meeting of how the Big
Ten solved some of its internal disputes. Bo McMillan and
Mal Elward were arguing over some alleged recruiting irregu-
larities, and Mal had laid out his case with some pretty com-

plete documentation. At that point, the commissioner, Major Griffith, rapped his gavel, asked for a motion to adjourn and closed the meeting. The matter never came up again. I guess it was an unwritten rule that no one was to bring up such matters before the whole group.

Naturally, everyone in the Big Ten—not to mention Columbus—was anxious to know how the Buckeyes would do under their new regime. The first three months of constant attention had built up a tremendous ground swell of curiosity, and a record crowd of 25,000 showed up for the annual spring game, even though it was nothing more than a scrimmage. It turned out to be a wide-open game, and everyone expressed himself impressed with our offense, but I was not pleased. It was a cold, wet spring, and coupled with some holdover distractions, we had not achieved the detail and timing that I wanted. So it was back to the practice field.

We trained harder than ever. As in Massillon, we worked in small groups so we could precision-machine the individual parts of our team before putting them together. It was a teaching point I had adopted from Jock Sutherland of Pitt, and it helped accelerate our development.

Before we went onto the practice field as a team—and every team I ever had always went on the field together instead of straggling out in twos and threes—I made sure each player was in his assigned seat in our football classroom. I just looked at an empty seat to see who was absent. I always talked to my players before practice, sometimes on subjects other than football, and laid out our objectives for that day and how long we expected to work. If a player knew exactly what was expected of him and how long it would take to accomplish, he would not try to pace himself. If we finished our work before the allotted time, practice was finished; if we didn't, we stopped, but it meant that either the players hadn't worked hard enough or we had planned too much. We refigured for the following day and started anew.

The Ohio State players were not used to this practice—Schmidt had always kept them on the field for a long time—but my rule was to spend no more than ninety minutes at a time. Anytime a practice exceeds an hour and twenty minutes a player's attention span and learning capacity quickly diminish. That's true in the classroom as well. Players also get tired standing around for long periods and begin holding back.

In the same vein, I never believed in long warm-ups before

a game. If a team does its stretching before going onto the field, all that is required then is getting the feel of things, checking how the wind is blowing and warming up on mechanics and team play. On hot days, ten or fifteen minutes often are enough for a pregame warm-up; otherwise, a team can boil out—wearing football equipment takes a lot out of a player.

We always opened our practices—not only at Ohio State but everywhere I coached—with what we called the routine warm-up drill, pairing off players by their positions and similar weights. Each player, in less than two minutes, went through a series of five exercises. The first two were tackles, in which the player being tackled learned how to roll to each side with each shoulder. Then there was the head-on tackle, in which the player walked with the man and put him down on his back, teaching the runner how to curl up and tuck in his head. The fourth and fifth exercises were different each day. One day it might be a long body block from each side, the next day a straight shoulder block, the next day a reverse body block. The basic idea was to get the feel of the ground, and of a man, so that contact work became natural. All this was done at a very slow speed so that no one got hurt. In this way the player's body was conditioned to the game of football, while injuries were kept at a minimum. Without this type of drill, some players wouldn't touch the ground or make contact with a man from one game to the next. The result, and benefit, from all these drills were some deadly tackling.

We worked on the drills every day, regardless of how wet or dry it was. There were days when we'd get down in the rain or mud or snow, and I'd say to the kids, "When you go hunting, you think it's great to be out trudging in this kind of weather. No one is going to melt, so let's go." Soon it became a way of life, though I do remember a practice at Ohio State when there was so much water on the field from a rainstorm that the ball floated away. The players looked at me, wondering what was next. "Let's go," I said, as if nothing had happened. The only time weather halted our practices was during a lightning storm, and then I'd got the players off the field immediately. Once a squad coached by my friend Jimmy Robinson was hit by lightning, and some of the players were killed standing in the huddle. This made a deep impression on me, and I never wanted to endanger anyone's life.

When our fall practices began, we had only thirteen letter-men from 1940, five nonlettermen and thirty-three sopho-mores. Our squad was smaller than previous Ohio State squads, but I've never believed in wasting time teaching people who were not going to play. I wanted to devote our time and effort to the first offensive and defensive units. Soon I had them responding to a new offensive style built on shift-ing from a T formation to the single wing, right or left, and on moving from a balanced to an unbalanced line. We used the same rhythm shift as at Massillon. Sometimes we'd run from the T formation instead of shifting.

A few eyebrows were raised at that and also because I made the passing game a more important part of our offense. Teams just didn't utilize it much then, but when I was a pas-ser in school and college, I had formed strong beliefs in its effectiveness, particularly if it was balanced with a good run-ning game. I never liked to play against a team that could throw the ball effectively. I insisted on one rule with all our passers, however: Don't force the ball if there is no open re-ceiver. Either take the loss or scramble. That was my first message to Paul Sarringhaus, our passer at Ohio State.

"Just so we understand each other," I told him. "One of the things I don't like is interceptions. At the same time, don't be afraid to throw the ball if you have a man open or see a man coming open. It is a judgment decision from that point on, but don't force it."

We won some games at Ohio State with our passing be-cause of those admonitions. It also helped that we had great receivers like Bob Shaw and Dante Lavelli.

As the season approached, my worries about any fallout effects from the previous regime disappeared. Deep down in my heart, I figured we were going to whip some teams, but rather than have everyone point a finger at us too quickly, I kept it low-key and talked about our lack of experience. No matter how much experience we might have had, however, no team could have been prepared for what awaited us on that first football Saturday afternoon in 1941 in Ohio Sta-dium.

FOUR

Glory and Gloom

THE GAME WAS AGAINST MISSOURI, and it finished a perfect
trifecta of misadventure for the start of my new career. The
string had begun a few days before at yet another "Meet
Paul Brown" night at the Palace Theater in Columbus. Ted
Lewis, who was from nearby Circleville, and his orchestra
were the featured performers, and they had dedicated their
show to our team before a packed house of nearly 3,000
people. Ted even had me try on his famous trademark top
hat. I found he could balance it so easily on his arm because
it was filled with tin foil, which made it heavy and simple to
handle.

Clyde McBee, the president of the Agonis Club, made
some opening remarks and brought the house down when he
said, "Paul Brown is going to be the pillow . . . er, pillar of
Ohio State football. . . ." I introduced each of our players
and coaches and said something about each man. Katy sat in
the front row, and as the program went on, I saw her eyes
beginning to droop. That was the signal that she was going
into insulin shock. She always carried a small container of
orange juice for such emergencies, but no one around her
was aware of the situation. I could only watch and fidget as
her eyelids got heavier and heavier, and I raced through my
part of the program, hoping to reach her in time. When I finished, I immediately excused myself from the stage, went
directly to her and had her drink the orange juice. She was
all right soon—but I have forever remembered that scene.

That wasn't all. As if surmounting all the emotions of
coaching my first game at Ohio State were not enough, I was
refused admission to Ohio Stadium on the day of the game.

When our buses arrived, I stepped off to say hello to Tink Ulrich and some friends from Massillon while the gates were being opened. The buses and their police escort went inside, while I shook hands and briefly chatted. After saying good-bye, I walked to the gate and passed one of the guards, completely oblivious to anything or anyone because I was so emotionally charged.

Suddenly the guard grabbed me.

"You can't come in here, sir," he said. "Where's your ticket?"

"I don't have a ticket. I'm Paul Brown," I told him.

"Is that right? Well, I'm President Roosevelt, and you still can't come in," he replied.

There was nothing I could do, so I walked to a spot below our locker room, which was on the second floor of the stadium, and waited for someone to look down so I could catch his attention. No one did, and I began tossing stones at the window. After a couple of minutes one of the players stuck his head out.

"Holy smokes, the coach is down there," he yelled to the people inside.

"Send someone down, and get me through that gate," I yelled to him.

The trainer came down and got me in, but those were be-littling moments, and for a while I worried that I might not make it. Of all the times to have to worry about a thing like that! And when I *did* get in, I never dreamed that I would have to go through such a wringer as I did against Missouri.

The split T formation helped revolutionize college football, and some of its principles, such as the wishbone and veer formations, are in vogue today. However, when Don Faurot and his Missouri team unveiled it for the first time ever against Ohio State in my first game as head coach, it gave me some of the worst moments of my coaching career. Though we won the game, 12–7, we were not prepared for this new concept, and we managed to survive only by the sheerest good fortune.

Missouri also had some emotional factors going in its favor, including Faurot's bitter disappointment over not being selected as the Buckeyes' head coach. Don wanted to show the Ohio State people they had been dead wrong about that, and he also had a strong desire to avenge a loss to the Buckeyes two years before that had cost his team a perfect season.

Of course, we had some emotion going for us, too, since this was my first game, and my players were as keyed up for this game as I was—but we had nothing to match his revolutionary concept in offensive football. Even emotions can disintegrate in such situations.

Faurot had used the Notre Dame box formation in his spring game, and we had seen nothing then that warranted any alarm. Of course, he had strategically hidden the split T and all its new techniques. The key to its effectiveness lay in its line splits. Instead of positioning themselves a conventional six inches from the center, the guards split a yard or a yard and a half, and the tackles split the same distance from the guards. Now at that time defensive linemen were always taught to take their spacing from the position of the offensive linemen—for instance, a defensive tackle might be taught to play off the inside shoulder of the man opposite him. If they did that now, however, huge splits would open up in our defensive line, into which the quarterback could easily pop through or hand the ball to a running back. To increase the line's effectiveness further, Faurot had also developed the brush block, in which the offensive lineman hit the defensive man hard enough to seal him off or knock him off-balance for just the instant it took the quarterback or halfback to bolt past.

We had never even thought about such things, and Missouri started ripping through us right from the start. Our players were totally confused, and we had to make an instant decision.

"Just keep your normal distances in relation to your teammate next to you," we told them, because we could think of nothing else at the time. "Let them split from sideline to sideline if they want to, but stay in your same relative position."

That desperate decision saved us, and from then on we played with the traditional 6-2-2-1 defense. Missouri drove up and down the field, with Don Greenwood, Harry Ice and Bob Steuber putting on a stunning show of offensive football. The first time Missouri had the ball, Steuber gained 67 yards in two plays, but we held at our 7-yard line. We stopped them again on our 4-yard line, and a tremendous 48-yard punt against the wind by Jack Graf got us out of trouble. He hit another for 72 yards that again took them from deep inside our territory.

At one point, in order to try to keep the ball from Missouri, we elected to run on a fourth-and-one situation near midfield and made the first down. Graf passed to Bob Shaw for our first touchdown in the second quarter, and Jack scored our second touchdown in the final quarter. We had beaten them.

After the game Tink Ulrich said to me, "PB, if all you can do is twelve to seven against this team, I'm afraid for you. You're in for a long season."

"I think you're wrong about that," I told him. "Missouri is a fine football team, and they are going to give people fits this year with that new offense."

As it turned out, Missouri didn't lose another game until Fordham beat them, 2-0, in the Sugar Bowl, and only one other team scored two touchdowns against them. I learned from that experience never to put total faith in what I saw of an opposing team in spring practice, and from then on we always tried to be ready for anything.

That game helped me in another way, too. I mentally cataloged the football capabilities of Greenwood and Steuber, and when I put together my first Cleveland Browns team, I signed them. As my college seasons went on, I found I could never forget anyone who played well against us, and the Browns benefited considerably from my memory.

The first time I ever saw Otto Graham play football, for instance, was in our 14-7 loss to Pappy Waldorf's Northwestern team—the only game we lost in 1941. Otto was only a sophomore, playing as a single wing tailback, but against us he looked like anything but a sophomore. In the first quarter, after we had held Northwestern on our one-yard line and punted from our end zone, he passed to Bud Hasse for a touchdown. We tied the score on Bob Hecklinger's touchdown, but late in the game Otto started to his left as if he were going to run a sweep, and while on the dead run he threw a long pass all the way back to the right side of the field for the winning touchdown. I never forgot Otto's tremendous peripheral vision and his ability to run to his left and then to throw far across the field with such strength and accuracy. Perhaps it is true you don't forget the players who beat you. I also saw him play football against us twice more and watched him play basketball for Northwestern, and each time I marveled at his athletic ability and his gift of peripheral vision, a must if a passer is going to survey a field quickly and pick out the correct receiver. Not only that, but he could run as well, thus making his passing all the more effective. Years later Otto was the first player I signed for the Browns because I knew he had all the skills to be a great quarterback.

I found the same skills in Edgar ("Special Delivery") Jones when we played Pitt the week after Northwestern had beaten us. We defeated the Panthers, 21-14, but Jones, already an acknowledged star, had a tremendous day. Like Otto, he was a great runner and passer as a single wing tailback and deservedly picked as an All-American that season. He was such a superb athlete he even pitched a few games for the Cleveland Indians during the time he played for the Browns.

There were other great games and players that season. After we had recovered from our opener against Missouri, we traveled to Los Angeles and defeated Southern California, 33-0, the first time Ohio State had ever won a football game on the West Coast. This was my first trip to the West Coast, and we were treated royally. Our kids had a tremendous time with movie studio tours and gracious hospitality, but that didn't sway us against the Trojans. Southern California got only 78 yards passing and *minus* 9 yards rushing that afternoon. When I saw the thousands who greeted our team at the railroad station upon our return, I looked at our players, and I could see some self-satisfied grins. That worried me.

"We just had a good day," I told that crowd. "We can't afford to get ripe. When you become ripe, the next step is to become rotten, and when you become rotten, you fall."

That is almost what happened. We had an open date the next Saturday, and we nearly lost our aggressiveness and desire. The only way to maintain this edge is by scrimmaging, but your own players can get hurt—when you play another team, there is only a 50 percent chance that any injury won't be to one of your players. I resolved never again to have any gaps on our schedule, as we headed into our game against Purdue.

In that Purdue game I found out for the first time what it meant to be a marked man—in the sense that I, rather than my team, became the object of the opposition. Perhaps that week's layoff plus the great victory over Southern California and the consequent adulation poured on the players had something to do with our ragged performance, but I also knew that many of my former Massillon players had gone to play for Mal Elward at Purdue, and two of the greatest, Rocky Snyder and Jim Miller, were just itching to show their old coach a thing or two. I tried to convince our players during the week's practice that they faced a street fight from these players, but my words went unheeded. Jim Daniell's blocked punt for a safety in the first quarter turned out to be the victory margin as we squeaked by, 16–14, and when the game ended, I was mobbed by those Massillon kids.

Our 46-34 victory over Wisconsin in 1941 also had a strong Massillon connection and was one of the most interesting and entertaining games we played all season. The Badgers were coached by my boyhood idol, Harry Stuhldreher, one of Notre Dame's Four Horsemen. Stuhlie, who had been several years ahead of me at Massillon High School, was a short, stocky guy, and I always marveled at how he got so much out of such a short body. He was a great leader, though—he had to be as the quarterback of that famous Notre Dame backfield—and I've always been grateful for our Big Ten association that introduced us and, eventually, made us dear friends.

Harry was a very good football coach, but he went through some difficult times at Wisconsin. One morning at breakfast my son Mike, while reading the sports pages, asked me if I had ever been burned in effigy.

"Why?" I asked him.

"Well, here's a story about Mr. Stuhldreher being burned in effigy at Wisconsin," he told me.

"No. I never have," I replied, and Mike's face fell in disappointment. He must have thought that was some big deal for a football coach.

When Harry brought his team to Columbus for our game, the university invited the Massillon High School band to play at halftime, but I had no time to think about any good old days at home because we had a real battle going with Wisconsin. We led, 20-7, at one point, but Wisconsin tied the score, 20-20, before Jack Graf, on a perfectly executed spinner play, ran 64 yards for a touchdown that gave us the lead for good. There were two amazing statistics in that game. We threw only four passes, and each one resulted in a touchdown. And Wisconsin had the benefit of a fifth, or extra, down when the officials miscounted and Wisconsin used it to score a touchdown. With touchdowns coming so fast, I protested vehemently when it happened, but since we ended up winning the game, I did not make an issue of the mistake later. The scorekeeper, as Dave Stewart had often said, was the most important man in the stadium.

Our next-to-last game that season was against Illinois, and it was Bob Zuppke's final game as head coach there. Bob had sent a scout to watch us against Missouri, and he had returned and told him, "Paul Brown is just another high school coach. He didn't show much against Missouri. Wait till he plays Southern California next week and gets run out of the Coliseum."

"Let's wait and see," Zuppke had told the coach. "Maybe he's pacing his team and just getting by this week, so everyone will not give him much of a chance against Southern California."

After we defeated Southern Cal, 33-0, Zuppke, who had also become a college head coach after a spectacular high school coaching career, called the scout into his office and said, "See, that's what I mean by pacing. This new guy must be some kind of coach if he knows how to pace already." That hadn't been the case, of course—we had been fortunate to escape with our lives against Missouri.

Zuppke went through a tough season in 1941, but his team played with tremendous courage and determination against us, before losing, 12-7. After the game I walked out on the field, and Coach Zuppke came toward me, totally disheveled, his hat crumpled and sitting sideways on his head, his tie askew. He had a little smile on his face, though.

"Congratulations, coach," I said, extending my hand. "It was a real battle. Your team played exceptionally well and really wanted to send you out as a winner. I commend you. You were more than we wanted."

"Oh," he said in his heavy German accent, "you remind me of myself many years ago when I came from high school football. I tell you what. If you got the boys"—and he raised his hand in the air—"you'll beat old Zup. Of course, if you're down here"—lowering his hand—"and Zup's got the boys, he'll beat you.

"Now," he said, putting his hand in the middle, "it's right about here. At this stage, old Zup will beat you."

He laughed and walked away, but he never did congratulate me. That was the first and last time I ever saw him, but Alex Agase, one of our middle linebackers with the Browns and the best I've ever seen at reading an offense, played for

Zuppke at Illinois, and we often talked about "old Zup's" coaching skills.

Beating Illinois or anyone else, however, really didn't mean much at Ohio State—and still doesn't—unless the Buckeyes ended their season with a victory over Michigan. This series has always attracted national attention and produced some of college football's greatest games, and certainly my first confrontation with them in 1941 was no exception. Ohio State with only thirty-six players healthy enough to be in uniform, and many of them limited because of football-related injuries, was a twenty-point underdog, playing before 102,000 people at Ann Arbor.

At that time I hadn't been involved with Ohio State long enough to realize fully the importance of beating Michigan. To me it was a game that had to be won, just like every other game on our schedule, and I made no effort to attach any special emotional significance to it during our practices, though I certainly didn't downplay it either.

I knew that our team was not as strong as the 1940 team that had been thrashed 40-0 and that Michigan wasn't much weaker, even without Tom Harmon. The day before we left for Ann Arbor I showed our team the films of that rout, not so much to stir them up for revenge as to show what Michigan could do to us if we played anything less than our best football. When we sat down to our pregame meal, I placed a copy of the *Detroit Free Press* at everyone's chair so they could see the statistics of that 1940 game spread out over the front page. It was my final reminder to the players that the same thing could happen to us unless we went all-out and literally died trying our best to win. Well, we didn't win—but we played to the most stirring tie I've ever seen.

Fritz Crisler's single wing offense was cleverly conceived. He had a spinner series built on trapping the defensive linemen, from which Michigan's backs would either run or pass. It was very effective in cooling down a pass rush and made their own passing game more effective. Two great backs on the Michigan team made this offense work: Bob Westfall, a 220-pound fullback, who had been a starter the previous year with Tom Harmon and was a very fine passer; and Tom Kuzma, who had succeeded Harmon as tailback and was a superb runner.

To counter it, Fritz Mackey conceived a defensive plan using a five-man line and utilizing a linebacker on the weak side of Michigan's formation. This alignment proved particularly hard to trap and twice in the first quarter managed to stop Michigan inside our ten-yard line without allowing a point, and again at our five-yard line early in the last quarter. George Cheroke played a tremendous game on defense as he continually broke up the fine tuning of those Michigan trap plays.

Still, Michigan led, 14-7, until Jack Graf scored his second touchdown midway through the third quarter, and in the final quarter, after stopping them on the 5-yard line, we drove 95 yards for the go-ahead touchdown. The play was Mackey's idea. We put our left halfback, Dick Fisher, on a deep swing pass after decoying Michigan's cornerback and safetyman away from the area, and when Dick caught the ball to complete a 52-yard play, there was no one within 15 yards of him. We missed the extra point, and that set up the astounding emotion-charged ending to this unbelievable game.

Our players were so wrung out they couldn't stop Michigan from tying the score, 20-20. All Michigan had to do was kick the extra point, and they'd win. I stood on the sidelines after that last Michigan touchdown and couldn't bear to see my team, which had fought so gallantly against overwhelming odds, come out as a loser. I tried to delay the inevitable for a couple of minutes by calling time-out and sending in a substitute while Michigan got ready for the extra point. When the time-out period expired, I still couldn't stand it, so I sent in another substitute, and again time was called. By the time Bill Melzow, the kicker, who had been standing idly on the field for nearly five minutes thinking about that kick, finally got to hit the ball he just flubbed it.

That was it. Later everyone thought I had been trying to psych Melzow out, but that hadn't been the case. When the game ended, there was a mad scramble for possession of the game ball—it had been a tie, after all—and Westfall, who was Michigan's captain, finally managed to scoop it up. But then he did a wonderful thing. He went over to our captain, Jack Stephenson, and, in the middle of the field, handed the ball to him.

"You deserve it," he told Jack. "You played a great game." Both men embraced in one of the most stirring displays of sportsmanship I have ever witnessed, which, to me, epitomized what college football really meant back then.

After the game, as I was talking to the press, a guard

tapped me on the shoulder and said, "Katy wants to see you and won't take no for an answer." I broke off the news conference immediately, left the room and walked right into a big, warm hug from my wife. Everything we had done that season and that day was worth that one wonderful moment.

Elation about that game was high throughout Ohio. Someone in Governor John Bricker's administration even thought it would be nice to give me a personal commemoration and issued me a license plate, PB-20, which I kept until I left Cleveland for good in 1963. That license plate was always very special to me. Many times later on I looked at it and thought again of the players on that 1941 team with tremendous warmth and appreciation.

One of the keys to our success in 1941 was that everyone made a contribution because the one quality that ran throughout that team was unselfishness. It enabled us to get the most from a limited amount of talent. I don't think many outside the team realized the feeling we had for Jack Stephenson, our captain, for instance. Jack was in and out of the lineup, playing behind Charley Csuri at tackle, but he was always in the spirit of his team and a fine leader. I'm sure it was a bit of a jolt for a captain not to be playing regularly, but he never once let down. It was the same with players like Thornton Dixon, our fourth tackle; or Leon Schoenbrum; or Sam Fox, a ball-hawking opportunist who played behind Bob Shaw at end; or Paul Sweeney, our third wingback. Tom Kinkade began the season as our starting wingback, but when Horvath came on, he had to split the job, and neither ever complained about not getting enough playing time. Kinkade was a strong, slashing runner who excelled in blocking, while Horvath was a tremendous runner and pass receiver, an ideal combination for certain situations. Wilbur Schneider, too, was a 175-pound guard who played excellently behind Lin Houston and Ed Bruckner. Though he was extremely quick, I used to ask Fritz Mackey. "Do you think he's big enough?"

Fritz would say with determination, "He sure is!"

I've often thought about Pete Hershberger and Don Steinberg as well. Both were good blocking ends who never caught many passes, yet they never complained. Pete's father was my friend, and he used to make arrangements for a group of us to take our children to a farm outside Columbus to cut down our Christmas trees. When the cutting was finished, we sat around a fire and enjoyed a special kind of togetherness.

Sadly, Pete was killed in World War II. Don Steinberg, who later became an outstanding surgeon, took a lot of ribbing about not catching too many passes, but he was a consistent, mistake-free player.

So were John Halabrin and Dick Fisher. Halabrin played behind Jack Graf and today is an insurance commissioner for the State of Ohio. Fisher came to Ohio State under Francis Schmidt with the title "the Columbiana Clipper" because of his great high school reputation in Columbiana, Ohio. He hadn't played much for Schmidt, but he bore much of the brunt of our offense in 1941 and did everything that we asked.

Jack Graf, who occasionally visits me today at the Bengals' training camp in Wilmington, Ohio, was a very special player in 1941. He was the hub of our team—the punter, passer and featured running back, particularly adept at ball handling and passing from our spinner series. Francis Schmidt hardly knew that Jack existed in 1940, but in our system he became a tremendous fullback. Katy and I used to get together with his parents in Massillon, and his father used to officiate at many high school and college games. Jack was the perfect example of how a good football player could also be a good person. He was class president, captain of the basketball team and an actor talented enough to play in *The Male Animal* on Broadway after graduation.

My pace at Ohio State never slackened after the 1941 season. There were recruiting trips and a mandatory whistle-stop tour through New York State to address the Ohio State alumni chapters.

One of the people we recruited was a high school lad named Lou Groza from Martins Ferry, Ohio. Lou was an all-state tackle in football, an all-state center in basketball and a member of the national scholastic honors society, and as a senior he stood well over six feet tall and weighed 220 pounds. He had also begun to excel as a place-kicker, thanks to some fine tutelage from his brother, Frank. Even then the kicking game was important to me, and I saw that Lou's talent could give us a tremendous advantage. I asked Gomer Jones, his coach and an Ohio State alumnus, to bring him to Columbus later in the year for an interview.

At the time Notre Dame was also interested in him, and Lou said he was thinking of going to South Bend.

"What has Notre Dame offered you?" I asked him.

"I'll get a full scholarship, plus room and board," he said.

"Lou, we can find you a job, and that is all," I replied.

Lou said he really wanted to play at Ohio State, but there were other problems.

"My brother was just drafted into the army, and I know I'll be next," he said. "So I can't guarantee that I'll be able to play for you until the war is over."

"That's all right," I replied. "We are building a team that will have the best possible boys, and we want you to be a part of it."

He finally agreed, and we arranged a job that paid him $60 per month, and Lou played for our freshman team in 1942 before going into the army. Even as an eighteen-year-old, he was something special as a kicker. His kickoffs sailed 70 yards, and his field goals, under pressure, went 40 and 50 yards. Unlike college football kickers today who use a platter, he kicked off the grass.

Lou illustrated something that would become a real problem for us, however: the war. On the first Sunday in December 1941, I had just finished signing a radio contract with WBNS in Columbus and was walking out the door of the University Club when I heard shouting that the Japanese had attacked Pearl Harbor. Like everyone, I was stunned, and I knew that the nation would have to go to war. I knew, too, that our lives would change, but again like everyone else, I probably felt the serious changes would affect someone else. How wrong I was!

The war had no startling effects on our football program in 1942 because a nation builds gradually for such a massive effort, but it always seemed to hover over us. We tried to ignore it as best we could and carried on. We were rebuilding our team again, though this time mostly with players of my own choosing. Only three starters were among the eleven lettermen reporting for our fall practice, the bulk of our team coming from twenty-six sophomores. Among those sophomores, however, were such players as Dante Lavelli, Bill Willis, Tom James, Gene Fekete, Bill Hackett and George Slusser. And among the lettermen were Bob Shaw, Charley Csuri, Don McCafferty, Hal Dean, George Lynn, Paul Sarringhaus, Lin Houston, Jack Roe and Les Horvath.

Shaw and Lavelli both performed brilliantly, not only at Ohio State but as professional football players. Lavelli was with the Browns, of course, and we tried to get Shaw, but he had already signed a contract with the Los Angeles Rams. Shaw was six feet five inches and the former state hurdling champion when we had him at Ohio State and teamed him with Lavelli, who had been an Ohio sprint champion; they were two of the fastest ends in collegiate football in 1942. Bob showed it in the 1942 Michigan game when he caught a pass, twisted from a tackler and ran away from the entire Michigan team to score the decisive touchdown. In recent years he has become a general manager in the Canadian Football League.

Don McCafferty, who later became head coach of the Baltimore Colts and the Detroit Lions, was a tenacious tackle. He and Bill Willis battled for that job throughout the season but still were the closest of friends. Mac was six feet five inches tall and nearly 240 pounds, which made him a bit willowy for drive blocking, but his speed was ideal for leading our power sweeps. The first time the Bengals got to the playoffs, we lost to his Colts team, which went on to win the Super Bowl.

Speed was our trademark. Willis was as quick as a snake's fang. Lin Houston ran a 4.6-second 40-yard dash. Almost as fast were Csuri, who became a renowned professor of fine arts at Ohio State, and Hal Dean, who went to the Los Angeles Rams and then became head of an energy company. Our center, Bill Vickroy, had tremendous quickness, which counted more than speed at his position since a center does not run as much as a guard or tackle.

Our backs also had tremendous speed. These included George Slusser, who had transferred from Dartmouth to be part of our program, and Tom James, both of whom had played for me at Massillon; our captain, George Lynn, the blocking back in our wing formation and the quarterback whenever we used the T formation; and our fullback, Gene Fekete. In his second varsity game against Indiana, Gene ran a spinner trap for 44 yards for one of his two touchdowns and set up a third score with a 43-yard run, which brought us from behind for a victory.

Then there were Les Horvath and Paul Sarringhaus, the perfect blend of speed and power. Sarringhaus weighed about 215 pounds, but with his low center of gravity, he just ripped through anyone trying to arm-tackle him. Defense was not his forte, but because players went both ways at that time, he played to the best of his ability and good-naturedly took some ribbing because tackling was not his strength.

Paul had to overcome some battle wounds and physical ailments from time to time, but we never felt they were as serious as he did. In 1941 he scared everyone in our game against Missouri when he allowed a man to run right past him for a touchdown. What had happened, though, was that he had been trying out contact lenses, which were new at the time, and he hadn't even seen the runner. We suffered along with him until he got used to them.

In another game that season Paul came to the bench with blood streaming from his nose. The doctor and I came to check the problem.

"Doc, what's wrong?" I asked.

"Well," our doctor said, "he's got a bloody nose, that's for sure."

'We don't count that,' I told them. "Come on. Let's go, Paul! Get back in there."

I had just come from Massillon, where we never paid any attention to a bloody nose; even a broken nose didn't make any difference—those were things to be taken care of after the game. My order made an everlasting impression on Paul, however, and he used to remind me of it at our team reunions. At our most recent gathering, which Paul missed, I commented, "I notice that Paul Sarringhaus isn't here, and I really was prepared to tell him how sorry I was that I had him go back into the game with that bloody nose."

It gave the players a laugh and is indicative of the fellowship that has endured from that tremendous season. Such camaraderie occurs any time a team successfully works together to achieve a goal. Whenever I meet my former Browns players from our championship years, I can sense the same feelings, and this has been one of my lasting rewards throughout the years.

We had to take the hard road in 1942 because we couldn't sneak up on anyone as we had in 1941, when we got by with sheer enthusiasm and with some successful gambles at key junctures of a game. Our system of football had become firmly implanted by the time we opened the season with a 59-0 romp over Fort Knox, a game that was scheduled to help the war effort by entertaining the troops. It also served to get us ready for Indiana and Bo McMillan. It would be the first time I ever coached against McMillan, and it turned out to be the most interesting game of our season.

I knew Bo from his recruiting trips to Massillon, though the players he wanted always seemed to wind up at Purdue. He was a fine gentleman in the southern style and a good coach. I particularly recall a golfing weekend I spent several years later with Happy Chandler, then commissioner of baseball, my friend Tommy Henrich and Bo. Bo and Happy were honest-to-goodness, good-ol-boy milk shake drinkers, but good enough at golf to beat Henrich and me during the three days we played. One night we were watching the Cleveland Indians play baseball on television when Chandler said, "My, this is pretty good. I've never seen this before." We all stared at him. He was the baseball commissioner, but I truly believe that was the first time he ever had seen a baseball game on television.

McMillan had a great team in 1942 with Pete Pihos, Lou Saban, Jim Dewar, Billy Cowan, Billy Hillenbrand and Lou Gambino, all on offense. As happened in 1941, when we had played against Otto Graham, Edgar Jones and Bob Steuber, I never forgot those players, and I signed Saban, Dewar and Cowan for the Browns as soon as we formed the team. Pihos, of course, played for the Philadelphia Eagles, but I often tried to figure a way to get him, too, because he was such a great tight end, and Hillenbrand in his prime, when he played for Chicago and Baltimore, reminded me of Hugh McElhenny because of his tremendous ability to reverse direction and evade tacklers. In this Indiana-Ohio State game he not only caught a touchdown pass from Saban but broke through our defense so quickly on another play that not one lineman or linebacker touched him. He gave Tom James, who had great quickness, one fake and ran past him, untouched, to complete a 54-yard touchdown run. He became a great star in the All-America Conference, but injuries cut him down before he could compete in the NFL.

Against all this firepower, we had to fight for our lives and it was two things—our conditioning and our plan to use T formation plays in the second half to combat Indiana's defensive tactics—that got us our victory. Throughout the first half we ran from the single wing, shifting right or left. The Indiana players stood at the line and then ran to their positions, depending on the direction of our shift. We let their coaches make adjustments to that offense at halftime; then we unveiled our T formation, without any line shifts. It totally baffled Indiana, and by the time they had figured out what we were doing Fekete had ripped them apart, and we had won, 33-21. Indiana had also begun to wilt in the fourth quarter from the hot September sun, but thanks to our conditioning, we never noticed it.

The following week, when Southern California came to Columbus, an unfortunate incident at halftime caused a furor and even touched the governor. It started in the final seconds of the first half, when Lavelli was injured at Southern California's one-yard line after catching a pass. Instead of stopping the clock, the officials allowed it to run out. The Big Ten and the Pacific Coast conferences each had two officials there, and it seemed to me the PCC guys were a little too involved in how their team came out.

The clock was reset to allow us ten seconds to run a play, but we couldn't score. As I started across the field, I saw Jeff Cravath, the USC coach, running after the officials and complaining. I was upset that we hadn't scored, and as I passed Cravath and the official, I said, "If I were you, I'd settle for that," meaning that the clock had expired without our scoring.

We went on to win the game, 28-12, as Bob Shaw caught two touchdown passes. Afterward, however, Cravath complained to the press.

"Do you know that the coach from the other team threatened me?" he said. "He said he'd settle with me for that."

Of course, I hadn't said any such thing; Jeff had garbled my remark to mean that I was going to get him personally because I thought his team had deliberately injured Lavelli. John Bricker, the governor of Ohio, came to see me after the game and said, "What's this I hear about you threatening Jeff Cravath as you walked off the field at halftime?"

"Threatened him?" I asked, incredulous. "I simply said to him that if it were me, I'd settle for us not scoring from his one-yard line, and I couldn't understand what he was beefing about. The officiating probably saved them from being scored on."

John just laughed, but the story, with me as the pugnacious villain who would fight anyone who crossed his path, made headlines for a few days on the West Coast. It also needlessly furrowed some brows in our own administration until we straightened out all the facts.

After that game we were ranked first in the Associated Press's new weekly poll, and we fought to keep our ranking as we swept past Purdue and Northwestern. Actually, with Otto Graham as their leader, the Wildcats gave us our toughest battle of the season before we won, 20-6. Everyone was gunning for us because that top ranking in the college polls made us a juicy target, but we could cope with that. What we did have trouble coping with was the war, particularly when we traveled. Our trip to Wisconsin the next week was the best—or worst—possible example of that because it contributed to our only loss in ten games.

The military had appropriated all the first-class railroad equipment and forced us to travel to Wisconsin in rickety old railroad coaches that looked as if they hadn't been used for years. In preparing those cars, no one had thought to drain and flush the rusty water tanks before filling them with fresh water. Nearly everyone drank the water en route—and within hours a massive attack of dysentery swept through our party. I had taken a sip, but the water had tasted funny so I'd dumped it out and felt no effects.

The night before the game we were in a state of emergency. Our team doctor couldn't treat everyone by himself, and we had to call in all the medical help available from around Madison, Wisconsin. Other misfortunes compounded the disaster. Some of our players had been caught in a melee while returning from a movie, and they had been victims of the tear gas local police had been forced to use to disperse the unruly crowds. It also was Homecoming Weekend at Wisconsin, and because of wartime living conditions, we had had to house our players in a hotel in the middle of the city—the very worst place to keep a team under any conditions—and we got caught up in all the hoopla.

Early on Friday evening the hotel's ancient elevator broke down, and everyone in our party had to climb six flights of stairs every time he went to his room. You can imagine what that did to everyone's legs, not to mention what it meant to players suddenly taken with dysentery. In the middle of the night some drunken fans got loose on our floor and started pounding on doors, while the desperately ill players tried to get some rest. The next morning the hotel's management directed us to their pub room for our pregame meal, and it still reeked of beer and cigarettes from the previous night. When some of the sick players walked in and got a whiff of that, they became ill all over again.

At the stadium some of our players couldn't even put their uniforms on for pregame practice because they were constantly going to the bathroom; others got dressed and then couldn't go out on the field for the same reason. During the game players had to keep running from the field to the dressing room and back again. My coaches were affected the same way, and we had all we could do to keep a semblance of control. When we finally got back to the dressing room after the game, we found many of the players just stretched out on the floor, too sick to move.

Even with a healthy team, playing Wisconsin, with its so-called H Boys—Elroy Hirsch, Pat Harder and Pat Hoskins—would have been tough. As it was, however, we never had a sporting chance in this game, and we lost 17-7. Some of my Massillon players, such as James and Slusser, played in a losing game for the first time in their lives, and they took it hard. No one had anything to be ashamed of, though, because that game had been out of our hands before we ever played it. From then on I never took a team on a train without bringing our own drinking water. All it would take would be one cuckoo to doctor the drinking water the night before a game, and there would be no way the team could perform.

That loss to Wisconsin cost us our top ranking in the polls, but it served to make us only more determined. The following week we defeated Pitt, 59-19, with 587 yards of offense. Fekete alone gained 139 yards, including an 89-yard touchdown run, and that was on only three carries in the first quarter.

A week later I coached a team in Cleveland Stadium for the first time in my life. I never imagined at the time that those sidelines would become my second home four years later. We defeated Illinois, 44-20, that day, with what seemed like every citizen from Massillon, Akron and Canton cheering from the stands. Tom James had a tremendous day—the first two times he carried the ball he had touchdown runs of more than 70 and 30 yards. Illinois just couldn't touch him on those sweeps because our weak side linemen, with their great speed, got downfield and mowed down the Ilinois defense. They were so much in control that when we watched the films of that game, it looked as if the plays were being run in a controlled scrimmage.

Unfortunately Tommy injured his shoulder in that game, and as he was lying on the ground being treated, Alex Agase, Illinois's great linebacker, frustrated with trying to catch him all afternoon, came over, looked down at him and said, "Now let's see you get up, you little red-haired runt!" Alex and Tommy later were teammates in Cleveland and used to rib each other about that game.

Tom's injury was especially unfortunate because it meant we were without five healthy running backs for the Michigan game the next week—and you know by now how much that Michigan game meant. There was even more at stake than usual, however. Fritz Crisler had found his wellspring of Ohio talent drying up because of our new program and the attention the 1941 tie had directed toward Ohio State, and he wanted to make sure he beat us to prove to the high schools that Michigan was better. His team had defeated unbeaten Notre Dame the previous week, and for the first time all his players were healthy. We were ranked third nationally, behind Georgia and Boston College, and a victory meant our first Big Ten title. Added to all this was the tremendous response the game always evoked around Columbus, and there was no way of calculating the full emotional impact the rivalry had generated by kickoff time. Both NBC and CBS had come to broadcast the game, with Bill Stern and Ted Husing, respectively, behind the microphones, and we found ourselves with a huge national radio audience of more than 300 stations.

I had never met Husing until a couple of evenings before the game, when he came for a briefing on our team. All I knew was that he was the nation's most popular football announcer and that he was supposed to be a master of the English language. He arrived with a woman companion, and when he began talking about some games he had broadcast, I was surprised to hear him say, about every fifth or sixth sentence, some four-letter expletive. Each time he used one, he turned to the woman and said, "Excuse me, dear," and then kept on for a few more sentences before using another expletive, and then added another "Excuse me, dear." He kept this up throughout our conversation. Perhaps he thought that saying "Excuse me" expunged the words, but the whole incident was quite a letdown to me.

We played splendidly in the rain that Saturday to beat Mchigan, 21-7, and win the Big Ten title. Shaw's touchdown pass broke open a tight game, and again Tom Kuzma was the victim of the game's decisive play, as he had been the previous year. Shaw was much bigger and stronger than Kuzma, and after catching the ball, Bob shook him loose on the sideline, tippy-toed for several yards trying to keep his balance and stay in bounds and then ran away from everyone for the touchdown.

Paul Sarringhaus and Les Horvath took care of the other touchdowns with their passing. Horvath passed to Paul on an option play after Charley Csuri's blocked punt gave us the ball at Michigan's 35-yard line in the second quarter, and then Sarringhaus and Horvath teamed up again for the decisive touchdown in the last quarter. Michigan's great halfback, Bob Chappius, set up the Wolverines' only score, and it was the first time I had ever seen him. After the war he became a great All-American running back for Michigan and was part of one of our greatest trades after we drafted him in 1947, then sent him to the Brooklyn football Dodgers for Dub Jones.

Our season still wasn't finished, though. Mr. St. John had added a game against Iowa Pre-Flight, a service school with a model physical education and football program for college and professional players who were in the navy. Many thought our team would let down after beating Michigan and winning the Big Ten title, but the opposite seemed to be true. All week the intensity stayed high, our players challenged by the opportunity to play against what really was an all-star team. They also knew there was a remote possibility we could finish the season as the nation's top college team, and that was important to them.

Many thought the game would be a mismatch. Iowa Pre-Flight, under Bernie Bierman's coaching, had lost only one game to Notre Dame all season, and their roster included such players as Forrest Evashevski from Michigan; Mal Kutner, an All-American end from Texas; Bill Daley and Clayton Tonnemaker from Minnesota; John Michelosen of Pitt; and two former Ohio State players, Dick Fisher from our 1941 team and Jim Langhurst from 1940—all this in addition to several NFL players. The team outweighed us by twenty-one pounds per man in the line and eighteen pounds per man in the backfield, according to the game program.

In the end, the difference—and it was a big one because we stunned them, 41-12—was our great speed. Trev Rees, one of my assistants from Ohio State who had joined Bierman's staff after going into the service, had tried to convince Bernie that he was making a mistake trying to stack his defense too tightly inside to try to stop Gene Fekete.

"Paul Brown will run us right out of the park if you put the defense in so tight," Rees told him.

"I don't know about that, Trev," Bernie replied. "I'd have to see that kind of speed for myself to believe it possible."

Trev later told me he could do only what his coach wanted him to do, but he knew our players and how I would utilize their speed if Pre-Flight gave us the chance. Tom James had a great day running to the outside. On our first play he ran right at Tonnemaker, and with his tremendous leg drive and speed he just bounced off the Iowa player and sped 54 yards. Later he returned a punt 56 yards for a touchdown and passed 46 yards to Shaw to set up a second touchdown. Fekete ran 52 yards with a pass for a third score, and Sarringhaus passed 42 yards to Horvath to set up a fourth touchdown, all in the first half.

That proved to me that we had a "November" football team, one that peaked and finished well at the season's end. That is the mark of every great championship team, and we used to plan for that at Cleveland. It is imperative that a team be playing at its best when the games become so decisive late in the season, and there is a fine touch to not getting a team to peak too early.

In 1942 that fine touch helped us win the national championship because on the same day we so decisively beat Iowa Pre-Flight, Georgia Tech upset top-ranked Georgia, 34-0, and Holy Cross stunned unbeaten Boston College with a 55-12 victory. Ironically, that loss probably saved the lives of the Boston College players because they had to call off the victory party they had scheduled at a Boston night club. The club was the Coconut Grove, where hundreds of people would die in a fire.

A few days after the season's final poll was released, naming us number one, I received a phone call from Lou Little.

"I'm going to ask you a favor," he said to me. "You have been voted coach of the year, but I'd like you to forgo it because Bill Alexander, the coach at Georgia Tech, is dying. We'd like to give him the honor because he's been a great credit to college football for many years and we feel this would be a fine tribute for him.

"You're going to be around for many years, and you'll have a chance again soon to win it. Bill never will have another chance, so if you'd agree to it, we'll keep this between ourselves."

I did agree, and only a few coaches that year knew that I was the one who had actually been chosen coach of the year. Ironically, I never again had a chance for consideration. The following season was our Baby Bucks year—my final season at Ohio State—during which we won only three of nine games with a group of seventeen-year-old kids and other players exempt from military service for physical or scholastic reasons. In almost every game they were forced to compete against older and more talented college and professional players.

Like most major universities, Ohio State had affiliated its programs with the military by 1943, but unlike our major football rivals such as Purdue, Northwestern and Michigan, which had joined the navy's V-12 programs, he had chosen the army's ROTC establishment. The schools under navy jurisdiction allowed their enrollees to play college football and also accepted transfers into the program from other schools. Not only did those, like Ohio State, Illinois and Pitt, which were in the army program, lose their players to the military once they had reached their eighteenth birthday, but once they had enrolled, they were forbidden to play football.

Many of my players from the previous year were in the army's ROTC program at Ohio State, and as a result, they couldn't play. In 1944 the army changed its rules, but by that time I was already gone from Ohio State. That opened some very tender wounds because I knew some people would look at our record in 1943, see a terrible year and not know the circumstances. They wouldn't know that we might have had a player for two weeks and just had begun to get him grooved into our system when he would reach his eighteenth birthday and have to leave our team to go into the service. Nor would they know that we had to play with seventeen-year-old kids such as Matthew Brown, Dean Sensanbaugher and Glen Oliver, none of whom weighed 160 pounds and who were literally ground up any time they played against the navy schools. I'll never forget Bill Hackett playing guard against Purdue and taking a tremendous beating from Bill Butkovich, a great running back who was much bigger, stronger and older. To his credit, Hackett later became an All-American guard at Ohio State, but he paid a terrible price for some experience in 1943. Nearly a quarter century later, incidentally, Hackett would be the driving force behind my return to professional football with the Bengals.

My sense of justice and personal pride rebelled at these inequities, and I didn't spare Mr. St. John my feelings. Not only were we being unfair to a group of seventeen-year-old kids, but we were exposing them to serious injury anytime they played against players like Butkovich. His justification was that we were performing a service to intercollegiate football and saving the program at Ohio State. In reality, we were providing money for the athletic department, and while we may have kept the continuity of Ohio State's football program, it was at the personal expense of those kids.

My complaints changed nothing, and we had to get our players ready. I drove them pretty hard throughout the season because I wasn't used to losing and I didn't like it, and I was bothered by the comedown from our great 1942 season. At the time I didn't realize just how hard I was pushing those kids. After the season ended, the injustice hurt me, and I realized I wasn't very proud of the way we had conducted the season, the only time during my entire coaching career that I ever felt that way. I probably owe those kids an apology for forcing them to try to make us a winner when no amount of work ever would have helped us against such overwhelming competition. It saddens me to think that we threw them to the wolves whenever we played those teams, and I hope they understand that it was never anything personal.

What made the situation worse, and angered me so much it influenced my decision to go into professional football instead of returning to Ohio State after the war, was that no one ever appreciated what they went through. Actually, the Baby Bucks were a victim of the war, but I never could reconcile myself to the fact that they never even bothered to give them a year-end football banquet.

The pity of it was we didn't play badly at all, under the circumstances. When we lost to Great Lakes, 13-7, 40,000 people gave us a standing ovation for our effort. The Iowa Seahawks, with their mixture of college and professional players, had all they could do to win, 28-13, and it was only the great play of Otto Graham that brought Northwestern to a 13-0 victory. In addition, whenever we played schools with an ROTC program, such as Pitt, Missouri, Indiana and Illinois, we were very competitive, and most often we were successful. Two of our most memorable games that year were against Pitt and Illinois, and for two different reasons.

Clark Shaughnessy was coaching at Pitt, and we went into that game fearful of his passing game because he was a master of the science of football. As it turned out, he had even less talent at Pitt than we did, and we won easily. It was my first real look at the T formation with flankers and men in motion, however, and it was the kind of football I later assimilated into my own system with the Browns.

Ripley's "Believe It or Not" had a field day for years with our game against Illinois because we were allowed to kick a field goal and win after time had expired. With the score tied, 26-26, we had tried to pass on the game's final play, and it had failed. When the gun went off, both teams went to their dressing rooms thinking the game was over, but only Russ Walker, a caption writer for the *Columbus Dispatch*, who had been working along the sidelines with his photographer, had seen what had happened before the gun: One of the officials had dropped a penalty flag.

Russ was a high school official, and he knew a game could not end with a defensive foul. The official who had thrown the flag, I found out later, saw everyone run off the field and just stuffed it back into his pocket, content to allow the game to end without enforcing the penalty. Russ told Jim Masker, the referee, about the penalty, and checking with the official, Jim found it had been against Illinois.

He came to our dressing room as I was talking to our players, knocked on the door and poked his head inside.

"Coach," he said, "could I talk to you a moment?"

"Sure," I said, and moved over to the door.

"The game has ended in a foul, and you have the right to one more play," he told me. "Illinois was offside, and you can accept the penalty and take the extra play if you want it."

"We'll take it; it's our play," I replied immediately, without thinking.

I knew that we would get the ball within field goal range and that it could well be our only play. Our kicker was a sev-

enteen-year-old kid named Johnny Stungis, and it never occurred to me until we were walking out of our dressing room
that John had kicked extra points but had never kicked a
field goal. It also never occurred to me until that moment
that Illinois could block the field goal attempt and run with
the loose ball for a touchdown. A tie would have been better
than a loss, but I dismissed the possibility and decided to go
for the victory.

On the way down to the field I said to Stungis, "John, I
never missed a field goal in my life."

"No kidding, coach," he said, very seriously. "Did you kick
many?"

"No," I said, "I never even tried to kick one."

We both laughed, and that might have eased some of the
pressure. About a third of the crowd was still in the stands,
and they were stunned to see both teams returning to the
field. It was a peculiar sight, the players, some of them in
uniform, some partially undressed, standing behind the end
zone with the spectators, everyone watching the officials re-
spot the ball where they thought it should be.

Illinois had been penetrating well against our kickers, so I
warned the eleven men on our field goal team, "You understand that they could break through and block this kick,
recover it and run with it, so this can boomerang on us, too.
Let's be particularly tight and solid at every position when we
line up."

They nodded, and as I walked toward the end zone, the
crowd that had jammed behind the goal posts formed an op-
tical illusion so that the distance from where Stungis would
kick the ball actually looked shorter. I prayed that it would
prove to be no illusion. When Johnny kicked, I watched the
ball and then turned and said to Carroll Widdoes, "I think
the darn thing went over."

The next moment I was being hoisted into the air by the excited fans because the kick had indeed been good and we had
won the game, 29-26. Ray Eliot, the Illinois coach, never
reconciled himself to that loss because he claimed the officials
erred in our favor in respotting the ball for the kick. I can't
blame him for feeling bad, but in those days we were in such
dire need of a victory that it didn't make any difference how
we got one.

For years afterward I answered phone calls and settled bets

on that game because people just couldn't believe something like this could happen. Ironically, two weeks before, Stungis had kicked what had looked like the winning point against Indiana to give us a 14-13 lead with two minutes to play, only to have Bob Hoernchmeyer throw a touchdown pass to Don Mangold in the final thirty-two seconds for the Hoosier victory.

Our final game in 1943 was in Ann Arbor against Michigan, and we knew we didn't have a chance. Though we played over our heads for the first half and trailed only 13-7, Michigan just wore us down in the second half with their tremendous personnel. After the game their players carried Fritz Crisler off the field, and I made the observation that if I were a coach of a team with his kind of advantage over a bunch of seventeen-year-old kids, I didn't believe I would have allowed anyone to carry me off a field. That didn't set too well with some people, but that's how I felt.

The wonderful years I had had in the only job I had ever really wanted ended a few months later when I was commissioned as a naval officer and sent to the Great Lakes Naval Training Center. I never returned to Ohio State. After the war, when Ohio State football ran into hard times, I was constantly being touted as the next head coach, but I was with the Browns then and had no intentions of leaving. I allowed all the speculation to exist only to get us some public attention.

Every time my name came up, however, friction arose between some factions at Ohio State and among the alumni, some of whom never forgave me or Mr. St. John for my not returning as head coach after the war. When Saint retired and was honored at the halftime of a game at Ohio Stadium, he was booed so loudly he had to turn off his hearing aid so he couldn't hear the crowd's reaction. It was a sad thing to have this fine man end his career in this manner.

Today I still have warm, fond memories of my time at Ohio State, and they have left me with a great feeling for anyone who coaches at a major university. I have always enjoyed the personal associations that have developed between me and the hundreds of these men I have met during my fifty years of football, and happily, I have seen scores of my own coaches and players join their ranks. That is why I find some of the injustices which befall the decent coaches in football to be repugnant and entirely outside the spirit of our game.

At some universities, when a coach is over fifty, he is automatically disliked. When he's over sixty, he is not supposed to be able to relate to young men, and there are many who want him fired. Having gone past those years, I know this is patently untrue as long as a man is willing, and given the opportunity, to work at this phase of his job.

Having also experienced the problems of college coaching, I know, too, that a great many good coaches will come upon lean years simply because they don't have the players or because of circumstances beyond their control. It distresses me to see that prior success and service over the years don't mean anything then and that suddenly they're being called "too old" and in need of replacement. It is even more distressing to see some of these fine coaches relegated to lesser jobs or, worse still, forcibly retired from the university. All those great Saturday afternoons they helped bring to their schools suddenly become meaningless, and that is not fair.

One of the saddest of these stories is the way Woody Hayes ended up after dedicating his life to Ohio State. One moment of frustration, and he was gone in a matter of hours, after close to three decades of service.

I first met Woody during those summers I went to school at Ohio State while I was coaching at Massillon. At the time he was the line coach for New Philadelphia High School. He was always very intense and involved, and every so often he would go into his room and lock the door, and soon we'd hear him snorting and moving about. We found out that he was shadowboxing just to rid himself of his excess energy and to keep himself in shape. Since that time our relations have always been cordial, and when I was coaching the Browns in 1948, I was asked for advice, and I recommended him for the job as head coach at Miami University, my alma mater, a position he held for three years.

Both of us had one thing in common when we became head coach at Ohio State—a special intensity for the school, though neither of us was a graduate. I know it wounded him deeply when he was fired. It is because of his experience, the experience of others like him and my own time at Ohio State that I have great empathy for all college coaches. Most of them approach their job with the same dedication and determination with which I approached mine during my years at the university. When I left for my assignment at Great Lakes,

I missed college coaching and all that went with being able to do the best possible job. However, there is no doubt that moving to this next coaching position reshaped my entire life in a very positive way.

FIVE

Great Lakes:
The Turning Point

THE WAR HAD TOUCHED EVERYONE as 1944 began, and I was no exception. Early that year my draft board in Massillon had advised me that I was liable to be drafted within a few months. I was thirty-five years old and close to the age limit for draftees, but I was told that I was a "prominent person" and that such people were being tapped by the military to set a good example for everyone else. When I told Mr. St. John the news, he called Commodore (and later Admiral) Robert Emmett, a good friend who commanded the Great Lakes Naval Training Center outside Chicago, to see if I could get posted there. The timing was right because Tony Hinkle, the Great Lakes football coach, was going to sea later that year and the commodore had been tremendously impressed with the Baby Bucks team that had played his superior team almost to a standstill in 1943. He sent word for me to apply for a commission as a naval officer so I could join the Great Lakes athletic department and eventually become the head coach.

My only exposure to the military had been one year of ROTC training when I was a freshman at Ohio State, but being primarily involved in athletics, I felt I could master whatever else the navy had in store for me. I passed my physical in March and left for Great Lakes a month later as a lieutenant, junior grade, wearing one of the two new uniforms Simon Lazarus, the head of Columbus's largest department store, had given me as a going-away present.

The next three years were sad for me. My life and my outlook on life were completely changed by my experiences in the navy and by what I had undergone during the 1943 season with the Baby Bucks. My feelings were still raw from that season, and I had not reconciled my mind to all that we had been forced to endure. I'm certain the chief reason for these feelings was my pride, which had been greatly inflated by season after season of unbeaten teams at Massillon and a national collegiate championship at Ohio State, but the injustices to those young kids really rankled me as well. Added to that was my first glimpse of what war can do to a person. Everything became bigger than life, and the overriding feeling was: Life is cheap; we're here today, and we may be dead tomorrow, so anything normal is forgotten. No one cared too much about the results of football games when our men were coming home in wooden boxes.

As a boy in Norwalk I had seen young men on railroad trains going to war, and I had never forgotten their faces: the looks of pride on some who were glad to serve their country, the exultant looks of others who thought that fighting a war was little more than a great adventure and the looks of fright on those who realized they might never return. That view through a child's eyes came alive again during my nearly three years at Great Lakes.

It shook my family and me not to know how this adventure was going to finish, and until the war ended in the late summer of 1945, I thought about only one thing: When was I going to sea? The thought hung like a pall over our lives because I had never had any assurances that I would be able to spend the duration of the war coaching at Great Lakes, and I'm sure that had the war lasted a little longer I would have been dispatched to the Pacific, just as Tony Hinkle and many other coaches who had worked with service teams were. There is no way of knowing what might have happened then.

Though I never saw a bomb dropped or a ship sunk, staying at Great Lakes did not insulate me from war's tragedies. Every ten days I strapped on my gun as officer of the day and saw some of war's real victims. There were times when I had to tell a sailor that his son had just been run over and killed by a car or that his wife had just been killed. I had to help cut down a man who had hanged himself because he didn't want to go to sea, and I remember the thing that struck me most was how far a man's neck stretched when he died from hanging. I saw men shot and stabbed to death from petty arguments, and I saw others come apart when they finally realized they might be killed fighting in the war.

Some took desperate measures to avoid going into combat. For a time I was in charge of the swimming program that was supposed to train every man to survive in the water. The night before one of the final tests, which would qualify a man for further duty, someone went to the bathroom in the corner of the pool, and we had to cancel the next day's work. It took us a full day to drain, clean and refill the pool, then schedule another test. The night before, the same thing happened, necessitating another delay. This time we posted some guards, and they caught a poor guy who had found a desperate way to stave off the inevitable.

One of our basketball players missed a trip because he overslept, and he was automatically taken off the team and dispatched to sea duty. Unfortunately he was lost at sea, and though I had nothing to do with the incident, I received a letter from the boy's mother years later blaming me for her son's death. Rollie Williams, who was the basketball coach and athletic officer at the time, tried to straighten out the matter, but the only Great Lakes coach the boy's mother knew about was Paul Brown, and she must have thought that I had coached the basketball team, too.

Even though I became the head football coach at Great Lakes, my duties as a naval officer took precedence. I was a battalion commander, and I often marched in review with others or reviewed parades as part of the staff. We had 110,-000 men undergoing training at one time, and I often reviewed their graduation exercises. Every time a group marched past I knew some of those kids would not return from combat. That was a sad and chilling thought, and it bothered me. I had three sons, and I knew my feelings for them were no less intense than those of the fathers of the young men I saw every day.

Though I was happiest coaching football, I did not have the kind of control over my players that I had been used to at Massillon and Ohio State, nor could I avoid other duties even on the days when our team played in the giant quadrangle that served as the centerpiece at Great Lakes. I was in the locker room while they donned their equipment; then I went on the field and seated the troops. When the game ended, our players returned to the locker room, but I had to stay and dismiss the troops. No one moved until I went through a checklist of procedures that began with Admiral Emmett and his party's leaving the stadium, followed by the senior officers and their families and so on, until the last company was dismissed. Then I returned to the locker room and talked to the players, who had to wait for me until all this was finished.

Before our high school and college games—and later in professional football—I always took our players to a movie to relax them, but that was out of my control at Great Lakes. Once, when we went to Milwaukee to play Marquette and helped my friend Tom Stidham raise some money for his football program, our players decided they wanted to go to a burlesque show. With a little coaxing—very little—they went up on the stage, rolled up their pants legs and danced with the girls. Since the game was a no-contest affair for us, I had been away scouting Notre Dame and knew nothing about the incident until the team returned home. We won the game easily, but the philosophy was: They can do what they want as long as they play, and that's it.

The players knew that football was only a means of delaying their departure for combat, and there were few other rewards, incentives or penalties attached. Nevertheless, I was as intense in practice as ever and continued my great emphasis on film study and playbooks. Most of the players gave us their fullest attention, and for most it was a brand-new experience in their football lives and one, many have told me, they have never forgotten.

I can only recall one real problem, and that was a violation of our rules against drinking. We had no control over the players once their football duties were finished each day, but I had made it clear from the start that a boozer had no place on our team, and if a man was caught violating that rule, he was gone. Dismissal from the team meant sea duty as quickly as the man's orders could be processed.

One afternoon in 1945, with the war over and everyone looking ahead to his discharge, two older players who had been shading our rules came to practice smelling like a distillery. That was enough for me, and I called everyone together in the middle of the practice field. Turning to the two men, I said, "In the opinion of the other coaches and myself, you two have been drinking. You are not fair to yourselves or our team. Get out, far, far away."

The other players cleared a path, and the two men went to

the dressing room, and by nightfall they were far, far away
... on their way to sea. We suspected that some of the other
players had also been drinking, but following that incident,
we never again had a problem. At the very least, they made
sure not to come to practice in that condition.

Still, Admiral Emmett wanted winning football teams, and
he gave me everything within his power to make my time at
Great Lakes as palatable for me and my family as the rules
permitted. He was a grand old guy and a real character of
sorts. Nothing seemed to bother him, not even being told that
the upper floor of his garage was being used as a bawdyhouse
by a group of sailors. He broke that up, with a few ribald
comments to anyone who seemed shocked, and went right on
managing that huge training facility. He loved athletes and
athletics and certainly never hindered our attempts to hold as
many good players as we could when they passed through the
base. A veritable who's who of major-league baseball served
as athletic instructors and players on the Great Lakes team,
men such as Bob Feller of the Indians, Pinky Higgins of the
Red Sox, Schoolboy Rowe of the Detroit Tigers and Mickey
Cochrane, a Hall of Fame player who had just finished his
major-league career at Detroit.

The admiral moved easily among these great athletes, and
he believed in the morale factor they represented. As far as he
was concerned, their overall objective was to entertain the
troops who passed through his command. Years after I had
left the navy and was coaching the Browns, I walked into the
clubhouse at Indian Creek Golf Club in Florida and found
Admiral Emmett playing gin rummy with some friends. It
was the first time I had seen him since leaving Great Lakes,
and we had a grand reunion, including a game of golf the
next day.

He smoothed my first day in the navy by having our
family quarters, which overlooked Lake Michigan, ready and
waiting when I reported to his office. I had made the mistake
of walking through the main gate en route to the base headquarters, and I must have saluted 5,000 sailors during my
trek. Fortunately it was one of the few things I had remembered from my ROTC days, though I soon learned there was
a back entrance in and out of the base which was less popu-
lated and required much less saluting.

One of the first persons I met at Great Lakes was an old
college acquaintance named Bob Steman, whom I was to

succeed. "The secret to success in the navy," he told me right off the bat, "is to have the right people working for you. I'm going to introduce you to a couple of crackerjack bootpushers who work for me, and they'll help you, too."

We went to his company headquarters to meet a man named Kolb, who, it turned out, wasn't in the office at the time. We were told he was eating lunch in the mess hall.

"Come on," Bob said, "let's wait for him at his barracks."

When we walked into the barracks, there was Kolb sacked out, and as soon as he saw Bob, his commanding officer, he leaped down from his bunk, and everything private flew out of his shorts. He stood there trying to salute and cover up at the same time, not knowing whether to be more embarrassed at being caught sleeping on duty or at exposing himself.

Kolb and I became good friends, and he did help me, but whenever I wanted to have some fun, I used to remind him of his jump from the bunk. When I became head coach of the Browns, he always came to our games when we played in Philadelphia, his hometown, and gave me tips about college players he had seen. He used to regale some of our coaches who had known him at Great Lakes with his stories, too—particularly the one about the day he was caught goofing off.

Aside from the day-to-day exposure to the atmosphere of war, our family life at Great Lakes was pleasant enough. Katy and the children left our home in Columbus and moved into our new quarters within a couple of weeks. Mickey Cochrane and Weeb Ewbank were neighbors, and Weeb was tremendously helpful in getting us settled. He later joined our coaching staff, of course. My sons were enthralled with living on a military base. They went to the drill halls and shot baskets, watched great athletes perform, saw movies every night and in general had the run of the base. My middle son, Mike, was the batboy for Bob Feller's baseball team and filled our basement with broken bats, cut-up baseballs and the remnants of drones which had been shot up during gunnery practice. He also had a badge that got him on and off the base and ran a little business fetching hamburgers and candy for the sailors, until we found out and canceled his accounts.

Admiral Emmett insisted that we have the best football team possible, and as long as we worked within regulations, he never refused any request for players or coaches. We found out which players were coming to Great Lakes, usually when their college coaches called to tell us, and then we "pulled their jackets," transferring them temporarily to the football team from boot camp, regular duty or one of the many service schools the navy ran on the base. When the season ended, their jackets, or service files, were placed back in the personnel pipeline, and they resumed their navy careers.

Tony Hinkle had already assembled our team for 1944, and I became an assistant coach on his staff until he left for sea duty just before the season began. Suddenly I had a team and a football system that I hardly knew, and twelve games to play. Tony used the Bears' numbering system for his plays—he had done some work for George Halas—and it was totally different from mine. The Bears numbered their backs 1-2-3-4 and the line 1 through 9, from left to right. If the No. 2 back ran outside left end, the play was referred to as 21. If the No. 3 back ran the same play to the right side, it was 39. I kept a piece of paper in my hand during the early games so I could remember the system, but I didn't dare change it because the players would have been totally confused at that late date, and our season would have been lost.

The 1944 team was not as strong as Hinkle's 1943 team, which had upset Notre Dame on the final day of the season and nearly spoiled a national championship for Frank Leahy. That Great Lakes team had had several professional players, but the rules had changed in 1944 because the colleges did not want to play what amounted to a team of all-star professionals, so we used only collegians or high school players.

Still, we had some talented players like Jim Mello, a smallish fullback from Notre Dame, who was a jiggly sort of runner; Jim Youell, a quarterback from Iowa, very intelligent and an excellent passer; and Eddie Saenz, a speedy 165-pound halfback. Both Saenz and Youell later played for the Washington Redskins in the NFL.

Our best lineman was George Young, a 240-pound end from Georgia who played offense and defense. I liked his defensive work so much I signed him for Cleveland a couple of years later, and he played as a defensive end for years with our great teams. Our other end at Great Lakes was Jim Keane from Iowa, who later played with the Bears, and there was this young halfback from Akron, Ohio, named Ara Parseghian. I later signed him at Cleveland when he finished his college career at Miami of Ohio, and of course, he later went on to quite a career as coach of Notre Dame. All this talent was good enough for us to win four of our first five games and tie the other, 26-26, against Illinois.

The biggest game for me in 1944 was against Ohio State because it meant going back to the school that I still loved, against players whom I had recruited and had known so well, who were using my system and being coached by Carroll Widdoes, one of my former assistants and dearest friend. It was an emotional wrench for me because my heart was not in it. In fact, I had told Tony Hinkle that if I were still his assistant, I would not have taken part in the preparations for this game because I knew where my real loyalties lay and I didn't think it would be fair to his players. Besides, I did not want to go back to Ohio State as an adversary. Hinkle had left, though, and I was the head coach. I had no choice.

Even my family's emotions were split. They always rooted for me, but my son, Mike, who was eight, told me flat out a couple of days before the game, "You might as well know, Daddy, I'm rooting for Ohio State."

Another reason for my ambivalence was the fact that shortly before the 1944 season began, the army changed its rules and allowed college players over eighteen years of age to play football at its schools. As I mentioned before, it didn't seem fair to me that the Baby Bucks had had to endure a season such as they had gone through before someone finally made the decision that would have saved them from being overmatched. I also had trouble accepting the fact that I had put in the system and recruited the players that Widdoes was using so successfully, while I was trying rather uncomfortably to master another system with a new team.

I put on my best face for the trip to Columbus, however, partly because I had to appear at three different functions the night before the game as part of the navy's recruitment and public relations program and partly because I would be seeing some old friends. I still had an empty feeling about the game, though, because I didn't know or have much faith in the people I had inherited. Our relationship was pretty impersonal, officer—enlisted man, and I knew that many of the players were involved in football simply as a means of staying away from sea duty, not because they loved the game.

All this became manifest the next day when Ohio State, playing with great emotion, as one would expect with its old coach on the other side of the field, won the game, 26-6, before nearly 74,000 people at Ohio Stadium, the biggest crowd since the 1940 Michigan game. Chuck Avery got Great Lakes' touchdown, but Les Horvath's running and passing and the play of the middle of the Buckeyes' line, particularly Bill Hackett, Warren Amling, Bill Willis and Gordon Appleby, helped put the game away in the second half. They dominated the Great Lakes' players and put such a pass rush on Jim Youell that our passing game became totally ineffective.

After the game, my friend Paul Hornung, who covered Ohio State for the *Columbus Dispatch,* visited our dressing room for my comments, and I asked him, "Does this look like a losing locker room to you?" He looked around and just shook his head. The fact that I had coached at Ohio State meant nothing to our players, nor had losing the game. They just wanted to have a little fun, and the dressing room was a bedlam as they talked about all the things they were going to do later. Who knows, perhaps they were right—things like football games tended to dim in importance to men who, two or three months from then, might be lying dead on some beach in the South Pacific. It was something I never could reconcile myself to while coaching service football.

Though we lost that day, we won nine of our twelve games that season, losing only one other to Notre Dame, 28-7, on the final Saturday. It was the first time I had ever coached against a Notre Dame team, even though I had tried to promote the idea at Ohio State. Mr. St. John and I once had a meeting with Father John Cavanaugh, Notre Dame's president, at which we discussed renewing the series that had been terminated after games in 1935 and 1936. I listened intently as the two men covered it from every aspect and became buoyed by what seemed the positive prospects.

After our meeting we bade Father Cavanaugh good-bye, and as he drove off, I mentioned to Saint that matters looked pretty firm.

"You must know," he told me, "that we never will play Notre Dame."

"Why?" I asked, rather astonished, considering the tenor of the discussions which had just taken place.

"Because when we played them in Columbus in 1935, our campus was split right down the middle," he said. "When Bill Shakespeare passed to Wayne Millner for the winning touchdown in the final seconds of the game, even some of our players stood and cheered. We just can't have that happen again."

In 1944 Notre Dame had lost only to Army and to Navy, and they quickly proceeded to defeat us, 28–7, but at least one good thing came from that game. Three Notre Dame players—end Bucky O'Connor, quarterback George Terlep and linebacker Marty Wendell—all came to Great Lakes the following year and played well. Terlep and O'Connor later played for the Browns as well.

The year 1945 was much more fulfilling for me, even though our team had to scrap from the very beginning to become successful because we lost almost every player that I had selected for the squad.

What happened was this: I had pulled the jackets of about three dozen of the nation's best college football players, including Buddy Young, before the season, and we thought we were ready to dominate the football scene. Just then, however, a Great Lakes officer who had been director of the service school was transferred to Fleet City in San Francisco and was told by his commanding officer that he wanted a great football team for his base. The commander knew where to look. As the season came closer, our players were transferred one by one to Fleet City, by some means which I never did understand. The explanation was something to the effect that Great Lakes was being phased down somewhat as a major installation, while the naval bases in California were being kept at full strength as the war's direction shifted from Europe to the Pacific.

The only player we got to keep was Marion Motley because he was unknown and had not been at the University of Nevada long enough to build up a great reputation. He became the cornerstone on which we built the 1945 team. Three hundred prospects showed up for our first practice, and we pared them down to fifty within a week, adding, in the process, O'Connor and Terlep, plus a swift halfback named Grover Klemmer, who is an NFL official today. One of our other prospects was a lean, blond-haired eighteen-year-old high school player from Superior, Wisconsin, named Harry ("Bud") Grant, who was recommended to me by my friend Harry Stuhldreher at Wisconsin.

Bud came to us as a fullback, but he told me years later, "There was this big black fellow who I had a very tough time tackling, and I became very interested in what he was going

to play when you finally called us by positions. I watched
him go over to where the rest of the fullbacks were, and at
that moment I became an end because there was no way I
was going to beat Marion Motley. I didn't know him and
hadn't heard of him, but I knew he was awful tough."

Bud knew what he was doing because no one could have
competed with Motley, and in fact, no one competed very
successfully with Bud once he broke into our starting lineup.
He was a great natural athlete with tremendous leaping ability, and once he got his hands on the ball, he never dropped
it. He had exceptional speed, too, and was the key to a play
we called TD-90. In it we used our backs and other ends for
maximum protection, and Bud ran an optional post or "go"
pattern as the lone receiver. With the extra blocking, our passers had enough time to throw the ball deep downfield and
allow him to run under it.

I sent him into one game with that play, and he scored a
touchdown, but it turned out we were offside, and the score
was nullified. So I sent him back and told the quarterback,
George Terlep, to run it again. Bud scored a second time, but
this time we were called for a motion penalty, and again the
score was nullified. "Run it again," I told Bud, and for the
third consecutive play he caught the ball and ran for a touchdown. This one counted.

When he joined the team, he was still in boot camp and
called me one day to say that he had been placed in a "den-
tal company" because they had told him he had to have all
his teeth pulled. The navy way in those times was to pull out
everything and put in a false set rather than spend time filling
and capping. I thought it would cause needless suffering,
however, and I knew it could put him into the infirmary for
several days, and I just didn't believe in treating personnel
like that.

"There is no way they are going to pull your teeth," I told
Bud. "Don't you do a thing."

I got after the right people, and he told me later they
treated him like royalty and took him to a dentist who re-
paired his teeth properly, the same teeth, by the way, that he
still has. I always liked this lean, rawboned young man, and
whenever he played against us when he was at Philadelphia, I
made it a point to wish him well after the game. Of course,
he has become one of the finest coaches in professional football now, and he has graciously told others that much of

what he saw of our coaching steered him toward obtaining a college education when he could just as easily have gone to work on the Great Lakes ore boats. I like to flatter myself that I can see some of our principles and techniques in Bud's football.

When our season began, we were still trying to put our team together and adjust to all our players coming and going, and as a result, we lost our first three games. Then we tied the fourth— and never lost again. Marty Wendell joined us for the third game of the year, and we moved him from full-back, where he had played at Notre Dame, to linebacker and offensive center, leaving the backfield to three exceptionally speedy runners, Frank Aschenbrenner, Klemmer and Motley. Perhaps the most notable game, other than our finale against Notre Dame, was our victory over Fort Warren, because that was when I first saw Mac Speedie. I remembered his dazzling moves and wonderful catching ability when we began putting together the Browns a few months later.

Our whole season boiled down to how well we did against Notre Dame, however. It was going to be the final game ever played in the Great Lakes oval, but frankly, sentiment for football history meant nothing compared to the overwhelming feeling on the base about that Notre Dame game. My intensity for winning certainly hadn't lessened and, if anything, had been sharpened by the tremendous response our players had given us during the season. In addition, there was a burr under my hide from the 1944 loss, and I knew that never again would I get a chance to coach against a Notre Dame team; my decision to enter professional football had long since been signed and sealed, and in fact, the Browns were then in the process of being put together.

For weeks before the game our players were bombarded with reminders from the base that the navy wanted a victory over Notre Dame, and no one had a chance to develop a ho-hum, let's-get-it-over-with routine. We were totally dedicated, and I never can say enough for their effort. Notre Dame had a fine team; its players, such as Terry Brennan, George Ratterman, Coy McGee, Bill Fischer, John Mastrangelo, Pep Panelli and a dozen others, would form the nucleus of a national championship team the following year, and I think they had very little regard for us.

We worked for three weeks to get ready for the game, even setting aside part of each practice session scheduled for our other opponents. As the game drew nearer, I arranged to ring the practice field with shore patrol personnel, so as to keep any prying eyes from watching our preparations. Before practice began, I called the patrol to attention facing the practice field, then gave the order "About face!" and they pivoted around and kept their backs turned while we worked. No one, friend or foe, saw our practices. It had the desired effect on our team.

Our players were just as intense. Motley and Klemmer were eligible for discharge a couple of weeks before the game, so I called them aside before a practice and said, "I've been notified that you men have finished your tour and may leave. Or I can arrange to delay your discharge until after we play Notre Dame. Which will it be?"

Both of them looked at me with a bit of steel in their eyes, and Klemmer said, with a big grin on his face, "Coach, we've gone this far, and I don't think the extra ten bucks the navy had to pay us is going to bust the government." Motley nodded his approval.

This was the only time while coaching at Great Lakes that I had a team so primed. For spirit and dedication they were as close to a collegiate team as I had coached in years, and they simply cut Notre Dame to ribbons, as a national radio audience of millions listened to Bill Stern's play-by-play.

Aschenbrenner, a small but tremendously fast halfback who later would be a star at Northwestern, hauled the opening kickoff 53 yards and three minutes later scored the first touchdown. When Notre Dame went ahead, 7–6, Motley took the next kickoff 37 yards, to start a 63-yard drive, climaxed by Klemmer's catch of a 29-yard pass from George Terlep and Aschenbrenner's touchdown from the 1-yard line. We never trailed again and broke the game open in the fourth quarter on Aschenbrenner's 13-yard touchdown run and a 44-yard burst by Motley for a touchdown. The final score was 39–7.

Notre Dame simply could not handle Motley that day and even had trouble knocking him down as he ran several trap plays that became his specialty over the years. We had particularly told Marion in practice, "If you come clear on this trap play, don't get fancy. If there is someone in front of you, just run in one end of him and out the other." That's exactly what he did. When he broke loose on his 44-yard touchdown run, there was only one man between Marion and the goal line. Motley never broke stride and simply ran over him en route to the end zone.

Afterwards our dressing room was positively flooded with emotion. The game now ranks as one of the special few in my career, alongside the first victory over Canton-McKinley, the 20–20 tie against Michigan in 1941, the victory over the Eagles in 1950 and the Rams for the NFL title the same year and the 1970 Bengals' victory over the Browns in Cleveland in the first regular-season game between the two teams. Those were precious moments, but few as sweet as that day in 1945. I still hear from many of the players on that team who have also marked that day as a special occasion in their memories. In fact, I still wear the wristwatch Admiral Emmett gave me after the game as a memento of my coaching years at Great Lakes. He gave watches to each of our players as well, and most of them still value them as keepsakes.

As we left the stadium for good that December Saturday, the huge oval in the middle of Great Lakes' parade ground was ready to be dismantled, and less than three months later I was discharged from the navy. It took some help from Admiral Emmett to do it, though. He had to intervene to keep me from being sent to the South Pacific to witness the atom bomb experiments at Eniwetok and Bikini atolls. He knew that I was anxious to begin my own experiments in Cleveland with a new football team and a new way of life.

SIX

Building the Browns: Hand-Picking a Champion

MY DECISION EARLY IN 1945 to enter professional football was guided more by my emotions than by any reasoned intention to better myself professionally or financially. I had no interest in professional football at the time, and Cleveland had a bad reputation as a professional sports town; it had not supported the Rams of the National Football League, and there was no apparent reason why it should support a second attempt at a pro football team. I really made a rash move, and making rash moves has never been my nature. However, in February 1945 my emotional balance had been tilted enough by my experiences at Ohio State and in the navy so that I was willing to consider an offer which even a year before I would have rejected automatically.

When I'd entered the navy, I had had every intention of returning to Ohio State and resuming my job as head coach, and Mr. St. John had assured me that it would be waiting for me when my service commitment ended. However, the chain of events that had been triggered in 1944 had left the matter far from cut-and-dried. I was still scarred emotionally by the Baby Bucks experience and by the army's subsequent reversal of its decision to let its ROTC players compete. The game between Ohio State and Great Lakes that year, in which no one on my side had seemed to care whether we won or lost, also left me crushed.

At Ohio State Carroll Widdoes was the toast of college

football in 1944, when the team finished an unbeaten season, and I was left on the outside looking in, even though I felt I had been greatly responsible for Wid's success since I had schooled him in football, recommended him as my successor and recruited most of his team. I began to wonder about my position at Ohio State because I knew that it would be unfair to remove someone whose team had just finished a perfect season and who seemed capable of producing future great seasons. I called Mr. St. John, seeking assurance.

"You're welcome to return," he told me, "but you must know it may be a bit sticky after Wid's unbeaten season and his fine coaching job. Still, we made an agreement, and we'll live by it."

I needed more than that. I needed to be pampered a bit and told that I truly would be welcomed. Someone had to say, "Gee, we'll really be looking forward to getting you back." No one said that, however, and it only added to my hurt feelings. I'm sure that Mr. St. John didn't mean anything bad in the way he presented the situation to me and that he was probably only revealing his true feelings, but it was this attitude, coupled with the emotional turmoil of 1943, that made me a willing listener when Arch Ward began wooing me to become coach of the All-America Conference's new Cleveland franchise.

Ward was the renowned and very powerful sports editor of the *Chicago Tribune* and a promotional genius who could turn a mere idea into success, as he had proved with the All-Star games in professional baseball and football. Now he was envisioning a second football league that, combined with the established National League, would help professional football become as prosperous as major-league baseball. His idea was basically correct, but unfortunately, as it turned out, a few years ahead of its time.

Arthur McBride and Dan Sherby were the moneymen for this franchise. McBride had become a wealthy man before the age of forty owing to his success in the newspaper circulation wars in Chicago and Cleveland, his real estate holdings in Florida, a sports wire syndicate and his acquisition of Cleveland's Yellow Cab fleet. His interest in football hadn't begun until his sons attended Notre Dame, but then he had started going to the games every weekend. McBride knew nothing about the game, but he fell in love with it and tried to buy into the NFL's Cleveland Rams. Dan Reaves turned

him down, but Arch Ward, whom he knew from his newspaper days in Chicago, sold him on taking the AAC franchise
for Cleveland.

McBride's first choice for a coach was Frank Leahy, whose
teams he had followed at Notre Dame—and who, he later
told me, was the only football coach he'd ever heard of.
Frank was in the navy when the two of them reportedly
made a handshake agreement on the job, but the school's
president, the Reverend John Cavanaugh, was anxious to
have Leahy back and convinced McBride to dissolve the
agreement.

McBride then turned for advice to John Dietrich, a respected sportswriter for the *Cleveland Plain Dealer*. John became so enamored of this new venture that he presented my
name and a glowing recommendation. McBride knew nothing
about me or my football, so he went to Ward. Arch knew
that I was probably Ohio's best-known football coach and
that my strong affiliation with the Massillon-Canton-Akron
area near Clevelend would guarantee a solid block of cus-
tomers for the new team—I had proved that at Ohio State.
Arch also staunchly believed that the nation's most prestigious
coaches came from the Big Ten, and he felt my presence
would lend the best possible image to his new league.

Arch visited me several times at Great Lakes after the
AAC's formation had been announced late in 1944. He laid
down his idea, citing the tremendous financial resources available from the prospective owners, as well as his own ideas
about the two major football leagues. He played to my ego as
well, and without actually realizing it, he started me thinking
that perhaps I should think of coaching where my talents
would be appreciated and I would be welcomed. I certainly
hadn't gotten that feeling from my conversations with Mr. St.
John, so I stayed interested during all our discussions.

Early in 1945, with eight franchises in hand but no
coaches or teams for his new league, Arch began pressing me
to make a commitment and sign a contract. I really wasn't
sold, but on February 9, 1945, I agreed to come to his office
to meet Sherby and McBride for the first time and talk about
a contract. When I left home that day, I had not yet made up
my mind about signing. I really knew nothing about the two
owners, and the idea of going into professional football still
left me a bit cold. As the meeting went on, Arch began
pressing me for a final decision, and Sherby and McBride

were sitting there, obviously anticipating some kind of action. I excused myself and called Katy at home.

"What are your feelings about this?" I asked her, after laying out the conditions that had been discussed.

"You do whatever you want to do," she told me.

That indicated to me that she felt our family could be comfortable with the job, so I went back and signed a five-year contract. My salary was to be $25,000 per year, plus 5 percent ownership of the team and a monthly retainer of $1,-500 for as long as I stayed in the navy. Most important to me, I had complete control of the team's operation, with total freedom to sign players and coaches. As was the case at Massillon and Ohio State, the money was secondary. I told Sherby and McBride that I wanted to build a dynasty from the start and that I wanted our team to have the very best of everything—players, coaches and equipment—regardless of what it cost.

"I'm sure you men are interested in making this go financially," I said, "but I'm not interested in your pocketbook. If we win the game and nobody is in the stadium, that won't bother me because I'll be satisfied with winning. If we lose the game in front of eighty-two thousand people, however, that's bad."

They never flinched, though I'm sure they must have wondered just what sort of person they had under contract. McBride never interfered with anything I did, and in fact, I rarely saw him after that day. Most of my dealings were with Dan Sherby, who was a fine man and whom I liked and respected very much. Both men always admitted that they knew nothing about football and simply enjoyed the excitement of owning a team. McBride had a great flair for promoting our team, and he was always content to involve himself in this aspect of the business alone. I've always felt that we had an unusual relationship—and a perfect one—and that it contributed greatly to building such a solid foundation for our team.

Of course, as I look back, I realize the best thing I ever did was to become a part owner because every time the team was sold—and it happened three times while I was with the Browns—I was paid for my percentage of the team, then given a larger number of shares by the new ownership. I also realized another profit when I liquidated my holdings, prior to starting the Bengals. That is the only way anyone can realize any financial independence from professional sports, and I was fortunate in both cases to get in on the ground floor.

When I went home to Great Lakes, however, I still wasn't so sure that I had done the correct thing, particularly since, as Arch Ward pumped up his promotion campaign for a new league that would not begin for another eighteen months, my name was the one he constantly used: I was the only football commodity the AAC had at that time. I began to get the hollow feeling that I was being used to sell the credibility of this new league, and I saw now why he had gone to such lengths to sell me on the idea. As the league began to slip in its later years, I think the other owners realized, too, that they had been sold a bill of goods. The AAC was Arch's dream, and he did everything he could to make it happen, but there just wasn't enough support for it in the real world.

Meanwhile, word had filtered back to Ohio State that I was considering signing with the All-America Conference, and the very evening after I had my contract, Ernie Godfrey called and urged me to withhold any decisions until matters had solidified at Ohio State. It was too late then, and soon I became a juicy target for some factions at the university who considered me a traitor for moving to professional football instead of returning to Ohio State. Some pretty bitter things were said and written, but Dr. Bevis disavowed these thoughts and publicly supported my right to determine my own future, even sending me a letter to that effect. Nevertheless, I'll never forget the wife of Harold Olsen, Ohio State's basketball coach, writing to me at the time: "How could you have done such a thing and joined the professionals?" A year later her husband, Ollie, left the university and became coach of the Chicago Stags of the new professional Basketball Association of America!

The net effect of this controversy was beneficial, however, because it called attention to our new team and helped build its visibility. As a matter of fact, this was an exciting period for me, albeit not as exciting as coming back to Massillon or going to Ohio State, because I was finally being allowed to put together a team that I wanted and that would operate under my principles.

Since I still had months of navy service ahead of me, I hired John Brickels, whom I had known as a coach in Ohio, to run our football operation from a small office in the Leader Building in Cleveland. One of my first mandates was to find a name for the team, my only requirement being that it be something we could animate as we had done so successfully with the Massillon Tiger.

McBride offered a $1,000 war bond to the winning entry, and a young sailor named John J. Hartnett submitted the name "Panthers." For several weeks we were referred to as the Cleveland Panthers in newspaper stories, until one day a man named George Jones walked into McBride's office and said that he had once owned a semipro team in the Cleveland area called the Cleveland Panthers and that the name belonged to him. It hadn't been a very successful team, but according to McBride, the man was willing to allow us to use the name if we paid him several thousand dollars.

McBride refused, saying he didn't want a name for his team that had smacked of failure, so we ran another contest, this time offering a new car as first prize. I had no further suggestions myself, and the three-man selection committee and I finally agreed that the name and thought appearing most frequently in the entries would be the one that we selected. The contest lasted for some time, and because I was well known from coaching at Ohio State and Massillon, it turned out that my name, or "Browns," appeared more often than any other, and so the contest's judges decided that "Browns" would be the name for the team. It has also been reported that we received many entries for "Brown Bombers," after Joe Louis, then the world's heavyweight boxing champion, and that we shortened that name to "Browns," but this was untrue.

Building a football team occupied all my free time during my last months at Great Lakes, and I talked to Brickels nearly every night about which players I wanted signed. The All-America Conference never got organized well enough to hold a player draft before the first season, and I had no idea what constituted a professional football player, but I had my own criteria—players with mental and physical ability who loved the game ahead of their paychecks. I felt sure about the players we set out to sign because I had either coached them or played against them, so I knew all about them. With players I did not know or had not seen play I got ironclad recommendations from football people whose opinions I respected to make sure the player was my kind of person.

The result was a hand-picked group that was more like a college team in their spirited approach to football. I have little doubt that this meticulous process of selection paved the way to our early successes, and that, together with the players we added in 1947 and 1948, was responsible for our unprecedented string of championships. All of them were hungry young men, most of them just coming from the service with great hopes for the future and eager and willing to try anything. To some like Lou Groza and Dante Lavelli, who had rubbed shoulders with death during some of the war's bitterest fighting, playing football was fun, and their exuberance and spirit were contagious.

Brickels did all the legwork, with help from Creighton Miller, a fine player from Notre Dame, whom McBride had put on our payroll at the behest of the boy's uncle, Ray Miller, the mayor of Cleveland, so Creighton could earn some money to pursue his law studies at Yale. Miller mostly advised us on the Notre Dame players he knew, but he was never, as was reported at the time, any real factor in my coming to the Browns, nor did he ever do any coaching. He was listed as an assistant coach for the 1946 season so that we could justifiably pay him.

While Brickels scoured the country, I traveled only a short distance from Great Lakes to Glenview Naval Air Station to sign Otto Graham. I remembered his tremendous peripheral vision and his great athletic skill, as well as his ability to throw a football far and accurately with just a flick of his arm, and I felt he was the best possible player to be our quarterback. He had been drafted by the Detroit Lions, but they hadn't even contacted him when we began our negotiations. Otto was finishing up his flight training and being paid only $75 per month. We clinched our agreement when we agreed to pay him a $250-per-month retainer for as long as he was in the service, plus a $1,000 bonus for signing, on top of a $7,500 salary. The retainer was the key because Otto planned to be married as soon as he left the service and he needed the money.

We gave monthly retainers to all the players we really wanted. Lou Groza and Lin Houston both were overseas when I sent them contracts and promised them $200 per month until their army discharges. Houston's company commander, an army captain who had to witness his signature, took one look at the figure and told him, "Kid, if you don't sign it, I will. You'll be making more than me, and you're only a private."

Houston had received questionnaires from both the Detroit Lions and the Chicago Bears, but when I sent him an actual contract with the promise of $200 per month for signing, he forgot about the NFL teams. Some players, like George Young, John Yonakor, Lou Saban, Edgar Jones, Groza and Houston, made more than $2,000 in bonus money; Graham and Groza made more than $5,000 during the remainder of their service hitches for signing with the Browns, and all these players repaid every cent with their efforts and loyalty. Some didn't even wait to join us. Groza, for example, wore out several footballs we sent him by working on his place-kicking in jungle clearings on Okinawa and in the Philippines.

Every player in the service was fair game in those days because the war had disrupted professional sports so severely. Many players had gone into the military after their contracts had expired, and since there wasn't any competition at that time, the NFL teams had figured they would return to their former teams. Contractually, however, most of them were free agents, and we went after the ones I knew could help us. We got into some conflicts with the Bears, the Chicago Cardinals and the Cleveland Rams before we finished, but we always resolved the question of which team held a valid contract. For instance, I had seen Vince Banonis play center for the Chicago Cardinals while I was at Great Lakes and signed him because he said he was free. The Cardinals produced a predated contract, however, and we freed him. We won, though, when the Bears battled us over the rights to Edgar Jones and Bob Steuber and backed off when we proved our contracts were valid. The most interesting case came when some of the Rams' players refused to play in Los Angeles, the city the team had moved to after winning the NFL title in 1945, and signed with us, arguing that their contracts had called for them to play only with the *Cleveland* Rams. The Rams went to court for a decision, but the judge upheld the players' position, and we got to keep such fine players as Chet Adams, a starting tackle in 1946; Tom Colella, a defensive back and our first punter; Mo Scarry, a center, who is now an assistant on Don Shula's Miami coaching staff; Ernie Blandin, a fine defensive tackle; Gaylon Smith, a running back; and Don Greenwood, defensive back.

I had seen Greenwood play at Missouri and Illinois and remembered he was fast and smart, a decisive player who rarely made a mistake and one of the best tacklers I had ever seen for a defensive back. Colella was a starting offensive back with the Rams but really blossomed when we made him a defensive back and punt return specialist. Tommy was also our punter until Horace Gillom joined us in 1947, though when Dante Lavelli broke his leg and Gillom had to play end full time in 1948, Tom again did most of our punting.

Colella and Greenwood are among the fifteen players from the 1946 team whom I rate as the best ever to play on my professional football teams. Five of them—Otto Graham, Lou Groza, Dante Lavelli, Marion Motley and Bill Willis— are in the Hall of Fame, and several others, including Lin Houston and Lou Rymkus, deserve to be there. Each of those fifteen players was a unique, special person who made tremendous contributions to our football in Cleveland.

As far as I am concerned, Otto Graham was the greatest player in the game's history. Playing the most important position—quarterback—he guided our teams into the play-offs every year of his ten seasons in professional football, seven times helping us win championships. No other player has ever achieved this, and the fact that his statistics rank first among all the passers who ever played professional football only further attests to his greatness.

Two other quarterbacks also belong in my select group: Ken Anderson of the Bengals, whom I'll discuss later, and Cliff Lewis, our second quarterback during our first six seasons. Had we not had Otto, Cliff would easily have been our starting quarterback, and in fact, he did open our first game since Otto had not had a chance yet to learn our system. Cliff was a marvelous defensive back, playing as middle safety, and in the early seasons, when Otto sometimes stayed in the game as a defensive back as well, we had the best secondary in the AAC.

Cliff's physical strength was awesome for someone who weighed only 165 pounds. One evening during our first training camp I heard a commotion upstairs in the dorm and walked up to find Cliff, Ernie Blandin, George Cheroke and Frank Gatski competing in an impromptu weight-lifting contest. Cliff was lying on the floor, and as I watched, he reached behind his head with both arms, lifted some heavy-looking weights up and over his body and then replaced them without breaking into a sweat.

Blandin, a tackle who weighed about 260 pounds, saw that and said, "Heck, that's easy. Let me at it."

Ernie flattened himself, reached back and grabbed the weight, but it never budged. He tried until he was covered with sweat and his face was beet red, but he still could not lift the weight. It dawned on him then that he couldn't match a mere 165-pounder, and I've never seen anyone more embarrassed, even though part of the difference was that Ernie had never learned the proper method of lifting weights and Cliff had.

Some of the others were no slouches in that department either. Cheroke, who played for us at Ohio State, was one of the first players I ever knew who built up his upper-body strength with weight lifting. One day Gatski, our center, saw George's weights and asked what they were all about.

"You lift them," Cheroke told him.

Frank leaned down, and as casually as if he were lifting a pencil off a table, he put one hand under the weight and lifted it off the floor.

"Now what do I do with it?" he asked George, who could only look on with amazement.

Gatski, a West Virginian who looked a bit like L'il Abner with his ready smile and tremendous physique, played center for us for ten years. He had another country attribute as well: The most fun in his life, outside of football, came from hunting with a bow and arrow, and he eventually became one of the country's best in this very unusual sport. He was as durable and tough as any player I've ever known—not one injury during his football career—and when he left us, it was to play for the Detroit Lions' 1957 NFL championship team. When the American Football League started in 1960, he just missed winning a spot on the Boston Patriots. He was thirty-eight years old at the time.

Eddie Ulinski also came to us that year. He had played with Gatski at Marshall College, and both were signed by Brickels. Ulinski was one of the most dedicated players I ever had, and a great guard, before becoming one of our coaches in 1950. He and Gatski had learned their football from Cam Henderson, a tough, hard-nosed coach, and Eddie was the same. He was also one of the finest teachers I've ever seen in football.

Ulinski was one of my all-time offensive guards, and so was Lin Houston. When he came to our camp at Bowling

Green College in 1946, Lin was an eager young man who had tested the poverty and hardship of the Depression years and knew that professional football was a way for him to help his family. As a result, football dominated his life, and he trained vigorously, impressing everyone with his technical excellence and his speed. He was supposed to retire after the 1952 season to pursue his sales career with a steel company, but we were in training camp only about three days the next summer when I got a telephone call from his wife, Edna Mae.

"Can you take Lindell back for another year?" she asked. "He is miserable. He can't sleep, he can't eat and all he does is pace the floor. He wants to come back and play, but he's afraid you might make him stick with his retirement plans."

"Okay," I told her, "tell him he can play one more season, and then he must call it off and get started on his life's work."

About six-thirty the next morning there was a knock on my door. I opened it, and there stood Lindell, his football shoes tied together and hung around his neck and a big sheepish grin on his face.

"Well," I said to him, "what do you have to say for yourself?"

"Aw, coach," he said, "I just like the life."

He had the greatest season of his career in 1953, but he had time during the year to prepare himself mentally for retirement after the season ended.

In 1948 we traded for Weldon Humble, another great guard who had been on the sprint team at Rice University. He also has a place among the greatest players I ever coached. I first saw Weldon when his Rice team defeated Tennessee in the 1947 Orange Bowl. He had already been drafted by Baltimore, but I saw something special in the way he played, and after the game we attended Rice's victory party, and I saw what a tremendous person he was. I made up my mind right then and there that I wanted him for the Browns, so I put together a package of five players who I knew would not play for us and sent them to the Colts to get him. A trade of this magnitude was unheard of in those days, but the Colts were a new team and needed help, and we got a great player. To me, a successful trade is determined by who gets the single best player.

Weldon was Texan all the way. He always wore cowboy boots and a big ten-gallon hat, and whenever he walked down

the aisle on our chartered airplane, someone up front was
bound to hum the *William Tell* Overture, the theme of the
"Lone Ranger" radio program. Weldon and Bill Willis sat together on every flight and shared a tremendous camaraderie
since both were guards and respected each other's ability. It
was a tremendous display of what people today call brother-
hood since Willis was black and Weldon was white, but it
was typical of the feelings all our players had for one another.

The friendship between Willis and Humble seemed perfectly natural to me. I never considered football players black
or white, nor did I keep or cut a player just because of his
color. In our first meeting before training camp every year, I
told the players that they made our teams only if they were
good enough. I didn't care about a man's color or his ances-
try; I just wanted to win football games with the best people
possible.

It was an issue that had to be faced in 1946, however, because Branch Rickey of the Brooklyn Dodgers had just signed
Jackie Robinson, and national opinion was running high, both
pro and con. Though the constitutions of the All-America
Conference and the National Football League did not forbid
black players from competing, none ever had in the fourteen
years since football's modern era had begun in 1932.

Nevertheless, I had made up my mind long before Rickey's
action that I wanted both Willis and Marion Motley to play
for us. Even though our sport did not have the same national
impact as major-league baseball at that time, I knew the
fierce attention we would receive would create some unfair
pressure which could in turn harm both players. I wanted to
avoid that dangerous ground, so, to soften the impact as
much as I could, I decided to wait until our team was settled
into training camp before asking them to join us.

We became the first pro football team of the modern era
ever to sign black players, just a short time before the Rams
of the NFL signed Woody Strode and Kenny Washington,
but I think the delicate way in which we did it helped both of
them to escape the tremendous pressure that Robinson had to
endure and to concentrate totally on becoming great football
players. Some people in our league resented this action and
tossed a few intemperate bars at me, but I felt those were
better answered by the players themselves when they played
against those teams. Unfortunately not every situation was

under our control. When we went to Miami to play the Seahawks in 1946, neither Willis nor Motley accompanied us because it was against the law in Florida at that time for blacks
and whites to compete against each other. Both men
handled this very sensitive situation with great dignity and
understanding, however, both then and throughout that season, and they made it easier for other black players to enter
professional football.

We almost never got a chance to sign Willis in the first
place, though. Bill had asked me about playing for the
Browns when he was finishing his first year as an assistant
coach at Kentucky State College in 1945, and I had said I
would contact him. When he didn't hear from me, however,
because I was waiting for training camp, he agreed to join
the Montreal Alouettes of the Canadian Football League. He
was ready to leave for Canada to sign his contract when I
asked my friend Paul Hornung of the *Columbus Dispatch*,
who knew him well, to bring him to our Bowling Green camp.

"Why don't you come down and join us?" I said to him
when he phoned prior to his coming. "I'll stake my reputation
that you'll be able to make our team."

"I can't do that, Paul," he told me. "I've already told Montreal that I'd go up and play for them."

I wasn't about to let him get away that easily, so I kept after him by phone to come to our camp, if only to be sure in
his own mind that he could—or could not—play for the
Browns.

"Okay," he finally said. "I don't have to be in Montreal for
a couple of days, so I'll come up to Bowling Green on my
way to Canada and give it a try."

When he arrived at Bowling Green, practice had just
ended, but I talked him into staying that night, signing a contract and taking part in our scrimmage the next morning.
Bill, who had the quickest defensive charge after the ball was
snapped of any defensive lineman I ever saw, lined up right
on Mo Scarry's head, and every time Mo tried to center the
ball, Bill was on him so quickly that Mo couldn't even make
the exchange with our quarterbacks. He told me later that he
watched Mo's hands, and as soon as they tightened to snap
the ball, he moved. I was so intrigued with this explanation I
got right down on my hands and knees along the line of
scrimmage to be sure Bill wasn't offsides. He wasn't, but he
moved with the ball so quickly it was hard to determine.

When Otto Graham came to our camp from the College All-Star game, he and Scarry had problems with the ball exchange during our early drills because Bill got off the ball so fast. Mo began anticipating Bill's move by snapping the ball, then quickly jumping back to begin his pass protection. Otto wasn't used to such a quick movement, and one time Scarry stepped on his toes, forcing Otto to howl in pain.

"What's the matter?" I asked him.

"Mo just stepped on my foot."

I whistled everyone to the center of the field.

"Now, men," I told the players, "someone stepped on Otto's foot, and we can't very well have a good practice if that keeps happening. So would you please take care not to step on his toes?"

Everyone laughed, but that's what Willis did to an opposing center. When we played our first AAC game against Miami, its quarterback and center never made one decent exchange. It was Willis's quickness, as well, that forced us to realign our own quarterback's stance as he stood behind the center, from a standard parallel-foot position to one in which one foot was placed slightly behind the other in order to push off and get away quicker from the line of scrimmage. This innovative move eventually became adopted throughout football.

Bill played for eight seasons with the Browns. He often played as a middle or nose guard on our five-man defensive line, but we began dropping him off the line of scrimmage a yard or two because his great speed and pursuit carried him to the point of attack before anyone could block him. This technique and theory was the beginning of the modern 4-3 defense, and Bill was the forerunner of the modern middle linebacker.

Though we almost lost Willis, Marion Motley was all too available for a man of his talent. Motley had returned to his Canton home following his navy discharge with no interest in returning to the University of Nevada and resuming his college career. He was nearly twenty-seven years old and, with a family to support, had taken a mill job. I called Oscar Barkey, a friend from Canton, and asked him to drive Marion to our training camp and have him ask for a tryout. I felt that was the best way to handle the situation, again in the light of the potential publicity, because there was nothing unusual in a player's coming to his former coach and asking him for a chance to play.

No other professional football team was interested in him at the time because he had not played enough in college or in the service to attract any attention. That was their loss. Marion became our greatest fullback ever because not only was he a great runner, but also no one ever blocked better—and no one ever cared more about his team and whether it won or lost, rather than how many yards he gained or where he was asked to run. I love him just for the way he blocked for us and the pride he took in being Otto's bodyguard on passing situations. No one reached our passers when he was blocking, and we often let him take on a defensive end man-for-man because he was big enough to handle anyone. After he hit a guy a couple of times, that player began looking for Marion first before he went after our passer.

Marion's tremendous running ability also was what made our trap and draw plays so effective. When he ran off tackle, players seemed to fly off him in all directions. He possessed tremendous speed for a big man, and he could run away from linebackers and defensive backs when he got into the open—if he didn't trample them first. I've always believed that Motley could have gone into the Hall of Fame solely as a linebacker if we had used him only at that position. He was as good as our great ones.

Several years ago I spoke at an affair in Canton at which Marion was being honored, and among the guests was his former Canton-McKinley High School coach, Johnny Reed. When John spoke, he recalled how he had played Marion as a guard before moving him to fullback. John had been fired after Canton had lost for the sixth straight time to Massillon, and when I got up to speak, I kidded him about it.

"You know, John," I said, "anyone who would play Motley at guard should get fired."

Marion came in for his share of good-natured ribbing, too. We defeated Los Angeles handily in a game in 1948, but Marion atypically lost three fumbles in the first half. After the game the players took some tape, made a handle from it, then stuck it on the ball and presented it to Marion. It was so unusual for him to fumble the players felt it might be their only chance ever to kid him about it.

Marion also had problems staying awake when he was

seated for any length of time. Once he fell asleep driving, ran into another car and bashed in his nose.

"I don't care about your nose," I told him after the accident. "But I do care about those legs, so you stay awake."

Sometimes he dozed off during our meetings, but I usually kept a wet towel nearby, and when I saw him beginning to snooze, I'd throw it at him, and he'd bolt upright. The other players always laughed and razzed him, and he took it without offense.

Lou Saban is another who rates a place on my list of great players. Lou, who has been an outstanding professional and college coach, was a very intense competitor and one of the deadliest tacklers we ever had. Although he had been a great college fullback, I remembered his skills as a linebacker the day Ohio State defeated Indiana, and that became his only position with the Browns; we put him into a game as soon as the ball changed hands, to replace Mo Scarry or Frank Gatski, our centers. We kept him on tap for other jobs, however. For a couple of seasons he was our backup fullback behind Motley, a third quarterback behind Graham and Lewis and the second place-kicker behind Lou Groza. He also did an outstanding job as our team captain after Jim Daniell left. If he thought a player was getting out of hand, he took him out to dinner and straightened him out.

Then there were Lou Groza and Lou Rymkus—Lou the Toe and Lou the Heel, they used to call themselves—a tremendous pair of tackles. I unabashedly considered them the best pair of offensive tacklers in professional football when they played together, and Groza is in the Hall of Fame as much for his play as a lineman as for his place-kicking. Rymkus should be in there with him.

That first season in 1946, however, Groza was almost exclusively a place-kicker and worked behind Blandin, Rymkus, Daniell and Chet Adams to learn his tackle duties because his only previous experience was as a freshman at Ohio State. I knew he could kick field goals of 40 or 50 yards, but early in that first season he used to get off the bench and begin exercising his leg when we had only reached midfield and it looked as if we might have to give up the ball.

"Do you think you can kick one from there?" I finally asked him.

"I think I can," he said. Actually, he knew he could because Lou was always certain of his own strength and ability.

So I let him try. In that 1946 season he kicked a 49-yard field goal against Los Angeles, a 51-yarder against the Chicago Rockets and one 50 yards through hurricane-force wind and rain in Miami. From that time on he was always a great potential weapon when we were inside an opponent's 49-yard line. I know that Lou won more games in clutch situations with his kicking than any player in the game's history.

When Blandin was sent to Baltimore in 1947 as part of the Humble trade, Lou moved in and played offensive tackle, too. Groza got his baptism in that position when Los Angeles Dons tackle Lee Artoe hit him right on the nose on the first play of a game. Artoe was wearing a face mask to protect a broken nose, so on the next play Groza unloaded on that mask and cut Lee's chin. For the rest of the game Lee chased Groza around, trying to get even, but Lou was so quick he blocked him and was gone without a scratch.

Lou Rymkus had been a starting tackle as a rookie with the Washington Redskins in 1943, the year they had won the NFL's Eastern Division title, but then the war had intervened. When the Browns formed, we sent him a contract with the promise of a $200-per-month retainer while he was stationed at Pearl Harbor. Lou returned to the United States a short time later and called George Preston Marshall, owner of the Redskins, to tell him of the offer.

"That league will fold in a month," Marshall told him. "Don't pay any attention to it."

"Well, they've offered me more than twice what you paid me, plus a monthly retainer until I get out of the service," Lou replied. "I'd like to know what your offer will be because I have a young family to support and I need the money."

"Forget what you heard from them," Marshall insisted. "I'm not going to try and match their offer. I paid you two thousand dollars as a rookie, and I'll offer you the same to sign with us again."

Lou signed with us, and it probably cost him a spot on the Redskins team that lost to the Cleveland Rams for the 1945 NFL championship. However, he certainly did well enough with us. Lou came to us with a big plus—excellent pass blocking techniques, drilled into him by Frank Leahy of Notre Dame. Within two weeks he was our best tackle and remained so for six years, including two seasons as an offensive and defensive tackle. He often bridled at not being allowed to play both ways more often, and occasionally, when our defense was in a short yardage situation, he would come to my side and ask, "Shall I go in and help them?"

"Go back and sit down, Lou," I'd tell him. "We need you more on offense."

He was one player who truly loved the game. During his first season someone fell on the back of his leg, tearing a cartilage in his knee and causing the knee to lock, but he never told anyone about it. Our trainer, Wally Bock, showed him how to snap the knee back into place. Sometimes Lou would have to do it six or seven times during a game so he could keep on playing.

When the season ended, he told me, "I'm going to need an operation."

I was stunned. "What for? What's wrong with you?"

Then he told me about the knee. I'd had no idea. That was typical, however, of this big, tough, rawboned guy who had come from the coal mines of southern Illinois and knew the meaning of a rough life. Leahy had nicknamed him the Battler, and that's what he was. His confrontations with Bob Reinhard when Bob played with the Los Angeles Dons, and later the Rams, were classics. They were two of the greatest linemen in the game's history, both about six feet four inches tall and 250 pounds. They went at each other with tremendous ferocity, yet never really got mad at each other until the third year, when Bob hit Lou with an elbow.

"Why did you do that?" Lou said to him, and on the next play he hit him. Players didn't wear protective face masks then, and they literally slugged it out for the rest of the game. Each of them was responsible for 45 yards in penalties, yet when the game ended, they walked off the field arm in arm.

In another game against the 49ers, Lou was being pounded with fists and elbows by one of San Francisco's tackles and started to get upset. Late in the game we needed a first down to keep one of our drives going, and Otto decided to use it to his own advantage.

"Can you take one more punch for the good of the team?" Otto asked him in the huddle.

"Okay," Lou said because he never refused his team one ounce of his energy or his blood.

Otto outlined his scheme. After the next play he would complain to the officials that Lou was being slugged and ask them to watch for the infraction. In the meantime, Lou was to say something particularly nasty to his tormentor and incite him to deliver the decisive blow.

"If they catch him, we get fifteen yards on the penalty and a first down," Otto told him.

Everything went off just as Otto planned. The 49ers' player tagged Lou, and he was out for nearly five minutes. When he opened his eyes, the first player he saw was Otto.

"Did we get the fifteen-yard penalty?" he mumbled.

"No," Graham had to tell him. "We scored on the play and had to decline the penalty.

Creighton Miller, who had recommended Rymkus to us, also brought John Yonakor, another teammate at Notre Dame who was taller and nearly as strong as Rymkus, to our first team. John ranks with Len Ford and Paul Wiggin as one of the greatest defensive ends ever to play for my teams. With all his size, though, John still had a high, squeaky voice, and naturally he got ribbed about it. Nothing bothered him more than an opposing team placing a flanker just outside his position, and when he saw it, he'd yell, "Flanker, flanker, flanker," in his high-pitched voice. Outside the game, our players began imitating him. "Flanker, flanker, it floats, it floats," they'd yell, referring to John's great ability to float along the line of scrimmage when someone tried to run a sweep to his side of the field. He was so strong the blockers could not knock him off his feet, yet so nimble he stayed with the backs as they tried to run around him. The players eventually nicknamed him Ivory because of his almost effortless floating motion.

There's a story I like to tell about John which illustrates one of my training precepts. Years after he had finished his career and was working for a steel company in Cleveland, I was walking through the airport with my three younger sons when I saw him coming down a corridor, smoking a big cigar. As soon as he saw me, he ditched the cigar, and as we chatted, I never mentioned that I saw him throw it away. That act really tickled me, though. Even years after playing for us, the moment he saw his old coach he reacted just as if he were still on our team.

I never smoked myself, and I never wanted our players to do so because it wasn't healthy. My players knew my strong feelings about it, and like John Yonakor, they often went to extremes to tone it down. Some went into the closets in their rooms at training camp to smoke a cigarette, so the smoke would not filter into the hallways; others walked to public buildings for a smoke. One day I was walking along the hall-way of the Sonoma Inn near San Francisco, where we some-times stayed before playing the 49ers, when I saw smoke coming through an open transom. I opened the door and saw some players in a card game and everyone smoking cigars. I didn't say a word, but as soon as they saw me, they all got up and threw their cigars into the wastebasket. I closed the door, and that was it. However, I've always suspected that they re-trieved them after I left.

The other two players from that first Browns team on my alltime list are Mac Speedie and Dante Lavelli, our two great ends. They complemented each other perfectly on the field, Speedie the "move" man, Dante with his tremendous speed and super hands. Mac was a very tough, determined player, as his childhood illustrates. As a young boy he learned he had a disease that affected the ball and socket of his left hip joint and caused the left leg to be an inch shorter and two inches smaller in diameter than his right leg. After a long period of being bedridden, he was given a pair of crutches, but Mac didn't care for that at all. He refused to use them or the arti-ficial brace an orthopedist had prescribed to help him walk with more comfort. Instead, he went out and climbed trees, jumped off roofs and did everything his pals did, just to prove to them he was not a cripple. Ultimately his condition was stabilized, though his left leg always remained shorter and smaller than the right leg.

It never affected his football ability, however. Mac may not have had Lavelli's great speed, but with his spraddle-legged running style he had the kind of great balance that en-abled him to stop, move laterally and come back and catch the ball. I think we were the first team ever to develop this type of pass pattern, an exercise in true precision because Otto had to throw the ball before the receiver looked for it or came back to meet it. Johnny Unitas and Ray Berry became famous for this kind of play when Weeb Ewbank coached the Baltimore Colts, and Weeb, of course, had learned it while coaching with us at Cleveland. Today such plays are routine in professional football.

Lavelli was one of the greatest natural athletes I ever knew—and one of my favorite persons. He turned down a contract from the Detroit Tigers to come to Ohio State and was just about ready to sign again with the Tigers after the war when I sent Fritz Heisler to recruit him for the Browns. He also had an offer from the Cleveland team of the National Basketball League to play with them, but we gave him a $500 bonus, and that sealed the deal.

I can't remember his dropping a single pass during the eleven seasons he played for the Browns, either in a game or in practice; the players used to call him Mr. Clutch or Glue Fingers. The reason was his geat concentration on the ball and the best pair of hands I've ever seen on any receiver. They had an almost liquid softness which seemed to slurp the ball into them. He always seemed to catch every ball that was thrown near him, and he took many away from defensive backs who thought he was beaten.

Dante had a high-pitched voice, too, and as soon as he thought he was open on a pass pattern—which was every pass that was called—he'd yell, "Otto, Otto, Otto," and his voice carried all over the field. He played at about 215 pounds and was the first of the great tight ends in professional football, though to take advantage of his speed, we often split him several yards outside the tackle.

Otto always called him Spumoni, and the way the two of them could adjust to shifting defenses in the midst of a play without ever saying a word or giving the slightest signal was uncanny. Dante had a great feel for running patterns, and he often broke into the open quicker than anticipated or at a different spot or angle from that planned. It didn't matter because Otto always had the ball at the precise spot. Once, in a game in Yankee Stadium against the AAC Yankees, we decided on a pass play to the right corner of the end zone. The Yankees' defense sensed the pass and set itself to stop it even before the ball was snapped, but then, in the middle of running his pattern, Dante suddenly broke the pass route and headed in the opposite direction toward the goal posts. Otto's arm was already in motion to throw the ball toward the corner, but amazingly he changed the direction of his throw without a hitch and passed to Dante for a touchdown. Otto came skipping off the field, yelling, "Did you see what that crazy sonnovagun just did?"

Lavelli, incidentally, was one of the five players—including Groza, Houston, Gene Fekete and George Cheroke—who were still eligible to play football at Ohio State when they signed with the Browns. Their decision to forgo this eligibility stirred another fuss at the university and, among other things, won me more accusations of sabotaging the school's football program. That was ridiculous. Those players had been through a war, they were older and their outlooks had changed totally from the days when they were fulltime collegians. Mine had, too, and I knew what war did to a person. Lavelli, for example, had been through the Battle of the Bulge and had fought at Bastogne, where he had seen row after row of decaying corpses when he finally walked out of that besieged city, Groza had participated in the bloody invasion of Okinawa and was earmarked for the invasion of Japan when the war ended. Life was completely different for them now, and college football no longer held the same allure it had had a few years before, when they were eighteen years old.

Every one of those Ohio State players eventually returned to the university and received his degree, however, a promise I exacted from them whenever we signed a contract. I even withheld some of their salary for them so they would have enough to pay their college bills. Even with their salaries and their GI benefits, it wasn't always easy for some of them to subsist because some had families. Lavelli, for example, used to play on pickup basketball teams several nights a week to supplement his income and pay for his college education.

This was the first layer of the Cleveland Browns then, a solid base of championship caliber. We added a second and third layer in 1947 and 1948 with players like Horace Gillom, Alex Agase, Dub Jones, Tom James, Chubby Grigg, Tony Adamle, Bob Gaudio, Bob Cowan and Ara Parseghian, and after that we were almost unstoppable. Such talent enabled us not only to hone old techniques to perfection, but to develop new ideas and innovations.

Dub Jones is a good example. With two ends like Lavelli and Speedie, I felt that our passing game could be even more effective if we got a third receiver into the play because it meant more pressure on the defense—no defense could effectively concentrate on three great receivers. I wanted to put that third man outside the tight end, either in a standing position or in motion as a halfback, and then occasionally I could allow him to stay as a running back to confuse the defenses further. I saw enough of Dub in his two years playing for the Miami Seahawks and the AAC Brooklyn Dodgers to know that he was the ideal man for this new concept, and he became the prototype of a new position in pro football—the flanker.

Getting Dub was one of the best trades I ever made, because we got him from the Dodgers, *plus* $25,000 for the rights to Bob Chappius, a great single wing tailback at Michigan who never really became successful in professional football. We had drafted Chappius because he had been the best player available at the time and we were looking for a quarterback eventually to replace Otto Graham, but he wasn't a sure thing by any means.

Branch Rickey, who was president of the football Dodgers as well, became interested in Chappius through his good friend Ray Fisher, the baseball coach at Michigan, who talked him into believing he really needed Bob after we had drafted him. When Branch asked about acquiring his rights, I told him we'd take Dub Jones and $25,000, and he snapped at the deal. That was one of the few times such a large amount of money had ever been involved in a football trade, but because of his baseball background, Mr. Rickey was used to such transactions.

Dub, another of our players who belongs in the Hall of Fame, had exceptional speed and was very tall, making him a great target for Otto's passing. He could run post patterns without ever getting tired, and no defensive back could cover him man-for-man. Dub was very scientific about developing his moves in a pass pattern. He worked to set up a defender, to force him to turn the wrong way or cross his feet—and then he'd go the other way. When Dub told Otto he was ready, we believed him and had Otto throw to him. Few realized, too, that he had a very strong throwing arm, but when he warmed up, he could throw a football great distances. It is easy to see where his son, Bert, the great young quarterback of the Baltimore Colts, who used to visit our training camps as a wee boy, got such great athletic skills and competitive instincts. He is every bit his father's son and just as fine a person as his dad.

Dub was a good example of a player who bothered me enough as an opponent to make me want him playing for my team. Two other players, Darrell Palmer and Chubby Grigg, came to us under similar circumstances, and they also rank among the best defensive players we ever had. Chubby had played with the Chicago Rockets in 1947, and Darrell with the AAC New York Yankees before we got him in 1949. Grigg was a ponderous man, the first truly big man to be quick and agile enough to control the middle of a line. He was no jolly fat man, though some players said he just absorbed a runner in his bulk and squeezed him to the ground. He had his own ways of succeeding. Often he spit tobacco juice in the face of the offensive lineman across from him. If the player took a swing at him, Chubby quickly pointed it out to the official, and the other player was ejected from the game; that gave old Chubby an easier day with a lesser player.

Each year he played for us I promised Chubby a $500 bonus for coming into camp at 275 pounds or less; each year he made the weight when we set him on the scale on the loading dock of the nearby hospital. As soon as he got his bonus, however, he made up for it in a hurry because he had literally starved himself for weeks beforehand to get down to the prescribed weight.

Chubby was also part of a personnel decision that cost us Art Donovan, who later became a great tackle for the Baltimore Colts and is now in the Hall of Fame. As we came toward the end of our 1951 training camp, Grigg and Donovan were battling for a place on our team and were rated about even, so, as was our custom, we talked over the decision in a staff meeting. Weeb Ewbank, our tackle coach, made the decision. Weeb felt he would be more comfortable with experience, and Donovan was a rookie, so we kept Grigg—though the responsibility ultimately was mine. He played well for us, but for only one more year, while Donovan played for thirteen years. I'm sure there are few who remember, though, that it was Chubby, replacing the injured Lou Groza, who kicked five extra points the night we defeated the Philadelphia Eagles, 35–10, in our first NFL game.

Horace Gillom, of course, had played for me at Massillon and with the Ohio State freshman and, after the war, for Jimmy Aiken at the University of Nevada. Jimmy told us after the 1946 season, however, that Horace didn't seem too interested in continuing his education, so we drafted him, and when he joined Groza, it gave us the greatest kicking game in the history of professional football.

Though he gained his reputation as a great punter, Horace, who weighted about 230 pounds, was also a tremendous all-around player and would have been a starter with any other team in professional football. He was our second tight end and for years filled in brilliantly whenever Lavelli or Speedie was injured. When we defeated the Dodgers, 13-12, in 1947, it was Gillom who broke through and blocked the extra point to prevent the tie game.

Gaudio and Adamle had also played for me at Ohio State, and both made wonderful contributions to the Browns. Gaudio, a technically perfect offensive guard, came from a wealthy construction business family in Cleveland and quickly became a favorite of Abe Gibron and some other offensive linesmen who always made sure that Bob had his Cadillac available so they could be seen riding around in style.

Adamle, who became team captain after Lou Saban retired, was our third fullback. One of the toughest and most hard-nosed players I've ever seen, he could barely walk on a sprained ankle after a game in San Francisco in 1951, but the next Sunday in Los Angeles he played one of the finest games I've ever seen by any linebacker. For all his toughness, though, he would later bring great sensitivity, skill and understanding to his medical practice.

Adamle joined Alex Agase on our linebacker squad, and when we lined them up with Saban, Willis and, on occasion, Humble and Motley, no one had a better corps. Agase, whom I had seen play in college and had obtained from the Chicago Rockets, was a particularly great help to us because of his diagnostic ability—it was so keen he could tell when a guard was going to pull out and in what direction he was going and would move toward the play before it even got started. To take one example, after we joined the NFL in 1950, we discovered from our films that Tommy Thompson, the Philadelphia Eagles' quarterback, positioned his feet a certain way every time he was going to drop back and pass. Alex just watched for it, raised his arm to alert our secondary every time he saw it and called for the pass rush.

He was not only a great diagnostician but a fierce tackler and a tenacious pass defender. When Tommy Thompson, no relation to the Eagles' Tommy Thompson, made our team as a rookie linebacker from William and Mary in 1949—the only rookie to do so that year—he and Agase formed a duo that our receivers called Hump Back Ridge because it was worth their lives to try to run through that area, even in practice. Alex also earned the nickname the Hook because he once wore a black cast on his arm and used it to hook players around the helmet enough to knock them off stride and make them aware of him. Even in practice, our receivers had to fight their way past Hump Back Ridge, and every so often there was a little battle because they were so proud they wouldn't concede a pass completion even to their own teammates.

Tom James came to us in 1948 and became an all-pro for years in our defensive secondary. He was also valuable as the holder for Lou Groza's kicks—Lou got so used to him that when Tom finally retired after the 1955 season, he just couldn't kick as effectively until he found a suitable replacement in Ken Konz. James was another of my Massillon–Ohio State players, and I've always had a special feeling for him. I knew his family very well when I coached at Massillon, and later he was a pallbearer at the funeral of both my mother and my wife Katy. I tried to get him for our 1946 team, but he had returned to Ohio State to play another season, then joined the Detroit Lions in 1947. That year Tommy broke his arm playing for the Lions, and when I met him at a New Year's Eve party in Massillon, his arm was still in a sling.

"Why didn't you contact me?" I asked him when he told me what had happened.

"I didn't know whether you wanted me," he said.

"Well, if you get your release from the Lions, I want you to come to our training camp," I told him most emphatically, and later that year he joined us at Bowling Green after the Lions placed him on waivers and none of the National League teams claimed him.

In 1947 Jim Dewar, Bob Cowan and Billy Boedecker joined us and gave us some tremendous speed in our backfield. Dewar lasted only a year because of a knee injury, but Cowan, whom we called the Sprinter because of his 9.6 time in the 100-yard dash, was a very effective back when we turned him loose as a receiver. Boedecker was one the most reckless runners who ever played for us and a terror when he ran back kicks. He would literally frighten an opposing kicking team because of his speed and wild abandon.

Also in that group was Ara Parseghian. He was a tough, chunky, bouncing type of runner, very strong, very physical and very determined. He had been drafted by the Pittsburgh Steelers after finishing his career at Miami University, my alma mater, but had turned down their offer, and stayed with us for two years, absorbing as much as he could. John Brickels, who later became athletic director at Miami, was instrumental in getting him interested in coaching, and when the opportunity arose, Ara cut short his playing career to start what became his life's work. Whenever we were interested in any of his players at Miami, Northwestern or Notre Dame, Ara would tell us straight out whether the boy could play, and he was never wrong. He replaced me as a member of Miami's board of trustees in 1978 after my nine-year term expired, and though his career is ended now, he certainly ranks as one of college football's greatest head coaches ever.

This new young group of backs blended well with Motley and with Edgar Jones. Edgar, who had earned the nickname Special Delivery at Pitt because of his race-horse style of running, was one of the finest clutch players we ever had. He was a chunky guy, at 212 pounds, and a "leaded runner" who ran with a low center of gravity, with his weight shifted forward, so it was difficult for a tackler to bring him down. He had been a fine passer as a single wing tailback at Pitt, and every so often during a game he'd get off the bench and begin loosening his arm, indicating to me that he wanted to go in and throw some passes. I'd look over at him, he'd nod and I would motion for him to sit down. I think he was hurt that we never gave him a chance to show his passing skill, but it never deterred him one bit from running with the football.

Edgar was such a good all-around athlete, incidentally, that he even pitched a few games for the Cleveland Indians while playing for us. He made the mistake, however, of trying that as a bargaining wedge when negotiating a contract. He never had a chance. I knew from Bill Veeck, the Indians' president and a good friend, exactly what chances he had for a major-league baseball career. Veeck, the master promoter, had allowed him to pitch as a gate attraction for his club, and while he was a good pitcher, Edgar was correct in investing his sports career with us.

Those were my players. You can be sure I was just as careful selecting my coaching staff. I always equated forming a coaching staff with working in a bank. You can hire people and teach them to add and divide, but you can't teach them to be honest. The techniques and intricacies of football come with experience, but the loyalties and the ability to survive the pressures of the game must be inherent. Working with my assistants was no different from working with our players. In both cases, it meant dealing successfully with people.

One of my first needs in 1946 was to hire someone who had had some professional football experience, so I brought in my friend Bill Edwards, who had been head coach of the Detroit Lions in 1941. I also wanted someone well schooled in our particular football principles and hired Fritz Heisler, who had been with me at Massillon and Ohio State. John Brickels was with me already, of course; I brought Blanton Collier and Bob Voights from Great Lakes; and for a time we had Red Conkright, who had been an assistant with the Rams. Voights left a year later to become a very successful coach at Northwestern, and Edwards left in 1949 for the head coaching job at Vanderbilt.

Our coaches became the first in professional football ever to work year-round. There was no dignity, I felt, in having a man coach our offensive line for six months and then sell automobiles for six months. This was part of my plan to make our team as collegiate as possible. In college the assistant coaches are full-time employees of the university, and they spend all of their off-season working on football. We did the same thing. Through films, each coach graded and evaluated the players under his control; then we graded and evaluated everything we did as a team. We found which plays worked and why others failed, and each coach was given the opportunity to offer creative input into every aspect of our football. We knew which players we could trade and whom we wanted to acquire. When it came time to discuss player contracts, I knew exactly who deserved a raise and had the data to back up our money offers. Our coaches also scouted spring football practice at the colleges. All that work kept them busy until it was time for their six-week vacation in the summer, and then training camp opened. This long period of evaluation and preparation was a key factor in our success each year because we never allowed our coaches or our players to fall into any ruts or continue faulty football techniques.

A team is made up of more than just football people, however. One of the most delightful men we hired that first season was Morrie Kono, our equipment manager. He came to our Bowling Green training site looking for a job on the recommendation of my friend Jackie Ranen, who had once lived in the same Cleveland orphanage as Morrie.

"What do you know about equipment and clothing?" I asked him.

"I just finished six years at the quartermaster depot near Columbus," he told me. "For the first three and a half years I handed it out; for the next two and a half, I took it all back."

Morrie, who also trained our Bengals' equipment manager, Tom Gray, was the master of the quick quip and the kind of person every team needs because he often created light moments and gave everyone a lift. Our players loved him and often made him the good-natured butt of their pranks, though Morrie gave as good as he got. He did everything for them, from baby-sitting their children to cooking their meals, because the Browns were his life.

When Morrie applied for the job, the only person working with our equipment was Tommy Flynn, a dwarf who had been hired by George Bird, our band and entertainment director, to walk the sidelines as "Brownie," our team symbol. After I had hired Morrie, I sent him to our equipment room, where boxes of new gear were waiting to be opened. He later told me with amusement that when he walked into the room, he had seen this little guy leaning over a huge box of pads abruptly lose his balance and fall upside down into the box. Later Morrie used to delight in tossing a helmet to Tommy, which simply knocked him down.

In training camp, and during our weekly practices, we often needed someone to fill in on one of the teams during our drills. We used no live tackling, so the players who were supposed to simulate the opposition all had dummies in front of them to give them a target for blocking purposes. Someone had to hold each of the dummies, however. At such times I'd say, "Morrie, get in there." He'd look at me as if I were sending him to the executioner because those players took an extra delight in really laying into his dummy and sending it and Morrie flying.

Before every practice our team assembled in full uniform in our classroom so I could talk to them about the day's work on the field. One day in training camp I was set to enter the classroom when I heard someone talking to the team who sounded an awful lot like me. It was Morrie. He was in front of the group giving them a lecture with the same phrases and word emphases I always used, and our players were breaking up. When I walked in, he looked at me a bit surprised, but not too shocked to say, "Okay, Paul, they're all yours now."

Morrie was the man I went to whenever I wanted anything done around our clubhouse. I never laid claim to being mechanically inclined, so I'd always say, "Fix it, Morrie . . . Morrie, fix it." We were in Chicago for a game once on a hot late-summer afternoon, but the heater in our dressing room was broken and running full blast, and the room was stifling.

"Morrie, fix it," I said to him, so he whacked it a few times with a hammer. After he had given it a half dozen blows, I said, "Okay, Morrie, that's fine." Some of the players around me knew he hadn't done anything, but as far as I was concerned, everything was all right. Pretty soon they were after him with all kinds of ridiculous requests, always saying, "Morrie, fix it."

One day during our film sessions at our League Park practice site the electricity went off.

"Fix it, Morrie," I called.

"Don't worry, Paul," he said. "It's a fuse. I'll go outside to the fuse box and put in a new one."

It had been raining outside, however, and there was a huge puddle of water under the fuse box. Morrie wasn't about to stand in it and change a fuse, yet he knew I expected the electricity to be turned back on as quickly as possible. Across the street from our practice field was John's Bar, so Morrie walked in and, looking around, saw four derelicts sitting on the stools.

"Who wants to make a couple of bucks?" he asked, and he was almost run over as all four charged him.

Morrie took one of them back across the street, and standing clear of the water himself, he let this poor guy stand in the puddle and change the fuse. I didn't know anything about it at the time, and I just figured he had done a great job, which, in his own way, he had.

One more person I should mention: A few years after Morrie joined us, I hired Leo Murphy, who had been with the AAC's New York Yankees football team, as our trainer. The two of them, Morrie and Leo, have been my loyal friends under all kinds of circumstances ever since.

So have nearly all those great players who helped bring the Browns to prominence. Hundreds of games and decades later, the times we spent together are no less vivid than in those years when we translated a flyer and a fancy into achievements which became a remarkable chapter in professional football history.

SEVEN

"The Paul Brown System"

THANKS TO THOSE PLAYERS AND coaches we had hired, our efficient front office and the fact that I had been privileged to prepare myself for an advanced look at T formation football during my two years at Great Lakes, the Cleveland Browns were successful from the very beginning. The success of the Browns soon had people talking about a "Paul Brown system," but I never laid claim to any such thing. I suppose they referred to our general philosophy encompassing such things as our practice procedures, sending in the plays with messenger guards and our belief in a wide-open offense, particularly in our passing game. Whatever the reference, many of the principles are in use today. For the last several years I have been able to look at the rosters of the coaching staffs in the NFL and count some thirty-five or forty of my former staff members or players who are now coaching. I take a great deal of satisfaction from this.

I've always felt that underlying any football system there must be a philosophy, a series of basic beliefs that set the tone for the players who make all of the game's technical aspects come alive. As for my own, it is really nothing more than those things I believe in myself, the bottom line of everything that is necessary to be successful in life, as well as in football.

The proper player-coach relationship is the first commandment in my philosophy of football, and when I was coach, I always put it into action on the very first day of training camp, which is the most important time a team spends together during the entire season. We never got involved in technical football matters until everyone understood what we expected of him off the field, in practice, in the locker room and in a game. My first lecture set the tone. It lasted about two hours and never varied much from year to year. In it, I told our team such things as:

"Starting a football season is a state of mind and heart as well as a physical experience. Don't ever get the idea that I'm trying to psych you with this talk. I believe in every word and everything I say. You veterans have heard these lectures many times, but when you get so that you can't pay attention or believe in it anymore, you're getting ripe, and you know what the next step is—plop! . . .

"We start all over—from the very beginning every year. It's a new season—nothing is taken for granted. Everyone starts equally, rookies and veterans alike. We figure that if you start a new house with a narrow foundation you can go only so high. We try to build a broad foundation. . . .

"Tomorrow it may be hot, and we'll practice. Later there will be snow, and we'll practice. It may be raining buckets, and we'll practice. Soon you'll accept this as a way of life. It's just part of our football. . . .

"My coaches are my partners, not assistant coaches. What they know, I will know. We have nothing to do at night but talk and think about you. Call us by our first names. We're all good friends—a happy family. We have just one objective—to win. And remember, if you're cut from the squad, be a man about it, and don't take it personally. We can't keep everybody. . . .

"Now for the training regulations. Beginning right now, you're in training for this football team. We want you to reflect a special image in pro football. We want you to be eager, enthusiastic—nothing more than a glorified collegiate team, not a bunch of tired old pros. . . .

"Keep your wives out of our football. Don't have your wife talk football with other wives. It breeds trouble. For example, I don't want one wife of a receiver complaining to the wife of the quarterback that her husband is being overlooked on pass plays. . . .

"We don't want thug football players. I'll take my players high-class, cold, deadly, smart, hard-hitting and hard-running. Always remember, when you meet an obnoxious football player, the meanest thing you can do to him is to beat him.

They can play dirty, call you names, violate the rules. Just beat 'em. They understand that more than anything. . . .

"We want to keep this one of the great football teams of all times, a team you'll be proud to say years from now that you played on. I don't want you to play for your paycheck. I want you to play for the sheer desire of licking somebody. You must sacrifice something to get to the top. That's why we ask you to train. I call it paying the price. . . ."

As the times changed, I altered some of the substance of my remarks to cover the problems of the day. At Cincinnati, when alcohol and drugs had begun to infect our young people, I let our players know that I could recognize these problems. We actually had a federal narcotics agent brief our staff on the entire spectrum of drugs. The player who reported in the morning wearing dark glasses wasn't too hard to figure out! Our rules were not for moral reasons. They were simply for the player's own good and for the welfare of our team, to give us the best possible chance of winning.

I never considered a training camp oppressive. Some people claimed players were treated like small children and given restrictions which were unnatural for grown men, but our training camps were never run that way. I always strived to make life as natural and as pleasant as possible during those few summer weeks. In our earlier years, many pro football teams held their camps in remote areas of the country, and players were supposed to work hard, get plenty of fresh air, sunshine and bed rest and live in what amounted to a monastic existence in order to build their stamina for the upcoming season. I agreed with the health aspects, but I thought that putting a group of men in the wilderness, cutting them off from their families, was a bit unnatural and unfair to them and their families. We sent our players home every weekend after a Saturday practice or preseason game, and they didn't have to report back until Sunday night. I wanted them to keep their families intact, to spend time with their wives and children. Sometimes my wife lived at camp with me because I felt that a woman's presence lent a certain tone to this kind of existence, and our coaches usually had their wives come and visit on Wednesday and join us for dinner. The coaches could also go home on weekends.

For years, the highlight of our camp was the family picnic, in which everyone's family participated. We had games for the kids—Marion Motley's little boys took most of the prizes.

I always kept a dish of candy on my desk and a few dimes in my top drawer for the Coke machine, and all the kids knew where to find them. All this was an effort on my part to show the players and their wives that we valued their friendship. It also helped foster a warm feeling within the team.

In addition, we wanted our players to work in good surroundings, and our three professional training camps typified what I considered the right atmosphere in which to train. We started at Bowling Green University in 1946, a picturesque, mid-American campus within reasonable driving distance from any place in Ohio; that meant the players who lived in the state had access to their families. We housed our players in the Alpha Xi Delta sorority house and heard some good-natured ribbing about it, of course, but it was a lovely building. A few years later we moved our training site to Hiram College, a tiny school outside Cleveland, and when I started the Bengals, I chose Wilmington College because I had remembered playing college baseball there, and it still appealed to me.

In training camp we constantly emphasized doing everything one proper and precise way, from how we assembled in the classroom and took calisthenics to our routine warm-up drill to how each play had to be run. Nothing was ever hurried because we wanted to make sure we got it right. In this way, the discipline and the tenor of our team were established at an early date.

In every camp I applied the basic laws of learning—seeing, hearing, writing, then doing again and again. All the players diagrammed the complete play and wrote their individual assignments in detail in their playbooks. We wanted them to know the play's complete concept, not just their individual parts. We checked those playbooks, too, and graded the players on their accuracy. They were then tested on Sunday by having to draw up the entire play. I usually told them on Thursday what plays the test would cover, and they always were from among those offensive plays or defenses we had taken on during the week. Most of the rookies had never been required to do this before, and they had to do some intense studying to pass and have a chance to survive. Over the years the veterans became used to it. Many thought it was an elementary-school approach, but to this day those players can recite the dicta that we laid down, from simple calisthenics to the most complex play. Our classroom procedures were the very basis of our football system.

When we went onto the practice field to put our offense together, we always took on one running play in the morning and one pass play in the afternoon and followed another principle: The more carefully these basic plays were presented, the better a team's entire structure would be. The first play was a basic handoff, following the old axiom that the best play in football is straight ahead. It established the importance of the offensive line charge, of blowing people out, and set the tone for our total offensive development. Our second running play was the off-tackle play, or almost straight ahead, which illustrated the offensive line charge with more people involved. Our third was the end run, or quick flip, which emphasized my belief that the quickest end run was the best end run. Our first pass play always utilized full protection for the quarterback, which established the blocking of the backs as well as the linemen. The second involved one flaring back, and the third used both backs as receivers.

The offense continued to grow on this daily basis. Starting the third week, we began our work on special teams in the mornings, always beginning with the punt, the most important play in football. We never tried to develop an extensive offense for the first preseason game. We were much more interested in how carefully we taught these few things, which would lay the groundwork for the entire season.

Meanwhile, we were developing our defense in the same meticulous day-by-day manner. Each offensive play that we took on mirrored the defense that we wanted to teach. This entire working schedule was laid out by the coaching staff before we went to camp, and I knew in advance what we would do every day of our training season.

I always gave the players the next day's plans at our evening team meeting. The offense and defense would then be broken into their respective groups, and the overall presentation given to each unit, after which the groups would split into still smaller units to work on the details. We used training films for this and put it all together the next day on the practice field. Two plays a day don't seem like much, but it didn't take long for some players to buckle under the accumulated mental burden. That's why we placed so much emphasis on the more intelligent athlete.

We never scrimmaged during the first two weeks of training camp. I always felt it took that long to condition the human body for the rigors of football. Even then, our first scrimmage was very controlled. Great emphasis was placed on avoiding injury because when a player was hurt, it set back our entire program.

Cutting a player was the toughest part of coaching for me. I saw more than my share of tears and shed some myself, particularly with the players who had been with me for many years. We always cut players as soon as we were sure they couldn't make our team. Some coaches like to keep such players around for "working numbers," but I wanted our coaching staff to expend its efforts on the people who were going to be playing.

I talked to nearly every player we released, usually with the assistant who had coached him sitting in. The two of us then tried to explain the reasons for the decision. Sometimes I told a rookie who was being cut, "If you were my son, I'd tell you to get on with your life's work. This could become a blind alley for you. You'll hang on for a year on some cab squad, and that's all. You're bright, you have the ability and you've got a college education. You've also had the experience of finding out what pro football is like. We hope that you enjoyed the experience and satisfied yourself."

Invariably the intelligent ones did; the others were sometimes more difficult to convince and usually disappeared after a season or two on another team as a fringe player.

When we made our final cut the week before the opening game, however, we operated a little differently. If we had room for two or three of five players competing for the final spots on our team, each of the players was told to come to our office at the stadium on Tuesday morning to pick up an envelope that had either their final paycheck and ticket home or a short note telling them they had made the team. I talked to all these players before making the final judgments, thanked them for their efforts and said good-bye in case I did not see them again. We did this, I explained, because we would be so busy preparing for the opening game that we had to work without interruption. I think the players understood.

Although the philosophical aspects were most important, the game's technical points also intrigued me. In formulating our technical football, I started with the solid offensive blocker; I never was a brush-block and scramble-block advocate. I always felt that you could teach the dessert easier than the meat and potatoes, and since the running game is the meat and potatoes of every offense, I favored linemen who were exceptional run blockers. I never liked the big, blubbery guy who could get back on two quick feet and absorb the pass rusher but who never had much ability for blasting out some-one on run blocking.

We wanted the "blow 'em out" run type of linemen be-cause they were important for the success of our fullbacks, and from my earliest days in coaching I always believed that the successful use of the fullback in any offense is the start-ing point in controlling a defense; otherwise, they spread out and come after your passer from good rushing angles. These basic technical aspects have always been a part of my foot-ball theory, and when I went to Great Lakes, I experimented with them as well as with anything else that intrigued me. For two seasons I worked in what amounted to a football laboratory. What emerged was a system of technical football that I then combined in Cleveland with my teaching philoso-phy, notebook and classroom work, the practice of grading films in the off-season and my never-changing belief in leav-ing as little to chance as possible. I suppose that all these ele-ments combined are what people referred to as the so-called Paul Brown system.

Over the years I was often asked about the key elements in our technical football, and one of the first things I pointed out was that our teams were always fortunate to have big, ex-ceptional fullbacks like Motley, Curley Morrison, Chick Jagade, Ed Modzelewski and Jim Brown. We also placed a special emphasis on the quick flip and run type of play, fea-turing halfbacks such as Dub Jones, Bobby Mitchell, Chet Hanulak, Bob Cowan and Billy Reynolds. We had many vari-ations of the play, but regardless of what play we used, we had a point of not locking ourselves into running first and es-tablishing a pass offense later, or vice versa. Our theory was: Move the ball, any old style.

I suppose the play that got us the most notice was the draw play. The play's origin was a total accident. During a 1946 game Motley and Graham collided trying to run a trap play on a muddy field. The collision created a broken play, and Otto, in desperation, seeing the linemen charging in on him, just handed the ball to Marion as they stood next to each other. The opposing linemen simply ran past Motley, and he took off for a big gain. We didn't think much of it at the time, but looking at the game films, Otto said, "I think that could become a play," so we developed the blocking assignments and the techniques which went with it. At first we called it a pick, but since that word was also part of the passing terminology, I changed the name to draw, because we wanted our offensive linemen to visualize it as drawing in the pass rushers. Then, after our play-off victory over the New York Giants in 1950, we added the quarterback draw using the same principles, because New York's defense had created some natural openings when their middle linebacker and defensive ends backpedaled on passing situations. Otto had seen them and, being an exceptional runner, had made some good gains in key situations. We incorporated the play into our game plan for the championship game against Los Angeles the following week, and it became a key to our final drive that gave us the victory. These draw plays have always been extremely effective in cooling off a pass rush, and it is important to note a distinction: a trap play cools off one man, a combination trap-draw cools off two, but a total draw slows down the entire defensive line.

One area where I had to change my beliefs in a hurry when I entered professional football was in the use of the forward pass from any point on the field. When we played the Brooklyn Dodgers in our first exhibition game in Akron, I tried to run the ball down their throats, but Glenn Dobbs put the Dodgers ahead by three touchdowns with his passing. I had never run into a passing offense like that before, and I became convinced, even before the first half had ended, that a team could not succeed in pro football by concentrating too heavily on the running game to the near exclusion of the passing attack.

It was not a hard adjustment for me to make, however, because I had always believed in the effectiveness of a good passing game. We soon became the foremost exponent of the forward pass, and I think we were more successful with it than any team in pro football during the ten years we were champions. Otto Graham, of course, was a big reason for that success because he was such a brilliant passer. Everyone marveled that Otto could work so well with our receivers, but he had learned to anticipate their movements by watching their shoulders. The intricate timing came from their working together for hours after the team had finished practicing each day. I always maintained that a receiver getting open wasn't just a matter of speed, but a matter of technique and knowing how.

When zone defenses became popular against us because no one could consistently handle Lavelli, Speedie or Dub Jones man-for-man, we developed new elements in our passing game. For example, we sent Otto rolling out to the right with a convoy of blockers. We called this roll-out, and when we did it to the weak side of our formation, we called it a waggle. In either case, Otto had the option of running or throwing the ball, utilizing his linemen as blockers. Again, his exceptional running and split-second judgment made these plays so effective. Later, when George Ratterman or Milt Plum was at quarterback, we had to take the plays out because neither player was mobile enough.

It is interesting to note that, years later, when the Kansas City Chiefs played in the early Super Bowls, the same plays reappeared under the name of a floating pocket or the offense of the seventies. It was nothing new.

Though I placed great emphasis on perfecting our offense, I never underestimated the importance of defense. The basis of any defense is how well a team can tackle, and we worked on it every day with the routine warm-up drill I described earlier, in which the players made physical contact with other bodies and the ground. When the game opened, we felt we could tell how well our defense was going to play if we saw gang-tackling on the first plays. If just one man tried to make the tackle and the rest watched, or the runner was hit and slithered for three or four additional yards, then we knew it might be a long afternoon. Another tip-off was in our defensive line charge. If our linemen exploded across the line of scrimmage and blew aside the opposition's offensive line, we knew it would be our day, but if we saw them patty-caking and "playing piano," as we called it, then we were in trouble. These things happened to us just as they can happen to any good team; you have to pay a physical price to dominate another team, and players, without meaning to, sometimes forget that.

In our early years in professional football we used the five-man line, but then we saw that by dropping Bill Willis off a few yards, we had a big advantage in getting him to the play's point of attack. This tactic became the forerunner of the 4-3 defense. Then, as defense became more sophisticated, we used blitzing linebackers—shooters, we called them—and added loops and slants and other stunts that made the Browns one of pro football's best defensive teams. This fact was often overlooked because of our open offense, but in our first dozen seasons we finished first in overall defense five times and second five times.

I was involved in our defensive game plan, though I left much of the detail to our defensive coaches. I remember one game in which I must have surprised Blanton Collier with my thoughts. It was against the New York Yankees, and he was showing me his plans for our goal line defense, in particular the options for covering Buddy Young, a "water bug" back, who was often used as a man-in-motion when the Yankees were inside the five-yard line.

"We can cover him a couple of different ways," Collier said to me, showing me his diagrams. "What do you think?"

I thought for a moment, and knowing that Buddy was not a great pass receiver and that the Yankees were often reluctant to throw to him in key situations, I told him, "The first time he goes into motion, let's not cover him at all. I don't think they want to throw to him, and it might confuse their offensive plans."

Blanton just looked at me when I said that because it seemed unthinkable not to cover a potential pass receiver at the goal line. The first time the Yankees got close to our goal line and sent Buddy into motion, however, they did not throw to him, though he was left uncovered. Of course, their coaches spotted this and, in subsequent plays, did try to throw to him, but each time we had him well covered. They were determined to catch us again, but we never gave them another chance. That's what I mean by mixing up coverages and alignments—never establish a patern, even to the point of doing something two plays in a row.

As for the special teams, I've already mentioned how important the kicking game was to us. I knew there were just so many times an offense had a chance to score, and I wanted to take advantage of every possible opportunity. If we couldn't get a touchdown, then three points were better than none and could spell the difference between victory and defeat. Lou Groza won games time after time for us because the opposition had no one to match him. In fact, after we had been in the NFL for a short time, George Halas noted with a sigh that when a team fought its heart out to get deep into our territory and was stopped, we sent out Horace Gillom, and he kicked the ball so far and high that it ended up back where it began. However, if the Browns drove past midfield and were stopped, instead of bringing out a punter, like most teams, we put Lou on the field, and he got three points with a field goal.

One of the reasons I particularly enjoyed pro football was that for the first time in my life, I was able to put all this together—the offense, the defense, the special teams—and take the time to refine it and develop new ideas because for the first time football was a full-time business. I liked having enough time to immerse myself in teaching, classroom work, the film studies and all that went with our football, as well as having the players' total attention and concentration all day and all season long. It was a full-time job for them, too.

I also encouraged full participation from the players and never disdained anyone's ideas. Our game plans were the work of many different people, including the players.

There were no great mysteries attached to our success. We were meticulous in all our preparations, and we even practiced how to practice. I took one complete session to show our players exactly how and where they should go on the practice field, and those routines remained the same whether it was a practice day or a game day. Everyone ran onto the field together each day. After calisthenics, each unit went to the same spot to go through its individual drills, and on Sundays before a game, that's where the players did their individual warm-ups. We even started our practices at one o'clock every afternoon, the scheduled time for Sunday's kickoff. I felt that our bodies became conditioned to this kind of routine and that a team played as it practiced.

As a coach I never believed in working into the wee hours of the night. I personally functioned and thought more clearly when I was well rested, and I think a coaching staff does, too. I've heard some professional coaches brag about working eighteen and twenty hours a day, sleeping on cots in their offices, and I've always wondered just how much they really accomplish during all those hours. They must feel insecure because I don't know any of them who has ever won a world championship.

During our years in Cleveland and Cincinnati we spent less time on the practice field than any team in football. Following a Sunday game in Cleveland everyone took Monday off because we never received our films until Tuesday. So every Monday Katy and I used to drive down to Massillon to visit our parents. All the coaches worked on Tuesday, but I tried to make sure that every coach had dinner at home with his family that night. Our players reported on Wednesday for film work and loosened up with touch-tackle games. Sometimes it seemed to me that they fought harder in those games than on Sunday! We used to match big guys against big guys and fast guys against fast guys. I honestly think in those days our players looked forward to practice, and it was a rare day when the practices weren't laced with enthusiasm, fun and vigor. There were times when I literally had to chase them off the field in the afternoon.

The one area of our football that drew a special amount of public attention was our play-calling and the use of messenger guards to shuttle the plays to our quarterbacks. On the basis of the number of victories and champsionships we won, it was a sound and very successful system, and today most of the NFL's coaches use it. Back then, though, we were belittled, and our quarterbacks, particularly Otto Graham, ridiculed for being something less than complete players. Much of this nonsense was based on ignorance, deliberate or otherwise, of how our play-calling system really worked and on sour grapes over our great successes. I know some coaches really wanted to adopt it but shied away at the time because they did not want to assume the responsibility. Others, because of their nonquarterback background, did not feel qualified. Ironically, I never understood why there was no criticism of defensive signals' being called from the sidelines. This was a commond practice for most teams for many years.

All this had nothing to do with questioning my quarterbacks' intelligence, nor was I ever worried about building character and initiative, two other criticisms that were tossed at us. I cared about winning games—period—and I stand on this record. We were a team, coaches and players together, and if we won, that's all that mattered. If we lost, then we went down together, and I never respected any quarterback who felt the system kept him from looking like the great leader. A quarterback is an important cog in the machine, but still a cog, and I wanted to give him all the help possible. I knew no quarterback ever worked as hard preparing for a game as our coaching staff did.

After he retired, Otto went through a period of being peppered with questions about having to work under the system, and he finally made some intemperate remarks for which he later was sorry. When he became head coach at the Coast Guard Academy, one of the first things he told me was: "Now I know why you called the plays." I know that Otto did not always like the system when he played for me, but he understood my reasons and appreciated the success. Winning makes believers of us all.

In professional football the substitution rules were more liberal in later years, and I chose the guards as messengers because they did not have to handle the ball. The last person I would have picked was another quarterback—and any coach who has tried that system would agree. We even used the messanger guards in practice, with me standing about ten yards away and sending the play to the huddle, so that everything could be close to game conditions.

In one game during the early fifties George Ratterman was playing quarterback, and I sent in a play with Lin Houston. When he relayed it, George, who never missed an opportunity for a joke, said to him, "I don't like that one. Go tell him I want another."

Lin was stunned for a moment and actually ran a couple of steps toward the sidelines before he stopped, realized what Ratterman had just said and came back to the huddle. "You go tell him yourself," he told Ratterman. Over on the sidelines I saw the players in the huddle laughing, but I had no idea what was so funny.

In another game, with a time-out on the field, I decided to send the play to the huddle with Morrie Kono, our equipment man. It was a pass play with some special terminology that was familiar to our guards, but a bit strange to Morrie.

"Now make sure you have it correct," I told him, and he repeated it before leaving the sideline.

All the way out to the huddle he repeated the play, and I thought nothing of it until after the game, when he told me, "I was about five yards from the huddle when Ratterman yelled at me, 'What the hell are you doing out here?' I was so flustered that I forgot what I was supposed to say.

" 'Why did you yell at me?' I said to Ratterman. 'You made me forget the play.'

" 'Tell me what you remember,' Ratterman said."

Morrie recalled the first couple of words, and Ratterman

said, "Okay, I got it," and he reconstructed it perfectly because the quarterbacks always knew our offense so well.

Contrary to common knowledge, I did not call every play on my own—in fact, the key to this system was the information that came from our assistant coaches in the press box and in the end zone. When a play was sent in, everyone knew what it was and what to look for. For example, if we sent in a trap play, the end coach watched the tight end's block on a linebacker, the guard coach watched the guard's trap block, the coach in the end zone looked at the line spacing and double-team block to see if they were effective and I watched the point of attack to judge that play's effectiveness. On a pass, the line coach watched the pass blocking to see where any breakdowns occurred, and why, the end and the backfield coaches watched the progress of the play and how well the quarterback followed the progression of receivers and I watched the overall pattern.

After every play we knew exactly why it had succeeded or failed and if it remained viable for our game plan. A quarterback not seeing all this might abandon an unsuccessful play when only a few adjustments might be needed to make it work, another reason why I preferred to call the plays. I knew just how little a quarterback saw of the overall defensive action once he handed off the ball or was buried by a tackler.

In our final game in 1959 in Philadelphia we had a first down on the Eagles' five-yard line. The play called for Jim Brown to run up the middle, but he was stopped for no gain. In our coaches' booth, Fritz Heisler and Howard Brinker noted that our quarterback, Milt Plum, had not called the Eagles' defense properly, and they told us to use the same play, but to remind Plum to check the defense. He did so the second time, which changed the blocking patterns, and Jim ran into the end zone without being touched. Another quarterback, calling his own plays, probably would have given up on that one.

The greatest myth about the system was that our quarterbacks were forbidden to change a play once it was sent in. That was totally false. Even if our quarterback came to the line of scrimmage with a play we had sent in, he always had the responsibility of calling an audible if he saw that the defensive alignment presented him with a better opportunity. In our early Browns seasons we didn't need much of a checkoff

system because we face only two or three defenses each
game, and we tried to have each play designed so it could
adjust to these minimal defenses. Our quarterbacks called out
the defense at the line of scrimmage, and each player knew
his assignment against it. In later years, as defenses became
more sophisticated, our quarterbacks, in making "check with
me" calls at the line of scrimmage, had their options tailored
in advance.

Sometimes, to loosen things up, my instructions to the messenger guard would be, "Surprise me!" and the quarterback
made his own selection. I don't know how often I was surprised, but with quarterbacks like Otto Graham, Tom
O'Connell, Frank Ryan and Ken Anderson, I never worried
about any mental errors. All our quarterbacks knew that they
were responsible for any call they made on their own,
whether it was a "check with me" or an audible changed at
the line of scrimmage.

Late in a 1951 game against the Chicago Bears, with
Cleveland safely ahead, I sent in a running play. Otto knew
that Dub Jones had already scored five touchdowns and
needed only one more to set a record, so he discarded the
call and selected a pass. Dub scored on the play, and I said
nothing about it because the play had been successful.

Sometimes our players wondered about the plays we sent
in. In a Bengals' game—against the Browns, as a matter of
fact—we were on third down and needed 13 yards for a
touchdown. I sent in a slow draw play, in which the quarterback actually passes the fullback and then hands the ball to
him in a forward motion. I substituted this play for the one I
had received from our coaches in the spotting booth because
from the sidelines I had seen the Browns' defensive line tee-
ing off. The players told me later there were some moans and
groans when the play came into the huddle, but they ran it,
and Booby Clark scooted right through the middle of Cleveland's defense for a touchdown. Our players came laughing
and shouting back to the bench, totally delighted that something a little offbeat had been so successful. There was a
sound reason why it had been called, however, and why it
had worked.

Another new term—taxi, or cab, squad—was born during
our early years in Cleveland. We had rosters of only thirty-
two or thirty-three players in those days and wanted to keep
some extra players around the city in case injuries cut down

our team. McBride and Sherby got them jobs driving taxi-cabs, and we paid them an additional hundred or so dollars a week to practice with us. There were no rules against this, as there are today, and these guys jumped at the opportunity because it meant they still had a chance to play professional football. We never kept more than two or three at a time, but it wasn't too long before other teams copied the idea, and the whole idea of a taxi squad burgeoned to outlandish propor-tions. Some coaches abused it, stashing twenty or more play-ers on a reserve roster. This cut down the availability of players to teams that needed them late in the season, and it wasn't fair to the players because it prevented many from playing for someone else and bettering their careers from.

It wasn't too long before some of our other routines had widespread recognition as well. I continued the policy that I had started back in Massillon of taking my players to a movie on the night before a game and, as I had done at Ohio State, of sequestering them in a hotel when we played at home. This was unheard of in professional football, but I be-lieved that a team should be together before any game, away from the distractions of family and friends, so they could concentrate better on what they had to do the next afternoon. Beyond that, I didn't want anyone talking about seeing any of our players in a bar the night before a game. I didn't con-sider it a hardship; it was for a very few Saturday nights each year, and most of our players welcomed the opportunity to prepare themselves in such an atmosphere.

Many times, when we went to a movie as a team, we got snickers from our opponents, who were out on the town by themselves that night. We usually had the last laugh the next afternoon. Everything we did together was for the purpose of unity and to remind our players that as a team they faced a very serious business the next day. Wives were always wel-come to join us for the movie, but when we returned to our hotel, the players kissed them good-night in the lobby, and they went home.

In the seventies the choice of movies became a bit skimpy for my taste, and when I complained publicly, a local theater owner in Cincinnati provided us with some private showings of decent movies, hoping that we would lessen our criticism.

I believe that we were the first team to travel by chartered plane, and I always made certain our players were served hot meals. Many teams simply handed out box lunches, and some of the players on those teams who later came with us told me they were always impressed with our effort to be first class. We never allowed—and still don't—any beer or liquor to be served on our flights, and it is not because I am against drinking. I know that some people simply cannot handle it, and they're often the ones who will get the extra beers not drunk by other players, and that is when the trouble begins.

When we traveled by plane, we gave written examinations on our game plan, again to emphasize to the players that they were not on a joy ride, but that we were taking them to another city for a very serious business. We marked all the exams, just as we checked and graded all their playbooks, and we knew who was doing the work and who was not. I knew that if a player did not know the answer to one of the exam questions, he would get it from someone around him, and though this might have been a bit deceitful on his part, it still served to make him think about football.

All these practices were part of our regular routine as the seasons rolled by and our successes piled up. All of them, too, were part of that first busy preseason in 1946, when there was still little notoriety about any "Paul Brown system," only great curiosity about a new Cleveland football team in a new league. Putting all my beliefs and ideas together in a totally new atmosphere had made me the most curious of all and, as it turned out, probably the most delighted with the results.

First day of practice at Ohio State, 1941: Paul Brown, Paul Bixler, Fritz Mackey, Carroll Widdoes in background.

Welcome to professional football: team mascot Tommy

Paul Brown

Browns' not game!

Flynn and I witnessing a less-than-spectacular moment in the Brown's history.

Our first AAC championship, 1946: left to right, Lou Rymkus (44), Paul Brown, Tom Colella, Lin Houston, Eddie Ulinski (36) and Edgar Jones (90). *Photo by John Nash.*

Paul Brown and Otto Graham.

Paul Brown and Dante Lavelli.

Celebrating our first NFL championship with Lou Groza in 1950. The arm coming in from the right is Arthur McBride's. *Photo from Pro Football Hall of Fame*

The new owners of the Browns, 1961. In front, left to right: Art Modell, Paul Brown and R. J. Schaefer. Standing: Robert Gries (left) and Dave Jones. *Wide World Photos*

Art Modell and Jim Brown. *Wide World Photos*

Sending in a messenger guard with the Bengals. *Photo by Danny Landwehr*

In front of Paul Brown Tiger Stadium in Massillon, 1979.

EIGHT

All-America Conference: Too Much Cleveland Browns

MY FIRST SEASON IN THE All-America Conference began a very special seventeen-year relationship with the Cleveland Browns. Through several hundred games and thousands of plays, that team was nearly as close to me as my family, and I dedicated myself totally to it. From the very first preseason game victory over the Brooklyn Dodgers, we dealt only in success, a fact that was evident the following weekend when we surprised many people with a 44–0 victory over the Miami Seahawks in the AAC's first regular-season game.

That win set a pattern that soon made us the most feared and respected team in the league. Our wide-open offense, particularly our passing game, became popular everywhere, and despite the attempts of some of the NFL people to downgrade our league's brand of football, the Browns' style of play became highly visible on all levels of football.

Nevertheless, even though we were successful and built the greatest franchise ever, my four years in the All-America Conference were not a particularly bright period in my life, and as the league became ever more beset by problems, it seemed to get darker and darker. It was an incongruous situation because I achieved everything I had ever hoped for in a football sense, yet I never had the security or sense of wellbeing that should have accrued from those achievements. There were great moments and great games during our four years of AAC domination, but I had always built my life on knowing where I was going and how I was going to get there, and the trip through the All-America Conference that ultimately brought me to the National Football League was a perilous journey through half-empty stadiums, bankrupt and ineptly run franchises and very hostile opponents who tried every way possible to beat us down.

Of course, I wasn't alone in this precarious existence, and there is a sense of achievement among those who were a part of this grand experiment that we at least survived—and that in the end we were the ones who became the dominant force when we joined the NFL.

Ironically, our battle cry was struck by Elmer Layden, the NFL's commissioner during the months when the AAC was still being formed. Someone asked if his league planned to play any games against "the new league."

"What new league?" he asked. "Let them go get a football first and then play a game."

A few years later Otto Graham was being honored by Washington's Touchdown Club as the AAC's most valuable player, and when he got up to speak, he held out a football.

"Gentlemen," he said, looking in the direction of George Preston Marshall of the Washington Redskins, who had steadfastly opposed any common scheduling or merger, "we have the football, and we have proven we know what to do with it. But I don't see anyone from the NFL too willing to test us."

The All-America Conference had some excellent teams, in fact, probably the three best teams in professional football when the Browns, the New York Yankees and the San Francisco 49ers were at their peak in 1948. When the league began, it certainly had greater financial resources than the NFL, its millionaire backers including Dan Topping of the Yankees; oilman Jim Breuil of the Buffalo team; Ben Lindheimer, a race-track scion who owned the Los Angeles Dons; the Morabito brothers in San Francisco with their vast lumber empire; Jack Keeshin, a trucking magnate from Chicago who was the Rockets' first owner; Bill Cox and Branch Rickey of the Dodgers; and, of course, McBride and Sherby in Cleveland. The media used to call our meetings "the millionaires' coffee klatch."

Some of those men, such as McBride, Breuil and the Morabitos, had sought NFL franchises before the AAC was formed and were genuinely interested in producing winning teams. Lindheimer was a great sportsman who did not know too much about football, but he was generous almost to a fault with players and money and with helping teams which had trouble surviving. Topping, who, with Del Webb, owned the New York Yankees baseball team, moved his Brooklyn team from the NFL into the AAC only after we agreed to chip in with some players and make his entry strong.

The Yankees, like the teams in Chicago, San Francisco and Brooklyn, built teams differently from the way we did in Cleveland. They stocked their rosters from the excellent service teams at El Toro Marine Base, Fleet City and March Field in California, Randolph Field in Texas and Sampson Naval Training Center in upstate New York. This brought them players such as Buddy Young, Elroy Hirsch, Joe Vetrano, Nate Johnson, Walt Clay and Harvey Johnson. At first, there was plenty of talent to go around for both pro leagues, but when the NFL continued its attitude of ignoring us and simply hoping we would go away, we began winning the battle for college talent. In addition to the players we were signing in Cleveland, the AAC soon attracted such outstanding collegians as Glenn Dobbs, Bob Hoernchmeyer, Frank Albert, Herman Wedemeyer, Len Ford, Bill Daley, Bill Hillenbrand and Burr Baldwin and convinced many former NFL players such as Norm Standlee, Charley O'Rourke, Bob Seymour, Joe Aguirre, Lee Artoe and Bob Nowaskey to sign. It wasn't too long before the NFL realized that it could not afford such parity, and the war for players began in earnest when the two leagues held player drafts in 1947.

The season was less than one game old, however, when I realized Arch Ward's new league was not as sound as he thought. The weak underbelly of the All-America Conference was a lack of football know-how on some teams, which ultimately sapped the financial and player resources of the entire league. Our first weak sister was in Miami, where the Seahawks lived on a dream that a southern team, manned solely by players from southern universities, would succeed. When the team, which was badly financed from the start, ran into an incredible streak of bad weather—three hurricanes on nights it was scheduled to play at home—nothing could be done to keep the franchise solvent.

I discovered all about Miami when we played them in our regular-season opener. Harvey Hester, a jolly, rotund man who was Miami's president and principal owner, met me on the field before the game and said, "I sure do feel sorry for you. You haven't got any good ol' boys from south of the Mason-Dixon line. How do you expect to win?"

I had never given much of a thought to where our players came from because I had picked the ones I had wanted, but I certainly did expect to win. With 60,135 fans watching, the Seahawks never had a chance. We had seen their quarterback squat down to take the center snap, and we knew that Bill Willis would devastate them much as he had us earlier in training camp with his quick defensive charge into the center. A couple of days after that game Frosty Froberg, our business manager, came into my office with a very worried look on his face.

"The Seahawks left town and didn't pay any of their bills," he told me.

I was stunned. I knew that Hester was outclassed trying to match bankrolls with out other owners because on our first trip to a league meeting in San Francisco I had watched him get wiped out in a card game with some of those men. However, we had given him a hefty check as his share of our gate, and I had expected he would use it to pay his bills.

"We have to pay the bills," I told Frosty. "We can't have the people in Cleveland thinking that this league is going to be fly-by-night. It will kill us."

Before that first season ended, the AAC wound up paying all the salaries of the Miami team, before finally selling it to a group from Baltimore.

Despite its millionaires, money sometimes became a scarce commodity in the AAC, though never for us, I might add, especially after Dan Reaves moved the Cleveland Rams to Los Angeles in January 1946. In our first season, we drew nearly 450,000 in seven home games, and in our second season, nearly 400,000. This was in stark contrast with the Rams, who never drew 100,000 in any season they played in Cleveland. McBride and Sherby orchestrated a vigorous promotion campaign, beginning with advertising carried by their fleet of taxicabs, then hefty newspaper and radio advertising, all topped off by a well-promoted group of pretty girls manning phone banks for call-in ticket orders. This kind of high-powered campaign was their style, the type of action that had made them so successful in the taxi business.

My own popularity from the Canton-Massillon area was

another strong area of sales, as predicted, and soon people were coming in special trains from as far away as Columbus. When the Los Angeles Dons came to play us for the first time in 1946, a crowd of 71,131 nearly filled what was then called Municipal Stadium, the largest crowd at that time ever to see a regularly scheduled professional football game. A week later 70,385 watched us defeat the 49ers in Cleveland. In 1947, 80,067 were at our game against the Yankees, and more than 76,000 watched our final game against the 49ers. Our biggest crowd ever was for our final 1948 game against San Francisco, when 82,769 saw us win 14–7.

Television had no impact in those days, and I have often thought that if it had been as popular as when the American Football League began in 1960, the AAC might have succeeded because of the constant exposure and the steady dollar flow that would have resulted. In 1949, the AAC's last season, I went out of my way to get our games televised and asked the public utility company, our chief radio sponsor, to give us $5,000 for the rights. In later years, before it was disbanded because of rules about network production and equal compensation to all teams, the Browns' television network reached eighty-four stations and became one of the most extensive in pro football, even stretching into New England.

In 1946, however, the medium was still radio, and I had our advertising agency set up a radio network that eventually extended to forty-three stations in every part of Ohio, including Cincinnati. Over the years I visited many of the stations when we renewed the contracts, and ironically, some of them are still part of the Browns' network in what is considered the Bengals' half of the state and compete with our Bengals' radio network. Likewise, we have some outlets near Cleveland for the Cincinnati broadcasts.

We gave the hundreds of thousands who saw and heard our games back in the forties something on which to build their loyalties; in the end we probably gave them too much because we were so successful we began to lose our fans. Still, we had some tremendous rivalries, particularly against the Yankees and 49ers, and spirited games against every team from that long-forgotten league. We also had tremendous players, but unfortunately their feats and abilities, individual statistics and records, including my fifty-one regular-season and play-off victories, have never been recognized in the National Football League record book. There was such feeling against us at the time of the merger that all references to our accomplishments were dropped. I've been told that since the two leagues never played each other and the NFL never had access to complete play-by-play compilations, the records would not be compatible, yet the AFL and NFL never played against each other, and all the AFL records are included in the current NFL book. I know, too, that the play-by-play sheets of the NFL were no better than those kept by the AAC; those year-end statistics are still available, and their accuracy has never been challenged. It's unfair, because the statistics compiled by Lou Groza, Dub Jones, Dante Lavelli, Marion Motley and Otto Graham, among others, during those years would give deserved added luster to their careers. At least, the Hall of Fame in Canton, Ohio, today recognizes our accomplishments.

But games, not statistics, occupied our efforts when we forged our success in the All-America Conference. The Browns' rivalry with the New York Yankees first captured everyone's attention, and our success in consecutive championship games against them brought national visibility to our team and our football. New York was then, and to a lesser extent still is, the nation's media center with its proliferation of magazines, daily newspapers, radio networks and wire services headquarters, and whenever we played the Yankees, and later the Giants, everyone in the country knew about it. Being successful only enhanced our reputation, but it also created some big-city hype to sell tickets. The New York media became frenzied and emotional because they weren't used to seeing their teams beaten with such regularity by a new, collegelike team from middle America. They couldn't understand my intensity for winning or my insistence on a precise and strict method of doing things.

As a result, we suddenly became the "big, bad Browns," and I was the "cold, deadly, cruel, brutal Paul Brown." One morning at breakfast my son Mike was reading the newspaper, and he asked me, "Why do they say those things about you?"

"That's the way it is sometimes when you are successful, particularly in sports where fans don't like the other team," I told him, "so don't worry about it."

It hurt me, though, that my own family was being affected, because I never was, or felt, cold or deadly. There are always those, however, who think it is bad if you continue to be successful and are forceful and demanding in achieving that success. Vince Lombardi went through this during the sixties, and it used to bother him when incidents involving him were blown all out of proportion.

"What can I do about it?" he asked me one day. "You went through it, and it didn't seem to bother you."

"There is nothing you can do," I told him. "It is part of being successful, and ultimately your success will quiet the critics. It is when you aren't successful that you should start to worry."

"I could just imagine what *that* would be like," he said, booming one of his laughs over the phone.

Bud Grant and Tom Landry have received the same treatment in recent years. Like me, they've often been judged on their facial expressions during a game. That is ridiculous. None of us has any control over how we look. I was too busy during a game concentrating on the plays to worry about whether or not I was animated. A football game is serious business, and anyone who would judge me, or any other football coach, by facial expressions under such conditions simply isn't making a sound judgment.

All this was new to me, of course, when I first came into professional football, and I was more engrossed with beating the Yankees than with my so-called New York image. Dan Topping had hired Ray Flaherty as his head coach, and Ray was well experienced in professional football, having guided Washington to three NFL championships. He was also well known and liked in New York at that time because he had played for the Giants and had coached for one of their most stirring rivals. A disciple of single wing football and now deservedly in the Hall of Fame, Ray had some very strong opinions about the game, how it should be played and who should be playing and coaching it, and I think it rankled him that we came in as brash newcomers and defeated his great teams, even though it was never easy for us. The media often tried to promote a feud between the two of us, quoting him once as having berated his team for losing "to a bunch of podunks coached by a high school coach." I never felt any animosity toward him, however, and though he may indeed have said that in a moment of frustration, I never took any of it personally. I let my players worry about those things.

The Yankees were like a who's who of professional football, its roster including such players as backs Orban

("Spec") Sanders and Buddy Young; linemen Arnie Weinmeister, Marty Ruby, Nate Johnson, Bruiser Kinard, Jack
Russell and Bruce Alford, who now is an NFL official; and,
in the team's last season, three defensive specialists named
Harmon Rowe, Tom Landry and Otto Schnellbacher, who
later formed part of the New York Giants' great defensive
team which would start another rich rivalry with the Browns.

We never lost a game to the Yankees, but several of them
were classic contests. We won two bitterly fought games for
the AAC championship in 1946 and 1947; once trailed the
Yankees, 28–0 at halftime before finishing with a 28–28 tie in
a game that was talked about for years. Players such as San-
der, Young, Weinmeister and Russell rate a place on my all-
time opponents team.

Sanders was an exceptional back, who ran with swift, long,
sweeping strides in a deceptive gait that made it seem as if
each stride measured four or five yards. He had the marvelous ability to pick an opening and dart into it before a defense's pursuit could fully react. Though he was the tailback
in Flaherty's single wing system, however, he was not as
adept at passing as he was at running.

Collaring Buddy Young was like trying to catch a water
bug. Buddy had tremendous acceleration and was particularly
devastating whenever the Yankees ran a short-side trap or an
inside reverse because he could get through the line so
quickly and dodge linebackers and defensive backs so well.
Buddy was never very big, but he had tremendously strong
legs that ripped through half-hearted tackles.

Weinmeister, who later became a great defensive tackle for
the Giants, ranks with Bob Reinhard as one of the two best
tackles we ever faced. He and Bruce Alford were the
Yankees' right tackle and right end, respectively, while Jack
Russell and Marty Ruby played the left side. There was no
better defensive line in pro football at that time.

In 1946 Flaherty had so much defensive talent that he often alternated an entire unit in each quarter, and in the second game against the Yankees that season it took a halfback
option pass from Special Delivery Jones to Lavelli to win, 7–
0. The game against the Yankees that meant the most that
season, however, was our 14–9 victory in the first AAC championship match. Not only was it the championship, but it
proved that there was room in professional football for a
team that combined the ideals of amateur players and the

soundness of the coaching system. We trailed, 10–7, midway through the fourth quarter, and it took a diving catch near midfield by Edgar Jones to get us moving in our winning drive. Shortly thereafter he and Lavelli hooked up on the same pass-option play that had won the second game and got a first down at the Yankees' 28-yard line. Two plays later Dante made a diving catch of Graham's pass between Jack Russell and Sanders, and his momentum carried him into the end zone for the winning touchdown.

The following year thousands of Browns fans went to Yankee Stadium in New York to watch us beat the Yankees again, 14–3, for our second title. The playing surface was icy that year, and I wanted to use sneakers instead of the conventional football shoes, but Flaherty refused, so both teams played with cleats. As it turned out, that was to our advantage, because our offense was built on passing, and Motley ran 51 yards with a pass to set up Otto's quarterback sneak for the first touchdown. Motley battered the Yankee's defense so badly with his running that they were easy bait for Edgar Jones's 4-yard trap play that scored the second touchdown.

As exciting and satisfying as that championship game was, however, the one game against the Yankees that engendered the most comment was the one we had played earlier that season before more than 70,000 people at Yankee Stadium. The Yankees had been successful in sealing off Willis and Humble, and their running game just tore through us for a 28–0 lead in the first half. As the teams were leaving the field, Buddy Young laughingly told Lou Rymkus what a bunch of bums we were. A few other wisecracks followed from other Yankee players, and our guys were steaming when we reached the locker room. So was I because we simply hadn't been working at the job. During halftime we made our adjustments to stop the Yankees' trap plays, and then I told Otto, "We're going to fire and fall back! Get ready!" He went out and put on one of the greatest exhibitions of passing that anyone had ever seen, and we scored twenty-eight points to pull ourselves up into a tie. That game, more than any other to date, helped establish Otto as football's premier passer.

Our players from that era have never forgotten that comeback game, but some of the greatest triumphs of all lay just around the corner. The 1948 Cleveland Browns team was the best Browns team of all, even greater than the 1950 NFL championship squad, and probably the greatest professional football team ever up to that time. It won every game and capped the season with a 49–7 victory over the Buffalo Bills for our third straight AAC title. We were the first professional football team since the 1942 Chicago Bears to go undefeated, but it wasn't even recognized when Don Shula's Miami Dolphins won all their games in 1972. I've never been one to dote on season records, but what we accomplished in 1948, just as what Don's team accomplished in 1972, was something special and certainly deserves to be acknowledged in the same light. As with our individual records, however, I've been told that since we didn't play in the NFL, it didn't count. I know this, though: The Browns, 49ers and Yankees were better than *any* of the NFL teams that year—and we beat those other two teams twice.

The real measure of our 1948 team was its ability to play and win three games within eight days, something no professional football team before—or since—ever has been asked to do.

This ordeal was Branch Rickey's brainchild. With his baseball background, he thought that a football team could play more than one game a week, and though I voted againt it in our league meetings, he convinced enough owners to give it a try. Compounding the problem was a schedule that began on Sunday in New York, followed by a sixteen-hour flight to Los Angeles, where we played on Thanksgiving Day, and ending on Sunday in San Francisco. Our preparation time was literally sliced in half, and we were given almost no time at all for any injuries to heal.

Compounding the situation was the fact that our game in San Francisco would decide the Western Division championship, and you can be sure I wasn't happy playing in a crucial game under such adverse conditions. Our only hope to meet the 49ers in some semblance of physical condition was to blow out the Yankees and Dons early in the game and rest as many players as we could. We managed it in New York, but things didn't look good when Lavelli got poked in the eye and his vision became blurred, while Special Delivery Jones and Chubby Grigg had to hobble out with leg injuries, joining James and Speedie, who hadn't played at all.

When we arrived in Los Angeles, I immediately put our players to work and skipped all the pleasantries usually associated with such a trip, including a special luncheon that had been scheduled to drum up ticket sales for the game. Noting my absence, one Los Angeles columnist dubbed me "the playboy coach," thinking I was out enjoying myself instead of attending to football duties. That was a real joke to our players, who knew only too well how much of a "playboy" I wasn't.

We broke open the Dons' game in the third quarter, but then disaster struck again when Otto was hit attempting to pass and the ligaments of his right knee were badly stretched. He could barely walk after the game, and I saw no way he could play against the 49ers in only three days. As I watched our players easing their sore and tired muscles onto our chartered plane for the flight to San Francisco, I knew there was no chance of serious physical preparation for the game. The only thing I could do was have our players soak in the mineral baths near the Sonoma Mission Inn where we were staying, about fifty miles from San Francisco. Miraculously, the soreness seemed to leave their muscles, and we began to gather hope after all.

Meanwhile, Otto could barely hobble, so I planned to start Cliff Lewis at quarterback. Right before the game, however, Otto worked out and saw he could still hand off the ball and move well enough to get back into the passing pocket, so he said to me, "Let me try it. Wally Bock said he'd give the knee some extra special taping support that should keep it from being reinjured. If I can't do it, I'll let you know, and you can let Cliff handle the offense."

"I don't want to take the chance of ruining you for good," I told him, "but if you want to play . . ." and I just nodded and walked over to Cliff.

"I think I'll start him," I said softly, "but be ready because I really don't know how long he can go."

We kicked off to the 49ers, and Jim Cason fumbled on the first play, giving us the ball. All our players expected Cliff to stay on the field—and then Otto hobbled out. They were stunned, then delighted, then positively elated when Otto passed to Lavelli for a touchdown on the very first play.

We fell behind, 21–10, early in the third quarter, but Otto was still hobbling back into the pocket to pass, and everyone was fighting to protect him. In the next ten minutes he fired three touchdown passes for a 31–21 lead, and when the 49ers scored to close within three points, he kept the ball for nearly ten minutes in the fourth quarter before surrendering it at the

49ers' 12-yard line with only fifty seconds to play. By then there was nothing San Francisco could do, and we won the division championship.

After the game Frankie Albert, Norm Standlee and Joe Perry of the 49ers came to our dressing room.

"We suspected you'd play," Albert told Otto, "but we were determined that if you did, there would be no dirty shots. Everyone on our team considers what you did a most courageous performance. We hated like hell to lose, but if it had to happen, there couldn't have been a more deserving way."

There had even been a rumor, one of the 49ers told Otto, that I had planned deliberately to hold him from the game so we would lose and thus force an extra play-off in Cleveland, which would have meant more money to the team and the players. Of course, none of us had heard anything about that, and Otto told me later that if he had heard it before the game, he would have insisted on playing even if it had meant being helped onto the field.

I never again complained about scheduling because I discovered that a team could, if it had to, play three games within a week. It's never something I would advocate, though, and I still feel strongly that professional football teams need a week between games to prepare themselves mentally and physically.

A week later we defeated the Dodgers in New York, where our odyssey had begun, and then trounced the Buffalo Bills for the AAC title to finish with our perfect record. Our unbeaten string, which had begun in 1947, eventually reached twenty-nine games and has never been equaled by any professional football team. Ironically, it was the 49ers who finally ended it, by defeating us, 56–28, midway through the 1949 season in San Francisco.

That was the game, incidentally, in which Edgar Jones, seeing me fuming about our lackadaisical approach, told me to relax and not worry because Otto would bail us out. Well, Otto didn't, and later that night, when we arrived at our quarters in Pasadena to begin a week of preparations for Los Angeles, I called a team meeting and threatened to fire every player—*including* Otto Graham—unless I saw a better effort in our next game. We won, 61–14, and one of my players later told me, "We found out that when you got upset, we got upset, and when that happened, the team we were playing was in big trouble."

Losing to the 49ers in 1949 was no disgrace—just the way
we did it made me unhappy—because San Francisco had
some fine players, and its coach, Buck Shaw, was my friend
and one of the best ever to coach in professional football. His
clean, sporting team reflected his own coaching style, and we
always had more trouble with his team than with any other.
In fact, anytime anything significant happened to us in the
AAC, we always seemed to be playing against Buck's 49ers.
There were the two games I've just described. Our largest
home crowd ever was at a game against the 49ers in 1948,
and our final AAC game in 1949, a 21–7 championship game
victory, came against them in Cleveland, just the day after
the merger of the two leagues had been announced. It was at
a 49ers' game, too, that I witnessed a most memorable event.
General Jonathan Wainwright, the hero of our World War II
Battles at Bataan and Corregidor, was honored at a game in
1946 and received a standing ovation that lasted nearly twenty
minutes. I have never heard anything like it anyplace.

Some of Buck's players were among the finest in the
league, and men like Frank Albert, Norm Sandlee, Joe Perry
and Alyn Beals challenged us in every game we played
against them. Albert was a tremendous quarterback. He
couldn't match Otto's passing ability, but he was the slickest
ball handler I'd ever seen. Being left-handed helped him because he went in an opposite direction from what our players
were used to, and we always had problems finding the ball
whenever he handled it because he had a very clever way of
hiding it against his body. He was also a very daring play-cal-
ler.

Standlee had played with Albert at Stanford and had also
spent a season with the Chicago Bears before joining the All-
America Conference. His running style was similar to that of
Larry Csonka with the Miami Dolphins; he started slowly
and seemed to roll through a hole, then gathered momentum
until it took three or four players to bring him down. He and
Motley were considered the AAC's two best fullbacks, but he
never could match Marion's speed.

When Joe Perry joined the 49ers, Standlee became a full-
time linebacker. Perry had tremendous quickness and accentuated it with speed and acceleration. He weighed about 208
pounds, but he ran with a low center of gravity and was one
of the deadliest runners I've ever seen on a trap play; if he got
even one step on a defensive player, he was gone. He did not

bother us much as an outside runner, but we had all we could handle when he ran between the tackles.

It was against the 49ers and a back named John ("Strike") Strzykalski that Mac Speedie first brought prominence to the down-and-out comeback pass. We knew that Strike was a good offensive halfback, but Buck decided to use him at cornerback in a 1947 game because of his quickness and speed. We decided to test that decision, and Mac caught nine consecutive passes against him. Each time he seemed to run right at Strike, then broke outside or inside, but the secret was that he came back to catch the ball. He did it five straight times to the outside, giving just a little head fake to get Johnny leaning the wrong way, and soon even the 49ers' fans began cheering this amazing display.

We had some other memorable moments in the AAC, particularly against the Los Angeles Dons during our first two seasons and against Buffalo in our final season. The Dons had captured the Hollywood movie crowd, several of whom became token owners, and Lindheimer had even named Don Ameche the team president. The team's general manager was Slip Madigan, a flamboyant and well-known coach from St. Mary's in California, and for the first two seasons Dud DeGroot, who had coached the Redskins to the NFL's 1945 division title, was the coach. He was later replaced by Jimmy Phelan, who had also coached at St. Mary's. With such fine players as John Kimbrough, Charley O'Rourke, Bob Reinhard, Burr Baldwin, Walt Clay and several from the Redskins' championship teams of the early forties, they outdrew the Rams and gave us some tremendous games.

We lost our first game in the AAC to them in Cleveland, 17–16, in 1946, and they cost us a perfect season in 1947, when Ben Agajanian kicked a "second try" field goal. Lou Saban had failed to get off the field in time before the first kick—a miss—and the penalty gave Agajanian another try. In 1947 the Dons obtained Glenn Dobbs from the Dodgers, a player I always wished I could have had because he had tremendous individual skills. Like Otto Graham, he possessed great peripheral vision and the ability to look one way and then throw back to the other side. He was also an excellent punter, but he played single wing tailback throughout his AAC career, and no one ever tapped his potential as a quarterback.

The Bills (who started as the Bisons in 1946) were a

worthy team, and they used to attract crowds of around 30,000 to their old War Memorial Stadium, which was used by the present-day Buffalo team until just a few years ago. Their star was Chet Mutryn, who had started with us in 1946 as a quarterback. We had thought he would be more successful as a running back, but he had resisted our suggestions, and since he wasn't as good as Graham, or Cliff Lewis, we had sent him to Buffalo, where, of course, he became a fine running back. I should have forced him to change because he would have been an even greater player with the Browns. My only other regrettable decision of that nature was cutting Bill McPeak before the 1949 season. Bill and his best friend, Bucky O'Connor, who had played for me at Great Lakes, were roommates in training camp, and both were vying for a job as offensive end. We decided to keep Bucky because he had more speed, but Bill later became one of pro football's best defensive ends when he played for the Steelers. I should have forced the issue with him, too, and put him on defense, but at the time he was determined to make it as an offensive end.

The Bills also had a receiver named Alton Baldwin who, in one game, caught several passes in front of Tom James. I was getting a bit impatient watching this, and I began yelling at Tommy, "Tighter, tighter, play him tighter." I had always warned our defensive backs, however, if a receiver caught three or four of those kinds of passes, to be wary of his *faking* a fifth and then taking off for a deep pass. Sure enough, Baldwin tried a fake after his fifth reception, and Tommy made a touchdown-saving tackle. After that, he used to tell our rookie defensive backs to be prepared for my griping about balls being caught in front of them, but never to get too close, because they could lose their jobs if they were beaten on the long pass.

When we got ready to play Buffalo again, I needled Tommy a little about his duel with Baldwin.

"Tom, I just got a telegram from your cousin," I told him one day after practice.

"My cousin?" he said with a frown.

"Sure, Alton Baldwin," I replied. "He wants to make sure you're going to be in the lineup."

Tommy bristled and bore down harder than ever in our practices. He never did let Baldwin catch any touchdowns against him.

By the league's final season the Bills had become a strong team with the help of such players as George Ratterman, Rex Bumgardner, John Kissell, Hal Herring, Abe Gibron and Bob Oristaglio, all of whom later came with the Browns and accelerated our rebuilding process when we joined the NFL. We played two regular season ties against the Bills in 1949 and then had to come from behind to beat them in a play-off game.

Unfortunately that was the third time we had played Buffalo that season, and no two teams can play each other three times in a fall and sustain interest among the fans. The reason was that the Dodgers had merged with the Yankees before the season began, and the AAC had now become a seven-team league with a reduced twelve-game schedule. Despite all our financial backing, the only thing anyone seemed to be thinking about was merging with the NFL; there was no plan for stability, not even for ways to solidify each team, so it could force a merger on equal terms. The leadership was nil. Arch Ward had persuaded the owners to select Jim Crowley as our commissioner because Elmer Layden, Jim's old teammate with Notre Dame's Four Horsemen, was the NFL commissioner, and he had thought we should match the Notre Dame affiliation. Crowley had no real interest in the job and soon left to join the Chicago franchise. Again we went the popular route at Ward's bidding and signed a prominent figure from World War II—Jonas Ingram, a retired admiral with family football ties to the Naval Academy, who really knew little about professional football. I always liked Jonas personally, but neither he nor his successor, O. A. ("Scrapiron") Kessing (who happened to have worked for him in the navy), had the football knowledge to lead our league and make it function.

There was no direction from the top, then, and it didn't help the league any that the players and financial resources of the successful teams were always being used to help the poorly run teams. At one league meeting Tony Marabito said he had a "case of the shorts," and McBride then told our accountant, Joe Lebit, "Write him a check for fifty," meaning $50,000. The word of both men was their bond, and that was all there was to it. At another meeting Arch Ward, who continually tried to upgrade the Chicago team, which never did become successful, asked if the Browns would send Otto Graham to the Rockets.

"He's from Waukegan and Northwestern, and his local popularity will help their gate," he said to me.

"No!" I said, and the way that I said it ended, for all time, any discussion on that point.

To help the new Baltimore team in 1948, a committee surveyed their player needs and forced us to give away a group of players that included Y. A. Tittle, whom we had drafted and signed just a few months before. We knew even then it was the most critical loss in the Browns' history because Tittle had been programmed to succeed Otto Graham when Otto finished playing. We never did find a suitable replacement after Otto retired in 1955, though Tom O'Connell did a commendable job in 1957. Had Y.A. stayed with us as our quarterback, there is little doubt our championship string would have extended long past 1955. Having to play with a poor team, as the Colts were then, early in his career helped him become the resourceful quarterback he would later be with the 49ers and the Giants; had he stayed in Cleveland, though, he would have been schooled under much easier conditions and could have been even greater. He and Norm Van Brocklin rate 1-2 on my list of opposing quarterbacks, though I'm sentimentally attached to Tittle because I drafted and signed him.

Being forced to lose players of Tittle's caliber was the type of thinking that crippled the All-America Conference and was the direct result of nonfootball people trying to succeed in a sport about which they knew nothing. And there were far too many nonfootball people managing teams in the AAC. Even Branch Rickey's shrewdness could not keep the Dodgers afloat. Although he tried to run his football franchise too much like his baseball team, I always liked him and found him to be a progressive and innovative executive. When he was president of the Pittsburgh Pirates during the fifties, he even asked me to manage his team. The idea intrigued me for a while, but I never really gave any serious thought to leaving professional football because it would have been a totally unfamiliar area.

The key blow to the AAC's hopes of survival was Chicago's failure to succeed on the field or at the gate. The team had some great players—Elroy Hirsch, Billy Hillenbrand, Bob Hoernchmeyer, Bob Dove and Bill Daley—but it had to fight the solidly entrenched Chicago Bears and the Chicago Cardinals, who were having their only successful season at the time. I've always felt that had Chicago been able to match the success of the Browns', Yankees', 49ers' and the Los Angeles Dons' first couple of years, and Buffalo's rise in the last two years, the AAC might have forced the NFL to concede to it. It never happened, though, and this just crushed Arch Ward.

Things became so bad in Chicago that when we played at Soldier Field in 1949 after a big snowstorm, our players had to work with the Chicago players to remove the tarpaulin because the Hornets could not afford a ground crew. Pretty soon both teams were engaged in a good-natured snowball fight, which might have been fun for them, but certainly wasn't what we were there for.

After 1946, Jim Crowley, Ed McKeever and Ray Flaherty each had a season as head coach at Chicago, but none succeeded. Crowley told me later that he had lost his zest for coaching football after seeing the ravages of war on the bodies of young men lying in military hospitals in the Pacific and that he really preferred to be an administrator. After his departure, Ward, hoping to capitalize on the Notre Dame influence around Chicago, hired McKeever, who had coached at South Bend in 1944. The night we played them in Chicago in 1948, he told me before the game, "We're going to whip your team." That was one of Ed's problems—he talked too much. We won, 28–7, played them the next week in Cleveland and won again. When he was released by the Rockets, who had no money to pay him, I insisted that our league at least honor his contract's salary terms, and he was always grateful to me for that favor, though I had done only what I felt was correct.

McKeever's situation illustrates again what the AAC was going through. It seemed through most of the league's four years that instead of talking about our football, we were always apologizing for the tattered state of the league or how much money we were losing or about our uncertain future. This bothered me, and I knew that it bothered our players, who were understandably concerned about that future. None of us ever knew peace of mind because of our involvement in that football war, and I never had any stomach for it. I was a football coach, and I wanted to expend my energies, and those of my players, on football, but there seemed to be endless rounds of meetings, desperate measures to save teams, continuous talk of dissolution or merger, and in our final season especially, it became one big nightmare.

Though I thought we might join the NFL—which found its situation becoming nearly as desperate as ours—the situation became so fraught with uncertainty that it even got to me. Even in 1948, when we had our greatest team, Katy and I often talked about the possibility of our venture, and at those times she was a tower of strength to me.

"What in the world have I done?" I asked her one night during that season. "The money doesn't mean anything, and I think I've led us into this frightful situation."

She reassured me in her own way that we would emerge unscathed, but I had to wonder, especially in light of all the unfounded news reports that were circulating about me. Many said that I wanted to return to Ohio State. Someone said that I had turned down that coaching job because I had not been given the athletic director's post as well. Another said that I wanted to leave Cleveland because I didn't like playing second fiddle to the baseball Indians, who had won the World Series that year and drawn more than 2 million fans. The Indians' success never bothered me because I was satisfied with our team's popularity at that time, and my relationship with Bill Veeck, the Indians' owner in those years, was most cordial. However, there was another thing that did bother me. I realized that very indirectly, I had been one of the reasons for the league's difficulties. In 1949 we had smothered the rest of the AAC and had taken away the one necessary ingredient that every successful league must have for its survival—competition, which fosters interest among fans. Now we were suffering with the other teams. Our regular crowds of 50,000 and 60,000 had dwindled to around 20,000, with the exception of the game against the 49ers, and one of the Cleveland newspapers ran a picture of McBride sitting alone in our bleachers, a very disconsolate look on his face, with the caption "What has happened, Arthur?"

I learned then that for a league to succeed, each team must be given the means to become as competitive as possible. In the AAC, we had nonfootball people trying to keep their teams going on a shoestring, hoping to gain some personal glory by being associated with a popular sport. In reality, however, it was men like Lindheimer, McBride, Topping and Jim Breuil who were really keeping the league afloat.

Years later, anytime the NFL added teams, I always made

a point of trying to give the new franchise the best possible deal in getting players, either in terms of an allocation draft or by making them available from among those who could not make our own team. Ironically, when the Bengals were admitted to the American Football League in 1968, we were given the poorest selection pool of any team, except possibly the Dallas Cowboys.

The only sensible solution for everyone's survival in 1949 was a merger, and McBride had been pursuing talks in this direction since our first season. Tim Mara and Art Rooney were his good friends, and they often agreed that the two leagues would inevitably get together, but they could not promote enough sentiment among the other NFL owners—principaly George Preston Marshall—to bring about the move. "I'd welcome the Browns in the NFL," Mr. Mara told McBride, "and Paul Brown is the kind of a man and a coach who belongs in professional footfall."

However, in 1948, when Jonas Ingram and I had discussions with Bert Bell, who had succeeded Layden as NFL commissioner, he told me that though many in the NFL would welcome the Browns and 49ers, it was Marshall's opposition that prevented it. So there it lay.

Nothing was done until the NFL itself began to wobble. It lost its Boston franchise, which moved to New York and later failed, and then it had to pump money into Green Bay to keep the Packers from folding. Mr. Rooney was being backed against the wall in Pittsburgh, and matters were grim in Detroit. We hung on, thanks mainly to the financial resources of McBride and of Lindheimer, who was financing both the Los Angeles and Chicago teams and who might have held out even longer had he not suffered a heart attack that took him from his daily responsibilities.

Our owners talked publicly of going forward into the 1950 season, I even signed a five-year contract and new interest was being expressed from Texas oilmen, notably Glen McCarthy, for new franchises in Houston and Dallas. When the NFL saw more millionaires on the horizon, they abandoned their hopes that we would die and that they could then absorb our remains piecemeal and turned instead, finally, to serious merger negotiations. The one incident that probably changed Marshall's mind was our outbidding him in 1949 for Lynn Chadnois, a fine running back from Michigan State, and Tommy Thompson, a linebacker from William and

Mary. He never forgave us or Tommy for hoodwinking him during what he thought were legitimate contract negotiations.

We had had no trouble signing Tommy because Dick Gallagher, who worked for us, had been one of his college coaches. Marshall didn't know this, however, when he invited him to Washington to discuss a contract. Tommy called us and asked for advice.

"You've signed with us, so there can be no conflict," I told him. "If you want to go and listen to what the Redskins have to say, see the city and have a good time in the process, that's your personal business."

The Redskins gave Tommy royal treatment. Later, though, when it was time to discuss a contract, he said, "Oh, I can't sign with you. I've already signed with the Cleveland Browns."

It was at this point that three of our teams were invited to join the NFL—the Browns, 49ers and Colts. There was some talk about allowing the competition for the dollar to take place in New York, Chicago and Los Angeles as well to determine which teams from both leagues would survive. However, financial fatigue had drained the interest from the owners of those teams in the AAC. Dan Topping, for example, was convinced by his partner, Del Webb, that it was wiser to concentrate their efforts on the baseball Yankees. Lindheimer was in poor health and unable to run the Dons on a full-time basis, so he became a part owner of the Rams. Chicago, with no money, simply folded. Jim Breuil had hoped to keep the Buffalo franchise, but when he found no sentiment for his city among the NFL people, he joined the Browns' ownership and insisted as part of the deal that he be allowed to bring along three players, Abe Gibron, Rex Bumgardner and John Kissell.

Once the merger was agreed on we battled to protect our interests, and in this I had Bert Bell's total cooperation, despite some vindictive attempts from Marshall to shortchange the AAC teams. This was my first real encounter with Marshall, and he never changed during all the years we attended league meetings. He was obnoxious; he insulted your intelligence and had a great habit of sleeping most of the day and showing up at the meeting late in the afternoon. We then had to stop the proceedings to brief him on all that had been accomplished. By that time all of us were pretty tired and ready to adjourn, but he was rested and mentally sharp. That was when he tried to work some of his little deals. At the player draft meetings, we all sat at separate tables, with our lists spread before us, and Marshall inevitably made the rounds of each table, coming up from behind, leaning over and giving the big hello. At the same time he would look over our shoulders at our lists, trying to get some information. After a while it became so obvious that everyone just closed his book when he saw Marshall coming.

Marshall almost sabotaged the entire merger when he insisted that the Browns be made a swing team and play each of the other twelve teams just once. We threatened to dissolve the agreement unless we got a square deal. I knew that being a swing team was a no-win proposition; no such team has ever been a success in the NFL. Marshall, as part of his price for allowing Baltimore into the NFL and within the seventy-five-mile limit of his team's territory, finally foisted the swing-team role on the Colts, and they won just one game all season and then folded.

We certainly expected no favors from Marshall, and we got none, but during these early organizational meetings Bert Bell never sacrificed our interests and was always fair-minded, open and totally honest in all his dealings. He held out no illusions that all would be sweetness and light when we joined the NFL, and he knew as well as we did that the prejudices of four years would last long afterward, but he worked to get us a fair deal. He told the owners at one meeting, "The Browns will not be kicked around as if they were the losers in a war. They will be treated the same as other NFL teams. We've engaged in a merger that is a victory for the public, not ourselves, and we'll treat it that way."

Bert knew that neither Dan Sherby, who with Lindheimer and Topping had represented the All-America Conference during most of the merger sessions, nor I would accept anything other than what we felt was best for our team.

I had insisted, and it was agreed, that we be put in the American Division of the thirteen-team league with the New York Giants, Washington Redskins, Chicago Cardinals, Pittsburgh Steelers and Philadelphia Eagles because the natural rivalries, as well as the sane travel conditions, made more sense to me. Our tremendous rivalry with the Giants, the still-prosperous rivalry between the Browns and the Steelers and our classic championship game in 1950 against the Rams were a direct result of this move.

In the allocation draft of players from the defunct AAC teams, I was greatly concerned about whether we would receive equal consideration because some of the NFL teams wanted to have them all to themselves. It again took Bert Bell's personal intervention to insure our full participation. Even then, every NFL team got first crack at the players before the three AAC teams did.

We picked last, but I had the advantage of knowing the good players. Our first choice was Len Ford of the Los Angeles Dons, who supposedly had an attitude problem. I've already described how his "problem" was really nothing more than hating to be on a losing team. He became a superb player for us and today is in the Hall of Fame.

We also picked Hal Herring, a center from Buffalo who turned out to be one of the best long snappers on punts and place kicks that we ever had. We took some others, too, but they didn't make as big an impact on our team as Ford and Herring.

At the same time the NFL decided to void all future draft picks the AAC teams had made and put them into a secondary draft. We lost Doak Walker to the Detroit Lions that way and Lynn Chadnois of Michigan State to the Pittsburgh Steelers. Everyone knows what a great player Walker became for the Lions, and Chadnois was a superb running back for some poor Pittsburgh teams for nearly seven seasons. There is no telling how truly great the Browns would have become had we been able to keep Y.A. Tittle, Walker and Chadnois.

Even without those players, however, the groundwork had been well laid for our seasons in the NFL, and our adventures in the AAC finally ended the day we defeated the 49ers, 21–7, in Cleveland for our fourth and last league championship. For the first time since I had entered professional football, I was truly happy, and that night, when Katy and I took our evening walk after supper, I said to her, "I feel safe now. I think we're on sound ground. Now we can quit worrying and concentrate on football."

NINE

The 1950 Season:
Welcome to the NFL

OUR FIRST SEASON IN THE National Football League in 1950 was the most satisfying football experience of my life. We began the season knowing that we would have to prove ourselves right away against the NFL champion Philadelphia Eagles, considered by everyone who didn't know us the best team in pro football. Beating them wouldn't be enough, however; every other team in the NFL, still smarting at having to accept us after years of disparaging our football, would want to make us pay its own particular price. I didn't mind the challenges because we had a few things to prove ourselves after being ridiculed and taunted for four years. We had only one thing at stake: our honor.

So did the NFL. It had bragged about its supremacy during the previous four years, and Greasy Neale, the Eagles coach, said it all when he disclosed soon after the merger, "We don't want Cleveland to win because it will make the NFL look bad."

Well, we did win. We took on everyone that year, and when the season ended, we were the new champions, called by commissioner Bert Bell "the greatest team ever to play the game."

That championship was won only after a lot of struggles, however, off the field as well as on. The feeling against us was so high that teams freely passed films and other information to each other, the only object being that we should lose. I was told that on a Monday following a game, the coach of our upcoming opponent would be briefed by the previous

week's coach, and by others who had played us, to give him
any help that might enable him to win. The strong feelings
even extended into the officiating, and I knew of several instances where AAC officials were confronted by NFL officials
in their dressing room before and after a game. On the field,
we found penalties being called where we couldn't find the
fouls. In our opening game against the Eagles, for instance,
we had touchdowns called back for apparent infractions, yet
when we looked at the films later, nothing illegal had happened.

That was all part of the price we had to pay for our newly
found stability, but we had waited so long it meant nothing
to experiment with our ideas, and by 1950 we had a pretty
game between the Browns and the Eagles. He knew the nation would be captive to what amounted to a grudge
match—for the first time, everyone would find out which
team, and which league's football, was the better.

We had pushed for this confrontation ourselves from the
very beginning. As I said at the time, "I don't care if we get
run out of the park, just as long as we get a chance to prove
ourselves." I never believed that anything very dire would
happen to us, however, because we had waited too long for
this confrontation. No one in the NFL knew it, but anticipating the merger, we had been preparing for the Eagles for
the past two years. Whenever possible, we had scouted their
games and studied films we received from various sources.
Every so often we had even taken some of our practice time
to experiment with our ideas, and by 1950 we had a pretty
good idea of what we could do against them.

The merger had been announced only the day before our
last AAC title game and a week before the NFL championship in Los Angeles between the Eagles and Rams. Philadelphia had never sent anyone to scout us when we beat the
49ers, but we had dispatched Fritz Heisler and Blanton Collier to the Rams-Eagles game. It was played in rainy conditions that precluded any passing, and the Eagles won it, 14–0,
on the strength of Steve Van Buren's carrying the ball thirty-
one times for nearly 200 yards. We saw nothing in that game
to cause us to change our plans, nor did we see anything in
the preseason games we scouted the following summer to
cause us much concern.

Neale had built a fine, wing T running attack around Van
Buren, the NFL's rushing champion, who had gained nearly

3,000 yards in three seasons. He had also designed the Eagle Defense, a concept that had become very popular in the NFL. It was built with a tight five-man line, two linebackers to jam the ends as they tried to release downfield and four defensive backs, which was innovative in pro football at that time. Neale pointedly declared that no team in the All-America Conference—and specifically the Cleveland Browns—could ever match his team. He brushed aside our great passing offense; it had no chance at all, he said, aginst the Eagle Defense.

Naturally, someone asked me for comment after one of Greasy's put-downs.

"Well," I said in what had to be my best low-key manner, "it just confirms my fears from everything I've read and heard since the two leagues came together. I presume we've won our last football game! But the last time I looked, we had ends who could catch and a guy who could throw. We don't claim anything. We'll be in the same league as the Eagles, and we hope we can win a few."

I deliberately low-keyed everything we did, but I also wrote to all our players in the off-season and told them I wanted them to report to training camp in the best condition possible—and why. I knew we would be engaged in a war from our very first preseason game, and when our training camp opened, I tried to set a tone for the upcoming season.

"We've established quite a reputation in four years of All-America play," I told the players. "But we've been taunted and disparaged about playing in an inferior league. We've heard that the worst team in the NFL can beat the best in the All-America Conference. There is not only this coming season at stake but four years of our achievement as members of the AAC. I'm asking that you dedicate yourselves more than ever to preserve the reputation the Browns have made. It won't be easy. We're new to this league, and things may get rough at times. But remember that the worst thing that you can ever do to an opponent is to beat him. An opponent understands that more than anything else."

It still wasn't very easy to underplay such a momentous opening game, and despite my words, our players were so keyed up that they were ready to tear into it when training camp began. I had to slow down everything and everyone—including the coaches, who wanted to do too much—and gradually build our preparations. I blanched one day when some writer asked Lou Rymkus if he wasn't afraid the NFL teams might be too rough on us, particularly the Eagles.

"I played against them when I was with the Redskins, and they never threw any chill into me," he told the writers, adding, "and neither did any other NFL team."

Our first preseason game was against the Green Bay Packers in Akron. Green Bay was one of the NFL's lesser teams, but when its players took the opening kickoff and moved down the field for a touchdown, I wondered for a moment if perhaps we really were in the wrong league after all. That doubt was erased, however, when we unleashed our own offense and wound up winning, 38–7. We won all our preseason games, but two in particular were very important. One was beating the Chicago Bears because of the impact of defeating a George Halas—coached team, though I was a bit unnerved when I went with a group to welcome George and his team to Cleveland. As the train pulled into Union Terminal, I saw him and his wife playing cards with Bill Downes and his wife. Bill was scheduled to be the referee for our game the next night! The other key game was against Detroit because it was a dress rehearsal for the Eagles. The Lions utilized every nuance of the Eagle Defense, and though they did not have the same talent, we were interested in the reactions of their defense to the game plan we were constructing for Philadelphia.

That game plan called first for us to attack the Eagles with our passing game, something Greasy Neale later told me had worried him much more than his public comments had indicated. In the game, he would pin much of his hopes on the ability of his linebackers to hold up our receivers before they got off the line of scrimmage and to allow the defensive backs double coverage on Dub Jones and Mac Speedie.

We decided to neutralize the linebackers by putting our left halfback, Rex Bumgardner, in motion and starting each play in a double wing formation to force single coverage. That would mean that Russ Craft, their cornerback, would have to cover Jones man-for-man, which was impossible. We tried this only briefly against the Lions, so as not to tip our hand, but each time their defense reacted as we had hoped.

The second phase of our game plan was built on spreading the Eagles' defensive line by imperceptibly widening our guards and tackles on each successive play. With no middle linebacker in the Eagle Defense, the center of the line was the weak area, even though their defensive tackles tried to compensate for this by charging to the inside shoulder of our offensive tackles. We knew their tackles were taught to line up opposite our tackles, and we reasoned that if we moved ours wider with each play, theirs would follow, and their middle guard would be isolated. With wider spacing along the defensive line, we could then run our trap plays with devastating effect. This is exactly what happened when we wanted to control the ball in the second half of the game, and I'll never forget Alex Wojciechowicz looking around for his defensive tackles and suddenly signaling for time-out. We could hear him yelling at his tackles to stay closer. They made the mistake—as the Lions did—of lining up on our offensive linemen instead of taking their normal spacing from the ball, and they never adjusted to it. I couldn't help thinking back to our first game at Ohio State against Missouri and how we had saved that day by keeping our normal spacing.

The hardest part of that first game was waiting for it to start. We had set aside parts of each practice day during the final two weeks of the preseason to polish our game plan, but the final week, when we concentrated on the game itself, the players were so quiet it got a bit eerie. The only thing that truly worried me was that we might peak too soon and leave our intensity and sharpness on the practice field.

Trying to cut some of the tenseness every so often, I'd tell our players, "Just think, it won't be long until you'll be able to touch the great Steve Van Buren."

Of course, that only served to get them a bit more fired up. As it happened, Van Buren didn't play because he had injured his foot in a game between the Eagles and the College All-Stars. Philadelphia had also lost Bosh Pritchard, its speedy halfback, but Neale's team was deep in talent, and he replaced those two runners with Clyde ("Smackover") Scott and Frank Ziegler. He also had Tommy Thompson, a veteran quarterback; Jack Ferrante and Pete Pihos as his ends; and the best offensive line in the NFL.

The game was played on a Saturday night in mid-September at Municipal Stadium, now named John F. Kennedy Stadium, a huge arena in South Philadelphia where the Army-Navy game has been played for nearly half a century. The Eagles were prohibitive favorites, despite the absence of Van Buren and Pritchard and despite newspaper reports from some Philadelphia writers who had covered our training season and seen what we could do. When we arrived in Philadelphia, we sensed everyone looking at us as at the victims of a huge sacrificial feast, and when our players reached the dressing room that night, they quickly dressed and then just sat and stared at the walls with barely a word to one another. After a few minutes of this morose silence I sensed they were about to explode and herded them onto the field for some pregame drills, deathly afraid that our emotion would be vented against the old steel lockers and gray concrete walls of our dressing room.

I was absolutely correct about their emotional pitch because never, in any game with which I ever have been associated, have I seen a team so keyed up, so ready to play. No one spared himself physically, and Eagles went sprawling play after play. The first time we touched the ball, on a punt following Philadelphia's first possession, Don Phelps ran for a touchdown. The officials ruled that Len Ford had clipped, however, and the score was disallowed, although when we looked at the films later, we saw, not a clip, but instead one of the greatest blocks ever thrown on a punt return—Len Ford had wiped out three Eagles' players in one move! Later in the first half, Phelps returned another punt 46 yards, and again we were penalized for clipping—and again it was another phantom call that never showed on the films.

The Eagles may have been lulled into a false sense of security early in the game because of two good drives of theirs, even though neither of them ended in a touchdown. Our defense was still at such an emotional pitch that it had not begun moving and reacting, though it did stop Philadelphia at the eight-yard line on the first drive and at the two-yard line on the second. The Eagles netted a field goal from the first, and nothing from the second, because Neale had elected to try for the touchdown.

In that second drive, the Eagles had a first down inside our five-yard line when we decided to send Motley into the game as an extra linebacker. On three consecutive plays, he met the Eagles' runners head-on and stopped them with hardly a yard. On fourth down, Marion was playing very close to the line again, and anticipating that Philadelphia might pass, we yelled to him from the sidelines, "Loosen up, Marion, loosen up," meaning that we wanted him to play off the line of scrimmage a bit.

Motley misunderstood, however, and while we watched, he

did the neatest body shimmy I had ever seen because he thought we meant he was to tight and we wanted his muscles looser. On the sidelines we just looked at one another, and some of the players laughed, and I think this helped relieve the tension. A little later, though, the sight of old Chubby Grigg coming off the field after badly scuffing a field goal try in the first quarter managed to dampen my spirits a bit.

Chubby had become our kicker when Lou Groza badly injured his shoulder early in the game and was unable to play. We'd never anticipated having to use him, however, because of Groza's great durability, and the fact was Chubby hadn't place-kicked since high school.

"What happened?" I asked him a bit impatiently because right then three points loomed very important.

"I just killed a damn mole with the hole I dug," he drawled in his Texas accent. I didn't find this homespun humor very funny just then, but fortunately I was able to laugh about it later.

While the Eagles looked as if they were dominating us early in the game, Otto Graham had been busy setting an ambush for their defense. It was time for the Russ Craft-Dub Jones duel we had rehearsed against Detroit. The Eagles always rotated their coverage toward a halfback going in motion (in our case Rex Bumgardner going toward Speedie's side of the field), and they felt that Russ Craft, their all-pro cornerback, could cover a receiver man-for-man on the other side of the defense. That receiver was Dub Jones, of course, and Craft had not yet learned, as the defensive backs in the AAC had, that Jones only made it *seem* as if he could be covered while he worked to set up an opponent. Then he'd tell Otto, "I'm open."

After we lost Phelps's 46-yard punt return late in the quarter, Joe Muha's second punt sailed out of bounds at our 41-yard line. After one play, Jones passed the word that he would be open. The next thing we saw was Dub making a fake to the outside, getting Craft to cross his feet and then taking off toward the goal posts. When he caught Otto's pass, he was 10 yards behind the Eagles' defensive back and easily ran for our first touchdown.

On our next possession, Graham went to work again. By now the Eagles' defense was becoming confused by Otto's pinpoint passing and was gradually deteriorating. Otto teased and probed and even got 21 yards on a screen pass to Motley that put us deep in the Eagles' territory. It was then that Lavelli, who had so bewildered their safety with his moves that he was getting free without any trouble, teamed with Graham for our second touchdown on a play I will never forget.

We had noticed that the Eagles seemed so fearful of our traps and draws that their pass rush suffered. We had expected just the opposite—that their pass rush would be so furious we would need our traps and draws to cool it off—but their strategy just invited us to stay with our deep passing game.

The play this time called for Otto to throw a hook pass to Speedie, but he had time to look at the other receivers because of the Eagles' hanging back and spotted Lavelli by the end zone.

The goal posts at that time were planted on two unpadded uprights on the goal line, and in practice, our receivers used to grab one of those posts and whirl around it and away from the defender. This particular time Dante swung around the first post and away from Frank Reagan and, while still going full speed, brushed the other as he caught the ball. For a moment, Dante was so intent on catching the ball I thought he was going to crash into the second upright.

"Did you know how close you came to running into that goal post while looking at the ball?" I asked him when he came off the field.

"Coach," he replied with the jagged edges of raw emotion cutting his words, "I didn't care where that goal post was."

When the second half began, the Eagles returned to trying to double cover Lavelli and Speedie, but we added another wrinkle that they failed to pick up—putting Rex Bumgardener at fullback and moving Motley to halfback, because a linebacker covered the fullback when he went in motion. Rex caught three straight passes for 30 yards before Philadelphia picked up the switch and altered its coverage. The moment the Eagles changed, Otto completed a 32-yard pass to Lavelli to their 12-yard line and then polished off the six-play drive with a touchdown pass to Speedie.

Our passing game was so dominant that we had run only ten times in the first three quarters, and when the last quarter began, we felt that it was time to get to our running attack and control the ball and the clock. We went to Phase Two of our game plan and began slowly spreading our linemen to give us better blocking angles and to isolate the middle of the Eagles' defense. Philadelphia then got a taste of Motley at his finest as he pounded at that defense. He and Jones alternated carrying the ball seven times, up to the Eagles' 1-yard line, and then Otto scored on a quarterback sneak. A few minutes later Jones broke off a 57-yard run around left end, and Bumgardner scored from the 1-yard line for our final touchdown.

Every phase of our offense and our defense was devastating that night. We drove Thompson from the game early in the third quarter and completely shut down the Eagles' proud running attack. At one point they even resorted to using a shotgun formation for their passing, but that didn't work either, and Bill Mackrides, who had replaced Thompson, got the Eagles' only touchdown when Pihos made a spectacular catch with Hal Herring and Lewis hanging on his back in the end zone.

I knew that we had embarrassed the National League, and I was quite pleased—and perhaps a bit surprised—when Bert Bell came to our dressing room and heartily congratulated us for our efforts. He told me later that he was genuinely happy that the Browns had won so convincingly because it made believers of his owners and of the public that the NFL would be stronger and more competitive with us in the league. As a former football coach he also told me that we had been the most intense and best-prepared football team he had ever seen.

I've heard claims by some old Eagles players that the team they lost to really was not the Cleveland Browns, but an All-America Conference all-star team. They had a better chance than we did, however, to select top players from the allocation pool, and they never took advantage of it.

Greasy Neale had mixed emotions after that game. I know that he was stunned and hurt that his proud Eagles team had not defended the NFL's honor, and he told some people, "Why, all they do is pass and trap, and they're like a basketball team the way they throw the ball around."

The next time we played the Eagles in 1950, however, during a rainy day in Cleveland, we didn't throw one pass, and even with Van Buren and Pritchard in their lineup, we beat them again, 13–7. Still, for all his testy remarks he was a realist, and when someone suggested to him that the first game might have been different had Van Buren played full time, Greasy demurred. "We might have scored another touchdown, possibly two, but as for winning the game, that was something else."

Our great passing game had wrecked the Eagle Defense and left a lasting impression on Neale. He told me later he thought Otto Graham the ideal passer because he hung the ball and allowed our receivers to run under it on our deep patterns.

"I tried for ten years to get our quarterbacks to do that, but they just didn't have the knack," he said. "I never saw a passer who hung the ball out there the way Graham does. Anyone who can put the ball up there for a guy to catch just a yard before stepping out of bounds, or put it right in his hands the moment a defender is beaten, is great."

When he picked his all-time team, he named Otto as the quarterback. He was a fine coach, but most of all, he was an honest man who had been very frank in telling everyone he didn't like the Browns because we had shaken the structure of the NFL and challenged its dominance. There were many others in the league who really disliked the Browns, but they gave us the phony handshake and the big smile, all the while waiting for their chance to get us.

His losing to the Browns twice in 1950 didn't sit too well with the Philadelphia owners, and they released Neale just before the 1951 season began. The University of Indiana was looking for a head coach at the time, and I wholeheartedly recommended him for the job. He didn't get it, but we remained friends until the day he died.

From the time we played the Eagles, the entire 1950 season became a tremendous personal experience, and it touched every facet of my life. Every week brought new surges of great emotion, fueled by feelings of relief that all the energies of our players and coaches were being funneled into football and not dissipated into worrying about our future. My own energies were no longer split between trying to keep a league alive and coaching at the same time, and life as I envisioned it was totally good.

Everything in 1950 did not come easily, however. Despite our victory over the Eagles and our subsequent fine record that season, we still were the interlopers who had crashed the party. It became obvious as the season went on that the NFL's worst fears were being realized—we were good enough to win it all. A lesser-talented team might not have survived, and as it was, we were in a precarious position. We had lost eleven players from our 1949 team through age, retirement or natural attrition, including John Yonakor, Edgar Jones, Lou Saban, Ed Ulinski, Mo Scarry and Ara Parseghian; only nine of our original players remained with us; and our rebuilding program had been hurt when we had lost the draft rights to Walker, Dick Kempthorn and Lynn Chadnois. Fortunately our program had also been helped a great deal by our getting Len Ford, Abe Gibron, Rex Bumgardner, John Kissell and Hal Herring from the AAC and then by an excellent draft that brought us running backs Ken Carpenter, Don Phelps and Emerson Cole, defensive back Ken Gorgal and linemen John Sandusky and Jim Martin.

Carpenter was used primarily on kick returns in 1950, but later he became one of our finest all-purpose runners and ranks among the best ever to play for my teams. His 210 pounds and mincy stride belied his great speed and his ability to cut and accelerate. The only time he ever disappointed me was in 1954, when he jumped our team and went to the Canadian Football League. I couldn't understand it because that previous January I had even brought him to Los Angeles to play for our East Pro Bowl squad, but like many young men, he did things at that stage of his life that he later regretted.

Gorgal, who was six feet two inches tall, and weighed 200 pounds, was one of the biggest safeties in the league at that time. He didn't have the speed of Tom James or Kenny Konz, but he had tremendous instincts for being in the right place at the right time. This made him a superlative defensive player and he was one of the nicest men I ever knew. The players called him Gurgles Gorgal because he added so much fellowship and good feeling to our team.

Ford, Gibron and Kissell were also among my all-time greatest. In fact, the only real heartache of that 1950 season involved Ford when, in our first game against the Chicago Cardinals, Pat Harder, without any justification, crushed his face with as vicious a blow as I'd ever seen in football.

Len was a tremendous pass rusher, and he had been running over the Cardinal blockers and getting to the quarterback. Jim Conzleman, their coach, had ordered Harder, a fullback to help with the pass blocking, and Len had begun running over him, too. Harder had tried every way within the rules to stop Len, without success, so he had just waited and, as Ford got around him, swung an elbow and hit him in the cheekbone, which crushed the side of his face. There were no face bars on helmets in those days, so Len took the full force of the blow, and it scarred him for the rest of his life. What made it even worse was that Ford, not Harder, was ejected from the game because the officials claimed he had flagrantly used his hands. When we looked at the films, we saw that everything Ford had done had been clean and that it had been Harder who had committed the foul.

I took those films directly to Bert Bell and was most emphatic in pointing out what Harder had done. After Bert saw the films, he agreed, and though he would not fine or suspend Harder, he issued an order for such tactics to stop. That didn't help Len, though, and he played little the rest of the season, until we got into trouble in our championship game against the Rams. Then he came off the bench and played magnificently, even though he was twenty pounds underweight because his facial injury had prevented him from eating properly.

Fortunately Len was able to come back and played for us right through the 1957 season, when Paul Wiggin replaced him in our defense. Ford passed away shortly before being elected to the Hall of Fame, and though he was one of my favorite players, he was also a bit of an enigma. Off the field, he was a gentle soul, but his own worst enemy in the way that he took care of himself. On the field, he was a fierce player and something to behold when he uncoiled and went after a passer. He used to convince himself before every game that no one could stop him from getting to a quarterback, and when he went into the game, it became a challenge, a matter of determination and desire, to prove it to himself.

Yet his gentle side often showed, too. In a game against the Washington Redskins, Len kept knocking down Eddie LeBaron, their little quarterback. Finally, Ed's nose began to bleed, and Ford just reached down, gently picked LeBaron off the ground with one hand and said, "I'm awfully sorry, but I hope you understand that I'm just doing my job."

Kissell was just the opposite, a hard, tough, strong defensive tackle who today is one of my dearest friends, despite some differences between us when he played with the Browns. John and I used to battle each year over his contract, and he was tough because coming from an eastern European family in which there had been little money, he was very frugal. Our players used to kid him about it, particularly when they discovered that his brother Ed, who was a defensive back with the Steelers, had sent him a three-cent stamp in the hope he might write him a letter.

One year I offered John what I thought was a good contract, but he still balked, so in near exasperation I said to him, "John, I'll bet that if I offered you a million dollars, you wouldn't think it was great right away because you'd want a million and one dollars."

He looked at me for a moment, and in his distinctive low, gravelly voice, he said, "You know how it is, coach. Everybody hates da boss."

Abe Gibron was an unusually built man. He weighed about 260 pounds, but stood just over six feet; his shoulders measured fifty-four inches across, and his physique tapered to a perfect V at his waist—all in all, he was a prefect physical specimen for a guard. His shoulder width made him a fine pass protector, but his greatest attribute was the explosive speed with which he came off the ball. His reactions on offense were like Willis's on defense, and no one ever matched his initial offensive charge. In fact, he often gave the appearance of being offside because he was the only offensive lineman who actually moved with the snap of the ball, and for a time the officials were calling him several times a game for the infraction. I finally took some films to Bert Bell and showed him that indeed, it was Abe's ability to move with the ball and ahead of the other linemen that made it appear that he was offside. Bert called all the officials and told them about it, and Abe got some relief. No guard was ever faster for the first five yards, and when he pulled out to lead our sweeps, he could stay in front of our fastest backs until he threw his first block.

Like Chubby Grigg, however, he was no jolly fat man. Abe was a very emotional player, totally wrapped up in the game. He was also very intelligent and, like Ford, a kind, gentle man, who probably had more friends among opposing players than anyone else in the league. However, when we had him, he ran around with a group of tough guys who called themselves the Filthy Five because they never allowed their practice uniforms to be washed, and the dust and mud of August training camp later blended with the snow and slush of November's practice field. The group included Frank

Gatski, Tony Adamle, Walt Michaels and Gibron. They were a throwback breed.

One summer, during a preseason game in Akron against San Francisco, Gibron got into a fight with one of the 49ers' players, who immediately jumped on Abe and began throwing some hefty punches. Lying on his back, Abe had no leverage, and his short arms flailed upward with no effect. Abe's mother was sitting right behind Katy and some of our friends, and as Abe's arms went up and down without making much contact, she stood up and began yelling, "Kill the sonuvabitch, Abe, kill the sonuvabitch!"

Katy told me the story, and when I saw Abe a couple of days later, I told him about a sign on the ceiling of the wrestling room at the Naval Academy that read: "If you can read this from your position, you're in bad shape."

"I wonder if you could have read that sign," I said to him.

"Aw, coach," he replied, "it doesn't make any difference. It was only an exhibition game, and you know that you always said that the nastiest thing you can do to an opponent is to beat him."

Gibron and I also had our moments over money because Abe never thought he was paid enough. I drove into our practice field one day in Cleveland, and next to my parking space was a brown Cadillac, the same color, size and style as my own.

"Who owns that?" I asked Morrie Kono.

"Abe Gibron just bought it," he told me.

At our team meeting before practice, I said, "Gibron, I know you can't afford that type of Cadillac, and I know it because I'm paying you."

"I know it too, coach," he replied, "and I know that you're not paying me enough. But the difference between my car and yours is that mine is mortgaged for the next ten years."

During one of our league meetings several years ago, when Abe was head coach of the Chicago Bears, we were standing next to each other in a buffet line, and I said to him, "Abe, think back to when you were playing and all the ups and downs you had, the emotional things that went with your life-style at that time. How would you handle a guy like that?"

"Aw, coach," he said, "we won, didn't we?"

That typified the spirit among those players; to them, winning was the only thing that counted, so I can never take ex-

ception to what they did because they were my kind of guys.
To give another example of that spirit, during our second
game against the New York Giants in 1950, Abe slammed
into Emlen Tunnell while he was waiting to catch a punt and
just splattered him. When I was coaching the Pro Bowl later
that year, Tunnell and I were talking, and he said to me,
"That Gibron is a madman coming down under punts. He's
crazy. A man just isn't safe waiting for the ball to come
down because he's just like a wild man."

Before our first game against the Giants the following year,
I recalled Emlen's remarks and said to Abe, "Tunnell thinks
that you're crazy when you run down under punts. It might
just be a smart thing to let him know you're coming when
he's getting ready to field a punt."

The first time Gillom punted, therefore, Abe gave a few
hoots as he got close to Tunnell, and Emlen, usually a sure-
handed punt returner, fumbled the ball. Hal Herring recovered for us, and a couple of plays later, Graham passed to
Lavelli for the winning touchdown.

After the Eagles' opener, the 1950 season really revolved
around our games against the Giants, and all season long we
three teams were in a close race for the division title. Steve
Owen, of the Giants, who became a good friend, had taken
the remains of the Eagle Defense and constructed an umbrella concept that received tremendous notoriety because his
team became the only one to beat us that year, twice. Because New York lost to the Cardinals and Steelers, however,
both of us were trailing the Eagles at the midway point of the
season, and it took victories by both of us over Philadelphia
in the second half of the season to eliminate them. We finished with identical 10–2 records, then played for the division
title in Cleveland the week after the season ended.

This game was perhaps Bill Willis's greatest ever. Late in
the fourth quarter we were ahead, 3–0, when Choo-Choo
Roberts, the Giants' fastest running back, started a dive play
at our 47-yard line. He saw everyone bunching up, however,
and bounced outside, and suddenly there was no one between
him and the goal line. Our closest player was 15 yards away,
and I was sure Roberts would tackle him on our 4-yard line.
Our defense stopped the Giants and forced them to kick a
field goal that only tied the score, instead of putting them
ahead.

Otto then moved us close enough, with just fifty-eight seconds to play, for Groza to attempt a field goal. The game had been played on a rock-hard surface at the stadium, frozen by temperatures with a wind-chill factor that dipped below zero, and everyone had worn sneakers for that game except Lou, who wore a conventional football shoe on his right foot for kicking. That big, hard leather shoe struck the ball and sent it spinning in a graceful arc through the goal posts, and we had finished our season of surprises by winning our division title. A last-second safety made the final score 8–3. The entire game, however—indeed, the season—had boiled down to Willis's catching Roberts from behind and preventing a touchdown.

This kind of heroics served as only the appetizer for the even more astounding events the following week, when we played the Los Angeles Rams, who had beaten the Bears in their play-off, for the NFL championship. The game ranks as the greatest I've ever seen, even greater than our opening victory over the Eagles, because of the remarkable array of players—nearly a dozen now in the Hall of Fame, aside from many others who belong there—and some of the most astonishing plays ever recorded in pro football history.

That game was a fiction writer's delight. We were the new guys in the league who had dethroned the champions and beaten them twice, we had won a playoff game from a team that had twice beaten us during the regular season and we were playing for the championship against the team we had replaced in Cleveland's affections—and on the same field where our opponents had last won a championship before leaving town. Now they were returning with the world championship at stake.

The 1950 Rams boasted five players who could run the 100 in less than ten seconds. Tom Fears, their superb end, had caught eighty-four passes from Norm Van Brocklin and from Bob Waterfield, who had been a hero in Cleveland, where, as a rookie, he had quarterbacked the team in the NFL title. The Rams actually had two backfields, one they called the Elephant Backfield, comprised of Tank Younger, Dan Towler and Ralph Pasquariello and specially conceived for this game because of our stadium's heavy playing surface; and the other called a Pony Backfield, with their fastest backs, including Glenn Davis, the famed Army star.

On the game's first play, Waterfield completed an 82-yard pass for a touchdown to Davis when Jim Martin, playing linebacker, missed his coverage assignment. That set the tone for the day, as both teams put on great scoring drives and tremendous surges of offense early in the game. Otto passed to Dub Jones for our first touchdown on our first possession, and Los Angeles came right back and scored in eight plays, one of them a 44-yard pass to Fears.

Mac Speedie had pulled a leg muscle in practice only three days before the game, so we wanted to get as much from him as possible before his leg gave out, and on every play we tried to isolate him and Lavelli on Tom Keane and Woodley Lewis, knowing that neither of the Rams could cope with them on a one-on-one basis. We also flared our backs, occupying the Rams' linebackers and creating natural openings for Lavelli in the middle of their defense. He caught a dozen passes that day, including one of 26 yards for our second touchdown.

After Dante's score, the center snap for the extra point try was too high for Tommy James to handle, and he picked it up too late for Groza to attempt a kick, so Tom, still trying for the point, just heaved the ball toward Tony Adamle. Tony had it for a moment and then dropped it. We trailed, 14–13, and that missed point changed the entire complexion of the game. We were still behind and would have to work harder than ever.

Early in the third quarter, Lavelli's second touchdown gave us a 20–14 lead, and it looked as if we could breathe a little more easily, particularly when Len Ford replaced Martin and, in one three-play sequence, threw Vitamin T. Smith, one of the Rams' ten-second backs, for a 14-yard loss, sacked Waterfield for 11 yards and then nailed Davis for a 13-yard loss.

The Rams bounced right back, though, and within a twenty-five-second span scored two touchdowns to take a 28–20 lead. Dick Hoerner ran seven straight times from our 17-yard line before scoring, and on our first play after the kickoff, Motley fumbled and lost the ball. Larry Brink, a great defensive end for the Rams, scooped it up and ran in for an easy touchdown. Though I was furious when Marion lost the fumble, he more than made up for it with the tremendous pass protection he gave Otto throughout that game after it became clear that the Rams had loaded up their defense to stop Marion's running and that we had to go elsewhere with our offense.

When we did, we found other heroes. Warren Lahr intercepted one of Waterfield's passes late in the third quarter, and Graham and Lavelli proceeded to beat a deadly tattoo on the Rams' pass defense with five straight completions. They so rattled Los Angeles it eventually allowed Rex Bumgardner to get free in the farthest part of the end zone for an unbelievable catch that cut the Rams' lead to one point.

In the final quarter, Otto Graham dispatched some of the greatest poise and heroics I have ever seen in a football game and became the centerpiece in the final act of this drama on Christmas Eve afternoon. After Tommy Thompson intercepted another of Waterfield's passes, Otto was driving our offense toward another score when he was blind-sided running a quarterback draw play, fumbled and lost the ball with only three minutes to play. He came to the sideline totally crushed because he felt he had lost the game with that fumble, and it hurt me to see this great player standing there so heartbroken. from the Rams' goal line.

I walked over to him, put my arm on his shoulder and said softly, "Don't worry, Otto. We'll get the ball back for you and win this thing yet."

It was the perfect tonic, the sort of unpreconceived thing a coach does in the heat of a game that happens to fit the moment. I had seen us battle harder in this game than any Browns team had ever battled before, however; I was completely confident we could still win and I wanted Otto feeling the same way when we got the ball back from him. That happened with less than two minutes to play, 68 yards away from the Rams' goal line.

Otto was magnificent, operating the poise and confidence that not only buoyed our players but tolled a knell the Rams' defense must have heard every time he took the center snap. Los Angeles was desperate to stop his passing and on the first play so overdeployed to cover it that he ran a quarterback draw for 14 yards to our 46-yard line. When the defense tightened a bit, he completed three more passes, two to Bumgardner, who made one diving, fingertip catch that I'll always remember. These brought the ball to the Rams' 11-yard line. The score was 28–17. Lou Groza needed only to kick the easy field goal to make it 30–28, and the game would be over. We told Otto to run the ball one more time and position it in the center of the field, and when he did that, he and several other players came skipping off the field, throwing their helmets in the air because they knew that Lou would make that kick.

"Stop that!" I snapped at them. I also felt he'd make it, but I took nothing for granted in this game. We didn't have to worry, though, because, with twenty-eight seconds on the clock, his kick was straight and true. Tom James, his holder, told me later that everyone had been so confident in the huddle that Hal Herring, our center, had even laughed when he asked him, "Where do you want the laces?"

"He put them right where I asked," Tom said.

Lou's kick hadn't even reached the goal post when Tommy began jumping in the air because he knew it was perfect, though he admitted that he was also doing a little politicking in case the officials had any doubts.

Lahr, whose interception had started our fourth touchdown drive, ended the game when he intercepted Van Brocklin's long pass to Bobby Boyd, and of all the passes he ever intercepted, that one is the most vivid.

It capped a great, exciting victory for us and Tex Schramm, who was general manager of the Rams at that time, has told me since that it was his bitterest moment in professional football.

"I could see it coming each time Graham handled the ball on that last drive," he said. "I could sense that it was inevitable that the Browns were going to win because they were just chopping us off a little bit at a time, and we were waiting for the final chop."

The thousands of fans at the game engulfed us, and we literally fought our way to the dressing room. "What the hell was the final score?" I asked as soon as I got inside because events had moved at such a dizzying pace that I didn't even know.

I knew that we had won, and that's all I cared about, though it pleased me even more when Bert Bell came in and told everyone, "You are the greatest team ever to play football." I was also pleased to get a letter from Branch Rickey a few days later, in which he wrote: "I want you to know how happy I am that you won the championship, partly because it vindicated the claims of our old league, but mostly because it was you who did it."

However, what I liked most of all was going home after that game to my family, while the rest of Cleveland celebrated long into the night, and later taking my usual evening walk with Katy. The night was cold but crystal clear, a perfect Christmas Eve, and she had her arm through mine and just squeezed me now and then as we walked along.

"You know, honey, I think we're going to be okay," I said to her. "Everything is going to be all right."

TEN

The Great Years
in the NFL

WINNING THE NATIONAL FOOTBALL LEAGUE championship in our first year began an unprecedented period of success for us, and for the next six years the Cleveland Browns *were* professional football in the minds of a public fast becoming more aware of our sport. We were a marvelously functioning machine, capable of successfully meeting challenge and change. Like every champion, we faced the burden of knowing that every opponent worked harder to beat us than anyone else on its schedule, but our veteran players, who had been seared tough by having to prove season after season that they were still the best, passed down a legacy of excellence and consistency that our new players accepted, and our fine traditions continued.

We played not only because we enjoyed the game and wanted to be successful, but most of all for our pride and the sheer love of whipping an opponent that challenged us. That didn't get any easier as the years went on because while we had written the book, everyone soon had a copy and not only paid close attention to it, but found new and different ways to attempt to stuff it down our throats.

Bert Bell saw all this as the game's first real opportunity to establish professional football as a popular rival to baseball in the nation's sporting preferences, and everything the NFL did from that point on was geared to showcasing its attributes. The greatest of these was its players, and so Bert instituted the Pro Bowl. Joe Stydahar, the coach of the Rams, and I opposed each other only two weeks after our championship game, and I welcomed the honor because it gave me the opportunity to meet the top players in our division for the first time. As the years went by, the game always produced some delicious bits of intelligence, such as Emlen Tunnell's wariness of Abe Gibron, that helped us prepare for our divisional opponents the following year.

In those years everyone took the Pro Bowl seriously, and the players were proud to be selected; some would have played simply for the honor of being named to the team and so being officially made "All-Pro." The money, in today's terms, was not very much: The players on the winning team each received $600, the loser $500, and of course, everyone got a week's expense-paid trip to Los Angeles. The Cleveland players who participated each year always had a good time and played hard, on and off the field. There'd be nights when I'd be home in bed in Cleveland and the phone would ring in the wee hours of the morning. It would be my guys telling me they were thinking of quitting and staying on the West Coast . . . just to shake up their old coach.

I took my Pro Bowl games very seriously, but I knew from the first that our biggest problem was finding a play-calling system that everyone could understand. I developed a talking offense, in which the play was described in the huddle. If we wanted to run a quick toss to the right, our quarterback would simply say, "Quick toss to the right." If it was to the left, he'd say, "Quick toss to the left," or "Off-tackle right," or "Off-tackle left." Defenses were restricted and simple, so everyone knew his assignment on each play and never worried about stunts or other gimmicks. I used this system in every Pro Bowl and Senior Bowl game I coached thereafter.

The first game lived up to its billing and our East team won, 28–27. Otto scored the deciding touchdown on a quarterback draw, and Lou Groza kicked the winning point. The most memorable moment was a 47-yard punt return by Bill Dudley for our third touchdown, and when Bill, who then played for the Washington Redskins, ran past our bench en route to the end zone, I caught myself running along with him, waving him on.

After the game I visited the University of Southern California, at the request of its chancellor and its athletic director, who were searching for a new head football coach. I had no intention of returning to college football at that time, but I knew when word leaked out, the Browns would be in the papers for several days, and I figured the publicity couldn't hurt us. I also visited Ohio State at the request of some media and a segment of the alumni who had begun a movement for my return. I told McBride on both occasions that I had no plans of leaving the Browns—I couldn't anyway because of the four years left on my contract—but that I just wanted to have some fun and get us some free publicity. I got that all right—it caused a stir in the papers for several weeks—but soon after, Ohio State named Woody Hayes as its head coach.

The final side benefit of winning our first NFL title was the right to go to Chicago in August 1951 and play the College All-Stars. I made sure everyone on the team took it as seriously as I did because I didn't want us to lose or even look anything less than professional champions. In front of more than 92,000 people at Soldier Field, we never gave the All-Stars a chance and won, 33–0. The game was so one-sided that Arch Ward, whose newspaper sponsored the game, met me in the runway near our dressing room at halftime, grabbed me by the shirt and said in a quivering voice, "Young man, don't ever hurt this game of ours."

Arch, who had been my friend during our time in the All-America Conference, still didn't understand that it simply wasn't my nature to go easy in a game that had the nation's attention and that anything less than our best effort would have embarrassed me. My players reflected my attitudes. We destroyed the popular belief that a good team of college players always had a chance to beat an established professional team.

Our key acquisition that season was Harry ("Chick") Jagade, a bustling fullback who put more enthusiasm and joy into his playing than anyone I ever coached. He had impressed me with his reckless running style when we had played against him at Baltimore and Buffalo in the AAC, and we signed him as a free agent, even though, with Marion Motley and Emerson Cole as our fullbacks, I really didn't know what we would do with him. At first we put him on our special teams, and it seemed he made most of the tackles whenever he ran down under punts and kickoffs. Soon even the fans were hollering, "Go Chick, go, Chick," and he responded. Motley at this time was beginning to have leg problems, so Chick got more playing time as a fullback. As Marion's legs continued to bother him, Chick became our most effective fullback with that same reckless, exuberant running style.

Chick played for the sheer love of the game because he was an executive in his family's business in Chicago, and he didn't need the money from football to supplement his income. His business commitments finally made it necessary for us to trade him to the Bears after the 1953 season for Curly Morrison, another ten-strike. Chick died a few years ago of a heart attack while trudging down a mountain with a felled buck around his shoulders. Knowing Chick, I'm sure that after he felled that huge buck, he just hoisted it up and told everyone, "I've got mine," and stomped off. That was his style.

In that same year Ken Konz was our top draft pick, but a service commitment kept him from playing until 1953. Ken became one of our best safetymen, a superb punt return man and Lou Groza's holder on place kicks. We also selected Walt Michaels, a fullback at Washington & Lee University in Virginia, but because we needed some immediate help at defensive end, we traded him to Green Bay. He stayed there one year before returning to us for a superb ten-year career as a linebacker. Walt was one of the most intelligent players we ever had—he eventually became our captain—and a no-nonsense player. As far as he was concerned, he often said, playing football was an easier way to earn a living than digging coal, and he later applied that no-nonsense approach to his own coaching career.

That year we also drafted Don Shula and Carl Taseff from John Carroll University outside Cleveland. Shula was a ninth-round pick and not as highly touted as Taseff, who had been his school's leading runner, but Don was physically suited to play defensive back. After the draft, I didn't contact either player for a couple of months, and both of them were concerned that I had forgotten them.

When we finally met to sign the contracts, I told each of them that his salary would be $5,000 for the season. The words had hardly left my lips when both reached for their pens and the contracts and quickly signed.

"I was afraid that you might change your mind if we talked another second," Don later told me.

Since both came from the same school, and Taseff was the better known, I had difficulty keeping their names straight during training camp. I always seemed to be calling Shula "Taseff," and one day during a scrimmage, Don tackled

Motley and was knocked out. I bent over him as he came to and said, "Great tackle, Taseff."

He looked up at me groggily and said, "Shula."

Both of them were called into the service after the 1951 season; Carl rose to the rank of sergeant, and Don became a corporal. Today, of course, Taseff is one of Shula's very fine assistants on the Miami Dolphins, and both have worked together for years in pro football. Don came back and played for us during the second half of the 1952 seasons, when we needed defensive backs, and later both were part of a mammoth ten-for-five trade with the Baltimore Colts.

Our second NFL season revolved again around our games against the New York Giants, following an opening-game loss in San Francisco that cost us an unbeaten year. Our defense in 1951 was the best in pro football and shut out four of our twelve opponents, including the Giants, 10-0, in our first meeting in Cleveland. New York's 6-4-1 Umbrella Defense had gotten all the headlines, thanks in part to some big-city media ballyhoo and its two victories over us in 1950, but we had long since solved its mysteries.

The four deep backs were Tom Landry and Harmon Rowe at cornerback and Emlen Tunnell and Otto Schnellbacher at safety. The two ends in the six-man line either blitzed on passing situations or dropped off to help on pass coverage, but the key to that defense's success was its two big exceptional tackles, Arnie Weinmeister and Al DeRogatis. We had had trouble rooting them out to establish our running game, which would have kept their ends from helping on pass coverage, but we noticed that if we kept our two setbacks in to block when their ends came on a pass rush, their only linebacker, Jack Cannady, could not effectively cover the short passes. Conversely, if their ends did not come on a pass rush, we could release our two backs into the short areas away from their coverage. The key in either case was to throw short and not to try to challenge them with our deep passes. Schnellbacher was especially effective against the long pass, and he burned Otto a few times before we finally convinced him that it was almost futile to try and go that route. In Schnellbacher, Tunnell and Landry, the Giants had three of the best defensive backs who ever played against us.

The rivalry between the two teams became a lively affair partly because several of the old AAC Yankee players had brought their feelings against us to the Giants. The New

York media tried to promote a bitter feud between Steve Owen, the Giants' coach, and me, much as it had tried to get something started between Ray Flaherty and me. When the Giants came to Cleveland for the first time, there was a big fuss about their having to work behind the stadium on an open field because we had refused to remove the tarpaulin from the playing field. Of course, no mention was made that we had also worked on that same field a couple of hours before, because it was raining and we hadn't wanted to expose the stadium's playing surface.

Steve went along with all this, but we became close friends, particularly during the years we coached against each other in the Senior Bowl, which I coached nine times. We always exchanged all the information we had about the players on our respective teams, and he never once held back anything. We'd also get together socially during the week we were together in Mobile and thoroughly enjoyed each other's company.

The most exciting game of that 1951 season was our 14–13 victory over the Giants in New York. John Kissell was so heroic in stopping the Giants on two consecutive plays inside the one-yard line with less than a minute to play that when the game ended, I walked onto the field and handed him the game ball. Bill Willis also so intimidated their center, John Rapacz, that he caused Rapacz's snap for Ray Poole's extra point attempt earlier in the game to go wild, and Ray flubbed the kick that could have given the Giants a tie. New York used both the A formation and T formation then, and when the Giants ran from the A formation, which was a modified double wing with the two wingbacks lined up deep in the backfield, Rapacz had to look between his legs while snapping the ball to the tailback. Before doing so, however, he also knew that he had to take one last check on Bill's position. After he did, Bill would move to get a different position and then just unload on him. I don't think anyone could have handled the assignment.

Another memorable game that year was our 49–28 victory over the Bears, in which Dub Jones scored his record-setting six touchdowns. George Halas, as was his custom during his coaching days, was roaming the sidelines and berating everyone. Finally, our captain, Tony Adamle, got tired of it all in the third quarter, when George walked on the field to protest a penalty. He tapped him on the shoulder and said, "Would you please get the hell out of here?"

I'm sure George was taken aback because he was used to having his own way during those years. He was a tough rival, who always knew what he was doing in football, and some have said that we feuded, but that is untrue. I always found him very friendly and easy to talk to, even when we were hammering out our merger agreement and there was so much ill feeling from other NFL people. Our views on the game were very similar. While our games against his teams were always spirited, we won most of them, so I never worried about there being anything personal, and I don't think he did either. He can truly be called the Father of the National Football League.

We wrapped up our 1951 division title in the next-to-last game of the year while the Rams and Detroit Lions had to battle to the end for the Western Division title. Our players were rooting for the Rams because the Coliseum's great seating capacity meant more money in play-off shares, but I wanted Detroit to win because the Korean War had made airline logistics a nightmare. On the final Sunday, Detroit lost a half-game lead by losing to San Francisco, and the Rams' victory over Green Bay set up a second straight championship game for us.

My worst fears about travel to the West Coast were realized when we had to split our team and send it on two planes for our early workouts in Los Angeles and then put our equipment on a third plane, which, of course, didn't arrive in time for our workouts. In addition, it was the third time that season we went to play the Rams in the Coliseum, having won in the preseason and in our second game following the 49ers' loss, and I never liked playing a team more than twice during any season. While I never believed in omens, perhaps all those things should have been a tip-off that trouble awaited us.

Los Angeles still had all its great offensive weapons from the 1950 season, but it had rebuilt its defense with younger players, who, by the end of the year, had become very competent. Nevertheless, we were still leading, 10–7, at the end of the first half, though we had lost a touchdown by Mac Speedie on a questionable penalty call. Our defense protected that slim lead in the third quarter, until suddenly Larry Brink sacked Otto, forced him to fumble, and Andy Robustelli picked up the ball and ran to the ten-yard line. Three plays later, Dan Towler scored to put the Rams ahead, 14–10, and Bob Waterfield's field goal at the start of the last quarter increased the lead to 17–10. Our defense got us back onto the game when it stopped the Rams on seven straight plays from inside the five-yard line without allowing a point later in that quarter, and Otto responded with a touchdown pass to Ken Carpenter that tied the score.

Three plays later, however, from our 27-yard line, Norm Van Brocklin passed to Tom Fears for the winning touchdown. It was our fault, a coaching mistake, that made it possible. For several years, our secondary had never declared a strong side of our opponent's offense formation until it saw which direction the fullback was going, and though we had gotten by with this strategy, it put a great burden on Cliff Lewis, the middle safety in our three-man secondary. This time the Rams' offense flowed one way, Fears crossed over from the weak side and it was simply impossible for Cliff to get back and cover him, though he just missed knocking the ball away by inches.

Tom James also reacted to that play, leaving his man as soon as he saw Van Brocklin targeting Fears. Many at the time blamed Tommy for allowing the catch because every picture showed him trailing Fears into the end zone when, in fact, he had made a gambling effort to prevent the touchdown. As it happened, this game was the first NFL title match to be televised nationally, and when Tom called home the next day, before we left Los Angeles, he found out all the news accounts and the television clips were pointing to him as the culprit. He was understandably upset and went to Tony Adamle, our captain, and asked him to speak to me about straightening out the story. It upset me, too, because he wasn't to blame, and I immediately talked to Harold Sauerbrei, who covered the Browns at that time for the *Plain Dealer* and who then wrote a story the next day absolving James of any fault and putting it on me, where it belonged. We changed our defensive coverage after that, but it was something we should have foreseen.

We had lost our bid for a second straight NFL championship, but our future was bright, even though for the next couple of years, particularly in 1952, we faced a myriad of problems that sometimes muddled our personnel situation. The only one I ever accepted as being outside my control was the Korean War, which delayed or interrupted players' careers with military service commitments. There was nothing we could do about that, and like every other NFL team, we coped with the problem as best we could.

The other difficulties, however, were more bothersome. I was still trying to find an eventual successor to Otto Graham, whose time for retirement was fast approaching, as was that of some of our other great veterans; I had to root out, and then stabilize, a disturbing morale problem that disrupted our team late in 1952, which meant a wholesale personnel shake-up; and as a capper, we fought a player war with the Canadian Football League that cost us three players and a first-round draft pick and eventually wound up in court.

My first concern ever since losing Y. A. Tittle in 1948 was to find and train Otto's eventual replacement. In 1951 we drafted Stan Heath, the nation's top collegiate passer from the University of Nevada, but he lasted just one week in training camp because he couldn't believe I was serious in demanding total attention to our classroom work. When I gave each player a written examination at the end of that first week, he couldn't answer one question correctly, and I put him on waivers that very night.

The problem was accentuated after Cliff Lewis retired following the 1951 season. We needed an experienced man behind Otto, and I obtained George Ratterman in a trade with the Dallas Texans. Ratterman, who had played against us in the AAC, had always impressed me with his great knowledge of the game, but I knew he often disregarded his coach's instructions and did as he pleased on the field. Still, I felt that with some firm handling and playing on a championship team, George might settle down and help us, and I was willing at that point to put up with some of his well-known pranks and practical jokes.

In that regard, he was already a legend when he came with us in 1952. I had been one of his victims when the Browns had played the AAC All-Stars in Houston in the final game of that league's existence. It had rained hard all week, and Ratterman had heard the Browns' players griping about working in the wet weather, so he called the switchboard operator, told her that he was the coach and asked her to call our players to tell them that practice was canceled. Our coaches waited to begin our meetings, but no one showed up, and it wasn't until that evening that we found out what had happened. I had heard stories about Ratterman's odd sense of humor in Buffalo, too. Once, in crossing an intersection, he found a car blocking his path and simply walked across the hood of the car without breaking stride. Another time he totally confused a friendly lady who asked him for directions in that city by pretending to be twins. He talked to the lady, then hurried to meet her by walking from another direction, then repeated the act until the poor soul was at her wit's end. In Baltimore he once crawled across an eighteen-inch steel span above some railroad tracks simply to win a twenty-five-cent bet.

No one ever faulted George for lacking courage. In our opening game against the Rams in 1952, I looked out on the field late in the game and found him running down under a kickoff and then making the tackle. He had inserted himself on the kickoff team, something none of our coaches would ever have done, to try in his own inimitable way, to tell me that he wanted to play, one way or the other. One evening en route to a movie in Washington, we walked across the Connecticut Avenue Bridge that spans Rock Creek Park, near the Shoreham Hotel, and George walked along the railing. One slip, and it would have been more than 100 feet into the trees and rocks below, but he was undaunted. When our bus had arrived at that hotel from the airport, incidentally, each of us had been greeted personally by a man decked out like a doorman. To strangers, it seemed we were getting the royal welcome. We were—from Ratterman's father, who was as much of a practical joker as his son.

George's pranks in the locker room never ceased. Someone was always getting "hot stuff," a jelly that contained medicated heat for sore muscles, in his jockstrap, which burned like fire. Horace Gillom was terrified of snakes, yet every so often a garter snake would tumble from his football shoes, and he'd scream bloody murder. Poor Morrie Kono once spent the night in our dressing room after George had locked him in, and when Morrie tried to get even by hiding George's clothes during a game at the stadium, Ratterman simply looked at his empty locker, turned around, bid everyone good-night, walked out the door to his car and drove home in full uniform. Even knowing these eccentricities didn't lessen our needs for an experienced quarterback, however, nor did it prevent him from offering some very incisive observations that helped us during our championship years.

I knew that George was not the real answer, though, and the search for a quarterback went on. In our 1952 draft we selected another record-setting passer from Loyola of Los Angeles named Don Klosterman, who is now general manager of the Los Angeles Rams. As a young collegian he had once written to me seeking advice on becoming a better T quarterback and saying that if I ever returned to college football, he would transfer to my school so he could play on my team. While in Los Angeles for a 1951 game against the Rams, I watched Don complete thirty-three of sixty-three passes in a losing game against Florida, and he impressed me. We later traded his rights to the Rams, however, when we decided to go with our experienced quarterbacks.

In 1954 we won the NFL's bonus pick. In those days a lottery was held each year for the draft's first selection, which a team could win only once. With our pick, we selected Bobby Garrett from Stanford, recognized by everyone that year as college football's outstanding quarterback. Bob stuttered badly under stress conditions, but George Lynn, one of my Ohio State captains who had become an assistant coach at Stanford, assured me that it had never been a problem with them.

Unfortunately it got worse when he came to us. The first time I met him, he could hardly say a word. My only hope was that he would relax when he got into a comfortable football situation, but that never happened with us. The harder he tried—and he really tried to overcome it—the worse it became. Sometimes during practice he'd go to the line of scrimmage to call signals and wouldn't even be able to get out the first word. It was the same in the huddle. I knew that this could be disastrous in a game, and I'd stand by the huddle, listening to him trying to call the play, and say "The thirty-second clock is running. . . ." Finally, he'd get the words out, but it soon became evident that even though he had all the other talents to be a good quarterback, this handicap just prevented him from being able to make it with us.

Our other first-round draft pick that year was a guard from Illinois named Johnny Bauer, who failed to make the team. For some reason, though, Green Bay coveted both him and Garrett, and when we suggested trading them for Babe Parilli, a quarterback whose passing ability had always intrigued me, they became wary and sent a scout to watch Bauer in our drills. That was forbidden by NFL rules. However, we spotted their scout in the stands, and I wanted Parilli, so Ed Ulinski, our line coach, worked out a signal arrangement with John Kissell. When Eddie turned the bill of his cap in the direction he wanted Kissell to allow Bauer to move him, Kissell then made sure he moved in a manner which gave the rookie guard his best possible blocking angle. As the Green Bay scout watched, Bauer had a field day against this great all-pro tackle, though after a while Kissell's patience began wearing thin. When he said, "To hell with this," he called off the drill. A couple of days later we made the trade with Green Bay. It eventually all went for naught because when Parilli, who had been in the service, finally came to us in 1956 as the well-publicized heir apparent to Otto Graham, he was too tense and nervous to be effective, and we had to trade him after that one season.

Though he never did find the surefire replacement for Otto Graham, our trades and draft choices brought us some fine players and kept us in championship form right through the 1955 season. In 1952, for example, besides getting Ratterman, we added three other great players in Darrell ("Pete") Brewster, Bob Grain and Ray Renfro. Brewster and Gain came in trades, and Renfro, one of the fastest men ever to play football, was a high-round draft pick. Brewster was a prime example of the role luck can play in obtaining a player. The Chicago Cardinals' new coach, Joe Kuharich, had just come from an unbeaten season at the University of San Francisco and wanted to gather as many of his players from that team as he could, including a linebacker named Burl Toler, whom we had drafted. In return, we asked for Brewster, a rookie of theirs from Purdue, and got him. As it turned out, Toler, who has been an NFL official now for several years, played in the College All-Star game and tore up his knee, ending his playing career, while Brewster had seven tremendous years for us, replacing Speedie in 1953 as our starting split end.

Bob Gain had started his career with Green Bay and became an excellent defensive tackle for us because he had such tremendous strength and big hands he simply tossed aside an opposing lineman. Added to that strength was great quickness and mobility. Bob, who is one of my closest friends, also had a tremendous sense of humor, albeit a bit earthy at times, and few ever got the last laugh on him.

When we trained at Hiram College, a barber used to come

once a week so our players could get their hair cut. Bob, who was balding prematurely, walked into the room where the barber, who was a bit of a wise guy himself, had set up his shop.

"Shall I take off my coat?" he asked.

The barber took one look and said, "You don't even have to take off your hat, if you don't want to."

Bob gave him an irate look, took off his hat and coat and sat in the chair. The barber stood behind him and began softly running one hand over Bob's scalp.

"You know," he said to Bob, "this feels just like my wife's butt."

When the barber removed his hand, Bob placed a hand atop his head and repeated the massaging action.

"By gosh, you're right," he told the man, "that's exactly what it feels like."

Ray Renfro was the man who succeeded Dub Jones as the Browns' flanker, though he had to work at mastering the position because he never had great hands like Jones or Lavelli. He ran the 100 yards in 9.4 seconds and played running back for the first couple of seasons before we moved him to flanker. My only regret with Ray occurred after he had dropped a sure touchdown pass one game, and I was so mad that when he came back to the bench, I said to him, "These days you never seem able to make the big catch!" Of course, I didn't mean it. But he was crushed, though he never let on at the time. I always told my players that anything said on the sidelines in the heat of a game should be forgotten when the game ended, but I realized that wasn't always easy to remember. He knows now that I never meant anything personal by it, and he had some spectacular games for us.

A festering mood of selfishness had infected our team by 1952, fostered by some players who were reaching the end of their careers and wanted to get as much for themselves as they could and supported by others who put money ahead of their team. The crusher came when, after a stormy team meeting, this group rammed through a vote that excluded the assistant coaches, trainer and equipment man from receiving any shares from the championship game money. I had the club pay these men, but it was a feeling that reflected itself in our attitude that entire season and in the way we lost to Detroit for the NFL title in 1952.

So we continued, trying to rebuild our team and infuse a

new spirit, without destroying its championship capability. Some people, like Lou Groza, and more recently, Jim Marshall of the Vikings, never seem to grow old, but basically football is a young man's game; a player reaches a certain age when he feels that it is just unnatural for him to be running into people. Spirited football—the kind I wanted—requires a blood-and-thunder type of person, and in 1953 we went after them, first in the draft by obtaining Doug Atkins, Billy Reynolds, Carlton Massey, Galen Fiss and, on our final pick, a blond-haired guard from Dayton University named Chuck Noll. We also traded ten players to Baltimore for Mike McCormack, Tom Catlin, Don Colo, John Petibon and Herschell Forrester, all of whom became starters for us for several years and served as the impetus that took us back to NFL championships in 1954 and 1955.

Ten players weren't too much to pay for the caliber of those men. Three of them—McCormack, Colo and Catlin—later became team captains and helped supply the kind of leadership that had begun to slip in 1952. I consider McCormack the finest offensive tackle who ever played professional football, a man who definitely belongs in the Hall of Fame, and when Bill Willis retired after the 1953 season, he became an equally fine middle linebacker for us, solidifying our defense. When he and Groza later were our starting tackles, we had a pair of 250-pound men who could run a 40-yard dash in full uniform in 4.8 seconds.

Tom Catlin and Don Colo were bruising defensive players, Tommy an outstanding linebacker, who simply whipsawed runners whenever he tackled them, and also a fine long snapper as center on our kicking teams. For many seasons now, he has been an excellent assistant coach with the Rams and Buffalo Bills. We had played against Colo in New York and Dallas and found in him a rough, almost brutal type of defensive tackle who punished offensive blockers. I knew our guys did not like to play against him; that made him the kind of player I wanted for our team.

Among the draftees, Massey became a regular defensive end, and Fiss, after a service hitch, came to us in 1956 and began an eleven-season career as an outside linebacker. Atkins, who was six feet eight inches and weighed 260 pounds, played only two years as a defensive tackle and end for us, but he was a fine player both seasons. I regretted having to trade him to Chicago in 1955, but his life-style became incompatible with our philosophy, though it never altered my respect for him as a player. Doug played in the NFL for seventeen years, finally retiring at the age of thirty-nine.

Chuck Noll was a Cleveland native, who had played at Benedictine High School and then at Dayton University. I always liked to take one or two local kids late in the draft, assuming, of course, that they were good players, but no one really expected Chuck to make our team—except Chuck himself. He was a very bright and determined player who became a tremendous technician as one of our messenger guards. No one ever worked harder in practice to perfect his skills. One day during his rookie season, I met some kids from Dayton University, and they asked me, "How is the Pope doing?"

"What do you mean, 'the Pope'?" I asked.

"That's Chuck Noll," they replied.

"Why do you call him the Pope?"

"Because he can do no wrong," they said, laughing.

I found out later that Joe Gavin, Chuck's coach at Dayton, had been the cause of that nickname because Chuck was so technically perfect Gavin constantly used him as an example when demonstrating line play techniques to his other players. In 1955 we moved him to linebacker, where he played with the same excellence, and he cut short a great career in 1960, when he joined Sid Gillman as an assistant coach for the American Football League's Los Angeles team. Of course, he now is one of the NFL's best coaches, and his own great determination and toughness are reflected in his team's style of play.

Billy Reynolds is another from that draft who played well for us, particularly when we played Detroit for the title in 1954. There is a funny story regarding him, though. He was sitting on the bench in a game against San Francisco, when he saw that Ken Konz, returning a punt near our sideline, was about to be tackled. In his excitement, Bill, who obviously had been bumped in the head on an earlier play, jumped from the bench and ran onto the field, hoping that Konz would lateral the ball to him before he was tackled. It was the first time I ever had seen that happen in football, and I was as stunned as the officials, who could only charge us with a five-yard penalty for having too many men on the field.

As if all this rebuilding weren't problem enough, we also

had to fight our war against the Canadian League. We lost Speedie and Kissell to them after the 1952 season, a year later Ken Carpenter jumped his contract and in 1955 Kurt Burris, our top draft pick, turned us down because he said he had a coaching job at the University of Miami, and a week later we found out he had signed with the Canadian League.

One day early in 1953 Speedie and his lawyer walked into my office, and the lawyer did all the talking, telling me that Mac was going to the Canadian League. If we tried to prevent him and force him to honor the one year left on his contract, the man added, he would take the entire matter to court and challenge the validity of NFL contracts.

Through all this, Speedie never uttered a word, but when his lawyer had finished speaking, I stood up, held out my hand and said, "Good luck, Mac." We shook hands, and he still said nothing, and that was the last time I ever saw or spoke to him for twenty-five years.

Carpenter, too, just abrogated his contract, and we didn't find out about him until we read about it in the newspapers.

In Kissell's case I decided we had to take a stand to prevent this wholesale player raiding. We swore out a subpoena for John to appear at a hearing in Ottawa, where he was playing, but when the Canadian process server went to the practice field and asked for Kissell, everyone on the field pulled his jersey over his head.

"I can't tell which one is Kissell," the man told our lawyer, and just walked away.

I have always believed that the Canadian judge was in cahoots with the team because he also refused our bid for an injunction that would have forced John to play out his contract with us. That was a blow to the entire NFL because it meant our players could go up to Canada, or be lured up there by promises of easy money, without any legal recourse on our part.

The next season John returned to play for us, and he told me something that nearly every American player has found to be true when he opts to play in the Canadian League over the NFL.

"Coach, it was like a foreign country up there," he said. "I was ready to come home after three weeks, and I wish that I had."

This business went on for another year, until I decided we had to do something and in 1955 signed Bobby Freeman

from Auburn, one of our draft picks, who had already signed
a contract with Winnipeg. I knew that he had the other contract, that the case would wind up in our court and that we
would probably lose, but I felt we simply couldn't afford to
sit back and allow them to raid us.

The judge who heard the case was Paul Jones, whom I
knew from riding into the city together in the morning from
Shaker Heights on the Rapid Transit. At least, I was on
friendly, if dubious legal ground.

Allie Sherman, the Winnipeg coach who later became head
coach of the New York Giants, told the judge how much he
needed Bobby, who was a quarterback, because he was in the
process of building the offense of the fifties in Canada and
could do it only with Freeman. I had never had any illusions
that Bobby could be a quarterback with us, and when I took
the witness stand, Judge Jones looked at me a moment and
then said, "What do you have to say for yourself?"

"Nothing," I replied, "except that we signed Mr. Freeman
in full knowledge that he already had signed a contract with
the Canadian League, and we did it in retaliation for their
signing our players."

"That's not a good enough reason," he told me, as I knew.
I was prepared for the verdict to go against us, but before it
could be rendered, Freeman was called into the service for
three years, and by the time he had finished his military commitment he was ready to come and play for us. He became a
defensive back for the Browns for several years. That slowed
up the Canadian League's incursions, and today we have mutually respected contracts.

While all this was going on, our rivalry with the Detroit
Lions had captured everyone's attention, and after we had
lost two straight title games to them in 1952 and 1953, every-
one said they were our "jinx." I never believed in jinxes be-
cause if one team beats another consistently, it is usually
because the winning team is pretty good, and in those years,
Buddy Parker had gathered some great players for his team.
Eight of them—flanker Doak Walker; tight end Leon Hart;
offensive linemen Vince Banonis, Lou Creekmur, Harley
Sewell and Dick Stanfel; defensive backs Yale Lary and Jack
Christiansen—are on my all-opponents team, and so are Joe
Schmidt, who joined the Lions in 1953, and Dick ("Night
Train") Lane, who came in 1960.

Banonis was the best run-blocking center who played

against us, and he could really move people from the middle of a defense. Hart, six feet five inches tall and 260 pounds, was the first of the truly big, mobile tight ends and a devastating blocker. When he came over the middle to catch quick look-in passes, he trampled unsuspecting linebackers and strong safeties. Christiansen had tremendous range against long passes, much like Schnellbacher, as did Lane. Lane looked like easy prey if we ran to his side for a while, but every time we thought we had him fooled there he was, back covering our receivers. Christiansen, Schmidt, Lane, Lary and Bobby Layne, the Lions' quarterback during those years, are in the Hall of Fame.

One of the Lions' most publicized players then, however, and the first raised to near folk-hero status by television, was their middle guard, Len Bingaman. Bingaman weighed 325 pounds, and though he was no big threat as a pass rusher, he liked to roam along the line of scrimmage making tackles. No one could move him because of his bulk, so we developed a scheme of "influence blocking," in which we blocked him toward the area where we wanted to run the play, knowing that he'd react against the pressure and take himself *out* of the play. A few years later we refined this concept to a much higher degree against Gene ("Big Daddy") Lipscomb at Pittsburgh.

A rash of injuries against the Giants in the final game of the 1952 season, including James, Kissell, Jones and Speedie, plus the bad attitude that had infected our team, had much to do with our losing to the Lions the first time we played them for the NFL title. Though we gained more yards and first downs than the Lions, mental errors crippled us. The worst came when we trailed only 14–7 in the second half, with a first down inside Detroit's five-yard line, and allowed our pass protection to fail. We never got a point from that drive, and the final score was 17–7.

In 1953, our rebuilding program helped bring us to the edge of an unbeaten season, but in the final game, we lost a seventeen-point first-half lead to Jim Trimble's Philadelphia team and were beaten, 42–17. I'll never forget one of our receivers running for an apparent touchdown, then dropping the ball with no one around him and the Eagles recovering it. I wasn't really crushed at missing a perfect season, however, because there had been too much talk about our being the greatest football team of all time, and that kind of talk could have hurt our mental attitude for the championship game. As it was, some strange turns of events cost us the title.

Of all the games Otto Graham played in Cleveland, there was never a worse one than that day against Detroit. He had an injured finger on his throwing hand, and his passes were sailing either too long or too short to open receivers, so in the second quarter, he asked to be taken out of the game, and I put in Ratterman. George was no better, however, so I gave the game back to Otto in the second half, and thanks to a pair of Groza's field goals, we led, 16–10, when the Lions got the ball with less than four minutes to play.

Earlier in the game Leon Hart had left with a damaged knee, and Jim Doran, nominally a defensive end, had replaced him and begun a bitter personal duel with Warren Lahr. Hardly a play went by without some contact between the two, even if the play was on the other side of the field. When Detroit started its final drive from the 20-yard line, they continued to battle, and when Doran threw an elbow, Warren got hot. On the next play Doran made a move as if to do it again, and as Warren rushed to retaliate, Jim cut around him and caught a perfect pass for a touchdown. Doak Walker's extra point was the winning margin in the Lions' 17–16 victory.

I never felt sorrier for anyone in my life than I did for Lahr as we rode home on the train afterward. He sat alone at one end of the coach, with no one saying a word to him, not because anyone blamed him, but because everyone saw he was just torn up inside. It was a shame because he was a very gifted defensive back, so speedy he stayed with the fastest receivers in football, and, unlike some cornerbacks, was an outstanding tackler.

Losing to the Lions as we did—it was the fourth game in two years we had played without beating them—immediately raised stories of a feud between Buddy Parker and me. I never enjoyed being beaten by anyone, but Buddy and I were always good friends. Our two coaching staffs had a golf outing each summer, and afterward we would sit around and talk for hours. Buddy never played golf, preferring instead to play the "nineteenth hole" with Buster Ramsey, his line coach, but he was a very engaging man and a fine coach.

That 1953 title game ended one of the most hectic seasons I ever experienced in Cleveland. It had begun in the spring, when McBride sold the Browns for $600,000 to a group headed by Dave Jones, and including Bob Gries, Sol Silberman and Ellis Ryan, who was part owner of the Indians. I was in Canada on a fishing trip when the sale occurred and didn't know anything about it until we came back through customs near Buffalo, New York, and I read about it in an American newspaper. I was furious for not having been told, and as soon as I got back to Cleveland, I confronted McBride.

"This is no way to do business," I told him. "And I certainly don't like having the club sold out from underneath me without so much as a word's advance warning or even any consultation."

"Dave Jones told me that you'd be willing to go along with the deal," he replied.

"Well, Dave Jones never told me a thing about it," I said. "And what you did is a far cry from the way we agreed our club would operate when you asked me to run it."

He had no answer for that, and I turned and walked out of his office. I never saw Arthur McBride again after that, though I found out later that his son, Artie, had convinced his father that our best days were behind us and that the club was getting too old to be a contender again. I wasn't the only one who was mad either. Everyone who had shares in the club was upset at the sale's price because we already had $300,000, or fully half the amount, in the bank in season ticket orders.

I still had seven and a half years remaining on my contract, however, and the new owners promised to honor all its stipulations, including the one that allowed me to run the team without interference. The new group had other businesses, and I saw them infrequently; they seemed content to bask in the glory from the team's success, though Jones was sometimes painful in his role as president. One day, I received a bill for $1,500 from a Shriners' magazine.

"What's this for?" I asked him.

"I had my picture on the magazine's front cover welcoming their convention to Cleveland and telling everyone to come and see us play," he replied.

"Don't ever do anything like that again," I told him. "That money belongs to our franchise, and our agreement is that I make the decision on how it will be spent. Your personal aggrandizement is not fair to the other owners."

He didn't like that one bit, and things were a bit testy between us for a while, but I was undaunted.

Gries also could be a problem. A man coarse in his manners, he was fired from his job in a large department store by his own father-in-law. Maybe he didn't like the sign Bob had on the wall over his desk: "Who says it doesn't pay to marry the boss's daughter?" Bob's big line always was that we needed someone to "merchandise" our team, and my reply to him was always that our best merchandising tool was putting more points on the scoreboard than our opponents did.

Silberman, who owned Randall Park Race Track, was no prize either. For a while he used to call me for information on our upcoming games, and I never understood why until I found out that he was betting on football games, forbidden for all owners by the NFL constitution. I reported these calls to Bert Bell, as required by the rules, and a short time later, Silberman was ordered by Bell to sell his Browns stock because of conduct detrimental to football.

Though our team was beaten only once in 1953, the season was far from easy. The worst moment occurred in a game against San Francisco when, before more than 80,000 people, Fred Burney pushed Otto Graham out of bounds, and while he was still on the ground, Art Michalik, a 220-pound linebacker, steamed into him and smashed a fist into his face. It happened right in front of our bench; the brutality of the act momentarily stunned our players, and then they almost lost control with anger. I was just as upset but had to expend my energy restraining our players, particularly Tommy Thompson, who wanted revenge on the spot. I spent most of our halftime break trying to restore some rationality; we were still involved in a close game, and I was afraid we would lose our poise and the game.

Otto left the field after the incident, and Dr. Vic Ippolito had to use fifteen sutures to close the vicious gash inside his mouth without administering any novocaine. Otto came back in the second half, looking rather grotesque, but proceeded to complete nine of ten passes in our 23–21 victory. Bill Johnson, who was San Francisco's center then, told me the 49ers' players were just as unhappy with Michalik as we were.

Before I allowed Otto to play in the second half, I had Morrie Kono attach an inch-thick piece of clear plastic to his helmet to protect his mouth, and he wore it for several games thereafter. Such injuries had bothered me ever since Len Ford had had his face bashed in by Pat Harder's elbow, and after the 1953 season I talked to my friend Jerry Morgan, who was with the Riddell sports equipment firm in Chicago, about manufacturing a special face protector. At first, they came up with a plastic mask somewhat similar to the one we had used the day Otto was injured, but it fogged up and, in the cold weather, broke. The players disliked it for another reason—they couldn't spit—and it was also too heavy to be worn in comfort.

"Give me something that will fit across the front of a helmet and will be about as big as my little finger, with tensile strength. I want it so it can withstand a stray foot, or a deliberately thrown fist or elbow, and take away the inclination to punch someone. But keep it light enough to weigh less than an ounce," I told Jerry.

The result was the single protective bar, and we were the first to wear it. Other coaches came to our training camp and saw it, and soon every team used it. A few years later we went to the double bar across the helmet. I have been under contract with Riddell from the start of this idea and for years collected a royalty on every one that was sold.

Later that season, in a game against the Steelers, Thompson tore up his knee, and though we did not know it at the time, his career was finished. Even in excruciating pain, though, and propped up on a stretcher, he refused to leave our bench and insisted on helping Marion Motley, who had replaced him. This one act epitomized the real spirit of the Browns.

Before the 1953 season ended, we had our annual war of words with the New York Giants, this time after we defeated them, 7–0, in an absolute quagmire at the Polo Grounds. The field was in a deplorable condition, even though all the weather reports had predicted rain, and I accused them of deliberately failing to cover it the night before the game. The Giants' official said the ground crew had mistakenly gone home without covering it, but I never knew of a ground crew abandoning a playing field in the face of a rainstorm. We won that game when we used a long count on a field goal attempt to induce one of their players, Joe Ramona, to jump offsides; the penalty gave us the impetus to continue our drive and score the only touchdown. In the season's final game against the Giants, we won again, 62–14, and Steve

Owen lost his job after the season ended. Many blamed me for running up the score, but Steve always knew that hadn't been my intention. In fact, I had replaced all our front-line players by the middle of the third quarter, and we scored only seven points in the final period.

Following our heartbreaking loss to the Lions in the 1953 title game, I went down to Mobile to coach the Senior Bowl game and took Weeb Ewbank, our tackle coach, as my assistant because he was in charge of our draft and would get a firsthand view of the top prospects. At the same time Don Kellett, general manager at Baltimore, offered the Colts' head coaching job to Blanton Collier, but Collier turned him down. Kellett's second choice was Weeb because, as I found out later, the team's owner felt the quickest way for his new team to succeed was literally to buy the Browns' system by hiring one of our assistants.

I never knew that Kellett was in Mobile talking to Weeb, and on the morning of the game Weeb said he had to meet someone, who turned out to be Kellett. When he finally did show up, the game was almost half over, and he told me after the game that he had signed a contract with the Colts. That was fine with me because it simply meant one of my friends had achieved success in his profession. The only problem was that Weeb had set up our draft, and since he was under contract to the Colts, I went to Bert Bell about the propriety of having him work for us under those conditions. We had paid for all the information we had gathered, and no one else on our staff had as much knowledge of the draft as Weeb, yet we didn't want him taking it to Baltimore.

"He must work for you until after the draft; then he is free to join the Colts," Bell ruled.

As the draft got under way, however, we noticed that the player we had planned to pick on every round was being chosen by the Colts. It wasn't until near the end of the first day's session that I discovered the system that was being used to relay the pick to the Colts' table from our table.

"Weeb, I know what's going on now, and I'm sorry about the way this thing has gone," I told him. "Tomorrow you go over to Baltimore's table and draft for them."

Weeb admitted it but said, "I did it for my wife and family." They were dear friends, too, so I couldn't take exception to that, but the personal hurt was great. In addition, our franchise was severely set back by what had happened.

We lost some players—notably Ray Berry and Ordelle Braase—whom we had planned on drafting. Of course, all that is behind us now, and we are very close friends. When Weeb was selected for the Hall of Fame in 1978, he asked me to present him, and I agreed, though the death of my oldest son, Robin, a day before prevented me from fulfilling that function.

Later that year, Collier left to coach at Kentucky, and there was another wholesale player influx. With all that happening, we probably had no right to expect a world championship season in 1954. In training camp that year, we were trying to sort out all the new faces when a strapping young high school fullback named Cookie Gilchrist, who had broken all the high school records in western Pennsylvania, came with his father to ask for a tryout. We were forbidden by NFL rules to sign anyone whose potential college class had not yet graduated, but his father insisted that the boy did not want to go to college and that we give him a tryout. We watched him run, just to ease out of the situation, but never scrimmaged him, as has often been reported. Nevertheless, the boy really intrigued me, and I even called Bert Bell to reaffirm the league rule. As I expected, Bert told me not to sign him. He left us, went to Canada, where he became a star, and stayed there even after he was eligible to sign with the NFL. Later he came back to play in the American Football League.

I don't even know if we could have used him, though, because both Curly Morrison and Maurice Bassett were excellent fullbacks for us that year. When we traded Dale Atkinson and end John Carson to the Redskins for defensive back Don Doll and then added Don Paul from the Cardinals, our secondary was secure. McCormack and Forrester came out of the service and joined halfback Chet Hanulak and guard Hal Bradley. We gathered steam slowly, and it wasn't until the season's eighth game, when we defeated the Eagles, 6–0, after a tremendous goal line stand at the end, that we held first place for good.

That victory was particularly satisfying because we had lost to the Eagles at the start of the season, and they were the ones who had cost us the perfect season in 1953. The Eagles, with their famed Suicide Seven Defense, were a physically tough team; I can even remember their equipment man going after one of our players with a water bucket following a scuffle near their bench. Bucko Kilory was still their great middle guard, ranging everywhere to make his tackles, but my all-time linebacking opponent was center and middle linebacker Chuck Bednarik. He was like a flaming torch on the field, one of the most ferocious players I have ever seen.

In one game he was giving such a tremendous performance against us, and it so intrigued me to see such a great football player in action, that I smiled. That really annoyed him, and he said to me after the game, "You laughed at me."

"I wasn't laughing at you," I said. "I just couldn't get over the way you were playing."

We both were installed in the Hall of Fame in 1967, and Chuck asked Greasy Neale to be his presenter. Greasy made a nice introductory speech for Chuck, and Bednarik spoke about his life and his time in football. Then he turned and, looking at me, said, "Paul Brown is the greatest coach who ever lived," with his own coach, whom he had asked to present him on this momentous day, sitting right there. I know Chuck simply forgot for a moment and said the first thing that had come to his mind, but it was an embarrassing moment for everyone, and I'm sure that Chuck has since wished he could have it back.

The victory over the Eagles in 1954 was one of several memorable games in a season that probably gave me more pure satisfaction than any during my years in Cleveland because we really had remade our team. We climbed back to the top with a substantially new group, but one that came very close to being as good as our great 1948 team. No one could have foreseen that early in the season, when we had lost two of our first three games, including a 55-27 trouncing at Pittsburgh that left everyone wondering whether our great days were behind us, but by midseason we were rolling.

A few incidents from that season stand out in my mind. One was the most amazing display of kicking luck and accuracy I have ever seen. In that miserable game against Pittsburgh, their punter, Pat Brady, put three kicks out of bounds inside the one-yard line. Of all the punters we ever faced, he is the one who tops my list, for that singular accomplishment.

Then there was Don Paul. Paul had come to us from the Cardinals with the reputation of being a problem player after some run-ins with his coach, though we never found any evidence of it. Despite his problems there, however, he always got along well with Vi Bidwell, wife of Card's owner Charley

Bidwell. During one of our games against Chicago, Don scooped up a rolling punt and was heading for the end zone when, running past the Bidwells' box, he held the ball aloft and waved it at Vi in good humor. She just waved back. I was a bit astonished at this display, but no more so than Tom James was a little later when he came up to tackle Ollie Matson, only to see Ollie accelerate and go out around and past him. The look on Tom's face told it all. Ollie was big and fast and used his speed like a maestro. He'd dip a little as if to run outside, and when the cornerbacks moved to get him, his acceleration left them dumbfounded. He and O. J. Simpson were the best runners we ever faced.

Our final game of the season was against the Lions and had been postponed from an earlier date because the Indians had been using the stadium for the World Series. Both of us were scheduled to play the following week back in Cleveland for the NFL title, so I really didn't care too much whether we won or lost, though as it turned out, the team felt differently. I kept our offense under wraps, particularly Ray Renfro, who had been sidelined with injuries. The game was played on a snowy field, and poor Warren Lahr was the victim of another last-minute touchdown that gave Detroit a 14–10 victory.

The frustration of another heartbreaking loss to the Lions was almost too much for some of our players, and big Doug Atkins wanted to go out and manhandle Lahr. I said very little to Warren because I knew he felt so bad, and in such situations I always believed it was better to let the matter lie, get a good night's rest and then look at it under less emotional circumstances. Later that week I called Lahr into my office and said, "That was one of those things that happens in football, and you can't let it destroy you."

That didn't change the team's mood, though, or that of the media, and we worked under a cloud all that week preparing for the title game. It affected the players so much that the night before the game, a group of them got together and drew up their own game plan, to be used only if our play selection from the bench wasn't working. They were as frustrated as the fans and had begun to believe all the talk about our play-calling's being too conservative. They were further motivated to this rather radical move by the fact that Otto had declared that this would be his final game with the Browns, and they wanted him to go out a winner and a champion as much as they wanted to beat the Lions for their own satisfaction.

Once the game started, however, they forgot about their plans. Otto completed nine of twelve passes, three of them for touchdowns. Two of them were scored by Renfro, who totally confused the Lions' defense because they never thought he would play and then tried to cover him man-for-man. Otto scored three more touchdowns, helped by Billy Reynolds's two tremendous kickoff returns and another punt return that gave us great field position for easy scores. Brewster and Hanulak also had a great game, and all the talk of the Lions' "jinx" over the Browns disappeared by the time we had a 35–3 lead. As the capper, I sent Otto back into the game late in the fourth quarter, allowed him to run one play, then called time-out and removed him from the game as the huge crowd roared for five minutes in tribute. After the game our players, in a grand gesture, presented me with the game ball, and that ended the play-calling problem.

I didn't want Otto to retire, but I couldn't deny him the right. I said, "Why not think it over because we want you to come back?" It had been on his mind, though, for nearly three seasons, and his wife, Beverly, also wanted him to step away, particularly after the mauling he had received in the 49ers' game that season. I knew that Otto was reaching the point where it was getting difficult for him to be up for every game, and I could always tell what kind of game he was go-ing to have as soon as I walked into the hotel dining room on Sunday morning. If Otto was reading the funny papers, I knew it could be a long day, but if he sat there biting his lips and then began peppering me with questions about what we were going to do, I knew we would win.

Ratterman was the heir apparent in 1955, but he had rarely played since coming with us and was rusty. George was a pinpoint passer, but he could not throw the long pass with Otto's authority or fine touch, nor was he as adept at ball handling. In addition, his mobility had become so limited he needed almost perfect pass protection, whereas Otto's abil-ity to maneuver away from a pass rush often gave him four or five extra seconds. These attributes, plus the tremendous leadership and confidence that Otto gave our team, were in the back of everyone's mind when we opened training camp, and I knew that every player kept waiting for him to return.

The feeling became stronger when it became evident in practice that our passing game simply wasn't functioning, and I knew even before our trip to Chicago to play the College All-Stars that it had to be Otto at quarterback, or else we were going to have a very difficult season.

That was borne out when, unprepared mentally for any kind of football, we lost the All-Stars, 30–27. I was embarrassed at how poorly we played, though it was against a fine All-Star team. The *Chicago Tribune* sponsors had allowed the grass to grow extra long, hoping to cut down on Groza's field goal kicking, while the All-Stars' kicker, little Tad Weed from Ohio State, had kicked off a platter, which flattened down the grass, and he had a fine night.

Three days later I met Otto and Beverly for dinner and asked him if he would give us one more year to help us make the transition. He wanted time to consider the request, because of some business commitments, and after a preseason schedule which saw us win one game, he agreed to come back. I paid him $25,000, which was more than any player in pro football made at that time.

The first day he stepped onto the practice field, it was as if he had never been away. Our offensive style, with improved blocking, had changed to a possession type of run offense with Morrison and Ed Modzelewski in the backfield. We moved Gain into middle guard, and McCormack became our starting right tackle, providing added power for our new offense. Chuck Noll moved to linebacker and solidified our defense, while Harold Bradley, who was also a fine artist and later moved to Paris to earn his living as one, became one of our new messenger guards. Living more on power than deception, we were never pressed and won our sixth straight division title, with only one loss.

The toughest moment of that year was having to let Motley go in the trade to Pittsburgh that brought Modzelewski to the Browns. Marion's injured knee had kept him from playing in 1954, and I had thought he would retire from football, but come training camp, there he was, wanting to play. I knew his days as a fullback were numbered, so we used him as a linebacker during our pre-season games, but his legs still caused him problems. Since Marion needed an extra year's salary to help him bridge a new career, we traded him to the Steelers.

I didn't handle the situation well, though, because I didn't have the courage to tell Marion firsthand that we had traded him, and before I could think of a better solution, he found out from another source, deeply hurting him. Letting him, and later James and Gillom, go were the most difficult things I ever had to do in pro football, and I handled all their situations badly; I regret it to this day. I just could not bring myself to tell these men, whom I had known since they were boys, that their careers were over. I know that Tommy would have broken down and cried, and I would have cried right along with him. It would have been better, however, had I suffered those emotional consequences, rather than carry the regrets with me for so long. All these players understand my feelings today, and I have told them how sorry I was for that action, but it didn't make it any easier at the time.

Motley finished his career as a linebacker with the Steelers in 1955, but James and Gillom were still part of our division champions which played the Rams for the NFL championship for the third time in six seasons. Nearly 88,000 people in the Coliseum saw Otto Graham have his finest hour as a player and us win our third title, 38–14. The Rams, under Sid Gillman, played right into our hands when they committed themselves to a zone defense, with four deep backs and a lone middle linebacker; we decided immediately to operate from a double wing formation, with Morrison, Jones and Renfro as the wingbacks. The middle linebacker in the Rams' secondary always flowed with the fullbacks, so we sent our fullback one way and threw to the opposite area. We had a 17–7 lead before the Rams switched to man-for-man coverage, obviously forgetting why they had used the zone coverage in the first place. Otto just riddled them after that, completing fourteen of twenty-five passes for 209 yards and two touchdowns.

Our defense smothered Van Brocklin and Fears, intercepting the Dutchman six times, including one which Don Paul returned for a touchdown. Three other interceptions set up two more touchdowns and a field goal, and when the fourth quarter began, we had the game put away. Shortly thereafter I brought Otto out of the game, and that huge crowd of Rams fans stood and gave him a thunderous ovation—a rare tribute to an opposing player, but certainly appropriate to this man's greatness.

"Thanks," he said to me when he came to the sidelines.

I looked at him and said, "Thanks" . . . and that was it, the end of an era that could never again be duplicated because, though we tried, we never found another Otto Graham.

ELEVEN

New Faces: Enter Jim Brown, the Players' Association and the AFL

THE YEAR FOLLOWING OTTO GRAHAM's retirement, we had our only losing season in Cleveland, finishing with a 5–7 record that was the direct result of Otto's leaving, Dub Jones's retirement, the loss of some of our players to the armed services and six consecutive years of drafting last or next to last.

It did give us the chance in the 1957 draft, however, to select Jim Brown, a once-in-a-lifetime player who became the best running back ever to play professional football.

Actually, Jim was our second choice. We desperately needed a quarterback, and John Brodie, Len Dawson and Paul Hornung all were available on the first round. Hornung and Brodie were picked immediately, and we lost a coin flip with Pittsburgh to see which team would get the fifth pick in the first round. The Steelers pondered for a bit over Brown and Dawson and finally chose Dawson. It was ironic that both of us needed a quarterback at that time because the Steelers had cut John Unitas in 1955 and we had had a chance at him. Shortly thereafter he had called me and asked for a tryout, but at the time Otto was back and perking along, so I had told John that we had no openings but that he was welcome to come to our training camp the next year. He later signed with Baltimore and today, of course, is in the

Hall of Fame. Though I lost him, he has said my willingness
to give him a second chance gave him the faith to continue
to the sandlots and to try again in the NFL.

There were no great quarterbacks on the board after
Dawson was picked, so we selected Jim Brown strictly because he was the best player available at the time and because I believed in having a strong, fast fullback for our
offense. Dick Gallagher had seen him play four times that
year and ardently believed that he was the best football
player in the country. In film study, I saw that he never ran
outside the tackles, but when he broke into the open, there
were quick glimpses of his incredible quickness and balance.
His strength also was apparent because every time he hit the
point of attack, the defense sagged and he always moved forward.

I signed him to a $12,000 contract and gave him a $3,000
bonus—the most we had ever paid any rookie up to that
time. And he was worth it. I have already made the distinction between Jim and Marion Motley, yet my strong feelings
about Jim's talents may surprise many because for nearly two
decades the public has been led to believe that our relationship in Cleveland was punctuated by open bitterness. The
common perception has also been that he was responsible for
my being fired after the 1962 season, whereas in reality Jim
allowed himself to be used as a pawn by Arthur Modell to
make my removal appear to be instigated from within the
team. Later Jim publicly stated that he had been used.

The real truth is that I never had a sharp word with Jim,
nor did he have any with me, during the six years he played
on my teams. That does not mean our years together were
problem-free—indeed, there were times when I regretted having drafted him, and before the 1962 season I seriously considered trading him because his outlooks and attitudes had had
such an undesirable effect on our team. However, there was
never any open hostility between us over these differences,
and I appreciated his football talent as much then as I do now.

I believe Jim now realizes that our team concepts were correct, and while I have not seen him since I left the Browns,
his public statements indicate that he regrets much of the
trouble that was attributed to his attitude as a player. Early
in 1979, when the press asked about our years together in
Cleveland, he said, "He was as great a coach who ever lived.
I still appreciate the things which he taught me. He was very

strict, a very classy guy. We learned a lot about class and carriage. He always called his team 'the Yankees of football.' "

Jim's life outside football since then has had so many ups and downs that I have come to feel sorry for him, and any hard feelings between us have been eroded by what has happened off the field. If he ever felt any resentment, I regret it because he was such a great, great player.

With the exception of his lackadaisical approach to practice and blocking, I never faulted his total effort in any game he played for the Browns and never hesitated to compliment him for his outstanding play. As a pure runner he stands alone—those who try to compare him with O. J. Simpson are comparing apples to oranges, no pun intended. OJ is more of a will-o'-the-wisp runner, in the same style as Bobby Mitchell, while Jim combined power, acceleration, speed and great balance with an inner toughness that never conceded the slightest edge to anybody.

The keys to his success were that rare combination of strength and speed we had noticed before drafting him. He was not a knee-pumping type of runner but had the ability to shuffle laterally if a hole was closed, and once he found an opening, his acceleration caused tacklers just to bounce off him. There were tacklers who thought they had him, but Jim had the unusual ability of allowing one of his legs to go limp, and when the tackler relaxed, he surged forward again, ripping apart the man's grip. Jim was also a most determined runner, who would have been even greater had he played on today's artificial surfaces. Though he played half his games on the heavy natural field in Cleveland, it never bothered him because he had such great balance; his feet were never far off the ground when he ran, so he was very difficult to knock down. Another key was the unusual muscle structure in his upper thighs that generated his power. His muscles were so tight he could not extend his legs more than two feet from the ground when he did our stretching exercises. That fact in itself gave rise to opinions that he was lackadaisical and lazy in his approach to the game and that I tolerated less effort from him than from the other players. In a game, however, his great second efforts were his trademarks, and he never once complained to me even after running twenty-five or thirty times a game. I couldn't get picky about leg extensions on a Tuesday afternoon after he had carried the ball so many times the previous Sunday.

Still, I could never excuse his lack of effort in blocking, which in some instances was so poor that pass rushers went right past him; other times, he failed to help other running backs when he was the lead blocker. He got miffed at me one day when I told him he was graded last among all our running backs as a blocker, but then I backed up the grades with some film clips. He said nothing, but I know he resented the criticism. His one excuse was that he had never had to do it at Syracuse, but he never really tried to learn with us either. Before the 1962 season began, we made a staff decision, fully supported by Blanton Collier, his backfield coach, that Jim had to carry out his share of the blocking, and it worked out well for the early part of the season. Gradually, however, he fell back into his old ways, and Collier was almost in despair. That didn't stop Blanton, though, when he became the head coach in 1963, from doing a complete reversal. He stated publicly at that time that Jim Brown didn't have to block for his team and would be used only as a runner. The year before, when he was backfield coach, his stated opinion to our staff was just the opposite. If Jim had worked at blocking, he would have been just as great as Motley; in my opinion, the difference between the two was that Jim didn't seem to care for his teammates as much as Marion did. If I had had both players on my team at the same time, I would have put Motley at fullback and Jim at halfback, where their skills and attitudes could have been best assimilated.

Jim's biggest problem was his attitude, and his worst enemy was himself. I often felt that he really couldn't stand himself and that this inner resentment touched everyone with whom he came into contact. By nature, he was an unhappy man, it seemed to me. Throughout his time with us he was a loner and never said much to anyone. He had few friends on the team, and none of any long standing. I've been told the roots of these problems were in his childhood, particularly his adolescent years on Long Island; his mother toiled as a maid in the homes of some of his high school classmates, who often taunted him about it, even though he was a great athlete who brought fame and recognition to their school.

This personal outlook, plus his awareness that he was a great player, created a peculiar atmosphere on the team. Until Jim came to the Browns, we never had any black-white is-

sues or attitudes, yet in his second year he told me that he no
longer wanted to room with Bobby Mitchell, another black
man, and demanded that we put him with a white player. I
told him to get any roommate he wanted, but the man had to
agree to room with him, too. It had to be mutually agreeable,
not forced. That was the last I ever heard of it.

In our training camp dining room Jim soon had most of
the black players on one side of the room, eating together,
and that had never happened before.

"Don't do this," I told him quite strongly. "You're hurting
your team, and I don't see any purpose in segregating our
dining room."

"I thought maybe you'd want me to go all the way with
it," he replied.

I was puzzled by what he meant until I recalled his com-
plaint about rooming with Mitchell, who himself later asked
to be switched because Jim wanted to fight every time Bobby
disagreed with one of his outlooks.

Jim was very conscious of his social standing. He once
complained that the big difference between the two of us was
our social status. "He's never even invited me into his home,"
he told someone. As I've mentioned, that was true, but I
never invited *any* of my players into our home during their
playing days, including those who are today my dear friends.

Jim also resented any authority or set of rules that required
he be given no special status—for example, our demand that
every player know all the assignments on each play. He publicly disparaged our IQ tests, claiming that some of the
veteran players cribbed on them. That was hardly possible
since we gave a different test each year; the only test that
really counted anyway was the one given to a player in his
first season so we could determine if we had any teaching
problems. I often felt the real reason he disliked those tests
was his concern about his own score and about whether the
black players, as a group, ranked high or low. Since we never
made the scores public or identified the standing of any single
player or group, it was a meaningless worry.

With all his attitude problem, however, in his six years
with me, he never challenged my authority to impose a rule
or procedure. In all that time I fined him only three or four
times, all for being late for meetings. Those were $50 levies,
and—as with every other player—I told him in front of the

entire squad why he was being fined and that it was nothing personal. I then went on with the meeting.

We knew from his first season that Jim had trouble accepting authority, because his college coach, Ben Schwartzwalder, said to me while visiting our 1957 training camp, "He's a great player, but I'm glad you've got him."

"What do you mean?" I asked.

"We put up with an awful lot during the week to get him to do the job in a game," he replied. "We had to let him have his own way during practice because otherwise, we were afraid he'd carry a bad attitude into the game and hurt our chances of winning. That caused a lot of headaches with the other players, but it was the only way we knew how to handle the situation."

We encountered the same problem as the seasons went by. In practice, other backs ran 40 yards with the ball on each play, but Jim ran 10, then dropped the ball and walked back to the huddle, hoping, I suppose, that we would call him for a lack of effort. When we did, he pouted for the rest of the practice. We finally treated him like a little boy, trying to get his best effort on game days by cajoling and overlooking his petulances.

I know our other players resented this, and I admit that he hurt us with his attitude in practice, but we tried to handle it because I wanted—and got—his best effort in a game. Collier, who later became his great champion, had the most trouble with him as our backfield coach in 1962 and was the first to urge we get rid of him. He often came in frustrated and discouraged from practice and would say to all the coaches, "Shall I take him on?" Everyone knew he wanted to call the shots with Jim, but he just didn't know how, nor did any of us have the answer without hurting our team. Finally, Blanton said, "I guess I'll just have to handle him like a kid." Before the 1962 season we were considering trading Jim, but all of us agreed we could never get comparable value for him and so decided to try to salve him for one more year and see if he responded. It didn't work, though. He began telling people, among other things, that he wanted to run outside, not inside, where his personal statistics might not be so gaudy, and had I stayed with the Browns, I would have resolved the situation. By that point Art Modell had undercut my authority with Jim to such an extent that he felt he could bypass the coach anyway. At that time this suited Modell.

Jim always had to be the man in the spotlight, but he often let it get the best of him. He resented Bobby Mitchell when Bobby's exciting running style became popular in Cleveland, and Jim got very touchy when everyone referred to Mitchell as the racehorse and to Brown as the workhorse. I could see the problem, but there was little I could do about it.

When we traded Bobby Mitchell to Washington for Ernie Davis, Jim came into our office a short time later and said, "Well, am I still on the team?"

"What do you mean?" I asked him.

"It looks like you're not too happy with me if you go get Ernie Davis," he replied.

I tried to explain to Jim that we were trying to take some of the burden from him and that he would be even greater if defenses had to cope with another big, fast runner. That didn't mollify him one bit, however, and our relationship deteriorated even further after that. Jim apparently felt I wanted to acquire a big back in order to get rid of him. I have to admit that one of the reasons, though not the chief reason, for the deal was that had we decided to trade him, we knew—or at least we thought we did until Ernie contracted leukemia and died—that we possessed a suitable replacement.

At the time those who figured that a deal for Jim was in the works suggested that the only equitable trade would be for Baltimore's Johnny Unitas. I wouldn't have made that trade on a player-for-player basis, though, because John had reached the age where his productivity was diminishing and Jim was still the best player in professional football. I still feel the same way.

One of our problems with Jim occurred when we had to intercede with the law on his behalf because he was forever getting into some kind of difficulty. By the time I left Cleveland his name had appeared on the police blotter many times. We actually saved him from serious injury, possibly death, during one training camp. Mike McCormack, our captain, told me he had learned that a man and his two sons were planning an ambush down the road from the camp to kill Jim because he was having a daily tryst with his young daughter.

"He's not my favorite person," Mike told me, "but if they get him, it will hurt our team, and that's the only reason I'm telling you."

I then had Eddie Ulinski, the assistant coach who was taking bed check that particular night, warn Jim in the hope that he would sever the relationship. This was to save him the embarrassment of knowing that I had found out.

"Those are big words," Jim said to Ulinski when Ed told him someone was waiting to kill him.

"I'm just trying to save you and help the team," Eddie replied.

"Thanks," Jim said, and just walked away. Forever after, things were never quite the same between Jim and the staff.

Back in the draft of 1957, though, we had no idea what was ahead of us. One thing we did know, however, was that the frustrations of 1956 could not be cured simply by drafting a good running back like Jim Brown. We had to have a solid quarterback. We had picked up Tommy O'Connell, a very willing, able player, as a free agent in the middle of last season, and we knew he would be adequate over the short term, but we needed someone behind him since Ratterman and Babe Parilli had not been able to do the job. When the second round came up, Milt Plum of Penn State was the best available quarterback left, so we picked him. He was not in the class of Brodie, Hornung or Dawson, but our scouts, particularly Gallagher, saw him as a competent, no-frills guy who had reasonable mobility and size and seemed to be mistake-free during a game. As it turned out, he was a very average quarterback without a strong arm, but he could have carried us farther down the road if he had only recognized his limitations and been satisfied to work within the scope of the offense we had prepared for him. As it was, instead of alleviating our problems, he only heightened them because, in truth, the team carried the quarterback. I have always felt that we had enough talent in the late fifties to win our division if we had gotten the quality quarterbacking we had hoped for.

Milt really was a nice man, but not cut out to be a leader. He had fair accuracy on short, quick passes to the backs, and his most effective season came in 1957, when he replaced O'Connell after Tommy broke an ankle. His completion percentages soared when he threw short, high percentage passes to the backs. Because his arm was not very strong, we could tell he avoided throwing the ball downfield into areas where accuracy and timing were the difference between an interception and a completion. As a result, though he often got five and six seconds of pass protection from our line, he would most often end up dumping the ball to one of the backs. His failure to get the ball effectively downfield thoroughly frustrated everyone, and he lost his credibility with our players when we lost too many games because of it; opposing defenses, knowing that he couldn't throw the long pass, began ganging up to stop Brown and Mitchell in our running game and taking their chances on the short passes. In 1962 we finally traded him to the Detroit Lions, where he had to carry the burden of playcalling and leadership by himself. They soon learned that he couldn't do the job, and he ended up as an unhappy and disillusioned football player.

Plum wasn't the only quarterback I tried out that year. In fact, I brought thirteen of them to training camp, the most I ever had in any year. It would have been fourteen had I been able to complete a deal with the Rams for Rudy Bukich. They were willing to accept a rookie linebacker from Michigan named Roger Zatkoff, but Zatkoff refused to report because he wanted to go back to Detroit, and the deal was canceled. That set us back years because we could have done a lot with Bukich and possibly made him a championship quarterback. As it was, we traded Zatkoff to the Detroit Lions before the season began for running back Lew Carpenter.

In trying to solve the quarterback situation, I even packaged seven players, including Carlton Massey, Sam Palumbo and John Petitbon, and sent them to Green Bay in exchange for Bobby Garrett again, hoping that time and experience had lessened his speech impediment. That didn't work out, though, and we released him, traded Parilli back to Green Bay and started the season with O'Connell and Plum.

Jim Brown's running and O'Connell's steady play before he was hurt helped us win six and tie one of our first eight games, and we clinched our seventh division title in eight years on the next-to-last weekend of the season. Our greatest game was a roaring 45–31 victory over the Rams, in which Jim Brown scored four times and amassed 237 yards rushing. That was an NFL record, which he later tied against Philadelphia in 1961 and which wasn't broken in NFL play until 1971 by Willie Ellison of the Rams. Jim finished his first season by winning both rookie of the year honors and the rushing title with 942 yards, the most ever by a rookie.

Brown wasn't the only successful rookie on our team that year. Paul Wiggin succeeded Len Ford at defensive end, and Paul has always been a special person to me: highly intelli-

gent, smooth, yet aggressive, one of the best ever to play on
my teams. Vince Costello, a quick, fast, sure tackler, also became our middle linebacker and played for ten years with the
Browns. He later became one of my coaches with the Bengals.

In addition, Milt Campbell, the 1956 Olympic decathlon
champion who had played some football at Indiana, joined
us. The decathlon championship had earned him the title of
the world's greatest athlete, but unfortunately that wasn't reflected in his football abilities. He had a million-dollar body
and fine speed, which we tried to use by letting him return
kicks, but he was not a football player. His fumbled kickoff
return in our championship game against Detroit that year
proved a costly mistake.

Campbell's mistake was nothing, however, compared to
Plum's careless action the Thursday before the game. He was
leaving the practice field and yelled to John Borton, our
third-string quarterback, to throw him a pass. It was very
cold, and the field was frozen, and as Milt slipped, leaping
for the ball, one of his hamstring muscles popped so loudly I
could hear it. Though we said nothing for the rest of the
week, we all knew we had little chance of winning even before we left for Detroit. O'Connell was still limping badly
from a broken ankle, and though the bone had calcified
enough for the doctors to allow him to play, he was so rusty
from inactivity we knew he could not be effective. Our only
hope was for a tight defensive game in which we might get a
couple of breaks and allow Jim Brown's running to carry us."

That just didn't work out. O'Connell gave it everything he
had, but his inactivity—as well as our own, because we had
had to wait a week while Detroit defeated the 49ers in a division playoff game—were too much. In the first quarter, with
the Lions ahead, 3–0, Tommy had Ray Renfro in the clear,
but he underthrew the ball, and Bob Long returned the interception to our 19-yard line. Detroit scored a minute later and
then took advantage of Campbell's fumble for another quick
score. Jim Brown ran 30 yards for a touchdown and cut the
deficit to 17–7. After Tobin Rote's fake field goal touchdown
pass to Steve Junker upped the Lions lead to 24–7,
O'Connell's timing failed him again by a split second and
Terry Barr picked off a sideline pass to Darrell Brewster and
raced for another score. Plum replaced O'Connell, but he was
immobile, and Borton had a bad arm, so we ultimately lost,

59–14. We never had a sporting chance going into that game, and from that day on I made it a point to warn our players to protect themselves from this type of needless injury before a big game.

The most intriguing thing that happened to me that season occurred one morning while I was riding downtown on the Rapid Transit. I kept stepping on an opened letter under my seat, so I finally reached down and picked it up, only to find it addressed to one of my own players! The letter was from Creighton Miller, who was then a young lawyer looking for some clients. Creighton had written that he and George Ratterman were forming a players' association to work for some undefined goals. The last line was the most interesting of all: "Be sure that you don't let Paul Brown see this or we won't get off the ground."

That shook me up, and I told our coaches about it, but we all reasoned that an association of players would be little different from any association of professional men, its efforts directed toward upgrading their professional status and other such lofty goals. Of course, that original players' association has now grown into a full-fledged labor union, and the players whom Miller and Ratterman helped organize ultimately kicked them out of the union because they were not militant enough. Every time I see them and remind them of what they started, I get the same answer: "If we had known what was going to happen, we would never have been a party to it."

At the time the players were vehement about not being identified as a union, insisting that they wanted nothing to do with that form of organization. Of course, all that is changed now, and the players' union has taken control of much of the game, and not for the good of the sport. I have never believed that the unions should have any part in professional sports because it is clear to me that players are individual contractors, who negotiate their own salaries. The football players' union once asked a powerful national union leader to become involved in their organization, but he demurred for that very reason: Football players are individual contractors.

As it stands now, the player has it both ways. He negotiates his own salary, and the union negotiates all his fringe benefits. I know the public is paying part of this burden with increased ticket prices, and it can look forward to even higher prices if our television revenues don't continue to increase.

The most serious damage has been to the spirit of the

game itself. Football is an emotional, competitive and highly physical game, yet unlike our earlier players, some of today's players are often more concerned about their own welfare than that of their team, their management or their city. It used to be, we went into a city for a game and our players had nothing to do with the other team. During the seventies, however, in Cincinnati, many times our opponents came to our hotel and got together with our players the night before the game, and then the next day tried to knock their heads off. I finally told our men. "This is ridiculous! Forget the camaraderie until after the game or, better yet, until after the season."

The two groups most attracted to the football union—the players who will never make it on their own in later life and the government—are the main reasons for its existence. Many well-paid players who have reached status in the profession ignore it and have opposed its strikes, walkouts and its general principles. Roger Staubach is a prime example. The government, on the other hand, with its labyrinth of bureaucracies which must find a reason for existence, fosters such a structure. Some politicians, looking for a cheap forum, have also seized upon it and helped sustain it. Because of this, the possibilities are bleak, at best, of professional sports' being freed from its bondage.

In the end the sport will succeed only to the extent that the players have a feeling for each other, their coaches, the management and the community in which they play. It is popular now to "buy" a championship, but that lasts only a short time. Any long-range success must be based on the players' genuine willingness to make sacrifices for each other and their team.

Professional football was nearly free of such problems when the 1958 season began, however, and had not yet become the dominant sport it is today. Before that season ended, though, football had finally achieved its great breakthrough with play-off and championship games that captured the public's imagination—and we, as usual, were a part of it, if not as large a part as we would have wished.

Going into that season, I believed that all we needed for another championship team was a breakaway runner in the backfield to keep the defenses from keying on Jim Brown and some added help at quarterback, since O'Connell had retired.

To try to solve the quarterback problem, I selected Jim Ninowski from Michigan State on the draft's second round. Jim had a much stronger arm than Plum, and though he was not as meticulous in his ball handling, I felt that would come with coaching and intensive work. We kept Jim for two years, but he was too jittery, and because he wasn't very tall for a quarterback and it bothered him to see over a tall defensive line, he wouldn't stand in the pocket till the last second before throwing the ball. In all, Ninowski actually played twice for us. We traded him to Detroit when we got Len Dawson from Pittsburgh in 1960, but Len's arm was never strong enough to suit me, and he did little in his two seasons with us. Before the 1962 season, he didn't even return the contract we sent him or answer our telephone calls, so we placed him on waivers. Apparently Len had decided to cast his lot with the American Football League. Consequently, we brought Ninowski back in the Plum trade with Detroit and made another stab at harnessing his great throwing ability. I always felt he could have been better for us had he worked at the game, without so many outside interests.

We had great hopes when we chose Ninowski in the 1958 draft, but as it turned out, our best pick was Bobby Mitchell, who didn't go until the eighth round. That may seem rather low for someone who belongs in the Hall of Fame because of a tremendous career as a runner and a receiver for eleven seasons, but he had acquired a terrible reputation at Illinois as a fumbler, and though he had dazzled everyone with his great speed and moves, no one wanted to take a chance on him. I had first seen Mitchell run the high hurdles for Illinois in a Knights of Columbus track meet in Cleveland, at the insistence of my son Pete, who was then attending University School. Bobby was a world-class sprinter at the time, and I was very impressed that night with his athletic ability as he skimmed over those hurdles. As the draft went on and his name stayed on the board, I kept waiting for someone to make the selection until finally, our turn came in the eighth round, and I said, "I've got to find out for myself." I was never sorry.

My fears about his fumbling were quickly assuaged, and very simply too, when we talked about the problem with his college coach. He told us that Bobby had played with three different quarterbacks during his senior year—one who was very tall and had made the handoff high on his chest, another who was very short and had given it beneath his waist and a third who had handled the ball properly. As a result, Bob had never developed any kind of consistency on the handoff and kept having to adjust his style to the quarterbacks—and fumbling. Personally, I never could understand why they were running him in the middle so often when his great strength was outside. In our system he became the greatest will-o'-the-wisp runner ever to play for my teams.

Even in 1958 preseason we knew we had something special, a player to supplement Jim Brown, when we watched Bobby and Leroy Bolden from Michigan State hook up in a tremendous battle to be the starting halfback. In one preseason game against Detroit, Bolden gained 113 yards; the next week against the Rams, Bobby gained 114—in the first half. Mitchell finally won the job, and for the first half of that season, while we were winning five of our six games, he and Jim were one-two in the NFL rushing statistics, averaging near 7 yards on each rushing attempt.

In one game against the Cardinals, Bobby was supposed to run an inside trap after Plum had faked a pitchout to Brown, but when Mitchell got to the hole, he found it blocked, and as he scampered to find more running room, he bumped into Milt and destroyed the play's viability. At the same time he saw Jim Brown standing alone in the backfield, tossed the ball to him, and Jim ran 41 yards for a touchdown; that play became known as the Bobby Mitchell Special. In the next-to-last game of the season at Philadelphia, we had Bobby returning kicks because we found he was less effective running from the backfield on frozen, slow fields, and he took the opening kickoff 98 yards for a touchdown and then returned our first punt 68 yards for another score in our 21–14 victory.

Everything else that season seemed secondary, however, to our games against the Giants, just as in the early fifties. New York, under its defensive coach, Tom Landry, had built its great defense utilizing the same "flex" concept Landry still uses with the Dallas Cowboys. Its key is the great discipline it exacts from each lineman and outside linebacker. They must control and stay within a defined area—whether or not the play comes to them—long enough for the middle linebacker and defensive backs to give support making the tackles. It is a very effective defense against a running game, and at that time the Giants had the linemen to make it work, including such players as Andy Robustelli (one of the best defensive ends we ever faced), Dick Modzelowski, Rosey Grier and Jim Katcavage.

When we played the Giants the first time in 1958, we were unbeaten in five games while New York had a 3-2 record. We knew Brown and Mitchell would not have an easy time against the Giants' defense, and we were counting on Plum's passing to give them help. We led, 17–7, at the half, as Jim ran 58 yards for a touchdown, but Plum began to show he could not be effective in key games and completed only four of fourteen passes for only 26 yards. Seeing that, the Giants concentrated on Brown and forced three fumbles by Mitchell, and it still took a roughing penalty against Wiggin to give them the life in the final touchdown drive that brought them a 21–17 victory.

When we met the second time at Yankee Stadium in the season's final game, our record was 9-2, and the Giants' was 8-3; that meant the Giants had to win just to get into a tie for the Eastern Division title. Jim Brown ran 65 yards for a touchdown on the game's first play, and Lou Groza added a field goal for our 10–3 halftime lead, and things looked pretty good. Since our defense was magnificent and we had the seven-point lead, I decided to try a fake field goal run, hoping to score a touchdown that would nail down the victory. The play had worked against New York in our first meeting, but this time Bobby Freeman, a former quarterback who was Groza's holder, slipped as he got up to run, and the play was smothered.

A couple of minutes later the Giants recovered Jim Brown's fumble and, using a pair of halfback option passes by Frank Gifford, tied the score, the touchdown pass going to Bob Schnelker, a tight end who had started his NFL career with us several years before. We weren't bothered by the tie, though, because we could still win the division title with it. We had a brief scare when Pat Summerall tried a 36-yard field goal with five minutes to play, but he missed.

The situation looked even better when the Giants got the ball again, because Gifford fumbled near midfield after catching a pass, and the ball popped out of his arms just as he was falling to the ground. It bounced five or six yards, and then Walt Michaels picked it up and started to run for a touchdown. New York's quarterback, Charley Conerly, saw the play, ripped off his helmet and threw it on the ground in disgust. Other Giant players were just as emphatic because they felt for sure the game was over, and so was their last chance to win.

But it didn't happen that way. Charley Berry, one of the officials, called the play an incomplete pass, and the Giants kept the ball. Our players were furious, and even some of the Giants' players were stunned at the decision. Shortly thereafter Summerall kicked the 49-yard field goal that won the game and made him famous.

When we looked at the films afterward, we clearly saw Gifford catch the ball, run for six or seven yards and fumble it forward as he was going to the ground, then Michaels pick it up and run with it. The films also showed Berry with his arms extended in front of him and looking around at the other officials, obviously waiting for a cue. When he saw no signal, he slowly began to wave his arms in front of him, still looking for help, but indicating that the pass was incomplete. I firmly believe he didn't know what to call, and when he saw no one ready to make the decision, he was reluctant to withdraw his arms and so made the signal very slowly, hoping that another official might take the hint. None did, however, and he was not very emphatic about calling the play; when he finally did, Michaels was well downfield and on his way to a touchdown. I took the film to Bert Bell and protested what I honestly felt was an unjust call. I noted with interest that Berry was never again assigned to work any of our games.

Our heart had been ripped from us by losing to the Giants that way, and there was a hollow feeling within all of us, having to prepare for another game in New York that shouldn't have been played. It was tough for our players to get up for it, and even more so because, as I was told later, they had begun to lose faith in Plum's ability to play under stress, reducing their confidence in their offense. In fact, it seemed to me that Plum, too, had lost his confidence. As it turned out, we reached the Giants' 4-yard line at one point, and when Plum tried a pass, he was sacked for a 12-yard loss instead of throwing the ball to an open receiver in the end zone. On the next play, he tried to throw across the defense, and the ball was intercepted by Sam Huff. The Giants went on to win the game, 10–0, and, of course, played Baltimore in the history-making championship game. Ironically, the cru-

cial call of that game, a ruling that Gifford had not made a
first down on a key third down run, thus forcing the Giants
to punt and allowing Baltimore to drive for its tie-making
touchdown that set up the sudden death overtime, was made
by—Charley Berry.

Some people have wondered, "What might have happened
had the Browns won the title and there had been no play-off
game or subsequent dramatic overtime championship? Would
the impact on the public have been the same?" That question
can never be answered, but one thing is for certain: The popularity of the Browns, and their great rivalry with the Giants,
were very responsible for the great surge of popularity that finally brought the nation's total attention to pro football.

Shortly after the 1958 season ended, the Green Bay Packers went searching for a new head coach, and Dominic
Olejniczak, the team's president, and Jerry Atkinson, a member of their board, whom I had known for years, asked my
opinion about a possible candidate. I recommended two
men—Vince Lombardi, the Giants' offensive coach, and
Blanton Collier, then head coach at Kentucky. They wanted
to know more about Lombardi, and the more I talked, the
more interested they became. I became interested, too, and
pushed full tilt for Vince because I really believed he would
make a good coach. When he got the job, I felt some responsibility for seeing him succeed, so I made a list of players
available to him, people we were willing to trade because I
knew they would have problems making our team in 1959,
and since they would be in the other conference, they
wouldn't play against us very often. He selected Henry Jor-
don and Bill Quinlan and, after the 1959 season, traded for
Willie Davis. They were young, fast guys with good potential,
but who needed a place to play regularly and a team that
could wait for them to develop. When the Packers won their
first two NFL titles under Vinnie, those three players made
up three-quarters of Green Bay's defensive line.

Vince and I became good friends as the years went by, and
when he first started, he often called me to solicit my opinions on certain problems or advice on how to handle situations that he had never encountered as an assistant coach. He
later helped me when we needed a back, after we found out
that Ernie Davis could not play, and traded Ernie Green to
us. Green played for the Browns for years and was a great
blocker for Jim Brown and Leroy Kelly. Later still, during

the five years I was out of football, he always invited Katy and me to watch his team play when it came to Los Angeles, and we often went up from La Jolla the night before the game and spent some happy evenings with him.

Our trades helped Vinnie to a winning season his first year at Green Bay, while our season in 1959 was spoiled by consecutive 21–20 losses to Pittsburgh and San Francisco and then our second loss of the year to the New York Giants, 48–7. With still about two minutes left to play in that game at Yankee Stadium, we were forced to leave the field when thousands of people, many of them drunk, poured out of the stands and began molesting our players. The lone policeman at our bench promptly disappeared the moment the crowd descended on us, and started milling and shoving our players and made me afraid for our safety. Finally, the officials told me to take the team to the locker room, and as I walked across the field, I had the pockets torn from my overcoat. We stayed inside for nearly half an hour before the field was cleared and the players could go back out and finish the game. I have often wondered what would have happened if we had not gone back out.

In that game, too, Jim Brown got kicked in the head in the first half and could not play, but our team doctor said it was all right for him to play in the second half, so we used him. The next day I was excoriated in the newspapers by Sam Huff for being cruel and brutal to Jim. It was none of Huff's business in the first place, but the important thing is that it is the team doctor—not the head coach—who has the final word in the NFL about whether an injured player can return to the game. Huff later wrote to me and apologized, but the incident had passed, and the word *cruel* was added to the list of adjectives which constituted my image in New York.

Huff's accusation was part of the Browns-Giants rivalry at the time, and there was also a big deal about Huff and Jim Brown having a personal feud, which was only newspaper talk. Huff played within the team concept of New York's defense, which at the time meant that the middle linebacker went to the point of attack and made most of the tackles. Since Jim Brown carried the ball on more than half our running plays, it appeared to many that Huff shadowed him wherever he went. Huff was a big hero in New York and even became the subject of a special television documentary, "The Violent World of Sam Huff," when the truth of the matter was that his linebacking talent benefited from the quality of the players in front of him and the system in which he played. In Sam's behalf, however, he unhesitatingly denounced anyone who tried to imply his southern heritage had any part in his feelings for Jim Brown. Both men dueled each other as hard as they could on the field, but they respected each other a great deal, and nothing personal ever tainted the rivalry.

Jim's greatest game that year was in a 38–31 victory over Baltimore when he scored five touchdowns and gained 179 yards. Though Unitas passed for more than 300 yards against us, we won the game by sending Mitchell outside Gino Marchetti and having Jim Ray Smith, one of our greatest guards, work on Big Daddy Lipscomb with our influence blocking. Jim Brown found some great holes to run through, as Jim Ray consistently took Lipscomb out of the play. When we arrived back in Cleveland, more than 1,000 people were waiting at the airport to greet us.

That 1959 season had a few other unusual moments as well. When we went to Washington to play the Redskins, George Preston Marshall protested to the officials that the cleats on our football shoes were illegal and demanded that we change them. The officials didn't know if there was anything wrong with them—there wasn't—but we had to change them anyway. Our players had to sit all over the playing field having their cleats changed, and we were charged with all our time-outs. That was Marshall's way of trying to upset us, but he did us a favor and made us mad. We had been playing poorly at the time, but with Mitchell gaining 232 yards in just fourteen carries, we beat the Redskins, 31–17.

I was proudest of our team the week after the Giants debacle when we finished the season in Philadelphia. Our defense stopped the Eagles on seven straight plays from the 1-yard line that day, and then we drove 99 yards to tie the score. Jim Brown's touchdown late in the fourth quarter nailed down a 28–21 victory. On the flight home, I thanked the players again for their effort. It was a special moment for me because I found that despite our problems that year, we still had some feeling for one another.

Professional football underwent some tumultuous changes that year. Not only had the players' association surfaced, but so had the American Football League, and just when we needed him most, we lost Bert Bell as commissioner. He died attending a game in Philadelphia, and Austin Gunsel, the league's treasurer, stepped in as acting commissioner, but with the game in rapid ascendancy and the threat of another league, we knew we needed the right kind of leadership to guide us through these troubled times. In February 1960 we met in Miami Beach to elect a new commissioner, and the battle lines were quickly drawn.

A group of eastern teams that included Washington, Baltimore and Philadelphia wanted to keep Gunsel, but the owners began to have doubts because of the way he conducted the meetings, particularly when he kept telling us how tired he was. I never felt he could do the job over the long run myself and belonged to another group, which included the Browns, New York, San Francisco, Los Angeles, Green Bay and Chicago, that wanted Marshall Leahy, the league's lawyer and a brilliant man. Leahy would have made a fine commissioner, but he refused to move to New York from San Francisco, and the other owners felt the NFL offices had to be in New York, the media center of the country.

We debated the question for a week, and even my name was proposed, though I never wanted any part of the job. Finally, Wellington Mara and I went to Dan Reaves, the Rams' owner, and asked him if he would allow his thirty-three-year-old general manager, Pete Rozelle, to consider taking the job. I had known Pete for several years and thought he was a very bright, capable personable young man. Our immediate problem was convincing Pete himself to take the job. "I don't know whether I'm ready for such a job right now," he told us.

"I'm sure you don't, but you'll grow into it," I replied. "You are the one person who has never indicated any interest in the job, so there are no active groups against you, and if you are elected, you can come into the job as your own man."

Pete finally agreed, and we went back into the meeting, offered his name and he was elected. He has been NFL commissioner longer than any of his predecessors and has done an outstanding job during some of the most trying times professional football has ever known. Few realize the personal toll that it has taken on him.

His first problem was coping with the American Football League, which had announced its formation before the 1959 season. Lamar Hunt and Bud Adams had approached Bert

Bell about securing a franchise, but when the matter had been broached at a league meeting, Marshall had shot it down just as he did everything he felt would cut into his share of the revenues. That turned out to be a grave error because had we admitted them, the American Football League would probably never have surfaced and we would have saved ourselves millions of dollars in contracts and legal expenses and still had a product worthy of public acceptance.

When Hunt and Adams were rebuffed, however, and announced establishment of their own league, I warned both sides that they had better be financially secure because I knew from my own All-America Conference experiences that as soon as one team fails, everything begins to crumble. The warning had little impact initially, but the Browns felt the first bite when Dick Gallagher left to become general manager of the new Buffalo team, and then Chuck Noll cut short his career at the peak to become an assistant coach at Los Angeles. Soon the AFL teams began signing every player available, and when we began looking for players late in the 1959 season, the market was bare. We knew then that this new league was a very real thing.

Throughout 1959 I urged our owners to add more teams and stop a foolish tug of war with the AFL over players, and after that league showed its strength in some major cities, we finally decided to add a franchise in Dallas in 1960 and in Minnesota in 1961. When we began discussing stocking the new Dallas team, I felt strongly we should give the Cowboys enough quality players in the allocation draft to make them reasonably competitive. "What good does it do us," I asked, "if they lose every game?" Ironically, I was opposed by my friend Weeb Ewbank of the Colts, who flatly turned down the suggestion, even though his team was the NFL champion and supposedly had more player depth at the time than any other team in the league. As a result, the Cowboys did not get a good deal and ended up tying only one of twelve games that season. It took them five years before they became truly competitive.

We also had problems with the awarding of the Minnesota franchise in 1960. The AFL had already selected the Twin Cities for one of its franchises, and Max Winter and his group were ready to accept when George Halas, the chairman of our expansion committee, told them they could join the NFL. Formal acceptance, however, required a vote by all the owners, and when it came time for the final tally, a straw poll revealed there were not enough votes for approval. Halas, in absolute despair, just laid his head down on the table.

I was equally upset and told the owners, "We have promised these people they could have a franchise in our league. If we make a promise like that, we must deliver."

When the meeting recessed, I saw how angry Max Winter and Charley Johnson, the sports editor of the *Minneapolis Tribune*, who had spearheaded Minneapolis's drive for a professional football team, were getting, and when the meeting reopened, I was more determined than ever to press hard for fulfillment.

"If we have promised these people, then we must fulfill that promise," I told them again. "We can't vote against this just because one or two people might not like the idea of having to take a lesser cut of the revenue pie. Our word has to *mean* something, and if we don't give them the franchise, the American Football League will move in and make tremendous capital of the way we mishandled this matter."

That did it, and the Vikings were voted into the NFL, but since I was so adamant about seeing them admitted, I felt a responsibility for their having a competitive team. Minnesota was a part of the same expansion pool dispersal as Dallas but, unlike the Cowboys, was allowed to partake in the draft as well, from which it got players like Fran Tarkenton and Tommy Mason. I also invited Joe Thomas, the Vikings' chief scout, to our 1961 training camp and made the unprecedented gesture of allowing him to watch the players I knew would have difficulty making our team. We arranged a trade, sending them Jim Marshall, who had played little with us because of encephalitis, Paul Dickson, Jim Prestel, Jamie Caleb, Dick Grencni and Bill Gault, and made an agreement that if those players were on the Vikings' roster for the season's first game, we would get some medium-round draft picks in return. The Vikings circumvented that agreement, however, by listing only Marshall and Dickson on the active roster when the season began, thus greatly reducing our compensation— and adding the other players the following week. That was quite a letdown to me after I had invited Thomas into our camp and made what I felt was a very generous offer. When I mentioned it to him later, he said simply, "I had to do it to help my team." Marshall, Dickson and Prestel were starters for years for the Vikings, and we gave them two more in 1962, when we traded defensive tackle Errol Linden and kicker Fred Cox. Cox is now one of the top five scorers in NFL history, but Groza was still our full-time kicker then.

Actually, Lou had retired in 1960 because of an aching back—but only for a year. I always believed the great thrust he put into every kick had been causing muscle traumas in his back, which were not alleviated by his playing full time as an offensive tackle, so when he returned in 1961, Dick Schaffrath replaced him at tackle, and Lou became a place-kicker only, until he retired after the 1967 season.

The Minnesota mishap and Lou Groza's return were still one year in the future, however, when we opened our season in 1960 with a team comprised of eighteen new players, including eleven draft picks, the biggest turnover of players in the Browns' history. We had lost three players to the Cowboys in the expansion draft and some aging veterans to retirement, so I had decided to go with youth, zest and vitality—and that's exactly what we got.

The opening game ended in a resounding 41–24 victory at Philadelphia, and when we played the Eagles a few weeks later, we were in first place with a 3-0 record (we'd had a week off), while they were second at 3–1. We battled them to the final minutes and a 29–28 lead in that game until a pass interference penalty against Vince Costello enabled Bobby Walston to kick the winning field goal for a 31–29 victory. The win gave the Eagles the impetus to begin the drive that ultimately brought them the NFL title. We were right with them until we lost to Pittsburgh, 14–10, in the season's eighth game. Still, we ended the year on a positive note when, in our last game, we scored twenty-seven points in the fourth quarter to beat the Giants, 48–34, for the right to go to Miami and compete in the first Playoff Bowl, a game devised to add more money to the players' pension fund. Considering that half our team was new, I thought our 8-3-1 record that year was a great way to begin the sixties and that even better days seemed to lie ahead.

How wrong I was!

TWELVE

Modell and the End of an Era

THE NEXT TWO YEARS, 1961 and 1962, were the darkest period of my life. A group that included Arthur Modell purchased the Browns early in 1961, and through the next twenty-four months, the situation gradually deteriorated to the point where it became to Modell's interest to discredit me and my coaching methods, so that he, as a "playing owner"—as he once described himself to me—could be the image of the Cleveland Browns. He told me on the day that I was fired: "This team can never fully be mine as long as you are here because whenever anyone thinks of the Cleveland Browns, they think of you. Every time I come to the stadium, I feel that I am invading your domain, and from now on there can only be one dominant image."

During the two years between his coming to the Browns and my dismissal, I lived through a period of almost constant "intrigue." Player was set against player; the loyalty of my coaching staff was questioned, and attempts made to find out which ones were "Paul Brown men"; public criticism of my coaching was encouraged among the players and steadfastly carried on by management through the media; discipline and control were torn apart by flagrant disregard for team rules; and the team itself was subjected to unfair and overwhelming pressures when the ownership twice "guaranteed" the public it would win the championship.

The relationship between the two of us has been described as a personality conflict, but it was much more than that. It was a basic conflict between two different styles and two dif-

271

ferent philosophies of operating—one from knowledge and experience; the other from a complete lack of either. In its place came some sort of cosmetic imagery that put one person ahead of the team and totally disregarded the feelings and efforts of those who had worked for years to maintain a state of excellence.

A team's president cannot guarantee the public a championship for the sake of selling a few tickets without making his team the target of everyone that it plays; he cannot give players a radio program and then let them criticize their teammates and coaches without tearing the team apart; he cannot constantly hobnob with the players, buy them drinks and dinner and curry their favor without undermining the authority of the coaching staff. Yet these were just some of the things I had to put up with during the 1961 and 1962 seasons.

Art was not a football person. I resented his lack of background in the football world and did not respect his knowledge, and I probably showed it many times, not helping the situation any. As we continued, however, I saw he was eroding my position with the result that I could not be successful and carry out my responsibilities. The player-coach relationship became progressively more intolerable, to the point where I was no longer able to call the shots, no longer in a position to demand from all our players all the things which make or break a successful football team. That had never happened to me before in all my years in football.

Until Modell's arrival in 1961 every set of owners had been content to allow me to run the team without any interference because they knew I knew more about it than they did, and they had other business interests that demanded their time and expertise. Most importantly, my methods had brought us unmatched success, both on the field and at the bank, so there was no reason to question anything I did. I was neither cavalier nor arrogant about this use of power because as a part owner of the team I had a stake in its success, and I worked just as hard to protect the investment of the other owners as I did my own.

Art could indeed have been "a playing owner," had he not breached my contract and become the instant expert in a business he knew virtually nothing about. Those two areas— his repeated violations of my contract's specific areas of responsibility and his insistence on saying and doing things which were destructive to the morale of our team—were our chief points of contention. Underlying all of it was his ultimate intention of becoming the dominant figure on the Cleveland Browns and of using whatever means necessary to achieve that end. In all my years there, such a thought had never entered my mind.

Some of his attitudes are different now, of course, specifically his relationship with players, because he was badly burned and disillusioned by some of those he used to bring about my demise. Our teams are now in the same division, and at league functions he goes overboard to be nice to me. He tells people that he holds me in the highest regard and that we are closer now than when he came to Cleveland in 1961. He has also said the biggest mistake he ever made was firing me. The success of the Cincinnati Bengals in such a short period of time—our won-loss record against the Browns was dead—even in ten years—might have moved him to that realization. The passing years and the far greater tragedy of losing my first wife, Katy, have drained away any bitter feelings, but they have never undone the loss of five years of my professional life or any of the heartache that my family suffered before and after he dismissed me.

I had no way of predicting any of this, however, when Modell's group bought the team from David Jones, Ellis Ryan, Herb Evans and Bob Gries for nearly $4 million in 1961. Jones, Ryan and Gries wanted to sell, they told me, "so we can get our estates in order," and though Gries eventually stayed as one of the majority owners, all three men died within a few years of the sale. Evans sold only because Nationwide Insurance Company, the owners of his radio station, WGAR, felt that pro football was "a brittle business" at that time.

The deal was put into motion by Curly Morrison, our old fullback from the mid-fifties, who was then working for the Columbia Broadcasting System, where he learned the Jones group was willing to sell the team "for the right price." Morrison told Vince Andrews, a New York theatrical agent and business acquaintance of Modell's, who knew that Art longed to be involved in professional football. Modell reportedly sold himself to Gries, who still had grandiose schemes about "merchandising" our team. Art advanced a variety of high-sounding ideas, including a plan for a pro football doubleheader. I

personally felt the idea cheapened our sport, and it later
proved to be a failure.

I first met Modell when the Browns were in New York for
our final game against the Giants in 1960. Phil Haber, a
member of the team's law firm, brought him over to our hotel, but I had no idea then who he was or that he was involved in the team's sale. I was led to believe on that
occasion that he was a football buff, and we had a very
pleasant chat. Even when he became an owner, I knew little
more than that he had worked for an advertising agency in
New York, dealing in packaged television shows, but when
the sale was completed, he told me, "I'm buying it really because of you. I think it will take me a year or two to find out
what pro football is all about." That is exactly how it turned
out.

At the time the team's sale was under consideration, I also
asked Gries what kind of money Modell had to invest. He
told me that Art and his family had about $28,000, but that
he would back him at the Union Commerce Bank in Cleveland for the rest of his share of the purchase price. One of
the heaviest investors was Rudy Schaefer for the Schaefer
Brewing Company, which wanted to open a new market in
Cleveland. Schaefer, who apparently knew Modell in New
York, became vice-president, but his main interest was selling
beer, and I seldom heard from him. Gries was the next
largest stockholder and also became a vice-president, but unlike Schaefer, he was involved in much of the chicanery that
eroded my position over the next two years. Gries really put
the deal together, but Modell secured a voting trust from the
group and became chairman of the board, and, in that role,
made all the announcements and let everyone believe he had
invested millions in the team. Shortly after the sale was completed, the NFL signed a two-year $9.3-million television
contract with CBS, so the group's investment was secured almost immediately. I never knew whether Modell had had any
advance word of this deal before his group bought the club,
but it was a fortuitous move at the time.

I had also thought, from time to time, about putting a
group together and gaining control of the team, but the circumstances had never been right, and I had always been involved with football and not really driven to become so
involved in ownership. Besides, I had my shares of the team,
which I kept when Modell's group took over, and I was satis-

fied that my contract protected my interests and duties, or at least so I thought.

I retained my duties as vice-president, general manager and head coach, and my contract was extended to ten years, at $82,500 per year, plus a $7,500 expense account and an option to purchase ten shares per year. My contract stipulated that I would be spokesman for the club at all league meetings and that I would retain control on all matters which were essential to the operations of the football team. In fact, I had my lawyer draw up the exact terms I felt protected my best interests, and when Modell read the contract, he said, "That suits me," and never quibbled over one word or phrase.

The part of the contract which spelled out my obligations reads:

Mr. Brown shall have the sole power, authority and discretion to act for the corporation in respect to all policies and details pertaining to the success as a football team of the Cleveland Browns, including without limitation the foregoing:

(1) The hiring, determining of compensation, releasing, selling, trading of players.

(2) The hiring, determination of compensation, the releasing of assistant coaches, personnel scouts, team physicians, team dentist, trainer, equipment manager and all other members of the field and clubhouse staff.

(3) The corporation's scouting and drafting activity.

(4) The purchase of all football equipment, medical training facilities and the mechanism, coaching aids, paraphernalia, including football movie programs.

(5) Selection of training camps, selection of all practice sites and facilities.

(6) League actions on playing rules, game officials, conduct of the game, size of the squads, allocation of players, player formulas in connection with distribution of any players to or from any team or teams that has to do with expansion.

(7) The approval of all hotel and transportation arrangements and team entertainment, and all matters involving the morale of the players, the coaches, the field and clubhouse personnel. . . .

Nor could I hire anyone for the front office for any period longer than a year without Modell's approval, and if I purchased the contract of a player, or players, that cost more than $25,000, I had to have his approval. Of course, this was no concern to me because players' contracts are rarely purchased in the NFL. In addition, the contract reads: "On any matters in the realm of Mr. Brown's responsibility that are discussed or acted upon at any league meeting, including executive, owner or committee meetings, Mr. Brown shall have the right to speak for the corporation and cast his vote for the corporation. . . ."

I cite the contract, with particular attention to Sections 1 and 7, because during the two years I worked for Modell, these sections were violated time and again. I discovered for the first time that the duties and stipulations laid down in a contract can truly not be worth the paper they're written on, as the phrase goes. To me, a contract was always a sacred document and a total commitment to every word and agreement contained therein. I never once infringed on his duties, which, under contract, were restricted to promotion and finance and which he proudly told everyone fitted his background and Gries's "merchandising" schemes. All the words and all the stipulations meant absolutely nothing, however, at the end of the 1962 season, when Modell made his decision to fire me.

When we first signed our contracts, though, I thought we had a healthy situation, and I was prepared to work with Art to make it successful. I should have known from the start—and indeed I was twice forewarned—that this arrangement was not going to work. Our group was less than a month old when we went to the NFL meetings in Miami Beach to gain league approval for the ownership, and the NFL's lawyer came up to me, obviously concerned. He warned me my association with the new group would not be compatible.

"They're not your kind of people," he told me, "and I hope you'll think twice before aligning yourself with them any further."

"Why do you say that?" I asked.

"Last night, at our cocktail party, Gries and Modell were saying disparaging things about you, and I think you should know it," he said.

Later that day I called a meeting of our group, which in-

cluded Gries, Modell and Harold Sauerbrei, and asked them
pointblank about the incident.

"I'm not responsible for what I say when I'm drunk,"
Gries replied. Modell said nothing, but I've always felt the
campaign to take over the club might have begun as early
as that meeting.

Almost immediately our team's front office underwent
drastic changes, in both style and methods of operation, and
not, in my judgment, for the better. For the first time since
the club was founded, I was no longer hiring some of the
front-office people, something which disturbed me because of
the loyalty aspects, and my concerns later proved true.

Modell and Gries made all the decisions of a nonfootball
nature. Art knew that Clevelanders were wary of outside
ownership, particularly of someone from New York, so for
window-dressing purposes he made sure all the top executives
were local people. Dave Jones was allowed to stay as
president, but he did nothing; Gries was vice-president; and
Marsh Samuels and Sauerbrei both had visibility. Jones and
Gries suddenly had offices at the stadium, something that had
never happened before, but that was a sham, and a year later
Jones was forced to step down, so Modell could become the
team's president.

In 1960 my son Mike had succeeded the deceased Russ
Gestner as business manager, but when he went into the service early in 1961, Sauerbrei got the job. That was a critical
loss for me because Mike, who had his law degree from Harvard by then, would have alerted me to the manipulations
that started soon afterward, and with him or Gestner in the
office, Modell's people might have been a bit wary about how
they operated.

I worked at being pleasant with Art when we began our
relationship, and I think he did, too. I didn't know at the
time how things would work out, but since it was very obvious he knew little about football, I expended every effort to
explain things and to try to help him fathom the unique
mechanics of our business. Still, the climate in which we
worked was different, and those who had been there before
Modell took over began to notice the change. I was very
low-key and never raised my voice or tolerated shouting or
vulgar language around the office, yet within a few weeks my
secretary, Mercedes O'Toole, complained to me that she sim-

ply could not stand the kind of loud language that was coming from the front office.

About that time I asked her to get a copy of my contract for reference purposes, but since photostatic copies had not yet been made, she went into Art's office and found the original lying on his desk. When she brought it to me, she said, "I think you should see these," and pointed to a series of check marks beside the paragraphs designating certain duties of mine which might be attacked. This was the first time that I began to have doubts about my situation, and from this point on I began to keep close track of the things I observed. A few weeks later my secretary walked into my office with her resignation already typed and told me, "I can't stand to be here any longer. The man has a Machiavellian mind."

Her loss was crucial to me because not only was she an outstanding secretary and a fine lady, but it meant that I no longer had someone inside the front office on whom I could rely. It wasn't long before we had an organization filled with petty intrigue, everyone in the front office currying favor and hoping to land on his feet, because it was now apparent that a struggle was going on.

Modell next went against my long-standing rule forbidding our players to have radio or television shows—something clearly within my purview as stated in Section 7, under team morale—and got Jim Brown and Milt Plum radio shows. It was also an opportunity to ingratiate himself with a couple of local newspapermen—or so it seemed to me—by paying them to write the scripts. I had always been opposed to such shows because it was unfair to the other players and the other media and was the quickest way to bring divisiveness to a team and ruin its morale. When I pointed that out to Art, however, he brushed me off by saying it was good for ticket sales and fan interest. Both shows hurt our football team because they criticized both players and coaches but, most of all, because there was constant criticism of our play-calling system. The furor that caused was fanned by Modell's own inflammatory statements while he sat in the press box at the games. Ironically, Modell was asked about the system at his very first press conference; that was a bit inane since he didn't know anything about our football team at the time or about the game itself. Still, he backed me down the line, noting, "I don't care if the plays go in by carrier pigeon."

A year later his tune had changed completely and he began

making speeches declaring that the messenger system was dead, that it had no place in football because of rapidly changing defenses and, furthermore, that the Browns were going to abandon it at his direction. Needless to say, it was clearly outside his jurisdiction to dictate to me how we called our plays. Art never understood, nor did he ever try to understand, what our technical football system was about, and his criticism was always based more on what he heard than on what he knew.

During one game in Washington he carried on in the press box about our offense. "Why is he doing that?" he'd yell. Or, "Doesn't he know any better than to do that?" That went on for the entire game, and when I was told about it by some media people, I took him to task both for the criticism and for losing his poise.

"Oh, it doesn't mean anything. I'm just a fan," he told me.

"You are not just a fan," I replied. "You're an owner, and the position requires an owner to conduct himself a bit differently in public from a fan, *particularly* if he sits among the press."

He ignored the admonition and began to start in on me with the players as well. He'd hobnob with some of them, buy them drinks and dinner and prowl the local night spots, and later some of them told me he'd ask them, "Is Paul Brown treating you all right?" . . . "Are you getting a square deal from Paul Brown?" . . . "What do you think of Paul Brown?" . . . "Has the game passed him by?" The seeds of discord were being sown.

All this was undermining my authority because there are always certain players just waiting for openings like this to go over the coach's head when they have a problem or feel they are being slighted. Modell kept it up even on our charter flights. He'd sit with different players, always wanting to know their feelings toward me; that gave them every reason to believe they could rely on a higher authority if they felt mistreated. It even spread to our practice sessions. Several times, as we ran our plays, we had to interrupt our practices and wait for Jim Brown or some other player to finish a conversation with Modell. The control I had once exercised over our team was disappearing before my eyes.

Modell also worked player against player. In 1962, before Jim Ninowski broke his collarbone, Ninowski and Mike McCormack were relaxing in a club with their wives after a game when Art sat down at their table. When Jim and his wife got up to dance, he leaned over to McCormack and said, "What about Ninowski? Is he over the hill? He doesn't look like he's playing too well."

A few minutes later, when Mike and his wife, Anne, got up to dance, Modell leaned over to Ninowski and said, "What's with McCormack? He got beat on a pass rush today. Is he finished? Do you think he can still play?"

Such tactics didn't work on a player like McCormack, but with others, it started trouble because there are always those on a team who resent some of their teammates, and with them, to encourage criticism is like pouring gasoline onto a fire. Modell never played football, or any other sport for that matter, and he did not understand how very delicate a mechanism a football team is and how quickly it goes off kilter if any of its parts involving morale are tampered with.

He was always trying to be pals with particular players. Some of them he promised big raises and jobs as player coaches. From his constant fraternization, he gleaned little nuggets about a player's unrest or disappointments and used them. For example, I've described the game in which I criticized Ray Renfro for not making "the big play," and how sorry I was that he had taken it so badly. I had totally forgotten about the incident—until our own publicity department issued a release referring to Renfro's unhappiness about the remark.

Trading players was clearly my responsibility under the contract, but I always kept Modell informed of what we did in that area. When we decided to trade Plum to Detroit for Ninowski, however, Modell and Sauerbrei went to Detroit to talk to Jim about returning to Cleveland, though that was not their responsibility. When the deal went through, Modell was the first to tell Plum, and then he told everyone how he had pushed for the trade when, in truth, he was no factor. Later he openly criticized and second-guessed our trades and encouraged players such as Jim Brown to do the same thing, all of which just chipped away further at the structure of our team.

As soon as Modell arrived in Cleveland, he began circling Jim Brown, seeing in him a juicy target with the "star quality" that show business and advertising people always try to exploit. He signed Jim to a series of contracts for publications and radio shows, again in direct violation of my rules, which encouraged him to be openly critical of the team and the coaching. It wasn't too long before everyone believed that Jim and I had drawn our battle lines and were in constant conflict.

That wasn't true—as I've said, Jim and I never had a cross word with each other. It was true, though, that as a coaching staff we had lost Jim Brown because he was now answering directly to Modell. Before the 1962 season began, Art publicly referred to Jim as "my senior partner," leaving everyone wondering where I stood. The ironic thing is, before the season, we had drawn up a new contract for Jim, which I had authorized for $50,000 per year. Modell got upset and said, "What are you trying to do, break me?" Yet after I was fired, he reportedly upped Jim's salary 50 percent to $75,000. This wasn't the only case of this type of thing.

In addition, I never believed in no-cut and no-trade contracts or in certain types of incentive clauses based on individual statistics, and I had told Art it was club policy. At the time Jim was getting a bit wary that we might trade him—indeed, our staff had discussed it—so he convinced Modell to insert a no-trade clause in his contract, though Modell had no right to do so. As a favor to Jim, he even arranged for a lawyer to meet with us and work out the tax problems to Brown's best advantage. Jim never showed up, however, and Art, who had become enamored with his new relationship with Brown, was crushed at being jilted because he ardently believed that he had become one of the man's best friends. Of course, their relationship has soured, and Art learned the hard way that you cannot buy or appease or play favorites with any player.

As a nonfootball person, Modell never understood—or else ignored—the fact that the quickest way to put a team in the hole is to guarantee its fans that it will win a championship. Since the claim comes from top management, they rightly begin to believe it, and their expectations become so high they are disappointed the moment the team loses a game or doesn't perform well. That puts intolerable pressure on the coaches and players because they have been given a public standard to maintain, regardless of whether it is maintainable, and the moment something goes wrong the coach is the first to be blamed. At the same time any team which makes such a claim becomes a ripe target for every opponent, making it even tougher for the team to win. That was another basic difference in our philosophies: He put selling tickets first in his priorities; I wanted to win—and knew people would come as a result.

As we went to training camp in 1961, I became increasingly concerned to see our publicity releases continually referring to us as having the best at this position and the best at that position, until any reasonable person could only assume the championship was a formality. Modell orchestrated all this, and just before the season began, I felt he really hurt us when he flat out predicted that the Browns would win the world's championship "because we have the best team and the best management in the league." That must have brought a laugh to the managements in Green Bay, Philadelphia, New York and Detroit, all of which were smart enough not to say anything.

Our PR department churned out these exaggerated claims each day, though everyone knew we had serious problems, beginning with inadequate quarterbacking and becoming worse when Gene Hickerson, one of my all-time guards, broke his leg and was lost for the season. Then Dick Schaffrath and Bobby Mitchell were called into the service. With Hickerson and Schaffrath gone, we had to juggle our offensive line all during the season, and it never did solidify. In fact, we were forced to use our ends, Rich Kreitling and Bobby Crespino, as messengers. Though Mitchell made most of the games, he never practiced with us because of his military duties and, as a result, was not nearly as effective. We got Schaffrath only on the weekends he could get a pass.

At the same time our foremost division rivals, the Giants, strengthened themselves when they obtained Y. A. Tittle in a trade with the San Francisco 49ers and then added Del Shofner, a marvelous wide receiver. I was surprised when I heard about the Tittle deal, because if we had known he was available, we certainly would have gone after him. Tittle became the key to the Giants' success in the years to come: three division titles over the next three seasons.

We lost our opening game to the Eagles, 27–20, on Jim Brown's 105-yard kickoff return for a touchdown, but nevertheless we were tied for first place in the fifth week of the season. Then the Packers beat us, 49–17, in a game Vince Lombardi later told me was the most perfect any of his Green Bay teams had ever played. "There was not a single mistake," he said, "and I had the curious sensation that I was watching our blackboard diagrams coming alive right on the field and literally executing themselves." That Green Bay team also had four players—fullback Jim Taylor, tackle Forrest Gregg, linebacker Bill Forrester and tight end Ron Kramer—who are on my all-time opponents team. When we lost to the Steelers, 17–13, to fall two games out of first place, the grumbling began because everyone felt he had been betrayed by those claims that we would win the title. It was at this time that reports began coming back to me of Modell's criticisms in the press box during a game.

Meanwhile, Plum was becoming progressively more critical of our play selection, even though he was the key player who was most falling short in performance. In our first game against the Giants, we were just a game out of first place again, but his swing pass to Jim Brown on the game's first play was thrown so softly one of the Giants easily picked it off and ran for a touchdown. When we trailed, 20–14, in the third quarter, Renfro was wide open in the end zone, and Plum's pass landed in the dirt, several yards short. Two weeks later, when we played the Chicago Bears, we were yet again within a game of first place, but after watching us build a 14–0 lead in the first quarter, the Bears discovered that he panicked when faced with a heavy blitz by the defense, and we lost, 17–14.

In our season's final game we played very well in tying the Giants, 7–7, at Yankee Stadium, in Modell's first "homecoming," as he put it, with his new team. Instead of being satisfied with the effort, however, he rushed into the dressing room immediately after the game and proceeded to berate me for my decision in the final seconds to punt the ball on fourth down from our own seven-yard line. We had needed seven yards for a first down on a frozen field, and if we had missed the first down, the Giants could have easily kicked a field goal and won the game. I knew the Eagles had already won their game, eliminating us from the Playoff Bowl, and since our men had played their hearts out against the division champions, I felt they deserved at least a tie from this game. I never had this happen before with any owner, and it upset me that this man had neither the knowledge nor the common sense to realize what our team had done.

As the 1961 season wound down, we began discussions with the Redskins about trading Bobby Mitchell as part of a deal to get Ernie Davis, who had broken all of Jim Brown's rushing records at Syracuse. The entire staff was thoroughly convinced that a team in our climate needed two big, fast runners to overcome the rough playing conditions late in the season, and it had become apparent that Mitchell, who weighed only 188 pounds, was having problems during the final weeks with the chopped-up fields and slick playing surfaces. In addition, Bobby was still strictly a game-day player because of his military service, joining us only when he was able to get a weekend pass and often not arriving until just a few hours before a game. There was another year left on his service commitment, and it seemed probable that he would miss our 1962 training camp and part of that season as well.

The Redskins were interested in him not only as a player—he had always impressed George Preston Marshall because of his great games in Washington—but because the team was under increasing pressure to break its color line. Marshall knew that Bobby was a class person, very intelligent and low-key, and felt he was probably the only player who could handle this special situation. Since Mitchell was stationed at Fort Meade, outside Washington, Marshall also felt he could get him an early release from the army. I discussed all this with Bobby beforehand and allowed him to discuss the situation with Marshall. He foresaw no problems, so it came down to structuring the trade.

Washington had the first pick in the draft, and we had two first-round picks. After some maneuvering about which of our picks they would receive, it was agreed that the Redskins would pick Davis for us, and we would pick Leroy Jackson, a swift running back, for them, and then send Jackson and Mitchell to Washington in exchange for Davis.

The trade appeared sound, but an act of God prevented us from ever finding out just how great Ernie would have been. After the draft Vince Lombardi called me and said, "If Davis plays to his potential, you've got it made next season. I still can't believe that Washington, a team in your own division, would do this." There is no doubt that the Browns would have had a tremendous combination with Jim Brown and Ernie Davis.

We had to sign Davis in competition with the Buffalo Bills of the American Football League, and since I was still involved with the 1961 season, Modell happily took on the job. I talked to Ernie first and knew from my conversation that Buffalo didn't have much of a chance, but I made a specific point again of advising Art, who never had done this before, that we had a policy against giving no-cut contracts, regardless of the player or the situation, and that we never announced salary terms because that created problems with other players. No-cut contracts are unfair because they deprive other players of a legitimate chance to make the team. I never wanted any player I released to be able to say he was cut because some no-cut guy—even a great player like Ernie Davis—was guaranteed a job even before training camp began.

Modell deliberately went against my wishes, however, and the newspapers soon splashed the news that Ernie had an $80,000 no-cut contract. As soon as I saw the headline, I knew Jim Brown's nose would be out of joint, but I'm sure Art never even considered that as he basked in the publicity photos, television interviews and newspaper stories, all the while "guaranteeing" that Davis would bring the Browns the title in 1962.

As it happened, Davis was on the College All-Star squad and, in his second day at their camp, had two wisdom teeth pulled and soon became very sick. His mouth would not heal, and after subsequent tests, the doctors in Chicago found he had "acute leukemia" and sent him back to Cleveland for further tests. One of my neighbors was Dr. James Hewlett, a hematologist at the Cleveland Clinic who helped conduct the blood tests, so I knew about Ernie's condition.

"Can the boy play football with this disease?" I asked.

"Don't let him play," Dr. Hewlett said most emphatically. "I'd hate to think of what could happen."

On Jim Hewlett's advice, I ruled out any chance that Ernie could play that season, even though he began medication that slowed the disease. All of us—including Ernie—knew he had only a few months to live, though we never made a public statement about the exact nature of his illness until after the season had started.

Ernie, of course, never played for the Browns, but for part of the season everyone was led to believe he might because Modell kept the possibility alive. We had played only three games, and were struggling, when Art announced that one of the doctors who was treating Ernie said he could play, followed, of course, by stories quoting other doctors saying it would be wrong to allow that to happen. Then came word that Ernie would begin working out under medical supervision when, in fact, I had ruled out any such possibility, on Dr. Hewlett's advice. Next we were told that Ernie "had recovered" and could play; that was deliberately misleading and built up only more false hopes.

Finally, Modell came to me one day and said, "Put him in a game, and let him play. We have a big investment in him, and I'd like a chance to get some of it back. It doesn't matter how long he plays; just let him run back a kick, let him do anything, just so we can get a story in the paper saying he's going to play and the fans will come to see him. If he has to go, why not let him have a little fun?"

I was concerned and called Pete Rozelle and told him, "I'm getting a lot of heat to activate and play Ernie Davis for a short time for publicity purposes. I don't want to do it, but I think you should know about the situation."

"Don't activate him," Pete said. "If you do, I'll step into this matter and overrule you, and I don't want to get involved."

Thus, my decision stood, but from that time forward, the Paul Brown—Art Modell relationship really went into the deep freeze. Modell went out of his way to avoid being with me; he sat on a different bus on road trips, or in a different part of the airplane, and rarely spoke to me, despite his claims later that he had done all he could to build a relationship.

The entire situation was unfair to Ernie, of course, whom I liked very much because he was such a pleasant and courageous person. He never once asked me if he could practice or play, but I'm sure all the needless publicity about his chances had to upset him. I know it upset our players and haunted us throughout that season. Our players saw him nearly every day at practice, where he'd don a sweat suit but do little more than warm up the quarterbacks or run laps. He was so ill the sweat just poured from him even as he stood watching us work. That frightened and unnerved many of our guys, who had never before watched a man in this condition. Sometimes, when he walked onto the practice field, they looked at him, and everything got very quiet. It became just heartbreaking.

The Davis tragedy was part of a season that was just one long period of personal distress. First came Modell's doubleheader idea. This, he said at the time, would be his claim to fame and of course, the idea failed, just as most knowledgeable pro football people said it would. I had opposed it from the very beginning because I've never been a $9.99 guy, and that was how I viewed this gimmick. From a practical point of view, it meant splitting our gate four ways instead of two, and I tried to convince Art that it would be better simply to make a tremendous production out of one game. "You are cheapening our product, and you can't give away what you are trying to sell," I told him. "That just gives pro football a bargain-basement look, and our game is better than that."

Surviving a profootball doubleheader, however, was child's play compared to surviving the pressures imposed on the team, our coaches and me by Modell's incessant "guarantees" of a championship long before we had played our first game. He actually said at one point, "No matter how much money or sacrifice it takes, I guarantee that we will win the NFL title." That had a ring of great sincerity to it, but it was strictly Barnum. We had no better chance that season than a lot of teams, and if taken on a man-for-man basis, what edge did we have sending Jim Ninowski against Y. A. Tittle? Add to that the unknown quantities of injuries, people being called into the service, weaknesses in personnel . . . and you knew there was no such thing as a guaranteed championship.

I even went to Art and told him to stop making those asinine public statements because it was only putting the team and me on the spot. "Oh, it's good public relations, and it helps to promote enthusiasm for season tickets," he replied, dismissing me.

The kiss of death for 1962 came just two days before the season began when Modell was reported to have told a Sigma Delta Chi journalism fraternity dinner, "The Browns will win their first championship since 1955 and the team will be the finest in years. Spectators will feast on a brand of professional skills unmatched since the golden days ten years ago. . . . If we don't win, we'll have a rough time finding excuses."

He said all this knowing my feelings about putting such pressure on the team, knowing we were starting the season without Ernie Davis, meaning that Jim Brown, "his senior partner," would again have to bear the brunt of the running game, and knowing that Ninowski at quarterback still hadn't proved he could win a championship. Selling tickets and drumming up interest may have been reasons for making those ridiculous guarantees, but putting everything into perspective, I'm sure now their prime purpose, from the very beginning, was to lay the groundwork for our showdown at the season's end.

Going into training camp in 1962, I had never felt so uncomfortable. What with Modell, and the pressure, and the constant carping throughout the off-season from some of our players about our football, my relationship with the team had greatly changed. The complete control and authority I had once held over them had worn dangerously thin. Meeting together, the coaching staff decided to ride out the storm until the season began, hoping we could find a way to regain gradually all that had been lost. We never did, though, and some of the things which happened to us that season reflected it.

We were all uneasy in that contrived atmosphere, and it was made worse when our players became so pumped up by all the publicity and grandiose expectations that they played their best football in the preseason while the other teams were experimenting and trying out rookies. That is the worst thing that can happen to any team. Though we won our five preseason games, it meant nothing because the team was brought along too quickly. Though I tried, I could not slow down because the players had begun to react more to what Modell said than to what we tried to tell them.

The biggest change was ostensibly scrapping our messenger guard system and allowing our quarterbacks to call their own plays. The furor over the play-calling system and our use of audibles had carried over from 1961, with the same tired and erroneous reasoning, and it was fueled again by Modell, who by that time had some Cleveland sportswriters doing Jim Brown's radio shows and sports columns, as well as blasting away on their own. I tried to straighten out one writer on how our system operated, if only to give him some facts on which to base any further stories, instead of the propaganda that was being fed from within our organization.

Any acquiescence on my part to changing our system, however, was only temporary because I never intended to go along with something I did not believe in, or was uncomfortable using. I bought some time by saying we would use our guards to bring in the plays only "some of the time." It was the best we could do in the preseason under the conditions that prevailed. The coaches, including Blanton Collier, felt as strongly as I did on this point and agreed to stay with this approach and then gradually to return to the former system once the season began; that is what happened. Later, however, when he succeeded me as head coach, Collier would go out of his way to point out that the nonmessenger system had worked so well when we were unbeaten in the 1962 preseason and that he had never understood why I had abandoned it. In fact, he was the most adamant among all the coaches against changing from our regular system.

I had rehired Blanton earlier that year after he had been fired as Kentucky's head coach. I must have been one of the first persons he called, and I could hear how upset he was when we talked on the telephone.

"Don't worry, Blanton," I told him. "Everything will work out fine. I'll make the arrangements, and you'll have a job with us again."

I didn't have an opening, in fact, but I rehired him anyway and made him our offensive backfield coach. Blanton had been my closest colleague for years, so I could not turn my back on him. When he had left us for Kentucky in 1954, I had hired Howard Brinker to fill his job as defensive coach, and I found out later that after he had returned to our team, Blanton felt I favored Howard over him and listened to his counsel more. I was never aware of any such differences, but I think the problem was caused by Collier's extreme deafness; not always being able to hear everything that was said, he imagined after a while that I was ignoring him.

Early that July, Blanton was invited to a local country club to play golf with Modell and Harold Sauerbrei, and after their match Art said to him, "Are you a Paul Brown man?"

"I didn't know what he meant," Blanton told us when he related the incident at our staff meeting the next day—but I did, and I confronted both Modell and Sauerbrei.

"What are you trying to do?" I asked them. "It only pits coach against coach if it becomes clear you have to declare your loyalty to the team president over the head coach. That's not right, and you *know* it is outside your jurisdiction to interfere with my coaching staff. You have sown the seed of discord."

I never got a satisfactory answer from either one of them, but from this point on, seeing what was happening, on the advice of my lawyer, I began carefully to note and record the moves which seemed directed against me or which violated my contract. I knew Collier had been deeply affected by his Kentucky experiences because Adolph Rupp, the school's great basketball coach, had apparently ridden roughshod over everyone in the athletic department, and he had always felt that Rupp was greatly responsible for his losing his job. Such experiences can develop the attitude "either get or get gotten," and as the 1962 season dragged on, the possibilities of what might happen to him and to me appeared to dawn on Blanton. He gradually withdrew from associating with the other coaches and said less and less at our meetings.

As we struggled through the terrible weeks of the preseason and then through the agony of the regular season, one of our prime football concerns was helping Ninowski and Frank Ryan, obtained in a trade with the Rams, tune into our system. Getting Frank was one of the best trades I ever made; the more I worked with him, the more I wished we had had him a few years earlier because we could have won big with him as our quarterback. As it was, Collier won the 1964 title with Frank as the starting quarterback. Another great trade that year was for Bill Glass, a defensive end good enough to rank among my finest ever.

The last player I cut in the preseason was a man named John Havlicek, who later, of course, became a great professional basketball player with the Boston Celtics. I first met him when he visited our locker room after a 1961 game. "What do you think of pro football?" I asked him.

"I wouldn't mind trying it," he told me.

"Are you serious?"

"Yes, I am," he replied, so I made some inquiries at Ohio State and was told that John had been an excellent high school quarterback and would have been just as formidable playing football for the Buckeyes as basketball. When we got to the late rounds of the draft that year, we were looking for pass receivers, but the "numbers" in front of us—height, weight, speed, body structure and so forth—told us to give Havlicek a try.

John was a tremendously competitive person and caught the football very well because of his very supple hands, but what finally caused us to cut him was his lack of great foot speed. I told him, "John, it would be a shame to have you play football as a fringe player, compared to what you could be in professional basketball."

He thanked me and left immediately for the Celtics' training camp. I never dreamed he would be such a phenomenal player with Boston, but again, I wasn't too surprised, not with his talent, competitiveness and intelligence.

When our season began a few days later, it was with a victory over the Giants. Modell was all smiles after the game, rushed into our dressing room, threw his arms around me and kissed me. His fawning thoroughly embarrassed me, and I couldn't stand to be around him, especially since I knew that while he was displaying all this affection, he was also working against me among the players. No wonder he told people I was "cold and unemotional" toward him.

Jim Brown had his poorest season with the Browns in 1962, and part of the reason was his freewheeling attitude of independence fostered by his relations with Modell. He also injured his wrist, which caused him to fumble an inordinate number of times. I made allowances for his injured wrist, but never for his attitude—sometimes after a lost fumble it appeared to me that he'd act nonchalant, as if he didn't care, and just walk away. Jim also did some thoughtless things at times, something he had rarely done in previous seasons. In our first Redskins game, for example, he started to run to the left, found himself hemmed in by the Washington defense and, as he was going down, tried to toss a lateral to Ninowski. One of the Redskins easily intercepted it and ran for a touchdown. That would never have happened if we had still been a disciplined team.

One of the most perplexing incidents to occur to us that year came after I had placed Howard ("Hopalong") Cassady, who had been obtained from Detroit before the season, on the waiver list. The Giants claimed him and, anticipating they might have the only claim, called our office and asked for his phone number, so they could have him come to New York once the waiver period expired. Modell talked with Jack Mara, the Giants' president, and assured him that we would not withdraw the claim so that New York—our foremost rival in the division and with whom we still had a game to play—could have free access to him. He had no right to do this, of course, but that meant nothing to him.

At ten o'clock the next morning, Vince McNally, the Eagles' general manager, called me about Hoppy, and we worked out a trade for a draft pick after withdrawing his name from the waiver list, all of which was within my realm of responsibility. Modell was furious, however, and publicly apologized to the Giants for our actions. I had acted for the

welfare of our team and had obtained a draft choice instead
of the token $100 waiver free, but all Art could do was raise
a fuss about "embarrassing me in front of my New York
friends."

Later, in a game against the Cowboys which we eventually
won, 19–10, we had taken the lead when Modell told one of
our ground crew that he hoped Dallas would run back the
ensuing kickoff for a touchdown. It was at times like this that
I made a point of keeping the league office aware of the situation.

Our team's efficiency was also cut down that season by
serious physical problems, in addition to Ernie Davis's terminal leukemia and Jim Brown's injured wrist. When Ninowski
went down with a broken collarbone, I had already been
leaning toward replacing him with Ryan, but Frank had still
not fully grasped our system. But he had to play anyway.
Our secondary, which did not have the great speed of previous years, was slowed even more when Bobby Franklin broke
his collarbone, and Ray Renfro suffered the entire season
with a psoriasis that afflicted his whole body. While it did not
dull his determination, it limited his effectiveness. John
Wooten, one of our young messenger guards, sprained his
ankle playing basketball on a day off—something that had
been forbidden in past years but over which I had little control now—and he was hobbling for a while as well.

One of my longtime policies was that no player whose injuries prevented them from playing could make our road
trips. These were business, not fun, trips, after all. I applied
the rule to Ninowski, yet when we got on the plane for our
first away game following his injury, there he was sitting with
the players.

"What are you doing here?" I asked him.

"Mr. Modell told me that I could come along," Jim said.

The worst trip of all was to our final game in San Francisco. Fog had closed San Francisco's airport, so we had to
land and wait in Sacramento for a few hours. While I sat and
talked with a couple of our coaches, another coach came up
to me and said, "You won't believe what I just saw. Modell is
in the airport bar buying drinks for some of the players."

That was the final straw. The last vestige of anything I had
ever stood for was destroyed. Art was totally aware of our
rules about drinking, yet he had deliberately gone against my
wishes. When we got to our hotel, I called Katy and told her

about it and the heartache it caused me. The next day we defeated the 49ers, 13–10, anyway, but Jim Brown missed a 1,000-yard season, which he had already achieved in the game, by trying to run outside—on his own—and getting thrown for a loss that left him with 996 yards. Still, after the game, I told our captain, Mike McCormack, to award him the game ball because he had played heroically with his injured wrist, and when he accepted it, I thought at the time that he looked a bit sheepish, I later found out why.

Considering all that we had gone through, a 7-6-1 record was not that bad, and the team had made more money in 1962 than in any year in its history. I honestly did not know what to do next, however. It was a question that became moot on the first Monday of 1963, when Modell called me into his office and fired me.

"I've made a decision," he began. "You have to step down as coach and general manager."

Naturally, I was stunned. "I really don't know what to say," I replied. "I have a contract with you for eight more years."

"You'll be paid for your contract," he replied, and then went on to say the words I have quoted at the beginning of this chapter: that the team could never be his as long as I was there, that whenever anyone thought of the Browns, they thought only of me, that from now on there could be only one dominant image—himself.

"Well," I replied, still trying to sort out what I was hearing, "now I know what you meant when you said it would take you a couple of years to learn about the business. The only thing I can say to you at this time is that I'll have to see my lawyer because I don't believe you can fulfill the terms of a contract just by paying me money." And I left.

That really was all there was to that final meeting. There were no loud words or recriminatory statements because that was not my style, but I walked out of the stadium and got into my car as if in a dream. I couldn't believe what had just happened; I had never imagined that anything like this could ever happen to me. I had never felt so hopelessly alone in all my life as at that moment. My entire life had been chopped from beneath me, and everything I had worked to attain swept away. I didn't want to be paid not to coach. The money meant nothing to me at the moment, though when I thought about it later, I wasn't even sure that part of the contract would be honored.

I had called Katy before leaving the office and told her briefly what happened, and when I arrived home, she looked at me and started to cry.

"It'll work out," I told her gently. "Just follow our old rule and say very little" . . . and we did. I never vented my feelings or talked about the usurpation of my duties and powers, and the deliberate attempts to take control of the team away from me, or about the thing that hurt me most—the heartache that it had brought to my family. That evening we went to visit Al Sutphin, a trusted friend, who owned the Cleveland Arena and whose farm in Florida we had often visited during our vacations. I took my contract with me, and after he had read every word, I asked him for his opinion.

"There is no question that it has been breached, which is something that should never happen in sports," he told me. "But I'm not sure what can be done about it legally, as long as he pays the money." To me a contract was a lot more than just money, though, so I hired a lawyer to look into the possibility of instituting a lawsuit. Pete Rozelle dissuaded me from it, however, when he pointed out that no jury would look favorably on the claims of someone who was being paid $82,500 a year for doing almost nothing, whatever the circumstances. Ironically, Pete had learned of Modell's intentions to fire me at our player draft in Chicago in late November. Art had told him at the time he was going to replace me with Blanton Collier, and Pete had tried to talk him out of it.

Modell had his reasons well prepared, though. He said he had not been consulted on trades, and the team had not reached its potential, neither of which was in his domain anyway. He said there was a question about whether I had been derelict in my duties as general manager because of some financial discrepancies in our ticket department; that, in fact, was something that came inside the category of financial affairs and clearly outside my responsibility. And he stated that seven players had come to him and said they would not return in 1963 if I were still the coach.

Bernie Parrish was supposedly one of those. Parrish was a very ordinary defensive back who spent more time politicking in the locker room, as the player representative, then preparing for a game. That season he had written to other player reps suggesting they have a say in assigning officials for a game. He had shown me a copy of the letter, and I had suggested he not send it, then called the commissioner, read it to him and, at his direction, straightened Parrish out on this ridiculous plan. Parrish later embarrassed Modell when he called for Rozelle to step down because, he claimed, Pete was not protecting the players' interests—and then proposed that I be named the new commissioner. That was some switch! Obviously, Pete and I paid no attention to it.

Here he was now, however, claiming he wouldn't play for the Browns if I were there. I don't know if Modell's promise of a pay raise and more responsibility on the team had anything to do with it. Who were the other players? No one knows. I did know, however, that Mike McCormack wasn't returning because he was unhappy with the whole situation. I also knew that Jim Ray Smith had business commitments in Dallas and had asked to be traded to the Cowboys and that it was usual, anyway, to have six or seven players want to leave or be traded for a variety of reasons.

All this was just part of the setup. When Modell and I met again two days later, we issued a one-paragraph statement prepared, at my insistence, by my lawyer, that I had been relieved of my coaching and general manager duties, I urged Modell not to bring any players into what I felt at the time was a purely legal affair. However, I was too late because as I drove home and turned on the radio, Brown and Parrish were already making statements which had been prepared in advance. It was obvious the orchestration of this act had been long planned.

Dick Schaffrath, too, made some disparaging statements about my tenure, but he later wrote me a letter:

"If I had killed my own son, I could not feel worse as I saw my name boldly supporting Art's actions," he wrote. "I know that Art used me then, and I tried to blame him for what I had done, but I can only say that I am not much of a man for not standing on my own two feet and keeping my mouth shut . . . I feel pretty cheap and I am sorry."

A newspaper strike in Cleveland at that time played perfectly into Modell's hands because most of our fans got very few details about what happened, so the subject was never aired in a prolonged public forum. The announcement was timed to take advantage of this news blackout, and Modell had organized a full-scale publicity force to back him up. He had hired out-of-work sportswriters from the struck newspapers, and they put out a pamphlet that was supposed to present all sides of the story. It was nothing but a thirty-two-page justification for Modell, with selected comments from players and a vague attempt to be objective with a couple of excerpts favorable to me from out-of-town columnists.

The tenor of this pamphlet was struck when it quoted team captain Mike McCormack as saying, "The Browns cannot win a title with Paul as coach," when what Mike really said was: "The Browns cannot win a title with Paul as coach *and Modell as the owner*." That was typical of Modell's methods of using the media for his own purposes, and the night my firing was announced, he even helped man a phone bank at the stadium with the rest of the executive staff, as calls poured in from all over the country.

Modell was in his glory during those days and even told a friend of mine, "Firing Paul Brown will be my claim to fame"—presumably in the same vein as his football double-header.

He said something else, too. "Why all the commotion?" he glibly asked one out-of-town writer. "Things happen like this every day in business. This is nothing more than an adjustment in the corporate alignment." Though this sounds like a clever explanation for a very volatile situation, it is a feeling that unfortunately still prevails among some owners in the NFL. To them, coaches are people only to be hired and fired—Modell told me himself that "coaches are simply for musical chairs." I once pointed out at a league meeting to the assembled owners that I was in both positions—coach and owner—and that I really resented the lack of respect and the general attitudes some of them had toward their coaches. My remarks were addressed mainly to one segment—the owners didn't know what being fired can do to a man, his family and to his career or care that he might have dedicated his life to that profession. The publicity was important to this group, and the owners were only too happy to take the victories the coaches had made for them. But respect? That was something else.

I had this excruciating experience the morning after I was fired, when I found the contents of my desk, and the pictures of my family, in a cardboard box on my front porch. The message was very clear: Don't come back to the office.

So ended seventeen years of my life.

THIRTEEN

Years of Exile

LIFE WITHOUT FOOTBALL BECAME A sudden and traumatic experience for me in 1963 and, if nothing else, gave me a tremendous appreciation of what really happens to a man who is stripped from the job to which he had devoted everything. I had seen it happen to other coaches, many of them close friends and associates, and I had had empathy for them, but because I had always been so careful to control all the elements which determined my own destiny, I hadn't been prepared to face it myself.

That is why one of my first concerns following my dismissal in Cleveland was for the future of my coaching staff. I hadn't yet grasped what had really happened and so assumed that all of us were being released. The day after the announcement became public, I called them all to my home, but before they arrived, I began calling teams throughout professional football, trying to get them jobs. Don Shula, who had just been appointed head coach at Baltimore, assured me he would have a spot for Blanton Collier, for whom he had worked at Kentucky. I didn't know that Collier might already have been told that he would be the Browns' new head coach. It did seem odd, though, that at the meeting at my home, none of the men seemed very concerned about their futures. I don't think any of them were disloyal to me, and they have assured me they had no inkling I was going to be fired. For one thing, Art Modell knew there were "Paul Brown men" among them and would never have tipped his hand for fear I would have found out before he was ready to make his move. I guess they just thought they were safe.

Modell talked about being interested in other candidates for *the* job, but the decision appeared to be cut-and-dried, and he finally announced Collier's name. At the time Blanton said he was taking it only because I was supposed to have told him. "You must do this for the good of your family. I understand." Actually, I never talked to him about the job.

In fact, I didn't hear from any of the coaches after they had left my home that day, and Katy and I couldn't understand why they didn't call or come to see us. Of course, I now realize that if Modell had heard about it, their jobs might have been in jeopardy. Finally, I said to Katy, "I've got to see these guys anyway," so I reserved a room at the Midday Club in Cleveland and invited all of them to lunch. I don't know what I really expected to accomplish, though I did ask them one favor: to tell the truth if they were ever called to testify in a damage suit. Other than that, very little was said by anyone, and it just tore me up. When lunch ended, about all I could say to them was "Good-bye," and with a hollow feeling, I left them. I guess that I was upset, too, that the men to whom I had given so much had offered me so little when I really needed it. I had brought every one of those men into football. They were my guys and my closest friends, and I couldn't understand what was happening to them or to me.

When I got home, I said to Katy, "I think those people put themselves in jeopardy even by having lunch with me." At almost the same time Collier was commencing a public about-face on some of the beliefs and principles which he had so strongly supported when he was on our staff. This fact, plus the prolonged silence from the coaches, finally drove home the realization that everything in Cleveland was finished. From then on I only wanted to cut the ties that had bound me so intimately to the city since 1945. I guess all of us understand the situation now, and one of those assistants, Howard Brinker, later joined my staff in Cincinnati.

I still had problems with Modell, too, about my future responsibilities. My previous contract had been breached, and on the advice of my lawyer, we drew up a new one that outlined my duties under the new conditions. It avoided a lawsuit. I was now to view a number of NFL and college games each year, "observe and recommend" any changes in our organization which I felt beneficial and give advice based on my expertise. All this was very vague and was designed only to offer some justification for paying me $82,500 a year for not doing much of anything. Modell agreed to pay all legal expenses, but I wound up paying my own and was never reimbursed.

When that was finished, I began a period I used to call my "dark years," though, in retrospect, they did offer a wonderful chance to put things into perspective and to spend some lovely times with Katy. I have often thought that God had a plan for us because I did not know, when that period of my life began, that she had only a few years to live. During the next five years we had a chance to do things together, to travel the world and enjoy afternoons swimming and evenings walking along the beach, that we never would have had otherwise. Though it was difficult for me at that time to see any real purpose in that almost languid existence, I feel different now.

Those first few cruel months after I was fired represented the low point of my life. I felt like Napoleon on the isle of Elba. We sat in our Shaker Heights home with no place to go; I had no office, no real job, and we never heard from anyone in the Browns' organization. I felt particularly sorry for Katy because she was not well, and my sons were just crushed by the whole chain of events and its aftermath. Finally, at the urging of my friend Dr. Bill Engle we went to La Jolla, California, in the late spring just to get away from the deadening atmosphere that had all but buried us.

La Jolla so captivated us we decided to make it our home. We returned to Cleveland, settled some affairs, saw only a few neighbors—there was nothing to be said—and literally sneaked out by nightfall. We soon made new friends in California. Our Shaker Heights home sat idle and almost unused until we finally sold it in 1964 after buying a home in La Jolla, and I have returned to Cleveland on a social basis only on rare occasions since then.

I deliberately went as far away from Cleveland as I could and was surprised how much time and distance helped me forget the experiences of my last season there. I had been so wrapped up in my own world that I hadn't even known the rest of the world existed. Now I was away from everything, and I had a chance to reflect on all that I had done. Traveling the world gave me a perspective on myself, and I'll always remember being in Hong Kong and seeing people there who had no idea who I was or even what "football" meant.

I liked that kind of anonymity because it enabled me to chop off my past completely. When we first came to La Jolla, we made it a point of having nothing in our home that would ever indicate to a visitor that I had coached a football team. I just wanted to shut off that phase of my life. Many of our friends in La Jolla didn't even know what I had done before coming there, until it was announced in 1967 that I had secured the Cincinnati franchise.

When we went to the 1964 Olympics in Tokyo, it was refreshing not to have anyone know me. I liked being just one of thousands of visitors, and the longer I did it, the better I liked it. We came home that year in time to have a family Christmas in Arkansas at the home of my son Robin, with Mike and his bride of just three months there, along with Pete, a student at Denison in Granville, Ohio. It was a lovely, happy time for all of us.

Katy and I were now living the kind of life that many men work all their lives to acquire. We lived at the Beach and Tennis Club for the first year or so until we found the home we wanted. Our first apartment was right on the Pacific Ocean, near the Scripps School of Oceanography, and we often strolled the Scripps Walk along the Pacific in the evenings. La Jolla has the most equitable climate in the continental United States, so I played golf four or five times a week. Katy often had her girl friends in for a bridge game while I was on the golf course, and in the afternoons we swam together and rested until dinner. Her daily swimming actually added years to her life, and I kept our pool temperature around eighty degrees so she could take advantage of it year-round. As her eyesight worsened because of her diabetes, I did the cooking and became pretty proficient at reading recipes and turning out a good meal.

We had our share of visitors, old friends from Cleveland and some of my former players like Otto Graham and Mike McCormack. Others called me when they came to San Diego on business or to Coronado Island for a convention, and Katy and I often went over to see them and spent some delightful hours. We explored the Baja Peninsula and Mexico; we shopped and walked and got to know some fine people through Bill Engle. It was a serene, pleasant existence, interrupted from time to time with trips abroad.

Our longest trip was to the Far East so we could see the Olympics, and that turned out to be the most unforgettable trip of all. We hadn't been in the air more than ten minutes on the plane carrying us from Hong Kong to Tokyo when Katy looked out the window and said to me, "Is that normal?"

I looked at the inside engine on our side of the plane and saw it was a mass of flames.

"I certainly don't think so," I replied, called the stewardess and pointed it out to her. She took one quick look and ran for the cockpit. In a minute the pilot came on and told everyone he would try to keep one side of the plane higher than the other to keep the fire from spreading, and after making a wide, slow turn, he headed back to Hong Kong.

Katy and I just looked at each other, both of us scared, knowing there was a good chance we might be killed. Knowing we were going to die in a few minutes was a peculiar feeling. We said our good-byes, and I told her I had had a wonderful life with her, and we kept talking to each other that way as the plane seemed to crawl back to the airport and the flames spread to the second engine.

This was the first time I had ever been in a truly life-and-death situation. We donned life jackets as we flew over the sea back to Hong Kong, while the stewardesses told us how to bend over to try to cushion the shock in case we made a crash landing. Some of the people lost control, pulled the cords on their life jackets and inflated them. It was pandemonium from then on because those poor people didn't know what to do.

Our pilot did a tremendous job getting us back safely, and I was told later we were very fortunate to have survived. He made one final sweep with the wing very high and kept it that way until the very last second, when he had to straighten out the plane for his landing approach. Fire equipment was all around us as we landed, and when I saw it later on the news, we looked like a flaming shish kebab coming onto a runway covered with fire-preventive foam.

As the plane slid to a stop, one or two of the men on the plane began climbing over women and children, trying to get off and, ironically, when we went into the terminal, they were the ones being interviewed on television and acting like heroes. One of my friends went up and grabbed one of those men, shoved him aside and threatened to punch him right in front of the television cameras.

We stayed in Hong Kong for about a week and changed from Japan Airlines to Air France. Wouldn't you know it, though? When many of the people who had undergone this terrible experience got on the new plane, the stewardess said, "Welcome to Air France, sometimes known as Air Chance." It was a macabre joke, and I know the laughter from some of us who had survived the other accident wasn't too sincere.

The Olympic Games were a very stirring experience, particularly when our team first marched into that huge stadium in Tokyo and, later, when our national anthem was played at the gold-medal ceremonies. As the games went on, it was interesting to contrast the feelings between the athletes; when they marched in, they were very stiff and formal, but as the competition went on, they became very friendly and seemed to enjoy each other's company. I watched Bob Hayes win the 100-meter dash, and though I knew that he had played college football, for once in my life I did not look at him then as a future professional football player. He was anything but a classic type of runner, because he just wiggled and wobbled all over the place—always moving, and moving fast enough to win the event in Olympic record time.

The most intriguing thing to me was the equestrian event, which was won by a Frenchman. He and his horse had a most unusual relationship at the medal ceremony. While the other two horses were prancing and restless, that horse had its head down and calmly looked over the crowd. The rider paid no attention to it, but when he stepped up to receive his gold medal, the horse followed, as one. It was obvious to everyone sitting around us that they loved each other, a true team.

We went to many other places, too—West Germany, Italy, France, Switzerland. In fact, we lived in Lucerne, Switzerland, for a month. We actually went to Europe twice, the second time with my friend Al Sutphin, who was making his thirty-second trip. Al was a walking travel book. He knew everything that we should see and do and knew all the right places to stay. I still have the itinerary from that trip because it was a rare privilege traveling with such a man.

With so much talk beginning to blossom in the mid-sixties about professional football expanding, Katy and I spent three weeks in Seattle and studied the area as a potential NFL city. It was a one-industry town, however, aerospace, which was not booming at the time. The NFL has since established the Seahawks in Seattle, and the team has prospered through its first few seasons, but I have no regrets about passing it by then.

Katy and I then drove to Canada, where I studied Canadian football very intensively, watching its games and its practices. The only thing I saw at the time that could be adopted by our game was the possibility of the wider field. As for the game itself, I couldn't see how any American player would want to become involved, unless he just couldn't make it in the United States. It was, as John Kissell had said, "like a foreign country." I also made a point while I was there of not seeing anyone I knew, though some of my former players, such as Bud Grant and Bob Shaw, were excellent Canadian League coaches then. One night I was a very anonymous observer at one team's practice session, and it reminded me of semipro football back in Massillon because the players practiced on a half-darkened field, after most of them had worked at other jobs during the day.

Watching the Canadian Football League was one of the ways I kept in touch with football during those years. I was lost when the late summer of 1963 rolled around because it was the first year since I had been in grammar school that I had not been involved in some aspect of the sport. I went on a physical activity binge, just to keep from dwelling on the situation. I played golf, hiked, swam every day; I did everything I could to keep me occupied and help me through the terrible withdrawal symptoms. I saw the Browns play only twice that year, both times on television, and it was a relief to move to California because their games were out of reach, and I was spared the heartache.

When we moved to La Jolla, I worked at forgetting the Browns. I more than fulfilled my contractual obligations to the team, however, by watching the Rams play a couple of times when the Vikings and Packers came to Los Angeles and by visiting Weeb Ewbank and Lou Saban when they brought their American League teams out to San Diego.

I also watched the Chargers work out, but if I went to a game in San Diego, I purchased my ticket and sat in the stands, where no one knew me, and I liked it that way. I didn't try to call the game in competition with the coach on the field. I was more interested in what the American League teams were doing, which was pretty much the same as what the colleges were doing, and I saw nothing that was revolutionary. All the "stacked defenses" and "floating pockets" were just so many words because I had seen them all before.

I included all this in my reports to the Browns, as well as opinions and observations for the better operation of the team and the game itself. My first recommendation was that Paul Warfield of Ohio State should be given particular attention as our top choice in the 1963 draft, and he was. I put together much of what I already knew about the team, and what I saw of it on television, to offer suggestions that might improve its quality. After 1963, I strongly recommended a way be found to change the defensive philosophy and to cut down the so-called elastic band style, which allowed opponents to maintain possession so much of the time.

In 1964, the Browns won the title, and several months following that game, Modell met my son Mike on the street in Cleveland and complained that I had not complimented him on the Browns' championship. I had, though, in the very first paragraph of my annual report, which was sent in mid-January. I had also added:

"I must admit that the success of the team gave me the feeling of at least leaving the Cleveland scene without the stigma attached to a loser. I can add that I also got some satisfaction out of the fact that the coaches, our football system and general procedures, draft choices and trades obviously turned out to be sound."

Until the American and National Football leagues agreed to merge in 1966, I urged in every report that the NFL consider some means by which to end its struggle with the AFL or, at the very least, to secure some legislation from Congress that would permit a common player draft. That would have stopped the intense bidding wars for players which were sapping the resources of every team and causing major problems in morale and competitive balance. Some of the teams simply could not afford to compete and often traded away their top draft picks to survive.

After the 1963 season I noted in my report that "if the NFL thinks that the American League will survive, then the quicker the matter is resolved, the better." After the 1964 season, I wrote: "The number one problem . . . is the question of getting together with the American League and solidifying the position of all pro football on the American sports scene. Right now, the National League is in a very strong position, an ideal time to force the terms that will be best for the professional game. The public will welcome the end of the pro football war. In fact, eventually it will force it."

I also suggested that the NFL consider expansion and suggested that if the league could not bring the AFL into its fold by asking it to drop its weaker franchises, then it should ask it to expand to worthy cities as a condition of ending the war. The following year the NFL beat the AFL into Atlanta and New Orleans, and Miami became an AFL city.

Having watched both leagues for two seasons by then, I firmly believed the NFL had better team depth, but I was surprised to find the public didn't know that, nor did it seem to care. All it was interested in was the excitement of the game that it watched every week.

Again in 1965, I urged that both leagues unite in lobbying Congress for legislation permitting the common draft, and it was possible "that this joint effort of the two leagues would be a start toward peace in the professional world." The following June the agreement was finally forged, and I called it "a great step forward for professional football, regardless of the many resulting problems and details that will have to be worked out." I think everyone has seen that the football of the seventies had justified that optimism.

From time to time during these years, writers called me to see what I was doing, columns and stories were written speculating about my happiness in retirement and there seemed to be an aura of general wonder about when I would eventually return to football and in what capacity. I know that some people in the Browns' organization worried at first that I would quickly reenter football and take some of the organization with me.

For the first couple of years I didn't do much about it because it took me that long to realize what had happened to me and that my Cleveland days were really over. I had no intention of rushing back, however, until I could control my own destiny. That wasn't so easy, though, because professional football had become a status object for many of the new young owners, who looked on it as a shiny plaything, with little thought as to what owning a football team really meant. Following the Pro Bowl in 1964, Jerry Wolman and Ed Snider had purchased the Philadelphia Eagles from Frank McNamee and came down to talk to me about joining their organization. I went to the airport to meet them; one of them got off the plane in shirt sleeves and wearing bedroom slippers, and the other was dressed in sloppy jeans. This non-business appearance threw me a bit. I don't know what I expected, but after seeing their casual attitude, I listened politely to their offer to become head coach and declined. A few years later Wolman was forced to sell the franchise when his businesses began to topple. In the meantime, he had given his coach a fifteen-year contract; that kind of business move and subsequent events were certain indicators that had I gotten involved, it would have been with another nonfootball person, and I had seen enough of that.

The following year I flew to Chicago at my own expense, expecting to talk with Rankin Smith, who had just been guaranteed a franchise in the NFL. I waited for an hour outside Rankin's hotel suite for him to see me and then was told he was unavailable that day. I left word that I was no longer interested and went back home, though I was disappointed because I had hoped that this would be the opportunity for which I had waited so long.

Ironically, as I was leaving the hotel that day in Chicago, I encountered Bob Gries. We greeted each other briefly, and I couldn't help noticing how sallow he looked. Though I didn't know it at the time, he had cancer and died just a short time later.

Another opportunity came in 1966, when Dan Reaves asked me to become head coach of the Rams, but his team was going through some internal ownership squabbles then, and I declined the job. I had been out of football nearly four years by then, and Pete Rozelle had encouraged me that I would have a place in a new franchise—indeed, the date with Rankin Smith was intended to help me get back into the game—but I wasn't going to jump into a caldron of trouble just to have a job. Reaves then offered the job to George Allen.

I still missed the game, and deep inside I yearned to become a part of it again. Katy and my sons sensed that feeling, but we knew the time and the conditions had to be right. I put on a good face whenever I went to the NFL games in Los Angeles, though a couple of times, when I met some friends, it was impossible for me to mask my disappointment. By 1966 I began to realize that regardless of how much Commissioner Rozelle tried to help me get back into football, it might never happen. I started to explore the possibilities of the broadcasting business, first looking into some radio stations, with the eventual goal of owning a television station. My life-style, I realized, was ideal, and I had proved to myself that I wouldn't die just because I wasn't coaching football. If that one, solid opportunity did not happen to come along in time for me to take advantage of it, I would have to reconcile myself that it just wasn't meant to be.

However, Bill Hackett, one of my former Ohio State players and a lifelong friend, who had become the veterinarian for John Sawyer's Orleton Farms in London, Ohio, helped change all that. When he and his wife, Bambi, left La Jolla after visiting us for a few days, late in 1966 he started a chain of events that shifted my whole world back to where it belonged . . . back to Ohio and professional football.

FOURTEEN

Back to Football: The Birth of the Bengals

THE IDEA OF RETURNING TO professional football in Ohio had never been too far from my mind. My son Mike had made a survey of areas in the country which did not have a professional football team, and of them all, he showed me that Cincinnati was the most appealing. It had 10 million people within a 100-mile radius, it was among the highest per capita income areas in the nation and had equally high per family buying power and it was located within an area of proved football interest.

I mentioned all this to Bill during his visit, and his enthusiasm could barely be contained. Bill always was a person to get things moving, so when he got back to Ohio, he began telling John Sawyer about our conversation, and John, who had heard many nice things about me from Bill, had his interest aroused. Then Bill contacted Jim Rhodes, the governor of Ohio, and a friend, and he was equally enthusiastic. I had known Jim since my coaching days at Ohio State, when he had been working for the city of Columbus, and he came out to visit me to see if I really was serious about starting a new team in Cincinnati.

When I assured him that I was serious enough to invest a sizable amount of my own money, he began setting up a series of meetings that really started the franchise on its way. It wasn't too long before I was commuting often between

California and Cincinnati in 1966, meeting prospective members of our ownership group and working on the details that attach themselves to such a massive venture. When I wasn't in Ohio, I was being awakened nearly every morning in La Jolla by Bill Hackett's phone calls giving me the latest news.

I also kept Pete Rozelle informed about our progress, and he encouraged me fully because the surveys he had commissioned for the league agreed completely with ours about the suitability of Cincinnati as a franchise. By this point it was pretty much determined that I would get back into pro football in Cincinnati or not at all because other prospective cities, such as Phoenix or Seattle, did not have suitable stadiums, and the universities in those cities were not inclined to allow theirs to be used by pro teams. As our group took shape and it appeared that Cincinnati could get a franchise, I was very excited about the prospect of resuming my career at a time when the sport was about to enter its greatest years.

My family was as deeply involved in all this as I was. Since everyone had been hurt by the affair in Cleveland, I felt everyone should have a say about whether I returned to football. When we were on the brink of getting our ownership together and securing the franchise, Katy and I brought our sons and their families to La Jolla to discuss our family future. I laid out everything that was involved, so that all of us could decide whether it would be best to go back into football or to invest ourselves fully in the broadcasting enterprises.

"We'll sleep on it tonight and decide tomorrow morning after breakfast," I said. "I want all of you to be a part of this."

The next morning we sat in our living room overlooking the Pacific Ocean, and I said, "Well, what should we do?"

"Oh," Katy replied, "we know what we'll do. We'll go back into football."

From the beginning, our group's intention was to join the National Football League, and my friends within the NFL worked on my behalf to convince the owners that Cincinnati was a worthy city. At one point Art Rooney of the Pittsburgh Steelers stood up at a meeting that was considering New Orleans, Seattle and some other larger cities and said to the owners, "Why are you fellows thinking twice? Cincinnati is a tremendous city, and it would be a fine addition to our league."

In 1965 the NFL had admitted Atlanta and the AFL had added Miami, but in June of the following year the two leagues agreed to merge, and each decided it would add one more franchise. The NFL chose New Orleans because it added another block to the tier of southern cities the league was building and because it had Tulane Stadium, with its 82,-000 seats, as well as an area that was rabidly interested in football. Commissioner Rozelle visited Cincinnati to tell me the news, but at the same time he brought along the members of the AFL's expansion committee, who said they were willing to admit Cincinnati as the tenth franchise in their league.

I wanted to consider the offer because we had sold our program on being able to bring NFL football to the area. I thoroughly studied the merger agreement and saw that it had a specific performance clause regarding games between teams from both leagues, which meant that when the merger was finally implemented, everyone would be under the umbrella of the National Football League and everyone would be competing against one another. That was good enough for us, and in May 1967 we agreed to join the AFL, though the official announcement was not made until July and the final papers were not signed until September. That "specific performance" clause became a critical issue a couple of years later, when the merger of the two leagues was being made final, and strong sentiment developed against realigning the teams and playing an interleague schedule. I successfully helped orchestrate a drive that overcame that opposition and brought about the promised realignment of both leagues.

Our group paid nearly $9 million for the Cincinnati franchise, but the price was actually closer to $14 million because we received no television revenues until 1970. Our ownership was comprised primarily of sportsmen, however, deliberately chosen to include men who not only represented some of Cincinnati's oldest families but did not view professional football as a quick-hit profit scheme and could also withstand the limited income for our first two seasons. John Sawyer, whose father, Charles, had been secretary of commerce during Harry Truman's presidency, was elected club president, I was head coach and general manager and my son Mike was legal counsel and assistant general manager.

Under the terms of our agreement, there was to be no majority stockholder. Therefore, I was given a voting trust because by NFL rule one person must be responsible for the club to the commissioner. In the event of my death, this control passes from me to my son Mike. This arrangement has proved beneficial to all of us because it was the only way I would return to professional football, and our owners needed me to get the franchise. Also, since I was the third largest investor, they knew I would do nothing to jeopardize the team's financial success. The original investments have been repaid.

All this sounds so simple now, but no one can ever fully appreciate the tremendous job done by Governor Jim Rhodes, Gene Ruehlmann, the mayor of Cincinnati, and Francis Dale, publisher of the *Enquirer*, in helping clear away all the obstacles. As governor, Jim pushed for us at every level and gave our venture a spirit of public acceptance, while Dale and Ruehlmann were moving forces within Cincinnati in getting the construction of a new stadium agreed upon.

That stadium was a key factor in our getting the franchise because the NFL's constitution mandates that every team must have a facility with a seating capacity of at least 50,000 people, and it was specifically stipulated that our franchise would be awarded only if a new stadium were ready by 1970. When we began priming Cincinnati as a potential franchise, we went to Bill DeWitt, the owner of the Cincinnati Reds and tried to convince him to become a co-tenant in a new stadium. The Reds owned Crosley Field, which was totally unsuitable for football, because the terrace in right field could not compatibly be used as a playing surface, and its seating capacity fell far short of the NFL's minimum figures.

DeWitt balked at the idea of moving to a new stadium in the center of the city, however, because he thought the risks might be too unreasonable. As a result, pressure from the public and the media, particularly from Frank Dale's *Enquirer*, became almost unbearable, and Bill suddenly found himself cast in the role of the bad guy who was preventing the city from acquiring an NFL team. Finally, we put together a group, which included many from our football ownership, including John Sawyer, Louis Nippert, Jim and Bill Williams, Dutch Knowlton and Barry and Pat Buse, that purchased the Reds from DeWitt, thus solidifying both professional sports franchises in the city.

Once the city saw it would have two tenants for the stadium—and once the league saw we would have a suitable stadium in which to play—barriers began to disappear. The agreement to build was flashed a few months before the NFL granted our franchise, and construction was begun soon after we were officially accepted. Riverfront Stadium stands today as a symbol of the city's health and a boon to the preservation of its downtown business, shopping and entertainment areas.

While Riverfront Stadium was being built, we had secured, through Jim Rhodes's help, the University of Cincinnati's Nippert Stadium, the only suitable stadium facility in the area. It had a seating capacity of slightly more than 31,000, and while it was far from being the perfect stadium for a professional team, it was fine for our temporary needs. Unlike New Orleans, we did not have to fill a vast arena, and our early crowds were college football fans, whose enthusiasm and spirit were the perfect adjuncts to our fight and determination. The two seasons we spent at Nippert were fun, happy years because we didn't have much of a chance to win, but we fought hard and played hard and ultimately established the core of fans who have supported us ever since.

I'm even sure that Nippert's limited dressing facilities helped us on more than one occasion. For the first couple of games, we occupied one that was so hot and muggy it simply drained the strength from our players. We subsequently moved up to the university's field house and put the visitors in the steamy dressing room. I think a couple of teams were actually beaten because their players had just wilted in that room even before the game started, while my young, eager beavers were full of energy.

Nothing could dim my enthusiasm at returning to professional football. I felt twenty-one years old again and like a new father, because I was coming home to Ohio. I had no worries about the franchise's being successful because professional football was riding a tremendous popularity boom, and everyone knew me in Cincinnati from my days with the Browns.

I had no delusions, however, about immediate championships, and I had steeled myself to handle in good spirit the adversity I knew would come from starting a new team. I knew what I was faced with, as did the public, and they accepted it, so it really wasn't too difficult to handle. Others had difficulty appreciating that, however. I remember my friend Tommy Davis, the coach at Western Reserve, wondering why I wanted to jeopardize my coaching record.

"The truth is," I told him, "records bore me. I've never once considered what my final won-loss totals might look like because I have always lived for the present and the future, not for the past. Besides, I had five years to think about my record and found it meant nothing when I wasn't doing the thing I loved most."

One NFL coach even commented: "Paul will find the game is far more complicated than when he left it. He could be eligible for Social Security before he fields a team that wins half of its games."

I never believed that, though, because I knew I had kept up with the game during my exile. I said from the start that we would be competitive within five years—and it took only three to reach the play-offs. While some wondered why a fifty-nine-year-old man wanted to come back into a profession that took a toll of younger men, I never worried a bit about my age. I was healthy, and I had the energy, experience and enthusiasm to help me circumvent problems that might have been too much for other men.

I couldn't wait to begin, even though there were a thousand and one details for us to resolve before we ever fielded our first team in 1968. Katy and I moved from La Jolla to Cincinnati almost immediately, and I set up our first offices on the eighteenth floor of the Carew Tower, where, for a couple of months, all we had were an old desk and chair, plus one telephone—a much more rudimentary beginning in the so-called golden age of pro football than when the Browns had started in 1945. It didn't bother me at all, though sometimes, when I was driving to work in the morning amid the belching fumes and smoke from trucks and factories, I thought of La Jolla and said to myself, "Brown, what in the world did you get yourself into?"

The first person we hired for our front office was our business manager, John Murdough who had held the same position with the Cincinnati Reds. Later, in the fall of 1967, we hired Al Heim, the executive sports editor of the *Enquirer*, as our public relations director. Both men are still with our organization, and so are Marv Pollens, our trainer, and Tom Gray, our equipment man, who joined us shortly after the team was formed. Marv was an assistant trainer at Miami University, and Tom had worked as a hobby for the Cleveland Browns for more than a decade, assisting Morrie Kono. Tom was the only person I hired then with any con-

nection whatsoever with the Browns because I wanted no repercussions. Even then, when he applied for the job, I made
sure he was still just a football fan who went to Cleveland on
Sunday afternoons to enjoy himself, not a bona fide employee. We also hired George Bird, who had been the
Browns' first entertainment director, to fill the same role with
us. George was in poor health at the time, but the job gave
him a tremendous lift, and when he retired, his daughter,
Shirley, a music teacher in the Cincinnati school system,
succeeded him. George died early in 1979, ending some forty
years of matching football and music to make first-class entertainment programs.

We had to find a name for our new team, so I formed a
committee of three, including myself, John Sawyer and Dave
Gamble, another of our owners, to make the selection. Both
men had graduated from Princeton, the mascot of which is
the tiger, so I said, "Why not Tigers?"

"Sounds all right with us," they said, "but it is kind of
common, so why not make it a Bengal tiger or Bengals?"

That was perfect because it was a name that could be animated and also one that picked up a thread of tradition that
went back nearly thirty years to when the city had had a professional football team named the Cincinnati Bengals. We
had received many suggestions for "Buckeyes," but I didn't
want anyone confusing us with Ohio State's team, and
besides, our following would be spread throughout four states
instead of just one, and I didn't want to limit us.

I was also involved in designing our uniforms, as I had
done at Cleveland. My one key principle was "nothing too
flashy" because nothing is worse than a bad team with a
crazy-looking uniform. The old Denver Broncos' vertical-
striped stockings had made them a laughingstock in the early
sixties, and I was determined to avoid anything that might
bring ridicule while we struggled to become respectable. I
know that many people have said I patterned the Bengals'
uniform and colors after the Browns, but that is not so. In
addition to our helmets' being different, our orange, black
and white colors are representative of our symbol, the Bengal
tiger, while the Browns' colors are orange, brown and white.

Team uniforms and nicknames were only two of the details
that swarmed about me then. I attended dozens of civic and
fraternal luncheons, oversaw the hiring of all our personnel,
helped set up our radio network, scouted college and pro

games and generally involved myself in every facet of our team's operation. We had so much to do and so little time to do it all in, and it seemed about all I ever did was get up in the morning, go downtown to work, come home in the evening and go to sleep. The time slipped by so fast I don't know what happened to it.

Yet our organization gradually took shape, and things did come together, even if sometimes by happenstance, as in the case of our finding Wilmington College for our training camp. Mike and I were returning from Cleveland one day when I saw the sign for Wilmington, and I recalled I hadn't been back there since my junior year at Miami, when we had played a baseball game against Wilmington's team. Several schools, including Miami, had invited us to use their facilities for our training camp, but I said to Mike, "I'd like to take a look at Wilmington. As I remember, it was a tiny school, like Hiram College, where we could have peace and quiet for concentration."

In fact, the school had changed very little since then, except for a new gymnasium-field house I spotted, overlooking three football practice fields. I wanted to see more, but the building was locked, and we were just about ready to leave when the custodian, a woman, showed up and became so caught up in our conversation about the place that she unlocked the doors and gave us a conducted tour. She didn't know who we were or why we were there, but she was so pleased and proud that someone took an interest in her building she couldn't do enough to help us.

The building had everything we needed, so we called the school's head, Brooke Morgan, and asked him about using his school for our training camp. He didn't know what to make of us, so I said, "I'd like you to call Dr. Paul Sharp [who had been president of Hiram College], and he'll tell you how we administered our program." Apparently, Paul couldn't say enough nice things about us, and within a short time Mr. Morgan invited us back to consummate the deal. We have trained at Wilmington ever since, and the size of the town and the school, its relaxed summer atmosphere, and its convenience for our fans have been perfect for us.

While all this was happening, our football operation was also well under way. Even before our front office and franchise had been solidified, I hired Al LoCasale, who had worked for the San Diego Chargers' personnel department, as our director of personnel, and my son Pete became his assistant. I put together our coaching staff from men I knew about or had seen work. The first to be hired was Tom Bass, whom I had watched when he was an assistant with the Chargers. The next was Bill Johnson, of the 49ers. I had seen him when Pete and I were up in San Francisco while Katy was confined to a hospital there. We had had time on our hands between visiting hours and gone out to watch the 49ers practice. Bill's work as offensive line coach, particularly his ability to teach and to command the attention of his players, had impressed me very much. He seemed like a man's man to me, and his people worked at their job with a tremendous amount of enthusiasm. I next hired Rick Forzano, who had just finished his second year as backfield coach of the St. Louis Cardinals and whom I had known since his days as a young coach at Kent State University. Bill Walsh became our recievers' coach when his semipro team, the San Jose Apaches, which he had coached and managed, went bankrupt. Jack Donaldson, who had worked for Weeb Ewbank in New York, became our defensive line coach.

In the beginning all of us worked in the basement of our town house in Glendale, a Cincinnati suburb, as we put our offense and defense together. Our system was basically the same as I had used at Cleveland, though I welcomed the input of every coach, most of whom had come from different backgrounds and whose suggestions were often incisive. I stayed with the same numbering and play-calling systems I had used at Cleveland, though we altered the cadence from rhythmic to nonrhythmic. The biggest changes were on defense, which had become more complex and sophisticated with alignment switches and different defensive secondary coverage.

The most difficult problem was having to plan strategy without ever having coached any of the players. When we put in our quick flip end run, somebody said, "How do we know we've got a halfback fast enough to run this?" When we diagrammed a power play up the middle, someone else asked, "This won't be any good unless we have someone strong enough to make it work." Another problem was being sure everyone understood the terminology. We basically used mine because I have to operate that way, but if one of the other coaches used something that sounded a little better or made more sense, we built it into our system. I cannot say enough for the contributions each of those coaches made during that time, and I have always been grateful for what they did to help us build our new team so successfully in such a relatively short period of time.

Of course, not too many people expected such swift success, particularly considering the paucity of quality players we received from the expansion draft and our nearly total reliance on the rookies we selected in the regular player draft. I had hoped the AFL owners would see the soundness of my long-held beliefs about allowing a new team to become reasonably competitive from the start, and even Pete Rozelle tried to help me by bringing me before the American League owners so I could make an appeal for an allocation draft at least as good as that given the Miami Dolphins two years before. After I had made my little pitch, carefully laying out my ideas and documenting the case with proved references from past expansion teams, Al Davis of Oakland stood up and said, "Oh, that's already been decided. What's the next order of business?"

What they had decided was to give us the bare minimum because they knew they faced a merger with the stronger NFL teams in just two seasons, and they did not want to sacrifice any of their quality players just to help the new guys. Only eight AFL teams participated in our player allocation draft, Miami being exempt, and each team was allowed to freeze twenty-nine players before we could choose one. Then they froze two more, and we got two more choices; on the last round, each team froze one more player, and we got our last pick; and then each of the eight teams "gave" us another player. In contrast, Miami had been able to choose after each AFL team had frozen only its first twenty-five players, and New Orleans and Atlanta had gotten to choose from a player pool that came from fourteen teams, so both the depth and the numbers of players were much larger for them.

The AFL player allocation draft held in Jacksonville, Florida, was also mismanaged and poorly run. We were given the names of the eligible players only the day before, and I had an inkling of what we were up against when I saw the lists arriving on scraps of paper, the backs of envelopes—anything that was at hand. We were supposed to have been provided with vital statistics, including injuries, and all pertinent information about every player, but they were often

missing, and some names were even wrong. The lists included
every cripple, bad actor, retiree or inept player in the AFL.
Several of the players had already told their teams they were
going to retire, and more than a dozen of the forty players
we eventually picked never even showed up for training camp
the following summer. We selected Cookie Gilchrist from
Denver, for example, and two weeks later the Broncos hired
him to sell tickets and do promotional work. Only seventeen
players from that group made our first team, and some, such
as Ernie Wright, Sherrill Headrick, Frank Buncom, Bobby
Hunt, Andy Rice and Fletcher Smith, showed some of the
quality we had hoped to extract from the draft. Headrick had
tremendous spirit and gave us everything he had, but prior
injuries had sapped his talent, and he lasted only one season.
Buncom died in his sleep the night before a game in 1969,
and I often wished I had had Bobby Hunt in his earlier days,
when he had first entered professional football with Kansas
City.

The teams that didn't want to do us any favors really
wound up helping us, though, because they forced us to build
a team as it should be built—through the college player draft,
the life's blood of our business. We were able to "raise our
own" and discard the others at the earliest opportunity.

At least, we were permitted to be full participants in that
draft, with a formula that allowed us two round picks, three
in the second, third and fourth rounds and two from the fifth
through the seventeenth, with the exception of the sixth
round, in which we had the pick of every AFL team except
Miami. Fourteen of the first fifteen players we picked made
our team, and in all, nineteen from that draft were on our
roster in 1968. With such an infusion of youth and quality, it
was little wonder we made the play-offs in our third season.

Our first choice in the draft was Bob Johnson, an All-
American center from Tennessee, whom I had personally
scouted and who eventually played eleven years for us,
through the 1978 season. A few people were surprised when
we made a center our top pick, but I had thought, "Well,
where do we begin?" and the answer was obvious: Since the
ball must go from the ground to the quarterback before anything else can happen in a game, we might as well start with
a center. There was more to it than that, though. From meeting him and talking to his coaches, I also knew that Bob was
a tremendous person, and he had been a team captain at ev-

ery level of competition. He was even captain of the College All-Star team that year, and before our first season, I appointed him our offensive captain, a rarity for a rookie. He held the job until his final game as a Bengal, and I never once regretted the choice.

The draft brought us other fine players as well. Essex Johnson, a sixth-round draft pick in 1968, played for eight seasons with the Bengals and became the team's all-time rushing leader. He had been underrated, however, because we were an expansion team, so he never got the full credit due a player of his ability and accomplishments. Somewhat in the mold of Bobby Mitchell, Essex had unusual balance and acceleration, looked slighter than his close to 200 pounds and ran the 40 in 4.4 seconds. I've always had a great feeling for Essex because he was so quiet and gave us everything he had.

We landed Paul Robinson in the third round, after I had seen him play against Ohio State as a wingback, and that he was in football at all was a stroke of good luck. Paul had gone out for football in his senior year at Arizona State only after he had exhausted his track eligibility, and I immediately liked his rawhide, slender build and excellent speed. Robbie was a tremendous competitor—he had to be to win the league's rushing title with a first-year expansion team. We gave him the ball most of the time, and he never complained, and I know he was disappointed that he never had that kind of season again. He became a marked man after that rookie year, however, and we had to spread out our running load, because we had neither the strength nor the experience to be successful with just one back carrying the brunt of our offense.

Of all our choices that year, Jess Phillips from Michigan State, in the fourth round, was certainly the most interesting. Jess was serving time in the penitentiary for passing bad checks. We felt, however, that he was basically a good person who had succumbed to some youthful temptation when he had seen some of his former teammates come back to school with plenty of bonus money, flashy clothes and big cars after a year of professional football. My son Mike talked to the prison officials and then to his lawyer, and we were told that if Jess, who was an exemplary prisoner, got a job with us and thus had an opportunity for rehabilitation, he would be released from prison. I had also talked with his coach, Duffy Daugherty, who had told me Jess was a fine boy and a fine football player—good enough to make the All-Big Ten team as safety in 1967—so we felt we were on safe ground.

Six days after reporting to Wilmington, Jess was in the starting lineup against Denver and stayed there throughout the rest of his rookie year; then we switched him from safety to offense in 1969, and he became our leading rusher for the next two seasons. Off the field, he took a job in a Cincinnati bank and became a valued employee. Jess stayed with us for several seasons, and was always an exemplary citizen.

Other players from that draft who started for us in our first season included our defensive ends, Bill Staley and Harry Gunner; two of our three guards, Dave Middendorf and Howard Fest; Al Beauchamp at linebacker; Tom Smiley, our starting fullback for half the season until he was called into the service; Bob Trumpy, our tight end; Dale Livingston, who did our punting and placekicking; and Dewey Warren, our starting quarterback for half our games that first year.

We had also paid a first- and second-round draft pick to get John Stofa, another quarterback, from Miami. It was a steep price to pay because we knew his limitations, but he had no military commitments, and he was the only experienced quarterback available from the AFL. Finding a quarterback was our single biggest problem that first season, and we probably got as much from Stofa and Warren as we had any right to expect. Warren was released the following season, when Greg Cook and Sam Wyche joined our team.

By the time the drafts were over we had a lot of players, but the biggest problem was how to marshal them all. I watched the New Orleans Saints being put together in 1967, when they practiced at Point Loma, near San Diego, and saw scores of players come and go within a month's time. Often players would arrive by plane in the morning, scrimmage in the afternoon and be gone by nightfall. I watched everything the Saints did, looking for the right way and the wrong way, and decided I saw no purpose in bringing so many players into camp or putting them through so much scrimmage work.

The Saints chose to build a veteran team, hoping to be successful immediately, partly because they had an 82,000-seat stadium to fill each week, and as a result, they sacrificed the long-range success of their team. I knew the moment we got our allocation draft that we had to go with our college draft choices and that we had to spend the bulk of our time working with the players who would be a part of our future. The main thing we learned from watching New Orleans was how "not" to do it. Tom Fears was a good coach, but with all the negative factors he was faced with, it was little wonder this team went for years before becoming competitive.

Even with my staunch beliefs in manageable training camp rosters, however, it was impossible not to avoid looking at more than 100 players as we opened camp in early July. Within ten days we had pared 50 players from the squad without even holding a scrimmage, because I was determined not to sacrifice my principles about how our team should be formed. Some players arrived in camp already expecting the worst. I'll never forget Ernie Wright telling one of the writers after he had been in camp a few days, "When I came from San Diego, I didn't know whether I would last ten minutes. I knew Jim Brown real well and wasn't at all sure whether I could get along with Paul Brown. But everything I heard was completely wrong because he treats us squarely."

I knew many players who join an expansion team think that since no one expects much of the team from a won-loss standpoint, they won't have to give much of themselves, but we worked at the outset to short-circuit those attitudes. At our first training camp lecture, I told our players, "We may be an expansion team, but we will *not* be a French Foreign Legion." At the same time I wanted every player to feel that he had an equal chance to make the team and that he was more than just a numbered jersey.

I had every player stand up at that first meeting and introduce himself, give his school and whatever team he may have played on in the pros. I didn't want any of them who left us to say, "Holy smoke, it was such a cold, impersonal place they didn't even know my name, and I never had a chance to get to know anyone." I wanted that first camp—as I did every camp I ran—to be a pleasant experience. I told them they were not in a life-or-death situation, that a dropped pass wasn't tantamount to expulsion and that one mistake didn't mean a plane ticket home.

I tried to emphasize excellence in everything we did and not hurry or rush anyone or anything. The overall mental outlook of that group was wholesome because each of them had been challenged to prove he could make an expansion team, resulting in a very competitive situation. Applying the same standards and beliefs I had used in Cleveland, we built very slowly, but always very carefully. We wanted the players to become familiar with and accept our philosophy of football, and as far as we were concerned, what they had done before didn't matter.

At one point we had to cut down the amount of material in our playbooks. "We're not coaching the Cleveland Browns with only two or three rookies trying to make the roster," I told our coaches. "This is a *team* of rookies, and we've got to slow down and give them a little bit at a time."

I don't think I ever felt discouraged during those two months. We knew exactly where we stood, and we just wanted to see how well we could do under very difficult conditions. I don't think I changed any of my basic outlooks, though it may have seemed so because I had to be so tolerant of younger, more inexperienced, or less talented players than I had coached at Cleveland. I'm sure my happiness at being back in coaching was reflected in my day's work and in my relationships with everyone who came to our camp. I also know that I appreciated my situation more by having been away, so I held nothing back in my second opportunity to build a team.

We had some problems—the severe heat, for one. The temperatures were in the high nineties day after day that summer. We also faced the threat of a players' strike, but my guys were fighting for their lives, and all the strike talk seemed to fall on deaf ears. The other American Football League teams didn't help much either, with their so-called buddy system, in which teams helped each other by not claiming players on injured reserve so the original team could keep them on its roster. In 1968, the AFL owners had agreed to abide by the NFL's no-recall procedure on injured waivers, and we claimed Ken Stabler from Oakland and Al Denson, a swift wide receiver from Denver, that way, only to be told by Milt Woodard, then the AFL president, that our claims were invalid because the teams really hadn't decided to go along with that rule after all. That was wrong because the waiver procedure is supposed to help the team that needs players, but there were actually threats of reprisal against those who wouldn't honor this "buddy" agreement. Eventually a stop was put to it, but I wore a black hat on the subject for a while.

During training camp we worked at our normal two-plays-per-day pace, and I decided that in the preseason games we would stay with our usual procedure on rookies, which was to put them into the game gradually and not destroy whatever cohesiveness we had established. I was totally realistic because we really didn't have much of a chance against established teams, particularly against a team like the Kansas City Chiefs, who were our first preseason opponent at Nippert Stadium.

The Chiefs took the opening kickoff and drove for a touchdown, but after Warren McVea made a good return of the ensuing kickoff, he fumbled and lost the ball, and the Chiefs kept it for the rest of the quarter and scored another touchdown. It was the first time in my career that any of my teams had not run at least one offensive play in a quarter. We did have a nice moment, though, when Solomon Brannan, a defensive back, scooped up a fumble and ran for our first touchdown in the second quarter, to close the Chiefs' lead to 14–7. We didn't even make a first down until the third quarter, but when we did, everyone in the stadium stood and cheered, and not derisively. Those people really meant it because they were behind us all the way.

We eventually lost the game, 38–14, and I know I surprised everyone afterward when I said, "We did better than I expected because we worked on specific things, and I am pleased that we showed a semblance of becoming a team." In our second game, at Denver, we battled so tenaciously that the Broncos elected to take a safety in the final five seconds, rather than risk a possible blocked punt, and though we lost, 15–13, we had progressed a bit further. We led Buffalo at the half of the next game but lost, 10–6; then we won our final two preseason games, 19–3 against the Pittsburgh Steelers and 13–9 over the New York Jets. We played the Steelers in Morgantown, West Virginia, and traveled by bus because the transportation was easier. On the way home, everyone was singing, and it reminded me of my days at Massillon, coming home after a victory. That win over Pittsburgh was one of the few by an AFL team over an NFL team in that preseason, and our victory over the Jets—who that season won Super Bowl III—came in the face of a desperate passing flurry by Joe Namath, which was turned aside time and again by our young defensive backs, Fletcher Smith, Charley King and Jim Williams.

Those final two victories were big moments—I still have the game ball from the Pittsburgh game—because we had proved that this untried group of young men had a chance to be successful, and it helped them believe in themselves. The next step was to apply all that we had learned and endured to our first season of play, and though we were no threat for the championship in 1968, I never doubted for a moment that we would ultimately become contenders. There were fence-sitters around the nation who weren't so sure and said perhaps I had made a mistake by coming back to the game.

For the next eight seasons, I was very happy to accept that challenge.

FIFTEEN

The Bengals—
and Good-bye

WHEN I STEPPED BACK ONTO the sidelines as head coach of the Bengals in 1968, it felt as if I had never been away. It was as if six years had vanished in an instant. There they were: the feelings of tension and anticipation as I waited to run onto the field with my team before the game . . . the rumble of the crowd . . . the almost-involuntary actions of the players as they slapped and prodded one another in their final acts of preparation . . . the backdrop of goal posts, scoreboard and white chalk lines over the green field . . . the black-and-white striped shirts of the officials . . . the air of anticipation as our kicking team ran onto the field—nothing had changed. I was a bit more excited and exhilarated because I had lived for the moment when all this would return to my life, but once I dispatched the first play into the game, it was just as it always had been—a chess game between "him" and me, a never-ending battle to do the right thing at the right time for the greatest possible number of times.

There was one difference, though. the plays might have been correct, the strategies sound and the desire total, but this team wasn't the Browns, or the Buckeyes, or even the Massillon Tigers. It was the Cincinnati Bengals, a group of green and growing young men—hardly more than a college team—together for just two months, still learning to know and like each other and trying to become skilled in a system that had once been used by far more talented and experienced players. It was a team trying to learn what professional football was all about even while it played the game.

For all that, however, we won three games—the most ever by a first-year expansion team in the NFL—and I was very satisfied with our efforts and our achievements. We had begun to grow, our players maintained a respect for each other and they stayed together through some tough times. No one ever let down or gave up in any game, and that is all any coach can ask. There were no surprises or disappointments for me in that first season. In fact, what Vince Lombardi had told me two years before was true—it is easier to build a team than have to maintain one as contender. In Cleveland we had never enjoyed the luxury of a patient and gradual approach to becoming a championship team.

When we started the 1968 season, I hoped very much that we could avoid the glare of the public limelight and the attendant pressures which often caused even experienced teams to falter. That didn't happen, however. Our very first game was scheduled for national television by NBC because the network had committed itself to an early-season game, and none of the other teams in the AFL wanted it. Only three games had been scheduled that first weekend in September 1968, and I always felt they decided to throw us to the wolves against a team of proved quality. I even called Julian Goodman, NBC's president, and explained, "We're just an expansion team, and we've been together for only a few weeks. We don't have a sporting chance in this game, and I'm afraid your network will get a black eye that could damage your image for the rest of the season."

"I understand your plight," he told me, "and I sympathize with you, but there is nothing we can do about it. The league made the schedule, and we must accept whatever game they give us for that date. I couldn't change it even if I wanted to."

"If we embarrass you and your network then, you'll know I was concerned beforehand and warned you about it," I said. He thanked me, but nothing changed, and even though we wouldn't share in the television receipts, we had to be a party to this scheduling. I was less worried about NBC's fate than about what might happen to us should we play badly and be embarrassed on national television. It was a difficult way to start, but it was just one more thing that went with being an expansion team.

As it turned out, we were not embarrassed and, in fact, played the Chargers to a standstill for nearly three-quarters of the game. We started Dewey Warren at quarterback because John Stofa, our only experienced passer, was injured. Dewey was a crowd pleaser because he had a certain swagger about him that made it appear he was exceeding his talent level. This quality, plus our own deepgut determination, and the Chargers' failure to take us too seriously made the game closer than it should have been. Our offense took the opening kickoff and marched for a touchdown, with Paul Robinson going the last seven yards and we left the field at the half with a 10–10 tie. We still trailed only 17–13 deep in the second half, when the Chargers finally broke open the game with a pair of touchdown passes by John Hadl, and we lost, 29–13.

I was pleased with what I had seen, "You gave everything that you had," I told our players afterward. "I thank you for your effort. It's a real credit to you. You played a team that all of us knew outmanned us, but you're still young, and your future is ahead of you. Let's not be discouraged in losing; just let us get ready to fight the next game."

Those players took my words to heart because we astounded everyone and won our next two games, including our home opener against Denver. We certainly didn't sneak up on them, as we had the Chargers, because the Broncos had barely beaten us in the preseason game. We went against each other just as fiercely this time, and the score was tied, 10–10, as the last quarter began. Then, after making a first down on a fourth-and-inches play, Stofa threw a 54-yard touchdown pass to Warren McVea. It was a true team effort because Rod Sherman, one of our flankers, who had to miss this game because of an injury, had told McVea that one of the Broncos' defensive backs usually took the first fake by a receiver. Sure enough, McVea gave him a quick move and then sped into the clear for Stofa's pass. A few minutes later Paul Robinson came out of the game to replace a lost shoe, and while he was lacing it up, his replacement, Essex Johnson, ran 34 yards for our last touchdown. When the game ended, I was hoisted onto the shoulders of my players and carried off the field. In the locker room, our captains presented me with the game ball, and the whole day was made even more special because Katy was there, and the victory was hers, too.

The Buffalo Bills came to Nippert Stadium the following
week, and Al Beauchamp and Charley King each returned
second-half interceptions for touchdowns that brought us
from behind for a 34–23 victory. The biggest play of the
game was a broken double reverse play, in which Stofa was
to hand the ball to one of the running backs, who would then
hand it to McVea. Stofa missed the first handoff, kept going
with the ball until McVea came along and then handed him
the ball himself. The play's different look seemed to confuse
Buffalo, and Warren scampered 80 yards for a touchdown
that gave us an early 10–0 lead. We had to rely on plays like
these to shake up defenses because we were not strong
enough yet to control the game. During the year we would
pull out all the stops, even throwing our triple-pass flea flicker
from the end zone—and completing it for a first down. We
used everything and anything.

We lost to the Broncos, 10–7, the second time we played
them that season, but I remember that game for another reason—all of us narrowly escaped death on our return flight to
Cincinnati. We were forced to land at Des Moines, Iowa, for
a short time because bad weather had temporarily closed Cincinnati's airport and, as we were ready to take off, another
plane landed ahead of us. Instead of turning off the runway,
however, the other plane just stopped. We were already under
way, and our pilot had to pour on the power to get us above
the stopped plane. Years later, when hundreds were killed in
a similar situation at Tenerife, in the Canaries, I thought
back to that moment in Des Moines and how close we had
come to a similar catastrophe.

Our season was a series of "near misses" because the following week, when we played Miami and lost, 24–22, a
missed 19-yard field goal by Dale Livingston at the end of
the first half turned out to be the difference. I had always
taken those field goals for granted when Lou Groza was our
kicker in Cleveland and often hadn't even bothered to watch
because they were so automatic. They weren't automatic anymore. As it was, we almost got a tie because Warren's touchdown pass to Bob Trumpy brought us within two points of
the Dolphins at the end of the game. The AFL had its two-
point conversion rule at that time, and Warren's pass for the
two points was batted around in the air between receivers
and defensive backs until it finally fell incomplete. The rule

has since been eliminated, but I thought it made the game more interesting for the fans.

We also sandwiched an exciting game against Kansas City between our losses to Denver and Miami and forced the Chiefs' great defense into a pair of goal line stands to preserve a 13–3 victory. Our losing skein ultimately reached seven before we defeated the Dolphins, 38–21, on a blistering hot day in Miami for our third victory.

One of our last games of the season was against the Patriots in Boston, where John Kissell, who now worked in the recreation department in Nashua, New Hampshire, and his wife met us at our hotel.

"Who's officiating the game?" he asked me.

I told him, and he said, "You're going to get screwed. Boston's coach plays poker with those guys once a week."

Sure enough, when Boston missed an easy field goal in the game, the officials ruled that we had twelve men on the field—that never showed on our films—and they made it on the second try. It seemed that every time we got something going that day, we were penalized.

After the game I met John and his wife, and he said, "What did I tell you? I knew it was going to happen."

He certainly had, so after viewing the films and seeing how many nonpenalties had been called, I called the league office and protested strongly enough so that the situation was never repeated.

That first season had brought me back to where I belonged, but sadly, it was Katy's last because she died very suddenly of a heart attack the following April while undergoing surgery in California. Suddenly I was very alone because I never thought she would die. The first thing I thought was, "I must take her home," and we arranged for her burial back in Massillon. That was our home, the place we had spent so many happy moments, the one place, above all else, I felt she would have wanted for a final resting place. I go back each year and tend her grave site, and afterward I often go over to the Massillon stadium and sit and replay the grand moments we experienced during our years living there. It renews my spirit and brings me close again to a person and a place I loved very much.

In the midst of this sudden ordeal, the future of professional football was being decided, and I was right in the middle of the struggle—the "blueberry in the milk," as some-

one described my role. In the spring of 1969 the final plans
for aligning the AFL and NFL were being hammered out because the merger had to be implemented by the start of the
1970 season. Instead of adhering to the terms of the original
agreement, however, both sides displayed considerable sentiment for retaining their own identities, meaning the NFL
would keep its sixteen teams and the AFL its ten.

That was not what we had been promised when our franchise had been awarded, however, and my lawyer-son, Mike,
and I pointed to the provisions of the "specific performance"
clause and insisted that the real merger of both leagues be
spelled out there. The clause stipulated a unified schedule of
regular-season games between teams from both leagues,
recognizing factors of geography, natural rivalries, stadium
size, gate attendance, weather patterns, team strength and
conflicts with baseball teams as considerations for scheduling
purposes, so as not to prejudice any franchise in the realigned
league. To me, that meant both leagues would be equal in
size, would have common scheduling, share equal television
revenues and have the same chance in building through the
draft. Otherwise, we weren't giving our fans all we had
promised when our franchise was born.

The sentiment against the realignment, however, seemed to
have the somewhat neutral support of Commissioner Rozelle,
who was willing to go along with what the majority of the
owners wished. The NFL owners were content with the status
quo because they had the big television markets, their sixteen
teams had an edge in numbers in drafting the future stars
and they knew they could get only stronger while the AFL
teams got weaker. On the other hand, many in the AFL went
along because the Jets' victory over Baltimore in the Super
Bowl only a couple of months before had given them a false
sense of independence and strength.

I refused to go along with either of them, and though
many of my friends among the NFL's owners tried to convince me to change my position, I never wavered and insisted
that the terms of the original merger agreement be honored.
It was a long, bitter and sometimes lonely struggle, and
because these matters reached deep into the pocketbooks of
every owner, it produced some of the bitterest infighting
professional football had ever endured.

To win the fight, I knew I first had to convince the AFL
owners that they were not really getting what they had paid

$18 million for three years earlier, when the merger agreement had first been drawn up. Consequently, I wrote a memo to their realignment committee—Ralph Wilson, Lamar Hunt and Bill Sullivan—and said:

We can understand the AFL's pride in the Super Bowl victory. Nevertheless, financial facts, not pride, should be considered. The AFL/NFL agreement is specific on realignment and it calls for a thorough mixing of present AFL clubs in order to evenly distribute the financially weak franchises among the strong. I can see keeping as much of a vestige of the league as possible, but I am fighting for my franchise.

Simple inter-league play does not create new divisions or groupings. What I want to emphasize is that we're open to any alignment that gives everybody an equal shot at victory and profits. I'll guarantee you one thing: If the leagues retain their present identities, the NFL will continue to control the major TV markets and the AFL franchises never will be worth as much. I don't blame some of the NFL clubs for wanting to keep their cozy little four-team groupings, but at the time of the merger, when everyone was afraid of going under, the AFL paid dearly.

I don't want to ruin the effect of the Super Bowl. There will always be a Super Bowl, no matter how it's arrived at. . . . But if you leave the merger, and allow the NFL to keep sixteen teams, and the AFL to retain ten teams, the NFL will always be stronger simply because it will have sixteen of every twenty-six draft picks.

I then presented my own plan for realignment, which split both leagues into four divisions. One included the New York Jets, Philadelphia, Pittsburgh, Cleveland, Buffalo, Cincinnati and Detroit; the second contained the New York Giants, Washington, Baltimore, Chicago, Minnesota, Green Bay and Boston; the third, San Francisco, Los Angeles, Houston, Denver, Kansas City and St. Louis; and the fourth, Oakland, San Diego, Dallas, New Orleans, Atlanta and Miami.

That arrangement kept together geographic rivals and teams with equal TV value, as well as those that paid comparable receipts to visiting teams. I pointed out that I wasn't against designating two leagues "American" and "National" if that helped preserve the Super Bowl, but I urged everyone not to worry about lessening the impact of that game. It would be a world championship no matter what the leagues were named.

Mike and I then took the eight-page merger agreement, boiled it down to a concise report and presented it to each of the AFL owners. In it, we listed five points we felt would be most crucial to our cause:

1. A financial summary of the visitor's share of the gate receipts for all twenty-six teams, which showed the AFL teams took home one-third less than the NFL teams.

2. A chart of AFL and NFL stadium seating capacities, which showed that only two AFL teams ranked in the top half.

3. Proof that NFL teams had a better average season ticket sale.

4. Home ticket sale attendance and receipts from rivalries within the NFL, which gave that league the edge.

5. Television ratings showing the NFL's games had consistently higher ratings because its teams were in the larger markets and reached more homes.

When we went to Palm Springs for our meeting, no one said too much to me until Gerry Phipps, the owner of the Denver Broncos, asked me to take a long walk with him the day before the meetings opened and spell out all my points in detail. He seemed very interested in my thinking and invited me to join a group of AFL owners at dinner that evening; again I laid out our arguments. When I had finished, Phil Iselin of the New York Jets said, "You're right, and I'm sticking with you." With Phipps and Iselin in my corner, the other AFL owners began to come around, and we succeeded in stopping the stampede within our own league.

Soon we had the AFL owners solidly lined up behind us, and it was time to tackle the NFL. I stood up at our meeting and said, "We will find out *legally* just what our position is regarding the specific performance clause in the merger agreement." The word *legally* was like a stick of dynamite, and the meetings were hurriedly adjourned, to convene again in early May in New York. In the meantime, the NFL owners knew they had to come up with a presentable plan.

In the time between the meetings, many of the owners rethought their positions and realized it had to be a 13-13 split, instead of the 16–10. The question was: How? They had my original realignment proposal, but the AFL owners, still proud and feisty after their league's Super Bowl victory and their successful fight to force a merger with the NFL, still wanted to retain as much of their league's identity as they could and felt that three of the NFL teams must join them, rather than have their own teams scattered about.

When the meetings reconvened in the first week of May, the deadlock continued. Finally, the commissioner sent both groups of owners into separate meeting rooms at NFL headquarters on Park Avenue and convened his now-famous "locked door" marathon bargaining session, which eventually lasted more than forty hours. Those rooms were something to behold: People slept on chairs and on the floor, no one shaved, collars rumpled, ties went askew or were discarded altogether and tempers got shorter as each exhausting hour passed. Each team had to keep its voting member present at all times, but since Mike and I both had voting power, we took turns getting some rest at our hotel, which kept us fresh and our mental resources sharp, so our position never weakend. Some of the others had to endure the hardship of living in one room for nearly two days. My most vivid memory of that time was Lamar Hunt sleeping on the hallway couch—a white flower across his chest that someone had placed there.

The pressure was on the NFL to come up with a solution. Art Modell was adamant that his team and some other old-line NFL teams would not move. "It would emasculate the NFL if the Browns were to leave," he stated publicly. However, Al Davis of Oakland finally came up with the answer, which was that the three teams that came into the AFL's group be paid for moving—and when the price was put at $3 million, Pittsburgh and Cleveland, I was told, were the first to volunteer. The fact that they switched together also made it more palatable because they were natural rivals.

Commissioner Rozelle then proposed the St. Louis Cardinals as the third team, but with $3 million at stake, there was no dearth of volunteers, and when we suggested the Baltimore Colts, the Colts snapped at the opportunity. "Have you ever seen a barracuda?" I joked.

The three teams were presented to the AFL owners, and in less than ninety minutes we had our alignments worked out and the commissioner's approval. It seemed almost *pro forma* when Pete brought representatives from the three teams into our owners' meeting so we could review the new setup and hold a formal vote for its consent—and then, to our surprise, Al Davis suddenly turned around and voted against it. It seems he wanted to have a veto over the ultimate realignment form for the entire league. Since unanimous consent was required, we suddenly had no agreement. The uproar was enormous, fueled by tempers tight from nearly forty hours without sleep. Al's reasons made absolutely no sense to the rest of us, so after going to the NFL meeting to explain what had happened, I contacted Commissioner Rozelle, his top aide, Jim Kensil, and Art Rooney to see if we couldn't find a way to break the impasse. After careful discussion, we came up with a plan we thought could work.

When the session reconvened, Lamar Hunt, who had used Al Davis for his proxy the first time around, this time spoke for himself and voted "yes" for the alignment. Then, instead of Davis, Wayne Valley, another owner of the Raiders, took control—and he too voted affirmatively. It was unanimous, a total victory, particularly for the commissioner, who had been on the spot to deliver an equitable solution that everyone— owners, fans and networks—could accept.

The end results of the 13-13 merger are evident today in the sport's tremendous prosperity, as well as in the success of our own franchise. We are in the same division as Cleveland and Pittsburgh, and our games against each other bring in the biggest crowds of the season. Under the fourteen-game schedule format that began in 1970, our fans got to see NFL teams, as promised, including the Browns and Steelers every year, the Colts every other year and three other NFL opponents. Under the new sixteen-game format, half our games are against former NFL teams. In the meantime, the American Conference has also become the dominant force in the NFL during the seventies, and the problems and ill feelings that existed among the owners when this agreement was being hammered out all have been set aside long ago and are now the subject of good-natured jokes.

Meanwhile, merger or not, we had another football season coming up. Our draft in 1969 had brought us some tremendous players, including our top pick, Greg Cook, a quarterback from the University of Cincinnati. I had seen him play several games at UC and couldn't help noticing his physical talents—quick feet, a fine throwing arm for both long and short passes and superior all-around athletic skills. He also had that indomitable quality that all great quarterbacks possess—like Otto Graham, he instilled so much confidence in his teammates they always believed he could find a way to win.

Greg had tremendous exuberance when things were going well, and when they weren't, he made no excuses. He was totally unflappable in tight situations—could stand and face the fiercest pass rush without flinching—but he also had enough mobility to roll out of trouble and still keep his pass play alive or to take off and run for whatever yardage he could muster. He was the first great young quarterback I had been able to select and have confidence in since we had picked Y. A. Tittle in 1948. When Greg played in the College All-Star game against the New York Jets that summer, he was selected as most valuable player. His coach in that game, ironically, was Otto Graham.

We had to battle to get Greg, however. A friend of mine tipped me off that the British Columbia Lions of the Canadian Football League were so interested in getting him that their owner and coach had chartered a plane and were flying to Cincinnati in hopes of signing him. I was in New York attending a league meeting, but this was an emergency situation so I had one of our assistant coaches bring him to see me, so we could discuss a contract on the spot. Things progressed rapidly, and Greg signed before returning to Cincinnati. The Canadian League people never did see him; after waiting several hours at his apartment, they gave up and returned home.

I knew we were pressing a bit in 1969, when we elected to allow a rookie to be our starting quarterback, but he had such outstanding qualities I didn't consider it an inordinate risk. Furthermore, his passing skills would allow us to begin building our passing game, something we had not been able to do in our first season, so, though I knew he would make mistakes, we tied our future to him.

It was then, in the cruelest of misfortunes, that a series of injuries cut him down. His first injury came in our third game of the season against Kansas City, when he was sandwiched between Willie Lanier and Bobby Bell and hurt his shoulder. He recovered from that within a month, however, and finished the season with some fine performances as our starting quarterback, even winning the honor of rookie of the year. Then, in an off-season pickup basketball game, he went up for a rebound with both arms, someone grabbed his right arm and pulled it back and the rotor cuff muscle in his right

shoulder was damaged beyond reclamation. He again hurt his
shoulder playing water polo, and though we finally sent him
to Cleveland for surgery to try to repair the torn muscle,
Greg was never the same after that. He did develop a good
throwing motion again, but his other skills became rusty. I
think, too, that he had lost his confidence and could not face
trying to succeed with diminished skills. He left our training
camp a couple of times without a word to anyone. On each
occasion I'd find a note under my door in the morning, telling me that he just couldn't go on anymore.

Cook was not the only great player to come from that
draft. Our first eight choices all played for us that season, including linebacker Bill Bergey, our second pick, on the
recommendation of my son Robin, who had seen him play
several times in Arkansas. Ken Riley, a defensive back who is
still with the Bengals, was a sixth-round pick, while our seventh choice, Royce Berry, played for us for seven years and
became our defensive captain. Two other players, wide receiver Speedy Thomas and guard Guy Dennis, each spent
four years with us, helping us widen the foundation that became the bulwark of our future success. We also obtained
kicker Horst Muhlmann, the team's all-time scorer, in a trade
with Kansas City after Hank Stram had decided he could not
displace Jan Stenerud.

When we went to training camp that summer of 1969, we
had no inkling of what would happen to Cook, and our mood
was upbeat. We knew we could win some games with a great
young quarterback; we had improved our kicking with
Muhlmann and our defense with Bergey, Berry and Riley;
and we still had the same spirit and determination that had
carried us through our first season. In our opening meeting, I
told the players, "We're no longer an expansion team. We
might be the newest team in professional football, but we're
grown-up now."

I don't think our players really understood that fact until
Cook, in only his third game, directed us to a 25–13 victory
over the Steelers in the preseason. Pittsburgh, with Chuck
Noll in his first year as head coach, threw blitz after blitz at
Greg, but he seemed to beat them all. When he followed that
with a victory over Denver in our final preseason game, our
guys finally believed we had no reason to take a back seat to
anyone in pro football.

None of us was prepared, though, for the death of Frank

Buncom, our starting right linebacker, the night before our season opener against Miami. Only twenty-eight years old, he died in his sleep at our hotel in Cincinnati. It was not a football-related death—in fact, I am told that Frank's father died in the same manner—but it was a terrible ordeal for our players to overcome, and we played with a heavy heart, though well enough to defeat Miami. I was told later that week the victory was the three hundredth of my career.

We also won our next two games, including a 24–19 victory over Kansas City, despite Cook's injury. For the second time our players carried me off the field after the win, and a few days later I received a letter from President Richard Nixon, in which he said: "I've been a fan of Paul Brown since the days of the Browns-Rams championship games. . . . A football season is much like a political campaign, it takes a lot of dedicated work to develop a winning spirit. The Bengals have made it through the primaries with flying colors. While I have to remain impartial, you can be sure I shall be following the action in the days ahead. . . ."

Those days pretty much depended on Cook's shoulder regaining its strength, and after sitting out two games, he came back and led us to a whopping 31–17 victory over the Oakland Raiders, the defending AFL champions. The following week he put on a tremendous show as we tied the Houston Oilers, 31–31, thanks to Muhlmann's 18-yard field goal in the final twenty-two seconds. Greg had been the whole show, on third-and-thirty, he ran a quarterback draw for 30 yards and a first down, and then passed 14 yards to Crabtree to set up Muhlmann's tie-making field goal.

That was our final thrust of the season, though. We finished with a 4-9-1 record—and I was picked as AFL coach of the year. I certainly appreciated the honor because it helped solidify our team for the next year: for competition in the realigned National Football League's American Conference, for our sparkling new stadium . . . and, for the first time ever, for our game against the Cleveland Browns.

We actually played the Browns three times in 1970, but our first one, in the preseason at Riverfront Stadium, was the one that caught everyone's imagination. We had been flooded with ticket orders, in fact, ever since the first announcement of the game in 1968. It was no secret how intense I felt about the game, though not as much as later in the year, for our regular-season meeting, but I tried to keep everything as nor-

mal as possible during our workouts at training camp. I never
said a word about making any special efforts on my behalf
because many of the players had been young teenagers when
I had left the Browns, and it would have been silly for me to
have tried to make this a crusade. Nevertheless, every player
on that team has told me there was something special about
our practices then.

The strong feelings for this first game were evident everywhere. The Browns arrived at their hotel in downtown Cincinnati to find the lobby dressed up with a rug resembling a
football playing surface; the assistant managers attired in the
striped shirts and white knickers worn by officials, complete
with yellow flags hanging from their pockets; all the wait-
resses wearing numbered football jerseys; and continual
showings of football highlight films in the hotel lobby. It was
a combination of college homecoming game and Super Bowl
to Cincinnati fans; my friends in Cleveland have told me the
intensity there was nearly as great, with one exception: Everyone in Cincinnati knew where his loyalty lay; in Cleveland
the feelings for the home team's former coach were also quite
strong.

I tried to be as nonchalant as I could on the night of the
game, and though I knew that eight years had passed since I
had last coached the Browns and that only four players still
remained from my 1962 team, it was a jolt walking onto the
field and seeing those brown jerseys, white arm stripes, solid
orange helmets and white pants. My first thought was: "They
certainly look familiar." I could not help recalling where
those colors had come from and how much of my heart and
my life had been invested in those suits.

Of course, it was all business once the game began, and we
did not start well, as we fell behind, 14–0, in the first quarter.
After Jess Phillips's touchdown had narrowed the score, however, Ken Avery recovered a fumble by Leroy Kelly, and in
two plays, Sam Wyche drove across to tie the score.

Then we went ahead, 17–14, at the half, when Bergey's
blitz of Bill Nelson caused an interception by Ken Riley and
set up Muhlmann's field goal. The Browns tied the game
shortly after the third quarter began, but when Avery blitzed
Nelson again, the wobbly pass was intercepted by Royce Berry, and he returned it for a touchdown. Wyche passed to Chip
Myers early in the fourth quarter for our final touchdown, and

we came away with a 31–24 victory, though our defense had to battle to the end to keep the Browns from scoring.

After the game Bob Johnson handed me the game ball, and I was touched, but I knew that, no matter how much I relished that moment, the two regular-season games against the Browns would be more important. In the first of them, before nearly 84,000 fans in Cleveland, we led, 20–16, going into the final quarter, before the Browns scored two touchdowns and beat us, 30–27. I was disappointed, but even more disappointed when an incident regarding me and Blanton Collier was misrepresented.

Standing on the field before the game, I pointedly told Collier that win or lose, I would go directly to our dressing room when the game ended because of a league directive designed to avoid an increasing number of nasty incidents by fans on the field after games.

"If there are any congratulations to be tendered, I'm offering them now," I said very specifically.

Collier, of course, was deaf, and I don't know whether he heard me, but I do know that Tom Gray, our equipment manager, who had come over to say hello to him and was standing nearby, told me later he had heard every word. Immediately after the game Collier complained that he had walked onto the field to shake hands and I had gone to the dressing room, and some of the Cleveland media made a big deal about it, insinuating that I obviously still harbored ill feelings about our past association. That made me look bad, even though I tried to explain, and I still feel I was undeservedly criticized for something that was clearly not my fault.

There were no problems later that year, however, when we met back in Cincinnati, however, and when I ran off the field following our 14–10 victory, I took off my hat and waved it to the crowd—something I don't even remember doing—because I was so exhilarated at our victory over a team with better talent and deeper resources. I can't recall our team's ever fighting harder against great odds than in this game. The turning point was our defense's stopping the Browns inside our 10-yard line in the first quarter and forcing them to kick a field goal for a 10–0 lead when a touchdown might have pushed the game out of control. We scored twice in the second half, keyed by Willie Lee Jone's sack of Mike Phipps that began our comeback, and our defense battled for its life to hold that lead. One of my friends told me afterward that I looked as if I were eighteen years old the way I ran off the field, and I told him, "That's exactly how I felt." I confess to having tears in my eyes when our players handed me the game ball for the second time.

Playing Cleveland three times, and winning twice in front of our fans, would be enough for any season, but 1970 was a monumental year for us in other ways as well. It started out with our players' being forced to stay out of training camp because of a labor dispute, and it finished in the American Conference play-offs. We bridged those two extremes without Greg Cook, but with a gritty job of quarterbacking by Virgil Carter, and with fine defense by our new players, Mike Reid, Lamar Parrish, Ron Carpenter, Nick Roman and Sandy Durko. Reid was our first-round pick, and though he was bothered by injuries during his rookie season, he was outstanding. A very emotional player and highly motivated to excel, though he did not like to practice, Reid, next to Bill Willis, was the fastest defensive lineman for the length of the ball who ever played on our teams.

Mike gave us several good years, but the acclaim he received for playing the piano with the Cincinnati Symphony Orchestra steered him toward a full-time career in music, instead, so he left us after five seasons, determined to write the big song. I also felt his unwillingness to subject himself to some of the physical pain which goes with football affected his decision.

Carter was a godsend to us in 1970, especially considering that we only picked him up two weeks before the season began, after he had been cut by the Buffalo Bills. He was an accurate short passer when he came to us, but he could not throw the ball deep with authority—he had a tendency to loop his passes and allow receivers to run under them—and we convinced him that by lowering the ball's trajectory, he could throw with more velocity and even greater accuracy. Combining this with a special roll-out type of offense we designed for him, we had an attack that no one could figure out until the season was almost over and our drive for the division title had ended.

His leadership qualities and his courage were even more impressive. In our next-to-last game against Houston, Carter suffered some broken ribs and had his tongue ripped open by what I considered to be a deliberate attempt by one of the Oilers' linemen to knock him out of the game. He could hardly speak for a week while his tongue mended, yet he was superb in our final 45–7 victory over the Patriots that clinched our first division title, and he battled valiantly the following week, when, with broken ribs that nearly prevented him from turning his body, he played against the Colts.

We weren't really ready yet to play in a title game against a team like Baltimore. The team, coached by Don McCafferty, who had played for me at Ohio State, was deeper, more experienced and more talented than we were, but it was a splendid opportunity to get our players used to the feeling of playing under championship pressure. Such a feeling is contagious: Once you feel it, the more you like it, and the more you want to feel it again. Of course, to some of our players it was exciting just being on the same field with John Unitas or even seeing him at close range because he had been their idol for years.

We arrived in Baltimore on Christmas Day, but when we went to Memorial Stadium, I think our kids were a bit surprised to see what amounted to a dirt field, frozen solid and barren-looking. This was not their idea of what an NFL play-off field should look like, but there was nothing we could do about it. The next day was one of the coldest, bitterest days I can remember, made even more so by our fortunes in the game. The Colts controlled us from start to finish. They had figured out that Carter could not throw normally because of his broken ribs, and as a result, our offense did little. Unitas passed for two long touchdowns, the last putting the game away in the fourth quarter, and Baltimore won, 17–0. The Colts, of course, went on to win Super Bowl V, but I was particularly gratified that we had gotten as far as we did because it put to rest for all time any insinuations still left over from the Cleveland years that the game of football had passed me by. That year I also received my second straight coach of the year award.

The draft the next spring produced mixed results but proved a bonanza for the Bengals in one very important respect—we finally got the quarterback we had been waiting for: Ken Anderson. Ken ranks just behind Otto Graham as my best quarterback ever. He has all of Otto's physical talents, as well as that one tremendously important attribute for any topflight quarterback—stability. Stability is the basis for leadership, and leadership is a quality that transcends even a powerful arm or swift feet. A quarterback can never be a problem child in my system. I don't take away the fact that fine quarterbacks like Bobby Layne and Sonny Jurgensen had their own life-styles, but Graham and Anderson epitomize the kind of man I've always wanted to build with. I've rarely met a player with a better attitude toward other people than Ken. He is purposeful, poised, well rounded and one of the pleasantest men I've ever known in any business. I've had a wonderful relationship with him ever since his first season with the Bengals.

In fact, we were lucky to get him because Norm Van Brocklin, then head coach at Atlanta, had also targeted him as a solid prospect. He felt, however, that because Ken came from a small college, Augustana, he would be around for a few rounds while the Falcons strengthened themselves at other positions. Bill Walsh and my son Mike had gone to Augustana to look at Ken and worked him out. Their reports had been unanimous in their enthusiasm, and after we had made our first two selections, a pair of offensive linemen, I began to get concerned that if we felt so highly about him, others might, too, and select him ahead of us.

"I'm not going to gamble any longer," I said to my staff. "If you still feel he is a great prospect, we'll take him now."

They all nodded, and that was it. If there was any gamble in taking someone from such a small school, it was simply that he hadn't been exposed to the pressure of big-time competition. As it turned out, it never bothered him a bit because he had been born with poise, and from the start, he looked like a veteran: perfectly relaxed, able to assimilate everything that we taught him, an all-around player.

He had to be all those things because in his first season Kenny got a crash course in NFL football that stepped up his progress several years. We still didn't know whether Greg Cook would be able to play, and we knew we could not be totally successful with Virgil Carter's limited passing range. When Virgil separated his shoulder in our third game against Green Bay and Cook was still recuperating, we knew we had no choice. Sooner or later Ken would have to go through a learning period, and it looked as if 1971 would have to be that year.

In the preseason of 1971, we took off on a hot streak, won five and tied one of six games, and when we bombarded the Philadelphia Eagles in the opener, everyone's expectations went skyrocketing. I had never deluded myself after our division championship in 1970 that we were still anything but a young, developing team that had to endure more growing pains before we became a bona fide contender—but nothing prepared me for the rash of misfortunes that was about to turn our season upside down.

As we went into the Green Bay game, our record was 1-1, and though we lost Carter with his separated shoulder, Anderson did a fine job of keeping us in the game. Then, with just one play left from inside the Packers' five-yard line and trailing, 13–10, we had to decide whether to kick a field goal and settle for a tie or to try to score on fourth down and win the game.

"I know what you guys want to do," I said to our players.

"Go for the TD!" they shouted, so we sent in a quarterback keeper play for Ken that sent a convoy of blockers out in front of him as he rolled around right end. That was some way to welcome a young quarterback to the NFL: giving him the pressure of winning or losing a game on one final play. The play worked perfectly, however, except that Ken, from lack of experience and not yet knowing his blockers, mistakenly cut inside near the goal line and was tackled before he reached the end zone. Had he stayed outside, he would have trotted over through the path his blockers had cleared for those final few yards.

Some said after the game that I had actually asked our players for an opinion on what to do, and many saw this as a sign that I had mellowed and was changing the way I ran a game. The players knew better, however. It was simply that they had fought so hard—under upsetting circumstances—I felt that consideration should be given to them as to whether they wanted to try to win the game or go off with a tie. Their decision didn't surprise me, and I think I would have been disappointed had they settled for the tie.

Those "upsetting circumstances" had nothing to do with the action of the game itself, but with a freak injury. Ken Dyer, a tall, lanky, hard-hitting defensive back had tackled the Packers' big fullback, John Brockington, but as he did so, he had turned his head the wrong way, and in an instant, the shock from the contact had paralyzed his body from his shoulders to his toes. We all were stunned as he was carried off the field on a stretcher, and his fate was more on our minds that day than losing the game. The doctors at first feared that he might die, but that crisis passed, and then they felt he might never walk again because he had snapped a vertebra near his neck and his nerves were damaged. Luckily Ken could eat and talk, and his mind had been unaffected by the injury, so when the other dangers had passed, he began his rehabilitation.

Ken's recovery is a remarkable and heartwarming story of how one man had to start almost from scratch and learn how to move again. We checked every day on his progress, and I even arranged for our game to be piped in by a special radio line so he could follow his team. Dan Devine, the Packers' coach, who was on crutches himself after suffering a broken leg on the sidelines in his season's opening game, also visited him often, and I am very grateful for that kindness.

At one point during his rehabilitation Ken's right leg suddenly turned blue and felt ice-cold. Ken thought it was a cramp and had his wife, Peggy, massage it to try to bring back some feeling. When it didn't improve, she buzzed for a nurse, who, immediately upon seeing it, summoned a doctor. The problem turned out to be a blood clot, and the worst thing you can do with a clot is rub it. The doctors were afraid for a time that the clot might ultimately travel to his heart and kill Ken or become infected and cause possible amputation of his leg. He was forced to stop his rehabilitation program and became so ill he lost nearly forty pounds until the condition was cleared up.

When he resumed his rehabilitation program to regain the use of all his extremities, his wife did not know how he was doing until one day he wrote on a piece of paper, "Go to hell."

"I knew then," Peggy told us later, "that he had his spirit back and he was going to be all right."

Shortly before Christmas 1971 he walked out of the hospital, and Ken today is just fine. It is a pleasure to see that big, smiling face when he walks through our locker room on his periodic visits, but it was a terrifying experience for all of us then. It was also a reminder that the dangers weren't only on the playing field because when I saw Devine on crutches at that game, I couldn't help thinking how close I myself had come during those many years to getting injured. On one occasion I was talking to Bill Johnson and not watching a punt when an official, following the ball's trajectory as it sailed out of bounds, plowed into me, and we both went sprawling. Another time, during a game at Nippert Stadium against Kansas

City, a wedge of players came rolling into me on the sidelines, but luckily I jumped high enough for them to roll under me and just sat down on top of them. In both instances, I was unhurt but more alert from then on.

The Green Bay game was a good example of how things went that season—a couple of yards, or a dropped pass, or a broken play, or a crippling injury were the difference between winning and losing time and again. Against Oakland, for instance, we had fought from a 17–0 deficit and tied the score, 24–24, with the ball at the Raiders' 10-yard line, when Anderson suffered a hip pointer that forced him to come out of the game. Our only available man was Dave Lewis, a punter who had been a quarterback in college, but who was strictly a last-chance guy with us. In two plays, he had us on the three-yard line, and we sent in the quarterback keeper play, feeling a big man like Lewis could almost dive into the end zone and score. He didn't make it, however, and we had to kick a field goal. It was the crucial difference because then George Blanda led one of his famed last-minute drives, and Oakland won, 31–27. The week before, we had had a 24–20 lead against Cleveland when we had lost a fumble, which the Browns turned into the winning touchdown in the final thirty-two seconds.

Perhaps our game in Houston during this seven-game losing streak best epitomized our entire season. Our chartered plane was several hours late and caused us to miss our day-before workout at the Astrodome. Next, the bus driver from the airport got lost; then we even had trouble getting into the Astrodome on the day of the game because the security guard didn't know who the Bengals were! After the game we discovered that our locker room had been broken into and some of the players had had money stolen. And when we arrived home, some of the players' cars had been towed for being parked in the wrong location. Worse than all that, we had lost the game to the Oilers, 10–6, in what I believe was the poorest professional football game I have ever seen—on the part of both teams.

I had never been through a season like that before, and though Carter came back and helped snap our losing steak by leading us to three straight wins, it was a relief to see it all end and have a chance for a fresh start in 1972. Our record also put us back in a favorable drafting position, so we resumed building our team, particularly our defense, and chose Sherman White, a big defensive end from California, and defensive back Tommy Casanova from LSU, on our first two picks.

We had sent our defensive line coach, Chuck Studley, to California to work out White, test him and see what kind of person he was, and Chuck had given him a good rating, so we were glad to get him. He played well for us for four years, but unfortunately, like so many players who come from the West Coast, he began making public statements about being traded to a West Coast team. We tried to make a deal but couldn't do it to our satisfaction, so finally, we got our first-round pick back when we traded him to Buffalo after the 1975 season. I was very disappointed in White's attitude, but I'll never forget his saying after he left us, "Those Browns, Paul and Mike, all they ever think about is the team and winning." What else were we supposed to think about?

Casanova was a splendid strong safety for us until he retired after the 1977 season to finish his medical studies. He would have been a first-round pick, but everyone was afraid he would forgo pro football for medical school. We agreed to allow him to finish his year's studies at LSU before reporting to training camp, and the decision proved to be good for us. That draft also brought us Jim LeClair, who finally replaced Bergey as middle linebacker when we traded Bill to Philadelphia after he had signed a World Football League contract. Jim has already made the Pro Bowl team and has many more seasons ahead of him.

All this young defensive talent kept us in contention through most of the 1972 season, and we finished right behind the NFL champion Miami Dolphins as the AFC's top defensive team. We vied with Pittsburgh and Cleveland for the AFC Central title until the next-to-last game, when the Browns defeated us, 27–24. Earlier that summer more than 84,000 people had watched us play Cleveland in a preseason game at Ohio Stadium, and in our three games that year against the Browns we played before more than 225,000 people. We have since discontinued the preseason game because both of us felt playing two games in the regular season was enough competition between our teams.

We finished the 1972 season with a resounding 61–17 victory over Houston, and with Ken Anderson playing quarterback full time, I finally felt our team was ready to become a legitimate contender. Our defensive team was solid, we had a quarterback who could throw the ball with strength and accuracy and, to top it off, Isaac Curtis, our first-round pick of the 1973 draft, was a world-class sprinter who could both catch and run with the ball. Isaac has since become one of the great stars of our era: a big man at 195 pounds, with the grace and balance of a ballet dancer and the hands of Dante Lavelli. I've often seen defensive backs start running with him and think they have him covered, only to have him turn on the "afterburners" in his legs and leave them looking as if they were standing still.

Curtis, who caught forty-five passes for more than 800 yards and nine touchdowns in his rookie season, was one of the springboards that brought us our second division title in 1973. Anderson had matured as a quarterback after just two seasons, Essex Johnson was at his peak and Booby Clark excelled as a rookie. Berry, Reid and White all also had their best seasons for us on defense.

That defense showed its real mettle in our first game against the Steelers, when it held Pittsburgh to only 138 yards and seven points. That turned our season around and gave our young players the confidence that they could beat a division champion. After struggling through a mediocre 4-4 record, we whipped through our last six games and captured the title. It was almost a replay of 1970, except that we had a better team, as did our closest rivals, the Steelers and Cleveland Browns. And this time, unlike 1971, we *won* the tight games, by whatever means necessary. Against Buffalo, Muhlmann's field goal in the final seconds was the difference, and we held O. J. Simpson, who that year had a record-setting 2,003 yards, to 99 yards; we beat the Jets, 20–14, as Joe Namath allowed the clock to run out while he waited for a center snap with the ball on our 1-foot line; and we played our best game in beating the Minnesota Vikings, 27–0. The Vikings went on to play in Super Bowl VIII.

Unfortunately, when we played the Dolphins in the first round of the AFC play-offs, our luck ran out before we even got started. Essex Johnson, who had gained 997 yards that season, torqued his knee on his second running play—without even being touched by a player—and was lost for the game. With our best running back gone, the Dolphins' defense concentrated on Clark and succeeded in shutting down our passing game by mauling Curtis before he could get five or six yards downfield. We trailed only 21–16 at the half, but with our offense so hampered, we could not control the ball, and we lost, 34–16.

Miami's style of pass coverage later became a subject of controversy. Developed by Don Shula and then taken up by Chuck Noll at Pittsburgh, who used to coach for Don, it was an offshoot of the bump-and-run, that started at the line of scrimmage and then continued downfield, with one or two defensive backs harassing a receiver until the timing of his pass pattern was broken. Shula termed it "rerouting the receiver." The theory for allowing it was that the defensive man could not be certain if the play would be a run or a pass, but that was false. Actually, defenders know early and untuitively what the play will be. In our play-off game the Dolphins made certain that Curtis could not get downfield because he was cut, grabbed, pushed and totally neutralized. After that game I worked hard on the NFL's Competition Committee to change the rule and allow only limited contact because this style of defense was hurting our game.

"What good is it for us to have performers who aren't allowed to perform?" I asked the committee. "The fans want to see receivers get downfield so the passer will have someone to throw to. Unless we change, we are not taking advantage of these great athletes."

Gradually the rule has been changed to limited contact, although I still think contact should be eliminated altogether, unless a running play is in progress. This matter is under constant review and always pits the teams with offensive-minded coaches against those who are defensively oriented. The adaptation of the rule, incidentally, has become known as the Curtis Rule, even though I wasn't thinking of just one player or one team when I was pushing for the change.

Though such football matters and coaching the Bengals had consumed most of my time and attention in the years after Katy died, my life away from football was pretty barren. I played a lot of golf during the winter in La Jolla, as well as bridge and gin rummy with our friends, but I was living only for myself, an empty existence. I came home each night and cooked my own supper, watched television if there was something worthwhile on or read before going to bed. If I was with friends on social occasions, it was always unaccompanied, and when the evening ended, I went home again to an empty house. I noticed this void particularly after games, most especially after a victory, when everyone scattered to enjoy himself and I was left on my own. I did not expect my sons to look after me, because they had their own families and friends, and though I was always welcome to join them, I felt it would be better if I went on my own way.

All this changed in June 1973, when I married my present wife, Mary, who was a widow with four grown children, including twin daughters. Her husband had died only two months after Katy, in 1969, and she had moved back to London, Ohio, where her parents lived. John Sawyer also lived in London at this time, and knowing we were looking for a secretary, he suggested she apply; she did and was hired. As I got to know her in our day-to-day association, I noticed how her happy nature brightened our office, and then our friendship blossomed and grew until we were finally married. I soon found that having twin teenage daughters around our home was quite different from having three sons, but I thoroughly enjoyed the experience, even if I couldn't always understand the words to their songs and often wondered why the music had to be played so loudly. Some of my happiest moments came when Mary and the two girls met me after I returned from a game or a business trip, and I know we boggled more than a few eyes as we all trooped arm in arm through the airport, laughing and chattering together.

My new life was a welcome relief from the problems which beset professional football early in 1974, when the World Football League began actively pursuing our players and causing economic turmoil because of their outrageous salaries and bonuses. Some of our teams have still not recovered from it. The WFL's first big coup was signing Larry Csonka, Jim Kiick and Paul Warfield from the NFL champion Dolphins, and it wasn't too long thereafter that Bill Bergey walked into my office and said he was about to sign a WFL contract with the league's Washington entry. We tried to dissuade him from signing, but he never gave us a chance to make a counterproposal because, as we found out later, he had actually already signed the contract, even though he had two more seasons remaining on his Bengals' pact.

We took Bill to court to try to enforce our contract and to void the other team's. Even if we could not win the case, as with the Canadian League case several years before, we felt litigation might force other players to think twice before signing with the World League, and thus slow down the wholesale raiding of our rosters. We lost the case and succeeded in that secondary aim, as we had expected, but the decision left us with a player under contract both to us and to another team. That was anathema to everything I believed in, and I could not possibly see how the welfare of our team was being served by this situation.

Meanwhile, during the litigation process, the WFL's Washington franchise had been moved because the man who had signed Bill and bragged about being able to pay him more than $100,000 a year really had little money and was happy to be able to sell Bergey's contract to the owners of another team for $10,000. That team, however, also had no money and wanted to rid itself of all such high-priced contracts.

One day, we had a call from the second team, telling us it was willing to accept $20,000 to tear up Bergey's contract. The man who called, however, wanted the money in small bills under the table. We told him we never did business in that manner and were not interested. I mentioned the incident to Mike McCormack, who then was coach of the Philadelphia Eagles and soon after, I got a phone call from Leonard Tose, the Eagles' owner, who said that he would consider making a deal with us for Bergey and that he would take care of Bergey's WFL contract on his own.

"This kind of thing doesn't bother me," Tose said. "I'm in the trucking business, and this goes on all the time in my world. What do you want for Bergey?"

We finally agreed on two first- and second-round draft picks, a deal that Tose made himself. McCormack later told me he understood that Leonard did indeed pay the $20,000 to get the other contract destroyed. I was severely criticized in Cincinnati for allowing Bergey to get away, but I certainly wasn't going to go against my principles and pay money under the table, especially to keep a player who had had no business signing a contract with another team in the first place. Later Bill would say to me, "Coach, I really liked living in Cincinnati, and I miss the Bengals because I miss the way things were done there. I guess you can call what I did a mistake, but the money was there. I was young, and I got carried away."

We felt that losing Bergey was not a major problem, however, because we believed LeClair could step in and play with the same excellence. Unfortunately LeClair developed a bone spur in his foot, in 1974, which prevented him from playing for the full season, and his problem was just symptomatic of what happened to us that year. We lost eight starters, including such players as Ken Anderson, Booby Clark, Essex Johnson, Vernon Holland, Bob Johnson and LeClair, and finished the season with just thirty-four players healthy enough to dress for our final game. I had never experienced such a devastating spate of injuries.

We were only a half game behind the division-leading Steelers, having beaten them, 17–10, with only five games to play, when it began. Anderson completed a record twenty of twenty-two passes against Pittsburgh, but his supporting cast disappeared over the next couple of games, and even Ken went down in our next-to-last match, and we finished with a 7–7 record. After we lost to Pittsburgh in the final game, there were some ill-conceived comments that we had not made an effort to win, but we'd never had a chance going into the game. By that time Wayne Clark, who had thrown fewer than 100 passes in five NFL seasons, was our only quarterback, and if anything had happened to him, our punter, Dave Green, would have been forced to play the position.

We threw only eight passes in the game and were accused of running the ball so we could get the game over with quickly. We tried to make as good a game of it as we could, though, and as for not passing, I don't believe Wayne really wanted to throw the ball; during the afternoon, we had sent in some pass plays which he checked off to runs, so I think he had convinced himself that he faced a hopeless situation.

The game was on national television on the final Saturday of the season, and I kept the commissioner informed of our plight and what we intended to do, just in case there were national repercussions. There were none, however, just some comments in Cincinnati.

Even with the rash of injuries in 1974, we had played well enough to be contenders for most of the season, so there was a great air of anticipation for 1975. That anticipation was dampened somewhat, however, by yet another players' strike, which forced a delay in the start of training camp. These actions had become a tiresome and demoralizing issue for me, but I was pleased that our players were the only ones, as a team, to vote against the strike. Of course, I was painted by the union leadership as working to convince our players to go against the action, but I never tried to sway our players one way or the other. All I did was keep them abreast of what was happening by reading or posting the information we re-

ceived from the league office and from the AP sports wire
that our radio people had hooked up for their own use.

I allowed our players to hold their meetings, and most
people didn't realize that it was the leadership core on the
team itself that was against the action and that these men
worked among the other players to discourage it. I didn't
have to say a word, and in fact, some of our veterans came
into camp voluntarily and worked with our rookie players.
Some, like Pat Matson, the players' representative, paraded
outside carrying picket signs, but they never got much sympa-
thy when people saw them driving Lincoln Continentals and
read about their making $80,000 per year. When a new con-
tract was finally signed, freedom was not even a factor. It
was strictly a monetary settlement, mandated by those who
were running the union and hiring its expensive law firm.

In the end I think the strike actually helped the spirit on
our team because our guys had to stick together in the face
of opposition from most other teams in the NFL. We also
added ten rookies that year, a young and happy group, and
they gave us a great zest to play. They brought a spirit of
competition and enthusiasm with them and made it difficult
for anyone not to get caught up in it. They pushed our
veterans so hard that we won our first six games, and by the
season's halfway mark we were in a three-way tie for the
AFC Central lead with Pittsburgh and Houston. Our passing
game was so devastating that in a 33–24 victory over Buffalo,
Anderson completed thirty of forty-six passes for 447
yards—and not one pass was intercepted.

We finished the year with an 11-3 record, second in our
division to Pittsburgh, the eventual Super Bowl champion,
but good enough to qualify as the AFC's wild-card team in
the play-offs against the Western Division champion Oakland
Raiders, whom we had beaten, 14–10, during the season. I
was happy—but I knew deep down within me that this might
be my last game as a head coach. I said nothing to the players, though.

Facing off against Oakland, we were behind, 31–14, early
in the fourth quarter, when Ken Riley's interception set up
Anderson's 25-yard touchdown pass to Charley Joiner, and
then five minutes later, Isaac Curtis took a ball from Oakland
defensive back Neal Colzie in the end zone and brought us to
within three points with about five minutes left to play. Soon
after, Ron Carpenter fell on Ken Stabler's fumble at Oak-

land's 37-yard line, and I thought we really had a chance to win. We called a crossing-pattern pass to Joiner, which had worked earlier, but as Anderson was about to throw the ball—and Joiner was in the clear—Ken was sacked by Raiders' linebacker Ted Hendricks, who had slipped off Booby Clark's block. That was our last gasp. Three more passes netted only six yards, and the season was over. The game still might have been ours, though, had Ken been able to get off that first-down pass.

I'm sure that as our players replayed that game, they were sure I would return in 1976 for another try at the Super Bowl, and if they had asked me three months before, I probably would have agreed. When the season had started, I had not thought about retiring, but the idea was kindled as we continued to be successful. The entire season had been a happy, wonderful experience for me, and I had always thought that when I did finish coaching, I wanted to go out on high C. By 1975 I was satisfied with what I had achieved since returning to the game.

Also, as I have noted at the beginning of this book, professional football had changed drastically since I had come back. The thoughts of the 1975 strike were still very vivid, and having had to go through player walkouts four times in eight years had been very discouraging. I think the disappointment from the Bergey incident also colored my decision because I saw that loyalty was becoming less and less important. In Bill's case, we had been very patient for the first three years while he had made his mistakes and become a good player, and I had believed in him because he had seemed to be so enthusiastic about playing for us.

There were other problem areas as well. I had found that regardless of how successful we were, the media didn't seem to be happy unless they could dig up some problems or criticize us. I'll never forget flying to a game in our chartered plane and overhearing one of the Cincinnati writers saying to the man sitting next to him, "I sure hope the Bengals lose tomorrow, I can write better if they do." Another media member, a beginning radio broadcaster, said, "I'm sorry, coach, I hate to attack you, but my superiors think that is the quickest way to advance my career." I couldn't understand that attitude because after all, we represented Cincinnati, and certainly life was too short for me to live in this type of atmosphere. Much of the pleasure was gone.

The increasing influence of some players' agents had also become a problem. As opposed to relatives, college coaches or bona fide lawyers, these people literally lived off other people's efforts, and I had no respect for them at all. I never dealt with them personally, but my son Mike did, and their influence was pervasive. Some told their players to complain publicly and demand to be traded because it would get them more public attention; others never even saw their clients play football and made unreasonable demands on the team simply so they could get more money from their percentage of the deal. I always thought the player's loyalty should be to our team and our community, not to some agent who just used him.

We have always wanted to be fair and honest in our dealings with our players because we know that if we aren't, we won't have their full heart and effort. We try to guide them and to help them stay within their financial capabilities, but we are not a bank that the irresponsible can use when they don't meet their normal obligations. For instance, we've had players who didn't pay their income taxes then come to us and want to renegotiate their contracts so they could meet their obligations. When we've refused, they've gone out and called us cheap and "insensitive" to their needs.

As the 1975 season wound down, I looked at all these factors and decided it was time to stop coaching. After the play-off game I spent the next two weeks putting everything in order. Bill Johnson was my choice for a head coach. I felt he shared my general coaching beliefs, even though he apparently felt otherwise about some of them. In the middle of his third season, of his own volition, he resigned. And Homer Rice, an assistant, was elevated to the head job. Homer has done a superlative job of putting the pieces back together, but in fairness to Bill, injuries at key positions had been disastrous. I know that when I appointed both, there were other assistants who thought they should have gotten the job, but I could appoint only one man, and I wanted to make the choice early, without any speculation, to avoid division within our organization.

Bill agreed that Mike McCormack and Charley Winner would be worthy additions to our coaching staff, and he arranged for them to be hired. After that, there was nothing to do but make the announcement, and I know I shocked Al Heim, our energetic public relations director, when I called him at home on New Year's Day in 1976 and told him to tell the media. I gave him a brief statement, hung up the phone and then disappeared from public view until the news had been digested.

I have not regretted the decision because I am well satisfied with my forty-five years as a coach. I can look back and feel that I never worked a day in my life because what I did wasn't work—it was fun. And as I look back over those many years, I find that no matter how people and times have changed, the words of Dean Elizabeth Hamilton of Miami University still ring true:

"The eternal verities will always prevail. Such things as truth, honesty, character and loyalty will never change."

I have tried to live my whole life by those words—and it has made me a happy man.

ABOUT THE AUTHORS

Paul Brown resigned as coach of the Cincinnati Bengals in 1975 to devote himself full-time to his duties as general manager and part owner of the team. The tradition has been passed on: his son Mike Brown serves as assistant general manager of the Bengals and his son Pete Brown is director of player personnel.

Jack Clary is a journalist/writer who has concentrated on sports for twenty years with the Associated Press, *New York World Telegram and Sun,* and the *Boston Herald Traveler.* He has also held management positions in professional football and public relations. He is the author of seven books, including THIRTY YEARS OF PRO FOOTBALL'S GREATEST MOMENTS, THE CLEVELAND BROWNS, and THE CAPTAINS.

Recommended Reading from SIGNET

☐ A GARDEN OF SAND by Earl Thompson. (#E9374—$2.95)

☐ TATTOO by Earl Thompson. (#E8989—$2.95)

☐ CALDO LARGO by Earl Thompson. (#E7737—$2.25)

☐ THE WORLD FROM ROUGH STONES by Malcolm Macdonald.
(#E9639—$2.95)

☐ THE RICH ARE WITH YOU ALWAYS by Malcolm Macdonald.
(#E7682—$2.25)

☐ SONS OF FORTUNE by Malcolm Macdonald.
(#E8595—$2.75)*

☐ THE EBONY TOWER by John Fowles. (#E9653—$2.95)

☐ DANIEL MARTIN by John Fowles. (#F8249—$2.95)

☐ COMA by Robin Cook. (#E9756—$2.75)

☐ THE CRAZY LADIES by Joyce Elbert. (#E8923—$2.75)

☐ THE FINAL FIRE by Dennis Smith. (#J7141—$1.95)

☐ SOME KIND OF HERO by James Kirkwood. (#E9850—$2.75)

☐ KINFLICKS by Lisa Alther. (#E9474—$2.95)

* Price slightly higher in Canada

Buy them at your local bookstore or use this convenient coupon for ordering.

THE NEW AMERICAN LIBRARY, INC.,
P.O. Box 999, Bergenfield, New Jersey 07621

Please send me the SIGNET BOOKS I have checked above. I am enclosing
$_____(please add 50¢ to this order to cover postage and
handling). Send check or money order—no cash or C.O.D.'s. Prices and
numbers are subject to change without notice.

Name _____

Address_____

City_____ State_____ Zip Code_____
Allow 4-6 weeks for delivery.
This offer is subject to withdrawal without notice.